Lightning Source UK Ltd.
Milton Keynes UK
08 December 2009

147228UK00002B/19/P

OXFORD MONOGRAPHS IN
INTERNATIONAL LAW

General Editors: Professor Ian Brownlie CBE, QC, FBA
*Former Chichele Professor of Public International Law in the
University of Oxford and Member of the International Law Commission,* and
Professor Vaughan Lowe, *Chichele Professor of Public International Law in
the University of Oxford and Fellow of All Souls College, Oxford*

HUMAN RIGHTS IN
INTERNATIONAL CRIMINAL PROCEEDINGS

OXFORD MONOGRAPHS IN INTERNATIONAL LAW

The aim of this series is to publish important and original pieces of research on all aspects of international law. Topics that are given particular prominence are those which, while of interest to the academic lawyer, also have important bearing on issues which touch upon the actual conduct of international relations. Nonetheless, the series is wide in scope and includes monographs on the history and philosophical foundations of international law.

RECENT TITLES IN THE SERIES

Just War or Just Peace?
Humanitarian Intervention and International Law
Simon Chesterman

State Responsibility for Transboundary Air
Pollution in International Law
Phoebe Okowa

The Responsibility of States for International Crimes
Nina H. B. Jørgensen

The Law of International Watercourses: Non-navigational Uses
Stephen C. McCaffrey

International Justice and the International Criminal Court:
Between Sovereignty and the Rule of Law
Bruce Broomhall

FORTHCOMING TITLE:

Universal Jurisdiction: International and
Municipal Legal Perspectives
Luc Reydams

HUMAN RIGHTS IN INTERNATIONAL CRIMINAL PROCEEDINGS

SALVATORE ZAPPALÀ

OXFORD

UNIVERSITY PRESS

*This book has been printed digitally and produced in a standard specification
in order to ensure its continuing availability*

OXFORD
UNIVERSITY PRESS

Great Clarendon Street, Oxford OX2 6DP

Oxford University Press is a department of the University of Oxford.
It furthers the University's objective of excellence in research, scholarship,
and education by publishing worldwide in

Oxford New York

Auckland   Cape Town Dar es Salaam   Hong Kong   Karachi
Kuala Lumpur Madrid Melbourne Mexico City   Nairobi
New Delhi Shanghai Taipei Toronto
With offices in
Argentina Austria Brazil Chile Czech Republic France Greece
Guatemala Hungary Italy Japan South Korea Poland Portugal
Singapore Switzerland Thailand Turkey Ukraine Vietnam

Oxford is a registered trade mark of Oxford University Press
in the UK and in certain other countries

Published in the United States
by Oxford University Press Inc., New York

© Salvatore Zappalà 2003

The moral rights of the author have been asserted

Database right Oxford University Press (maker)

Reprinted 2008

ISBN 978-0-19-928093-3

General Editors' Preface

Criminal proceedings are widely regarded as an epitome of the power of the State. Steps are commonly taken to prevent the abuse of that power by the entrenchment of constitutional safeguards against violations of fundamental human rights and by the answerability of police powers to democratic processes. In recent years international criminal tribunals of various kinds have been established, which sit aside from the safeguards ordinarily secured within natural legal systems. The question of the manner in which the rights of persons who are tried by those tribunals are to be secured is an important one, which will have to be resolved if international criminal tribunals are to succeed in their task of delivering justice. Dr Zappalà's study is an important and timely contribution to the debate on this topic.

IB
AVL

Contents

Abbreviations

ACHR	American Convention on Human Rights
AFDI	*Annuaire Français de Droit International*
AJIL	*American Journal of International Law*
An.-Am. LR	*Anglo-American Law Review*
BJIL	*Brooklyn Journal of International Law*
BYIL	*British Yearbook of International Law*
CJTL	*Columbia Journal of Transnational Law*
CLF	*Criminal Law Forum*
CLR	*Criminal Law Review*
CMLRev.	*Common Market Law Review*
Cor. ILJ	*Cornell International Law Journal*
CYIL	*Canadian Yearbook of International Law*
DJICL	*Duke Journal of International and Comparative Law*
ECHR	European Convention on Human Rights
ECJ	European Court of Justice
ECommHR	European Commission of Human Rights
ECourtHR	European Court of Human Rights
EHRLR	*European Human Rights Law Review*
EJIL	*European Journal of International Law*
FJIL	*Fordham Journal of International Law*
FRY	Federal Republic of Yugoslavia
GeorgiaJICL	*Georgia Journal of International and Comparative Law*
HILJ	*Harvard International Law Journal*
HRQ	*Human Rights Quarterly*
ICC	International Criminal Court
ICCPR	International Covenant on Civil and Political Rights
ICC RPE	International Criminal Court Rules of Procedure and Evidence
ICC St.	International Criminal Court Statute
ICJ	International Court of Justice
ICLQ	*International and Comparative Law Quarterly*
ICRC	International Committee of the Red Cross
ICTR	International Criminal Tribunal for Rwanda
ICTY	International Criminal Tribunal for the former Yugoslavia
IJIL	*Indian Journal of International Law*
IL	*The International Lawyer*
ILC	International Law Commission
ILJ	*Indiana Law Journal*
ILM	*International Legal Materials*
IMT	International Military Tribunal, a.k.a. Nuremberg Tribunal

IMTFE	International Military Tribunal for the Far East, a.k.a. Tokyo Tribunal
Int. JHR	*International Journal of Human Rights*
IRPL	*International Review of Penal Law*
IRRC	*International Review of the Red Cross*
Isr. LR	*Israel Law Review*
Isr. YHR	*Israel Yearbook of Human Rights*
JACL	*Journal of Armed Conflict Law*
LJIL	*Leiden Journal of International Law*
Mich.JIL	*Michigan Journal of International Law*
Mich.LR	*Michigan Law Review*
MLR	*The Modern Law Review*
NILR	*Netherlands International Law Review*
Nur. Ch.	Nuremberg Charter
NYUJILP	*New York University Journal of International Law and Politics*
NYULR	*New York University Law Review*
PrepCom	Preparatory Commission for the Establishment of the ICC
RBDI	*Revue Belge de Droit International*
RDIDC	*Revue de Droit International et de Droit Comparé*
Rec. des Cours	*Recueil des Cours de l'Académie de droit international de La Haye*
Reports	*Reports of Judgments and Decisions ECourtHR*
RGDIP	*Revue Générale de Droit International Public*
RHDI	*Revue Hellénique de Droit International*
RIDP	*Revue Internationale de Droit Pénal*
RPE	Rules of Procedure and Evidence
RSCDPC	*Revue de Sciences Criminelles et de Droit Pénal Comparé*
RTDH	*Revue Trimestrielle des Droits de l'Homme*
SFOR	*Stabilization Force*
TJIL	*Texas Journal of International Law*
TLR	*Temple Law Review*
Tul. LR	*Tulane Law Review*
UDHR	Universal Declaration of Human Rights
UNTAES	United Nations Transitional Administration for Eastern Slavonia
UPLR	*University of Pennsylvania Law Review*
Vand. JTL	*Vanderbilt Journal of Transnational Law*
VJIL	*Virginia Journal of International Law*
VLR	*Virginia Law Review*
Yearbook	*Yearbook of the European Convention on Human Rights*
YJIL	*Yale Journal of International Law*
YLJ	*Yale Law Journal*

Tables of Cases

UN INTERNATIONAL CRIMINAL TRIBUNALS

ICTY

ICTR

INTERNATIONAL COURT OF JUSTICE, HUMAN RIGHTS COURTS, AND HUMAN RIGHTS MONITORING BODIES

International Court of Justice

European Court of Human Rights

European Commission of Human Rights

European Court of Justice

Tables of Legislation

1

Introduction

I. A HUMAN RIGHTS APPROACH TO INTERNATIONAL CRIMINAL PROCEDURE

This book is based on the assumption that *human rights law* is the ideal lens for investigating the structures and functioning of international criminal justice. This body of law provides one of the best interpretative tools for the analysis of the procedural mechanisms of international criminal justice, since it helps identify the proper balance between the rights of individuals and the interests of society. And indeed, with regard to national law, commentators have already taken human rights as a parameter for assessing criminal procedures.[1]

In the following chapters the structure of international criminal proceedings is analysed—from the initiation of investigations to the enforcement of sentences—in order to establish how the protection of the rights of individuals operates. The analysis has been carried out taking into account the influence of the classic *models of criminal procedure* (*accusatorial and inquisitorial*[2]) in shaping the relevant rules.

I have primarily examined the practice of the UN *ad hoc* Tribunals (ICTY and ICTR),[3] the principles and rules governing their activities, and

---

[1] Cf. J.A. Andrews (ed.), *Human Rights in Criminal Procedure: A Comparative Study* (The Hague–Boston–London: Nijhoff, 1982); G. Conso, 'Diritti Umani e Procedura Penale', in SIOI, *L'Italia e L'Anno Internazionale dei Diritti dell'Uomo* (Padua: Cedam, 1969), 25–42; M. Delmas Marty (ed.), *Procès Pénal et Droits de l'Homme* (Paris: Presses Universitaires de France, 1992); B. Emmerson and A. Ashworth, *Human Rights and Criminal Justice* (London: Sweet and Maxwell, 2001).

[2] On the use of the terms accusatorial and inquisitorial or adversarial and non-adversarial cf. note 53 below.

[3] The International Criminal Tribunal for the former Yugoslavia (ICTY) and the International Criminal Tribunal for Rwanda (ICTR) were established by Security Council resolutions 827 (1993) and 955 (1994) respectively. On the *ad hoc* Tribunals literature is abundant. On the process of establishment of the ICTY see generally V. Morris and M. Scharf, *An Insider's Guide to the International Criminal Tribunal for the Former Yugoslavia* (Irvington on Hudson, NY: Transnational Publ., 1995) and for the ICTR see V. Morris and M. Scharf, *The International Criminal Tribunal for Rwanda* (Irvington on Hudson, NY: Transnational Publ., 1998). See also M.C. Bassiouni and P. Manikas *The Law of the International Criminal Tribunal for the Former Yugoslavia* (Irvington on Hudson, NY: Transnational Publ., 1996). For a thorough presentation of the jurisprudence of the *ad hoc* Tribunals see J. Jones, *The Practice of the International Criminal Tribunals for the former Yugoslavia and Rwanda* (2nd edn., Andsley, NY: Transnational Publ., 2000). Systematic reviews of the activity of the Tribunals are published on many law journals. See, e.g., H. Ascensio and A. Pellet, 'L'Activité du Tribunal Pénal International pour l'ex-Yougoslavie' in 41 *AFDI* (1995), 101–136; and subsequently H. Ascensio and R. Maison, 'L'Activité des Tribunaux Pénaux Internationaux' in 43 *AFDI* (1997) 368–402, in 44 *AFDI* (1998) 370–411, in 45 *AFDI* (1999) 472–514, and in 46 *AFDI* (2000) 285–325. See also

the provisions of the ICC Statute[4] and its Rules of Procedure and Evidence.[5]

At least since the creation of UN *ad hoc* Tribunals, respect for the rights of defendants has been one of the distinctive traits of international criminal justice. Initially, the accusatorial model was chosen for two main reasons. First, the judges originally adopted the Rules of Procedure and Evidence of the ICTY, primarily based on a draft submitted by the US Department of Justice,[6] which was very close to the US Federal Rules of Evidence. Secondly, the judges, mainly of common law background, were inclined to approve such a draft on the basis of the widespread assumption that the accusatorial model offers better protection to individual rights (an assumption that, at least to a large extent, I share).[7] Subsequently, however, practice evidenced the drawbacks of applying a purely accusatorial model to international criminal proceedings, and thus amendments were required. In amending the procedural system of the *ad hoc* Tribunals and in drafting the ICC Statute some inquisitorial elements were upheld, thereby diluting the originally adversarial imprint.

F. King and A.M. La Rosa, 'Jurisprudence of the Yugoslavia Tribunal: 1994–1996', in 8 *EJIL* (1997) 123, and on the *EJIL* website: <**www.ejil.org**>. Summaries of most relevant decisions may be also read, in Italian, in S. Zappalà (ed.), 'Osservatorio sul Tribunale penale internazionale', published monthly in *Diritto penale e processo* (starting from September 1997).

[4] The ICC Statute was adopted by the UN Conference convened in Rome (15 June–17 July 1998). On the ICC Statute see O. Triffterer, *Commentary on the Rome Statute of the International Criminal Court—Observers' Notes* (Baden-Baden: Nomos, 1999); R. Lee (ed.), *The International Criminal Court—The Making of the Rome Statute. Issues—Negotiations—Results* (The Hague: Kluwer, 1999); A. Cassese, P. Gaeta, and J. Jones, (eds.), *The Rome Statute of the International Criminal Court: A Commentary*, 3 volumes (Oxford: OUP, 2002).

[5] For a more theoretical approach to international criminal procedure, mainly based on the practice of the ECourtHR and other human rights bodies, and a comparative analysis of various national systems with the ICTY and the ICC, see C. Safferling, *Towards an International Criminal Procedure* (Oxford: OUP, 2001).

[6] It was noted that 'the United States submitted by far the most comprehensive set of proposed rules with commentary, numbering approximately seventy-five pages. This proposal was particularly influential because of its detailed coverage of procedural and evidentiary issues, the explanation of the reasons for the proposals contained in the commentary and the timeliness of the submission': see Morris and Scharf, *An Insider's Guide*, note 3 above, at 177. See also A. Cassese, *International Criminal Law* (Oxford: OUP, 2003) at 380.

[7] As noted by L. Leigh, 'Liberty and Efficiency in the Criminal Process—the Significance of Models', in 26 *ICLQ* (1977), 516–530, 'all free societies balance these criteria [liberty and efficiency] in their criminal procedures', at 529. However, whilst in accusatorial systems protection of individual liberties is the overriding concern of procedural rules, in the inquisitorial tradition criminal procedure is seen as a means for imposing societal values on the culprit. In other words, in inquisitorial systems, criminal law protects the values of the society and criminal procedure is the tool for ensuring compliance with those values. On the other hand, accusatorial systems, which are closely related to liberal ideals, do not require that criminal trials should aim at imposing the views of society on individuals. Moreover, the underlying idea is that rules of criminal procedure must protect the individual against abuses by public authorities. From this standpoint, the right of an innocent person not to be convicted is considered as one of the most basic rights, cf. R. Dworkin, 'Principle, Policy, Procedure' in C. Tapper (ed.), *Crime Proof and Punishment* (London: Butterworths, 1981), at 212. Other differences between the two models are discussed in more detail in Section IV below.

The main goal of this study is to establish to what extent these amendments and the resulting procedural system succeed in enhancing the protection of the rights of defendants. To this end it will be necessary to clarify the general scope of human rights protection before international criminal courts and highlight problems which may cause infringements of the rights of individuals, thereby putting in jeopardy the principle of 'fair trial'. Finally, it seems important to try to suggest possible means of addressing such problems, within the international criminal justice system.[8]

II. THE EXTENSION OF THE NOTION OF FAIR TRIAL TO INTERNATIONAL CRIMINAL PROCEEDINGS

As is well known, the right to a fair trial is strictly connected to the concept of due process of law and can be traced back to the Magna Carta (1215).[9] Through the provisions of the Carta the King promised that no free man would be taken or 'imprisoned or deprived of his freehold or his liberties . . . except by legal judgement of his peers and by the law of the land' (Article 39).[10] Today, however, these concepts, which are intertwined, are much more

---

[8] In recent years the UN has been involved in the creation of other forms of tribunals that operate on a national basis to adjudicate on international crimes; this occurred in Cambodia, in East Timor, in Kosovo, and in Sierra Leone. These courts, which are tailored to each specific situation, are also referred to as 'internationalized' or 'mixed' tribunals, since they are not truly international courts in that they function on the basis of a mixture of national and international features. For example, some of the judges are national and some international; the substantive and procedural law they apply is both national and international. On the basis of their specificity it was decided to leave them outside the scope of this work, which aims at dealing with the main bodies of international criminal justice. Therefore, at least for the purpose of this study international criminal justice is limited to the procedural systems of the tribunals created by the Allies after the Second World War, the UN *ad hoc* Tribunals for the former Yugoslavia and Rwanda, and the International Criminal Court. On mixed tribunals see M. Frulli, 'The Special Court for Sierra Leone: Some Preliminary Comments', in 11 *EJIL* (2000), 857–869; S. Linton, 'Cambodia, East Timor, and Sierra Leone: Experiments in International Justice', in 12 *CLF* (2001), 185–246; H. Strohmeyer, 'Collapse and Reconstruction of a Judicial System: The United Nations Missions in Kosovo and East Timor', in 95 *AJIL* (2001), 46–63. See also the Conference on Internationalized Courts and Tribunals organized by the Amsterdam Centre for International Law, the Project on International Courts and Tribunals and No Peace Without Justice, Amsterdam (25–26 January 2002).

[9] See P. Van Dijk, *The Right of the Accused to a Fair Trial under International Law* (Utrecht: SIM Special, 1983), and J. Niemi-Kiesilainen, 'Article 9', in G. Alfredsson and A. Eide (eds.), *The Universal Declaration of Human Rights: A Common Standard of Achievement* (The Hague: Nijhoff, 1999), at 209 ff.

[10] This provision has a mainly symbolic value and should not be overestimated; see in this respect, G. Alessi, *Il Processo Penale—Profilo Storico* (Rome-Bari: Laterza, 2001), at 51. For the text of the Carta and discussion of its constitutional significance see J.C. Holt, *Magna Carta* (Cambridge: Cambridge University Press, 1965).

developed and have been the subject of a great deal of international law-making.[11]

International provisions on the protection of individual rights in criminal trials are very similar,[12] and through their content a solid international under-

---

[11] On the historical developments and for a comparison of the fundamental international texts cf. P. Sieghart, *The International Law of Human Rights* (Oxford: Clarendon Press 1983), at 268. The Universal Declaration of Human Rights (UDHR) established some general principles on the rights of persons facing criminal charges. These are contained in three key Articles: Articles 9–11. Article 9 deals with protection against arbitrary arrest, Article 10 expresses the right to be tried in public and in full equality by an independent and impartial tribunal, whilst Article 11 provides for some more detailed provisions, such as the presumption of innocence and the right of the accused to have 'all the guarantees necessary for his defence'. Furthermore, Article 11 also contains the principles of *nullum crimen* and *nulla poena sine lege*. Despite the fact that the provisions of the UDHR on the rights of accused persons are rather terse, these were the cornerstone for the subsequent codification of more detailed norms. On the provisions of the UDHR on the right to a fair trial see extensively D. Weissbrodt and M. Hallendorff, 'Travaux Préparatoires of the Fair Trial Provisions—Articles 8 to 11—of the Universal Declaration of Human Rights', in 21 *HRQ* (1999), 1061.

[12] In the ICCPR the key Article on the rights of persons accused in criminal proceedings is Article 14. This Article, much more detailed than the corresponding Articles of the UDHR, was also accepted by communist countries, despite the fact that it was mainly based on liberal principles. It provides for the right to a fair trial and specifies what the requirements and the conditions for a trial to be fair are. Traditionally, these have been identified as (i) conditions having to do with the character of the jurisdiction, which shall be impartial, independent, and established by law, and (ii) the position of the accused before the court and *vis-à-vis* his opponents, the public prosecutor, and—where it exists—the *partie civile*. The rules specifically laid down in Article 14, paragraphs 2 to 7, are further specifications of what a fair trial is and of the minimum guarantees for an accused person. Paragraph 2 of Article 14 establishes the presumption of innocence, a fundamental principle that should extend its effects beyond the actors of the trial and should be a principle also governing the perception of the media and public opinion. Paragraph 3, which is divided into letters a) to g), provides for 'minimum guarantees' for the accused in the determination of the charges against him (or her). These guarantees are: the right to be informed of the charges, the right to have adequate time and facilities for the preparation of the defence, the right to be tried without undue delay, the right to legal assistance, the right to examine witnesses and to obtain their attendance, the right to have an interpreter, and the privilege against self-incrimination.

The European Convention on Human Rights (ECHR) Article 6 establishes the principle of the right to a fair trial and basically provides for the same safeguards as the text of Article 14 of the ICCPR, with two main differences, however. These are, on the one hand, the absence of a provision on the privilege against self-incrimination, which has, however, been recognized by the European Court of Human Rights (ECourtHR), cf. for example the case *Funke* v. *France* (25 February 1993 Series A, no. 256) and more recently *J.B.* v. *Switzerland*, 3 May 2001, **www.echr.coe.int/Eng/ Judgments.htm**, and, on the other, the absence of an express norm on the right to be present. Moreover, Article 5 refers to the right to personal liberty and protection against arbitrary arrest.

In the American Convention on Human Rights (ACHR), Article 8 establishes the same fundamental protection as that provided for in the Covenant, with the difference that it adds, in conformity with Article XXVI of the American Declaration of the Rights and Duties of Man, the requirement of the pre-establishment by law of the tribunal with a view to forbidding the creation of special tribunals. This difference, however, should not be over-emphasized, as the provision of the Covenant should also be interpreted in the sense that special tribunals are forbidden (cf. M. Bossuyt, *Guide to the* 'travaux préparatoires' *of the* ICCPR (Dordrecht: Nijhoff, 1987), at 283). It seems that the reason for excluding the requirement of prior establishment (prior to the commission of the crime) was due to the intention not to hinder the action of the legislator when trying to reform the organization of tribunals. Another characteristic that differentiates the

standing has evolved. It has been noted, in referring to the ICCPR, the ECHR, and the ACHR, that 'the three human rights treaty texts between them define the right to a fair trial in criminal proceedings in full and basically satisfactory terms. There are no important omissions . . . Of the three, the UN text is the most complete. The remaining two, however, guarantee all of the essential features of a fair trial. . . . There is . . . a common core of meaning of sufficient dimension as to permit a detailed statement of the scope of that right which can command widespread international consent'.[13]

With regard to the extension of due process principles to *international* criminal trials, it is submitted that although there was no one specific rule imposing on States the obligation to extend human rights safeguards to the international level, there were (and are), nonetheless, several good reasons to support this extension.[14] In particular, in the case of UN *ad hoc* Tribunals it would have been inconsistent for the Security Council not to impose respect for UN standards.

In any case, some arguments can be set forth in favour of such an extension. First, due process is a fundamental protection for the individual, to be

American text from the others is the absence of a provision granting the right to a public trial. On the right to a fair trial in the ACHR see A. Cançado Trindade, 'The Right to a Fair Trial under the American Convention on Human Rights', in A. Byrnes (ed.), *The Right to a Fair Trial in International and Comparative Perspective* (Hong-Kong: Centre for Comparative and Public Law, 1997), 4–11.

Additionally, it should be noted that in the Convention on the Rights of the Child similar provisions regarding fair trial for juvenile justice have been adopted. In particular, the norms of Article 40 reiterate the right to a fair trial before an independent and impartial tribunal. Naturally, the provisions of the Convention add guarantees more specifically addressed to juvenile offenders.

Moreover, again at the European level, but this time within the framework of the European Union, a non-binding text issued by a committee of jurists appointed by the European Parliament has been adopted. This text, called the '*corpus iuris*' and relating to the protection of the economic interests of the Community, also contains procedural provisions which confirm and reinforce the right to a fair trial, and express reference is made to the ECHR (Article 6 ECHR). With regard to the extension of the notion of fair trial to EC law see F. Jacobs, 'The Right to a Fair Trial in European Law', in 4 *EHRLR* (1999), 141–156. Finally, again at the EU level, the EU Charter, adopted in December 2000, contains provisions on fair trial guarantees very close to the abovementioned international texts. In general on the EU Charter see K. Lenaerts and E. De Smijter, 'A "Bill of Rights" for the European Union', in 38 *CMLRev.* (2001), 273–300.

[13] D. Harris, 'The Right to a Fair Trial in Criminal Proceedings as a Human Right', in 16 *ICLQ* (1967), at 352. The same opinion is shared by Van Dijk, note 9 above, at 1, where the author considers that 'the terms of . . . Article 6 [ECHR] are almost identical with those of the other provisions mentioned above [i.e. Article 14 ICCPR and Article 8 ACHR]'. On the right to a fair trial in the ECHR see D. Poncet, *La protection de l'accusé par la Convention Européenne des Droits de l'Homme: étude de droit comparé* (Geneva: Georg, 1977). More generally on the right to a fair trial see D. Weissbrodt and R. Wolfrum (eds.), *The Right to a Fair Trial* (Berlin: Springer, 1997).

[14] In this respect cf. more broadly Safferling, note 5 above, at 40–42.

restricted only in exceptional circumstances and to a limited extent.[15] For example, the right to due process applies even during periods of armed conflict.[16] Of course, one could argue that criminal proceedings for international crimes are of such extraordinary nature that most of the due process rights should be suspended. This argument, however, is not convincing, particularly when one considers that both the *ad hoc* Tribunals and the International Criminal Court (ICC) were created to contribute to international peace by doing justice in situations where the national system has collapsed or is otherwise unavailable due to an exceptional situation.[17] Arguably, the suspension of due process rights before national tribunals for crimes within the jurisdiction of the Court could constitute a case of unavailability of national jurisdiction that may justify intervention by the ICC. The *ad hoc* Tribunals and the Court aim to ensure due process in these situations. Therefore, it would be illogical to believe that the Tribunals or the Court could avoid complying with due process guarantees on account of the extraordinary nature of the crimes within their jurisdiction.[18] It would be arduous to maintain that an international body, which has been created to avoid the use of national criminal justice as an instrument of vengeance by one of the parties involved in the conflict, may do without due process rules.[19]

Secondly, as further explained below (in Section III), the extension of due process principles to international criminal trials allows States to co-operate with, or execute requests of, international criminal courts without running the risk of not being able to comply with their obligations under human rights provisions.[20]

[15] On this issue, see 'The Siracusa Principles on Limitation and Derogation Provisions in the International Covenant on Civil and Political Rights', in 7 *HRQ* (1985), 3–14, and the comments therein by A. Kiss *et al.* (15–131). See also S. Stavros, 'The Right to a Fair Trial in Emergency Situations', in 41 *ICLQ* (1992), 343–365.

[16] Cf. S. Stapleton, 'Ensuring a Fair Trial in the International Criminal Court', in 31 *NYU-JILP* (1999), at 550.

[17] See ICC Statute Article 17.

[18] This view was clearly expressed by A. Cassese, 'Opinion: the International Criminal Tribunal for the Former Yugoslavia and Human Rights', in 2 *EHRLR* (1997), at 331–332.

[19] A similar feeling was aptly described by Justice Murphy of the US Supreme Court, in his dissenting opinion in the well known *In re Yamashita* 327 US 1, 66 S Ct. 340, 90 L Ed.499 (1946), where he wrote '[i]f we are ever to develop an orderly international community based upon a recognition of human dignity it is of the utmost importance that the necessary punishment of those guilty of atrocities be as free as possible from the ugly stigma of revenge and vindictiveness. Justice must be tempered by compassion rather than by vengeance. . . . We must insist, within the confines of our proper jurisdiction, that the *highest standards of justice* be applied in this trial of an enemy commander conducted under the authority of the United States' (emphasis added). The decision and dissenting opinions in *Yamashita* may be read in F. Deak and F. Ruddy (eds.), *American International Law Cases* (1783–1968) (Dobbs Ferry, NY: Oceana Publications, 1978), vol. 18.

[20] Finally, it could be contended that at least some of those human rights safeguards amount to *jus cogens*, and thus they could not be superseded by any other contrary obligation. In this respect see G. Hafner, 'Limits to the Procedural Powers of the International Tribunal for the Former Yugoslavia' in K. Wellens (ed.), *International Law: Theory and Practice* (The Hague: Kluwer, 1998), 651–677, at 657.

In any case the starting point adopted in this book is that this is more a *policy* issue than a legal question. And the policy choice has been made in favour of an extension to international criminal proceedings of international human rights provisions on due process. This choice must be taken for granted, since the Statutes and the Rules of Procedure and Evidence of both the two *ad hoc* Tribunals and the ICC impose full respect for the right to a fair trial and other internationally protected rights of individuals.[21]

III. WHAT TYPE OF RELATIONSHIP EXISTS BETWEEN HUMAN RIGHTS MONITORING SYSTEMS AND INTERNATIONAL CRIMINAL COURTS?

1. General

An often unspoken question, underlying debates about the protection of human rights in proceedings before international criminal tribunals or the ICC, is whether individuals whose rights have been allegedly breached by organs of the Tribunals or by States enforcing Tribunals' requests, may file complaints with regional or universal human rights monitoring bodies, such as the UN Committee on Human Rights or the European Court of Human Rights (ECourtHR). For example, one may wonder whether The Netherlands could be brought before the ECourtHR for not preventing violations of rights protected under the ECHR committed by officials of the ICTY (or the ICC) on its territory.

In this respect, a general principle, already affirmed by the ICJ in 1949 in the *Corfu Channel* case,[22] provides that a State is not automatically responsible for all acts committed on its territory.[23] Moreover, it is a well-settled principle that the only conduct attributed to the State at the international level is, at least in general, that of its organs.[24] Hence, a State is not answerable for the actions of third States or international authorities even if these operate on its territory, unless, of course, the State in question explicitly allows or condones, or otherwise endorses such acts, thus becoming, to some extent, an 'accomplice'.

---

[21] On the importance of complying with human rights standards in the *ad hoc* Tribunals regulatory framework see G. Abi-Saab, 'Droits de l'Homme et Juridictions pénales internationales: convergences et tensions' in R.J. Dupuy (ed.), *Mélanges en l'Honneur de Nicolas Valticos—Droit et Justice* (Paris: Pedone, 1999), 245–253, at 247.

[22] See ICJ Rep. (1949), at 17–23.

[23] In this respect see, in general, L. Condorelli, 'L'imputation à l'Etat d'un fait internationalement illicite: solutions classiques et nouvelles tendances' in 189 *Rec. des Cours* (1984–VI), 9–281, and, on this specific issue, H. Dipla, *La responsabilité de l'Etat pour violations des droits de l'homme: problèmes d'imputation* (Paris: Pedone, 1994), 77–97. See also G. Gaja, 'Articolo 1', in S. Bartole, B. Conforti, and G Raimondi (eds.), *Commentario alla Converzione Europea per la tutela dei diritti dell'uomo e delle libertà fondamentali* (Padua: Cedam, 2001), 23–34, at 30–31.

[24] ILC Commentary to the Articles on State Responsibility, Chapter II Attribution of conduct to a State, **www.un.org/ilc/texts/State_responsibility/responsibility_commentaries(e).pdf**, at 80.

Although this issue poses problems that are outside our procedural perspective on international criminal trials, and therefore does not fall exactly within the scope of this study, it is appropriate to address, albeit briefly, some of these concerns in this introductory chapter.

2. The Nuremberg and Tokyo experience

At the time of the Nuremberg and Tokyo trials rules on the protection of human rights at international level were insufficient and no general human rights monitoring body existed. Furthermore, in the framework of those Tribunals there were no internal mechanisms for redress. In fact, neither the Charters nor the Rules of Procedure for the Nuremberg and the Tokyo Tribunals contained provisions for a right of appeal or revision,[25] although only the Charter of the Nuremberg Tribunal clearly provided that the judgment would be final (on this issue cf. *infra* Chapter 4 on appellate and review proceedings). Those convicted by the Tokyo Tribunal filed an appeal, first, with the Supreme Commander, General MacArthur, who rejected it, and subsequently with the US Supreme Court, which declined jurisdiction. This led to additional criticisms of the fairness of those trials.[26]

After the Second World War the normative situation at international level changed and the right to redress assumed greater relevance, with regard not only to the right to appeal and revision, but also to other forms of international supervision of national jurisdictions. These include institutions such as the Human Rights Committee, and, at regional level, the European, and the Inter-American, Commission and Court of Human Rights.

The European Commission of Human Rights (ECommHR) was confronted with an application regarding the detention of one of the persons convicted by the Nuremberg Tribunal: Rudolf Hess who was serving a life imprisonment sentence in the prison of Spandau, in Germany, under British control. The Commission, however, excluded the responsibility of the United Kingdom for the alleged violations of the rights of Mr Hess.[27] The reasoning of the Commission hinged on the fact that the prison where Hess was being detained and his personal status were regulated by an international agreement between France, Russia, the UK, and the United States. Therefore, the Commission concluded that even if violations of human rights had been committed, they were outside the jurisdiction of the UK in the sense required by the provisions of the ECHR; and the case was thus dismissed.

---

[25] On this issue cf. Chapter 4 below. [26] Abi-Saab, note 21 above, 247–248.
[27] See ECommHR, *Ilse Hess* v. *United Kingdom*, 25 May 1975 (Application no. 6231/73) [1975] 18 *Yearbook* 146.

3. The UN ad hoc Tribunals and the ICC

As already mentioned above, the principles contained in the major human rights instruments have been applied in the procedural systems of the *ad hoc* Tribunals and the ICC, which include internal mechanisms of redress in the form of appeal and review proceedings. Nonetheless, these systems have not been placed under the supervision of human rights monitoring bodies. It therefore seems that there is no form of external remedy against violations attributable to the Tribunals or the Court. In particular, there is no possibility for individuals to file complaints directly against the Tribunals or the ICC, for these institutions are not party to any human rights convention and monitoring system (only contracting States may be complained against, subject to certain procedural requirements). Conversely, States party to human rights monitoring systems, either at universal or regional level, may indeed find themselves to be the object of such complaints.[28]

In the event of an individual filing a complaint against a State that is enforcing (or otherwise complying with) a request by the *ad hoc* Tribunals' or the ICC, a problem of compatibility between two or more different international obligations arises. Obligations under the Tribunals' or the ICC Statutes may turn out to be inconsistent with obligations under the various human rights instruments (and customary law on human rights).

For an appropriate solution to this conflict let us first examine the case of UN *ad hoc* Tribunals. It seems correct to argue that, as these Tribunals were set up by a Security Council decision under Chapter VII, member States have no choice other than to comply with the Council's decision and co-operate with the Tribunals. This co-operation may entail occasional restrictions of individual rights, where absolutely indispensable. Of course, if one were to consider the individual right involved as protected by a rule of *jus cogens* (i.e. that cannot be derogated from by a treaty-based provision),[29] the conflict should be solved in the opposite way.[30] However, leaving aside the case of *jus cogens* provisions,[31] the State concerned would clearly be confronted with the

---

[28] It is interesting to note that the International Law Commission in its Commentary to the Articles on State Responsibility, note 24 above, stated that 'article 6 [of the articles on State Responsibility] does not concern those cases where, for example, accused persons are transferred by a State to an international institution pursuant to a treaty. In co-operating with international institutions in such a case, the State concerned does not assume responsibility for their subsequent conduct' (at 98).

[29] On the concept of *jus cogens* in international law see A. Cassese, *International Law* (Oxford: OUP, 2001), at 138–148.

[30] See Hafner, note 20 above.

[31] It seems difficult to consider provisions relating to fair trial and due process as being *jus cogens* in their entirety, since even human rights treaties explicitly provide for the possibility of derogation under specific circumstances. Of course the reasoning would be different for certain rights, such as the right not to be subjected to torture or other degrading treatments, or the right not to be punished without trial.

situation referred to in Article 103 of the Charter, according to which Charter-based obligations prevail over any other treaty obligation.[32] Even in this case nothing prevents the competent human rights bodies, if any, from reviewing the actions of individual States in order to assess whether State authorities have acted properly. In particular, monitoring bodies may establish whether, in implementing their obligations under the Charter or the ICC Convention, States have also complied with obligations provided for under the ICCPR or the ECHR or the ACHR; eventually they may even oblige them to pay compensation.[33]

The case with the ICC is more complex. The ICC jurisdiction may be triggered either by a State or by the Prosecutor *proprio motu*, or by the Security Council. In the last event the solution would be the same as that adopted in the case of the *ad hoc* Tribunals. In the other two cases, on the other hand, States would be faced with two conflicting obligations that are—at least in principle—on an equal footing. In such a case, States may have no alternative to violating one or the other rule. Nonetheless, first, one should consider that in negotiating and drafting the ICC Statute States have provided for a thorough extension to international criminal trials of human rights guarantees in the administration of justice. Secondly, one should refrain from general solutions and rather analyse the conflicting obligations in every single case. In this respect, it is submitted that, in general, from a theoretical and value-oriented standpoint, it would be appropriate to give more weight to individual rights, for human rights law was born to protect the individual against abuses of public authorities, including when they act upon the order of an international court.

The ECourtHR has already examined two applications regarding the accountability of States parties for violations of the rights protected by the ECHR in their relationship with the ICTY. In both cases it has found against the appellant.

In 1999, a defendant transferred by Croatia to the ICTY, Mr Naletilić, filed a complaint against Croatia on three grounds.[34] First, his extradition to the International Criminal Tribunal for the former Yugoslavia (ICTY) implied the suspension of internal criminal proceedings against him, and thus a violation of his right to be tried within a reasonable time in Croatia. Secondly, he complained under Article 6(1) ECHR that the ICTY was not an independent and

---

[32] Article 103 UN Charter reads '[i]n the event of a conflict between the obligations of Members of the United Nations under the present Charter and their obligations under any other international agreement, their obligations under the present Charter shall prevail'. The President of the Arrondissementsbank (District Court) of The Hague applied a similar reasoning in deciding over an application filed by Mr Milošević against the Netherlands: see note 40 below, para. 3.6.

[33] A different problem is that of determining what would happen to proceedings vitiated by the violation of individual rights. On this issue see Chapter 2 below.

[34] Application no. 51891/99 by *Mladen Naletilić* v. *Croatia*, 18 October 1999, **www.echr.coe.int**.

impartial tribunal established by law.[35] Thirdly, he raised the issue that his rights under Article 7 ECHR were in jeopardy, since the ICTY could impose on him a heavier sentence than that which could have been imposed in Croatia. The Court considered that the application was manifestly ill-founded.[36] On the first part of the complaint, it held that the applicant had referred to hypothetical future proceedings in Croatia (which would take place only in the event that the Tribunal dismissed the case).[37] On the second issue, the Court stated that an applicant might exceptionally raise an issue under Article 6 where, due to an extradition decision, he risked suffering from a flagrant denial of fair trial. However, the Court held that in the present case it was not an extradition proceeding that was at issue, but 'the surrender to an international court'. In addition, the Court clearly affirmed that the ICTY 'in view of the content of its Statute and Rules of Procedure, offers all the necessary guarantees including those of impartiality and independence'.[38] Finally, on the third issue raised in the application, the Court referred to the text of Article 7(2) ECHR, which clarifies that 'this article [Article 7] shall not prejudice the trial and punishment of any person for any act or omission which, at the time when it was committed, was criminal according to the general principles of law recognized by civilised nations'. The fact that the applicant might receive a heavier punishment from the ICTY than the one likely to be imposed by Croatian authorities was thus clearly not contrary to the provisions of Article 7 ECHR.[39]

In August 2001, the former President of the FRY, Mr Slobodan Milošević, filed with a Dutch court a complaint challenging the lawfulness of his detention and the legality of the ICTY. In particular, he requested the President of the District Court of The Hague to issue an order directed against The Netherlands for his unconditional release, on the grounds that his transfer to the ICTY was illegal and lacked any basis in international law. The President of the District Court rejected the claim of illegality[40] and declared that he had no jurisdiction to hear the plaintiff's claims,[41] since The Netherlands had lawfully transferred its jurisdiction over ICTY's indictees

---

[35] The ICTY Appeals Chamber responded to the objection that the Tribunal was not 'established by law' in its decision on the interlocutory appeal on jurisdiction, *Tadić* (IT–94–1–AR72), 2 October 1995, where it held that 'established by law' in international law means established 'in conformity with the rule of law' (paras. 45–48).

[36] The main reason was that the proceedings against the applicant in Croatia would have been re-opened only in the event of a termination of the proceedings before the ICTY, and thus the violation of the right to be tried within reasonable time was only potential.

[37] See Decision as to the Admissibility of Application no. 51891/99 by *Mladen Naletilić* v. *Croatia*, 4 May 2000, para. 1.a. (*Reports* 2000-v) **www.echr.coe.int/Eng/Judgments.htm**

[38] *Ibidem*, para. 1.b.   [39] *Ibidem*, para. 2.

[40] See Judgment in the Interlocutory Injuction Proceedings in *Milošević* v. *The Netherlands*, 31 August 2001, paras. 3.3 and 3.4, reprinted in 48 *NILR* (2001), 357–361. The President of the District Court referred to the Appeals Chamber Decision on Jurisdiction, *Tadić* (IT–94–1–AR72), 2 October 1995, and clarified that the plaintiff had 'by no means established that [such a] decision is incorrect or that the grounds on which it was reached were unsound': para 3.3 (at 360).

[41] *Ibidem*, para. 4 (at 361).

to the ICTY itself.[42] Moreover, the judge noted that according to national (Dutch) and international law the ICTY offered sufficient procedural guarantees; furthermore, it was for the Tribunal to decide on the legality of the detention of suspects.[43]

Subsequently, Mr Milošević brought his case to the ECourtHR. He complained under 'Article 5.1 ECHR that his detention on the territory of the Netherlands, with the active connivance of the Netherlands authorities, lacked a basis in Netherlands domestic law, and that a procedure prescribed by Netherlands domestic law was not followed'.[44] In addition, he argued that the ICTY had been unlawfully established, that his transfer from FRY to The Hague was unlawful, and that he should have been granted immunity from prosecution as former Head of State. He also complained about the unfairness of ICTY's procedures and lack of independence (shown, in the applicant's opinion, by the failure of the ICTY Prosecutor to investigate NATO's bombing against FRY).[45] The ECourtHR, however, did not pronounce on the merits of the case. It held that the complainant had not exhausted domestic remedies, such as filing an application to the Court of Appeal and subsequently to the Supreme Court on points of law.[46]

4. Human rights and international criminal courts

In the system of international criminal courts as it currently stands, respect for human rights in international criminal trials must be preserved within the system. In the alternative, individuals may only file complaints against States acting on requests of international courts. Of course, there is no reason of principle for such complaints not to be heard, e.g., by the ECourtHR. It is submitted, however, that for such applications to be successful the applicants should be able to show that the system of the ICTY does not meet the standards of the equal protection test, as enshrined, for example, in *Waite and Kennedy* v. *Germany* and *Beer and Regan* v. *Germany*.[47] In applying this test,

---

[42] *Ibidem*, para. 3.5.   [43] See *ibidem*, paras. 3.4 and 3.5.

[44] See Decision as to the Admissibility of Application 77631/01 by *Slobodan Milošević* v. *The Netherlands*, ECHR Second Section, 19 March 2002: see **www.echr.coe.int/Eng/Judgments.htm**.

[45] *Ibidem*, at 2. On the decision of the Prosecutor not to open investigations see P. Benvenuti, 'The ICTY Prosecutor and the Review of the NATO Bombing Campaign against the Federal Republic of Yugoslavia', in 12 *EJIL* (2001), 503; and N. Ronzitti, 'Is the *Non Liquet* of the Final Report by the Committee Established to Review the NATO Bombing Campaign Against the Federal Republic of Yugoslavia Acceptable?' in 82 *IRRC* (2000), 1017.

[46] In particular, the complainant had originally filed an appeal with the Court of Appeal, but decided to withdraw it because it considered that it would not have been effective. The ECourtHR, consistently with a number of precedents, held that 'mere doubts as to the prospects of success of a particular remedy . . . is not a valid reason for failing to exhaust domestic remedies'.

[47] In these cases the issue concerned the right to access to court in the framework of the European Space Agency, cf. Judgment 18 February 1999. The same approach has been adopted in *Matthews* v. *UK*, also on 18 February 1999, on which see the comment by H.G. Schermers, in 36 *CMLRev.* (1999), 673–681.

the European Court must verify whether the organization concerned ensures a level of protection for individual rights equal to that provided for under the European Convention.

If one looks at this situation from a regional perspective, there emerges a very close parallel between the protection of human rights before international criminal bodies and the relationship between the EU and the system of the ECHR. The European Court of Justice (ECJ) held that the EC has no competence to adhere to the ECHR,[48] but those rights enshrined in the ECHR are also substantially protected by the ECJ in the framework of Community law. Thus, the tendency is more in the direction of ensuring (or, at least, trying to ensure) equal protection rather than submitting one system to the jurisdiction of another. Of course nothing prevents individuals from triggering monitoring procedures, where available, before appropriate international bodies against individual States. Eventually such States may even be obliged to pay compensation by the monitoring body. Even in the case of a violation, however, it does not seem that this would deprive the Court of jurisdiction (see in this respect Chapter 2 below, on the rights of persons in respect of an investigation).

If the option to create a connection between legal systems was rejected at regional level (EC–ECHR), where there exists a context of high legal homogeneity and shared common values, this rejection may be even more justified at universal level. As the Appeals Chamber of the ICTY put it in *Tadić*, the international legal order is not an integrated system,[49] hence every international legal system of adjudication is a sort of 'self-contained system' that cannot be subjected to the supervision of organs belonging to a different system. Among international judicial bodies there cannot be such vertical relationships as those that would be introduced by allowing review of their procedures and judgments by external bodies. In general, it seems that it is more effective to try to find solutions to the infringement of the rights of the accused within the system itself. As will be shown in this book with regard to the system of international criminal justice, the main objective should be the strengthening of internal guarantees.

5. *Summing up: a plea for a realistic perspective*

At this stage of development of the international community, an institutional relationship between human rights monitoring systems and international

---

[48] See ECJ, *Opinion 2/94*, 28 March 1996 [1996] ECR I–1759; on which cf. the comments by G. Gaja, 'Accession by the Community to the European Convention for the Protection of Human Rights and Fundamental Freedoms', in 33 *CMLRev.* (1996), 973–989.

[49] Appeals Chamber decision on jurisdiction, 2 October 1995, *Tadić* (IT–94–1–AR72), 'international law, because it lacks a centralized structure does not provide for an integrated judicial system' (para. 11).

criminal tribunals or the ICC does not exist, nor is it realistic to think it will be set up in the near future. Experience shows great resistance by each subsystem to accepting external supervision. For example, when the ICTY had to discuss the legality of its establishment, it did not refer the matter to another body, nor did it decline jurisdiction, but assumed the task of legally appraising the UN Security Council resolution by which it had been created. In so doing the Appeals Chamber of the ICTY underscored that at this stage of development of international law there is a high degree of independence among each subsystem.[50]

As pointed out above, the experience of the relationship between the EU and the system of the ECHR bears out the notion that there is no room for mechanisms of external review of the system of international criminal justice. In the international legal order each subsystem tends to be self-contained and to operate as a 'monad'.[51]

Additionally, there does not seem to be an appropriate international organ to conduct such a review: regional human rights courts, on account of their non-universal character, are not suitable as they do not have international legitimacy, while the UN Committee does not really operate as a judicial body.

The most realistic perspective is to strengthen human rights protection within the system and ensure that rules are thoroughly respected both by national and international organs. Nonetheless, a monitoring process need not be realized perforce on an institutional basis, but may be effectively conducted by States, NGOs, international media, and the academic community.

IV. ACCUSATORIAL AND INQUISITORIAL ELEMENTS IN INTERNATIONAL CRIMINAL PROCEDURE—TO WHAT EXTENT DO THEY IMPINGE UPON THE RIGHTS OF INDIVIDUALS?

1. Introduction: models and realities

Among concepts usually adopted in comparative criminal procedure the distinction made between *accusatorial* and *inquisitorial criminal proceedings* stands out.[52] The purpose of this paragraph is not to discuss the validity of

---

[50] *Ibidem.*

[51] This is the incisive term used by L. Condorelli, 'Le Tribunal Pénal International pour l'ex-Yougoslavie et sa jurisprudence', in 1 *Cursos Bancaja* (1997), 241–276, at 262–265.

[52] In this study the terms adversarial and accusatorial are used as synonyms, although it must be noted that their meaning is not entirely equivalent. As pointed out by M. Damaška, 'Adversary System' in S. Kadish (gen. ed.), *Encyclopedia of Crime and Justice*, i (New York: The Free Press, 1983), at 29, 'the conventional position . . . attributes the same meaning to the words adversarial and accusatorial. [However] comparativists should draw a distinction between the two. . . . Under this approach the adversary process is said to denote only a method of

such categories;[53] on the contrary, it is accepted that this dichotomy is appropriate, at least for descriptive purposes. Our intention is to adopt this categorization and apply it to international criminal proceedings to try to explore the relationship between the provisions on the rights of the accused and procedural mechanisms derived from one model or the other.

In this section, an attempt will be made to clarify whether it is possible to speak of a model of international criminal trial and where this model fits in the ideal line that runs from a purely adversarial model to inquisitorial proceedings.[54] The other question is naturally whether it would be appropriate and, in the event, useful to discuss international criminal procedure in terms of models. These models were born in a national context and it may therefore be questioned whether they are applicable to international criminal justice.

Certainly it is nowadays universally accepted that models in criminal procedure have only an indicative value. However, a form of dialectic between these two different conceptions of the regulation of criminal proceedings does exist and, as will be shown, has had an important influence on the drafting of the Statutes and Rules of both the UN Tribunals and the ICC.

Most scholars agree that models only point to tendencies rather than describing realities with accuracy.[55] It is precisely in this light that it is important to explore the influence of the adversarial and inquisitorial models on international criminal procedure. Moreover, it is interesting to determine how the tension between the two models, which is also linked to the opposition between common law and civil law systems, has affected the development of the rules of procedure of international criminal courts.

---

finding facts and deciding legal problems, and is characterized by the two sides shaping issues before a relatively neutral judge. The accusatorial system, on the other hand, is a more encompassing concept, which includes the adversary method as its constituent element.' This said, as the present study does not aim at drawing on comparative methodology, there should be no problem in using both terms as synonyms.

[53] This traditional classification has been criticized by several authors, cf. e.g. M. Damaška, 'Evidentiary Barriers to Conviction and Two Models of Criminal Procedure: A Comparative Study' in 121 *UPLR* (1973), 506, and subsequently in the more comprehensive study *The Faces of Justice and State Authority* (New Haven, Conn.: Yale University Press, 1986), at 3–6. See also the well-known distinction by H. Packer, *The Limits of Criminal Sanction* (Stanford, Cal.: Stanford Univ. Press, 1968), between crime control and due process models, on which cf. M. Angel, 'Modern Criminal Procedure: A Comparative Law Symposium—Foreword', in 62 *TLR* (1989), 1087–1097, at 1089. See also L. Leigh, 'Liberty and Efficiency', in 26 *ICLQ* (1977), 516–530 and F. Tulkens, 'La procédure pénale: grandes lignes de comparaison entre systèmes nationaux' in Delmas-Marty (ed.), note 1 above, 33–55, at 37–42. More recently along the same lines see M. Findlay, 'Synthesis in Trial Procedure? The Experience of International Criminal Tribunals', in 50 *ICLQ* (2001), 26–53. Nonetheless, it should be noted that generally speaking all attempts to supersede the accusatorial–inquisitorial dichotomy did not reach the same level of diffusion among legal scholarship.

[54] Cf. J. Pradel, 'Inquisitoire—Accusatoire: Une Redoutable Complexité', in 68 *RIDP* (1997), 213–229.

[55] *Ibidem*, at 214.

Generally speaking it may be recalled that these models historically reflect different conceptions of 'judicial truth'. The inquisitorial perspective generally considers that the objective of the criminal process is ascertaining the truth; this is and should be the overriding concern of the rules of criminal procedure. These rules must enable the 'inquisitor' to extract the truth from the suspect.[56] On the other hand, from an accusatorial viewpoint the process *per se* is what really matters. The establishment of historical truth cannot be ensured other than through respect for procedural rules, which constitute the method for reaching 'judicial truth'. In the end, this differentiation reflects two opposing epistemological beliefs: while for the inquisitorial paradigm there is an objective truth that the 'inquisitor' must ascertain, for the accusatorial approach the truth is the natural and logical result of a predetermined process.

It is generally recognized that the adversarial system is more suitable when it comes to offering protection to the rights of the accused.[57] However, it will be shown in this study that a merely adversarial procedure does not fit perfectly into a system of international criminal justice. This is a system which is substantially different from national criminal justice for a number of reasons: first, because it has to deal exclusively with very serious crimes; secondly, because crimes under the jurisdiction of international judicial organs are usually connected with complex and delicate political issues; thirdly, because, as a consequence of their connection with politics, often these crimes are also linked to the national security interests of various countries; and fourthly, because in international criminal proceedings gathering evidence may involve missions in various countries, with corresponding costs and occasionally difficult diplomatic relationships. Additionally, international criminal trials are conducted before professional judges, the jury system having been thoroughly rejected. Thus a number of rules designed for jury trials are not appropriate.[58]

---

[56] This approach implied and justified resort to torture and other instruments of physical pressure on the suspect '*ad eruendam veritatem*', that is to obtain the truth from the suspect. The individual is the bearer of an historical experience, which must be known by the judge for the purpose of establishing the facts. See F. Cordero, 'Stilus curiae (analisi della sentenza penale)', in *La sentenza in Europa—metodo tecnica e stile* (Padua: Cedam, 1988), 293–312, '*comincia tutto da un'idea ovvia: colpevole o no, l'imputato detiene una verità storica; ha commesso il fatto o non l'ha commesso; nei due casi l'accaduto costituisce un dato indelebile, con le relative memorie; se quanto lui sa trasparisse, ogni questione sarebbe liquidabile a colpo sicuro; bisogna che l'inquisitore gli entri nella testa*' (behind the inquisitorial model there is an obvious idea: guilty or not, the accused knows an historical truth; although he may not have committed the crime, the events which took place are in his memories. Should it be possible to know exactly all the elements he knows, it would be easier to answer all questions: therefore it is necessary for the investigator to enter his brain) (at 297).

[57] F. Cordero, *Ideologie del Processo Penale* (Rome: Università della Sapienza, 1997, originally published in Milan: Giuffrè, 1966), at 196.

[58] On the jury system see the Hamlyn lectures by P. Devlin, *Trial by Jury* (London: Stevens, 1966).

To sum up, whilst it can be denied that models furnish an exhaustive reading of the reality of international criminal justice and occasionally may be even misleading, it must be admitted that they do help in the discussion of procedural issues.

Of course it could also be argued that it is reductive to limit the study of the rules of international criminal procedure to this antinomy (accusatorial/ inquisitorial or adversarial/non-adversarial). It is true that there are forms of criminal procedure other than those based on these two models.[59] In this respect it may be admitted that the choice made is not necessarily acceptable. However, the main reasons for this choice are the belief and awareness that these are the most common paradigms in legal science. Furthermore, these models have to an overwhelming extent dominated the debates in the relevant international *fora* in which the Statutes and Rules of the Tribunals and the Court were drafted.

Notwithstanding the efforts made by certain authors (within western legal culture) to find new interpretations and replace these traditional models with new paradigms,[60] it is not possible to conclude that these models have been superseded. At present the accusatorial–inquisitorial dichotomy still prevails.

2. *The rights of the accused and the procedural model of the Nuremberg and Tokyo trials*

The experience of the Nuremberg and Tokyo trials has always been taken as a reference point in international criminal law and procedure, even if its value as a precedent should not be over-estimated. It is well known that the international proceedings instituted against the major war criminals after the Second World War were essentially justified by the control of the victors over German and Japanese territory and their institutions. Therefore, these trials were deeply influenced by the matrix of victor's justice. Irrespective of any bad faith on the part of the main actors in the proceedings, it was certainly impossible to create, in such a very short time, truly supranational and impartial institutions for the investigation and prosecution of such complex cases.[61]

With reference to the Nuremberg trial, it should be noted that in London the decision was taken to divide those areas subject to investigation into different parts and to assign to each Allied Power a specific portion of the

---

[59] Cf. in this respect F. Malekian, *The Concept of Islamic International Criminal Law: A Comparative Study* (London: Graham and Trotman, 1994), at 9. See more generally M. Lippman, S. McConville, and M. Yerushalmi, *Islamic Criminal Law and Procedure* (Westport, Conn.: Greenwood Press, 1988). With specific reference to the rights of the accused, see T.J. al Alwani, 'The Rights of the Accused in Islam', in 10 *Arab Law Quarterly* (1995), Part I, 3–16, and Part II, 238–249.

[60] See e.g. Damaška, note 53 above, at 20 ff.

[61] On this issue see Chapter 2 below, notes 18–20.

forthcoming indictment. Accordingly, each contingent contributed to the whole process by conducting the investigation with respect to its own part of the indictment. The procedure followed at trial was largely based on the Anglo-American tradition, even though a large number of affidavits and depositions were admitted into in evidence, which seems to be in contrast with the adversarial model.[62] Moreover, the adversarial character of the proceedings had some negative effects on defence counsel who, trained in civil law systems and used to a different kind of procedure, had difficulties in promptly reacting to the needs of the adversarial system, for example by timely and apposite interventions during cross-examination. Also the conditions for defence investigations, which have great importance in an adversarial trial, were very poor. There were no resources for defence counsel, and the court did not take steps to support the efforts of defence lawyers. Furthermore, these lawyers, mainly from civil law countries, were not used to a system that might require them to undertake investigations.

Due process guarantees in the International Military Tribunal (IMT) system had nothing to do with the protection afforded before municipal courts in the USA or in Great Britain.[63] The rights of defendants were far less detailed than in the Anglo-American system.[64] The Charter of the IMT, which was attached to the London Agreement, laid down the fundamental principles of organization and procedure according to which the Tribunal was to function. The Tribunal consisted of four members, each with an alternate (Article 2 IMT Charter), who were individually appointed by each of the Signatories. The accused had no right to challenge the judges or the prosecutors, but each signatory had the right to replace its member of the Tribunal, with the only limitation of not being able to do so during trial, other than with the relevant alternate. This might indicate a lack of independence, affecting in the end the impartiality of the judges, or at least the appearance of impartial-

---

[62] For a penetrating discussion of the procedural systems of the Nuremberg and Tokyo trials cf. E. Wallach, 'The Procedural and Evidentiary Rules of the Post-World War II War Crimes Trials: Did They Provide an Outline for International Legal Procedure?', in 37 *CJTL* (1999), 851–883, and A. Cassese note 6 above, 372–380.

[63] This was clearly reflected in the words of Robert Jackson in his Report to the president on Atrocities and War Crimes, 7 June 1945, para. II.2, where he wrote 'these hearings, however, must not be regarded in the same light as a trial under our system, where defence is a matter of constitutional right. Fair hearings for the accused are, of course, required to make sure that we punish only the right men and for the right reasons. But the procedure of these hearings may properly bar obstructive and dilatory tactics resorted to by defendants in our ordinary criminal trials'. The Report can be read on the internet site of the Avalon Project at the Yale Law School, **<www.yale.edu/lawweb/avalon/imt/imt.htm>**.

[64] Although it has been correctly noted that even the US Supreme Court had not yet thoroughly developed its conception on fair trial safeguards: cf. D.M. Amman, 'Harmonic Convergence? Constitutional Criminal Procedure in an International Context', in 75 *ILJ* (2000), 809–873, at 820.

ity (which is as important as impartiality itself).[65] Section II of the Charter (Articles 6–13) contained provisions on the Jurisdiction of the Tribunal and a few general norms, among which were Article 12, which provided for trials *in absentia*[66] and Article 13, which conferred upon the judges the power to adopt the Rules of Procedure of the Tribunal. The judges had, under the Charter, wide discretion, with the only condition that the Rules must not be 'inconsistent with the provisions of the Charter'. Section IV, entitled 'Fair Trial for Defendants', contained only one provision, Article 16, which listed the guarantees that were necessary to ensure that the accused were given a fair trial. It included rights such as that to be informed of the charges and translation in a language spoken by the accused. Article 16(b) provided for a right of the defendant 'to give any explanation relevant to the charges made against him'. Additionally, defendants had the right to conduct their own defence or to have the assistance of Counsel (Article 16(d)), and the right to present evidence at trial in support of their defence, and to cross-examine witnesses (Article 16(e)). Other provisions in the Charter had the indirect effect of protecting the right of the accused to a fair trial, imposing duties on the Tribunal. Under Article 17, for example, the Tribunal was given powers such as the authority to summon witnesses, to order the production of documents or other evidentiary materials, or to appoint court officers for the purpose of collecting evidence.[67] However, it has been contended that these powers did not help in achieving the goal of ensuring the defendant a fair trial, as they were

---

[65] It is interesting to note that the Russian Judge, Nikitchenko, had previously been in charge of drafting the Charter, and, more surprisingly, also of drawing up the list of persons to be included in the Indictment. The French alternate too, Robert Falco, had been the representative of France in the London Conference and had participated in the process of drafting the Indictment: cf. D. Irving, *Nuremberg: The Last Battle* (London: Focal Point, 1996), at 116–117. On this issue see also R.K. Woetzel, *The Nuremberg Trials in International Law* (2nd edn., London: Stevens and Sons, 1962), at 44.

[66] This provision was inserted into the Charter, in spite of its being contrary to the American Constitutional tradition, because at the time of drafting the Allies were not absolutely sure of the location of all the possible indictees. Eventually one defendant, Martin Bormann, was tried and convicted *in absentia*. However, he was never found and thus the sentence never enforced.

[67] Consistently with this provision, Rule 4 of the Rules of Procedure provided for a right of the defence to file an application with the General Secretary of the Tribunal to obtain the attendance of witnesses or the production of documents. When necessary, it would have been possible to achieve this goal through the assistance of the governments of the Signatories or those of the adhering States. It should, however, be pointed out that the norm provided for witnesses to be summoned only 'if possible' and therefore attributed to the States a wide margin of appreciation that did not seem to be subject to any control by the Tribunal. The issue of the co-operation of States in the activities of International Criminal Tribunals has been the object of a decision of the Appeals Chamber of the ICTY in a matter brought to the attention of the Court by the Republic of Croatia, which did not want fully to comply with an order of a judge of the Tribunal, perhaps improperly titled 'subpoena'. In this decision the Appeals Chamber—reversing the decision of the Trial chamber—affirmed several important principles concerning the obligation of States to co-operate with the International Tribunal and the possible remedies for non co-operation.

not exercised in favour of the defence.[68] The Rules of Procedure adopted by the Tribunal did not substantially modify the situation. The general rights of the accused were reaffirmed and the conditions for their implementation specified (Rule 2 IMT Rules).

Parallel to the creation of the International Military Tribunal for the punishment of the major war criminals of the European Axis, another International Military Tribunal was established for the Far East (the so-called 'Tokyo Tribunal').[69] Section III of the Charter of this Tribunal dealt with the issue of fair trial and specified which procedures had to be followed to ensure that the accused received a fair trial. The guarantees offered by the provisions of this section were similar to those contained in the Charter of the Nuremberg Tribunal.[70]

When asked about the fairness of the Tokyo trial (but the reasoning can be extended to the Nuremberg trial as well) the prominent Dutch jurist, B.V.A. Röling, who served as a judge in that trial, admitted that the provisions of the Statute were very general; however he concluded that 'it was a rather fair trial'.[71] Nonetheless, one should note that the defendants in both Nuremberg and Tokyo had no possibility of obtaining exculpatory evidence from the Prosecutor.[72] Although the procedure was essentially inspired by the tradition of common law, the vast majority of evidence offered at trial was documentary, the reliability of which did not always prove satisfactory. Furthermore, some of these pieces of evidence subsequently even turned out to be false.[73] There were also problems with the translation of documents[74] and with the application of the rules of evidence. In principle, the Tribunals were not bound by rigid exclusionary rules (which are essentially created for

---

[68] Cf., e.g., the allegations reported by Irving, note 65 above, at 173–177, and M. Marrus, *The Nuremberg War Crimes Trials 1945–46: A Documentary History* (Boston, Mass.: Bedford Books, 1997), at 247.

[69] For ample documentation and references on the Tokyo trials see R.J. Pritchard, 'The International Military Tribunal for the Far East and the Allied National War Crimes Trials in Asia', in M.C. Bassiouni (ed.), *International Criminal Law*, (2nd edn., Ardsley, NY: Transnational, 1999) iii, 109–146, in particular at 127–133.

[70] The time limits were further specified by the Rules of Procedure, adopted on 25 April 1946, that stated that each accused should receive the indictment, the charter, and any other documents lodged with the indictment (so that copies could be taken) not less than 14 days before the Tribunal began.

[71] Cf. B.V.A. Röling and A. Cassese, *The Tokyo Trial and Beyond—Reflections of a Peacemonger* (Cambridge: Polity Press, 1993), at 54. Professor Röling, however, when speaking of a fair trial clearly refers to the kind of trial in the prevailing circumstances of the time and gives a substantial evaluation of the trial itself in light of the fact that it was in the end 'victor's justice' (at 87). It could be said that as an example of victor's justice it was fair.

[72] *Ibidem*, at 51.

[73] Irving, note 65 above, at 72 refers to a document that turned out to be a forgery.

[74] Cf. Röling and Cassese, note 71 above, at 53, where Röling explains how he discovered that one document was badly translated and how the majority of the judges disregarded the correct translation. Irving argues at 210 that the transcript on which the judges worked for their decision was not accurate and often wrong. Kranzbühler (who, however, was Defence Counsel for Admiral Dönitz) criticized the deficiencies in the proceedings, particularly in so far as the findings reached by the Tribunal are concerned, see Marrus, note 68 above, at 248–249.

jury trials),[75] but the problem seems to be that occasionally exclusionary rules were applied, especially when the defence was offering evidence.[76]

Two issues, however, must be distinguished: on the one hand, the question of the fairness of the rules of procedure in abstract; on the other, their concrete application which allegedly led to the substantial unfairness of the trials. It has been argued that the Rules were theoretically adequate to give the defendants a fair trial and that it was in fact their application that was unfair.[77] On the contrary, it is submitted that, although some of the rights of the accused were protected, some were instead lacking, such as the right to remain silent, or the right to provisional release. Additionally some of the provisions of the Charter and of the Rules of Procedure were intrinsically unfair or at least incomplete or unfairly administered. There were no provisions on disqualification, and there was no express rule on the presumption of innocence. Moreover, the lack of a detailed procedure for discovery and of any provision on the duty of the Prosecutor to seek or, at least, communicate exculpatory materials had an adverse impact on the rights of defendants. All these elements support the conclusion that these trials were not 'fair' in the current understanding, even if it could reasonably be argued that they were the fairest trials that defendants of vanquished powers might have had at that time.[78]

The rather scarce provisions protecting the rights of the accused in the 'international legislation' governing the trials of the major German and Japanese war criminals from the Second World War can be explained by taking into account three elements: first, the haste with which the victors set up the Tribunals after having considered various options for dealing with such novel, widespread, and large-scale crimes, allegedly committed not only by servicemen in the field, but also by military and political leaders, as well as civilians (such as industrialists etc.). Secondly, the heinous character of the events of the Second World War meant that an in-depth and thorough reflection on the protection of the rights of persons accused of crimes against

---

[75] In this respect see Wallach, note 62 above, at 855, note 12, where he quotes a memorandum by Justice Robert Jackson in which the American Prosecutor at Nuremberg explains why 'the United States reluctantly acceded to the abandonment of common law rules of evidence'.

[76] Other disparities of treatment are reported by R. Minear, *Victor's Justice: The Tokyo War Crimes Trial* (Princeton, NJ: Princeton University Press, 1971), at 118–124. Irving underscores that the right of the defendant to call witnesses was not appropriately supported by the Tribunals. The defence could only call a minority of the witnesses it wanted to call (at 188–189). Cf. Röling and Cassese, note 71 above, at 51. See also Wallach, note 62 above, at 869, where he writes 'the rules of evidence and procedure which governed the trials were flexible beyond not just the norms of criminal trials in democratic systems, but beyond the bounds of fairness as well . . . the underlying problem [was that] too malleable rules were applied . . . open to abuse because they were so flexible'. The dangers of flexibility are still present in the system of international criminal procedure. In this respect it will be argued that there should be an attempt to restrict such flexibility. This seems particularly justified absent any form of external supervision on the activity of international courts.

[77] Cf. again Kranzbühler, in Marrus, note 68 above, at 249, and, for the Tokyo trial, Minear, note 76 above, at 121.

[78] Cf. Röling and Cassese, note 71 above, at 54.

humanity, crimes against peace, and war crimes was not easy.[79] Thirdly, although already existing in many States, the concepts of fair trial and due process had not yet received international proclamation and were not yet as detailed as they would be a few decades later. It is precisely this process of international 'law-making' on the rights of individuals in the administration of criminal justice, described above, which created the imperative for stricter adherence to the adversarial model in the systems of UN *ad hoc* Tribunals.[80] Moreover, it was necessary to provide for a more developed catalogue of rights for the accused.

3. *The tension between accusatorial and inquisitorial aspects in the system of UN* ad hoc *Tribunals and in the ICC Statute*

(a) UN *ad hoc* Tribunals

The Statutes of the twin Tribunals created by the Security Council do not contain detailed rules of procedure. The task of adopting the Rules of Procedure and Evidence was left to the judges meeting in plenary session.[81]

Originally, the Rules of Procedure and Evidence (RPE) of the Tribunals were mainly based on *common law procedure*; in particular, they bore strong resemblance to the American model.[82] However, since their adoption they have undergone several significant amendments, and thus to a large extent it can be said that a new procedural system has been created: a sort of hybrid that fits somewhere between adversarial and inquisitorial.[83] It is, therefore, very difficult and certainly incorrect to refer to the RPE of the Tribunals as a static reality. Since 1993 the RPE of the ICTY have been amended twenty-five times and, since 1994, those of the ICTR twenty. This continuous process of amendment has been criticized and has consequently led to the suppression of such a 'law-making' power for the judges of the ICC.[84] However, the experi-

---

[79] Irving reports passages of correspondence between State officials before the establishment of the Nuremberg Tribunal from which it appears that some officials had the feeling that the trial, if any, should only be a formality. There was great fear that defendants would use a trial as a podium for justifying the atrocities and as a m eans of propaganda; on this issue see also M.C. Bassiouni, 'The Nuremberg Legacy' in Bassiouni, note 69 above, iii, 195–213, at 201–203.

[80] Such as e.g. the adoption of detailed Rules on pre-trial discovery (Rules 66–68 RPEs).

[81] See Article 15 ICTY St. SC Res. 827 (1993) and Article 14 ICTR St. SC Res. 955 (1994).

[82] In this respect see V. Morris and M. Scharf, *An Insider's Guide to the International Criminal Tribunal for the former Yugoslavia: A Documentary History and Analysis* (Irvington on Hudson, NY: Transnational, 1995), i at 177.

[83] Judge Robinson clearly affirms the *sui generis* nature of these rules and even refuses to consider them somewhere in between adversarial and inquisitorial: P. Robinson, 'Ensuring Fair and Expeditious Trials at the International Criminal Tribunal for the former Yugoslavia', in 11 *EJIL* (2000), 569–589, at 588.

[84] In this respect cf. F. Guariglia, 'The Rules of Procedure and Evidence for the International Criminal Court: A New Development in International Adjudication of Individual Criminal Responsibility' in A. Cassese, P. Gaeta, and J. Jones (eds.) note 4 above, ii, 1111–1136.

ence of the *ad hoc* Tribunals, and in particular the process of adjustment of the RPE through amendments, have been and will continue to be of invaluable importance for any system of international criminal justice.[85]

The procedure before the Tribunals remains *adversarial* in many respects. The investigation process is left to the Prosecutor, who has wide discretion in selecting the cases for investigation and in the conduct of the cases brought before the Tribunals. Only after completion of the investigative phase does the Prosecutor have to submit the indictment to a judge for confirmation. In the initial form of the RPE, the judicial organ intervened in the pre-trial phase only as a 'confirming Judge' (Article 19 of the Statute and Rule 47 RPE). Subsequently, through progressive amendments of the Rules, a judge of the Trial Chamber is assigned the task of 'organizing' the proceedings. Rule 65-*ter* introduced the 'Pre-Trial Judge', who 'shall co-ordinate communication between the parties during the pre-trial phase' (Rule 65-*ter* B). Moreover, the Pre-Trial Judge also has a whole set of functions aimed at regulating the entire phase between the initial appearance of the accused and the opening of the trial. Furthermore, in the ICTR system a similar role has been designed for a Judge of the Appeals Chamber, the Pre-Hearing Judge, who is entrusted with the task of supervising the preliminary phases of appeals proceedings (Rule 108-*bis* ICTR RPE).[86] Even without an explicit amendment to the ICTY RPE, the same role may be played in appeal proceedings before the ICTY by a Judge of the Appeals Chamber acting, *mutatis mutandis*, as Pre-Trial Judge, applying the rules set out for trials.[87] In addition, now, according to the new text of Rule 15, the confirming judge can sit as a member of the Trial Chamber hearing the case he or she has confirmed. This amendment, although not entirely persuasive in terms of respect for the principle of impartiality and the presumption of innocence, confirms the movement towards a more inquisitorial style.[88] Judicial practice has moved towards the adoption of some other inquisitorial elements, such as a more extensive use of documentary evidence and court transcripts, and the extension of the possibility of

[85] President Jorda, Address to the ICC Preparatory Commission, 19 June 2000, SB/P.I.S./511-E, suggesting that 'whatever Rules of Procedure and Evidence [the Commission adopts], it is important that they be sufficiently flexible to allow the Judges to deal with the unexpected events to which the prevention of serious violations of humanitarian law falling within the jurisdiction of the Court will inevitably give rise'.

[86] Strangely the ICTR has not adopted Rule 65-*ter* on the Pre-Trial Judge, although in practice Chambers operate a delegation of powers to one of their members. In this respect, see, e.g., Rule 65-*bis*, whereby 'a Status conference may be convened by a Trial Chamber or a *Judge* thereof' or Rule 73 establishing that 'the Trial Chamber, or a *Judge* designated by the Chamber from among its members, may rule on . . . motions based solely on the briefs of the parties' (emphasis added).

[87] As provided for by Rule 107 RPE ICTY.

[88] This amendment implies that a judge who has full knowledge of the materials supporting the charges against the accused is allowed to be a member of the Trial Chamber. In this respect, this seems a clear move towards a more inquisitorial system.

relying upon depositions. Often, as in the case of depositions, the decisions of Chambers have been followed by an amendment to the Rules.

(b) The ICC Statute

The choice made for the ICC was to rely on a model still based on adversarial inspiration, but with important inquisitorial elements. The investigation and presentation of the case are entirely within the purview of the Prosecutor. The Prosecutor has the widest discretion whether or not to prosecute. There are provisions for organizing the proceedings on admission of guilt. Evidence may only be given in court before the trial judge, subject to constant confrontation between prosecution and defence. The judicial organ at trial is a third party, which, in principle, should have no knowledge of the evidence prior to its presentation at trial. However, it is also certain that the adversarial paradigm is not pure. Many corrections have been made, such as the role of the Pre-Trial Chamber, or the possibility for the accused to apply for disqualification of the Prosecutor. Moreover, other elements, such as the duty imposed on the Prosecutor to seek evidence in favour of the accused or the provisions on pre-trial admission of evidence in case of risk of destruction, are tributes to a non-adversarial philosophy. Finally, it is unclear whether the Trial Chamber may have access to the materials submitted to the Pre-Trial Chamber for the confirmation of charges. Should this be admitted, it would be a major deviation from the adversarial model.[88a]

As mentioned above, the adversarial model is generally considered to be more protective of the rights of the accused. However, whilst conceding that this is true at national level, it is less certain at international level. The unique features of international criminal justice make both necessary and desirable some changes that, whilst not in perfect accord with the abstract model, are indeed essential in ensuring effective protection of the rights of the accused. By way of example it is interesting to refer to difficulties of conducting a defence investigation in international proceedings. This illustrates the limit of a system that would see the prosecutor only as a party and the judges as detached umpires. In international criminal trials both the prosecutor and the judges are bound to take all those measures designed to assist the accused in the preparation of his or her defence, which are imposed by the notion of fair trial.

[88a] See A. Cassese note 6 above, at 412–413, who seems to support the view that this should be the correct interpretation. On the other hand, P. Lewis, 'Trial Procedure', in R. Lee and others (eds.), *The International Criminal Court—Elements of Crimes and Rules of Procedure and Evidence*, (Ardsley, NY: Transnational, 2001), at 540–541, suggests that the drafting of Rules 121 and 131 ICC RPE is deliberately ambiguous, and argues that only the Court's practice will shed light on this issue (at 553).

4. *Conclusion: the need to strike a balance between adversarial and inquisitorial elements, for fair and expeditious international criminal proceedings*

From Nuremberg to Rome there has been an incredible improvement in the level of protection of the rights of defendants in international criminal proceedings. This is certainly not due to fundamental changes in the trial model. Since 1945 the general model has theoretically not changed. Basically, the procedure adopted for the ICC, just like its Nuremberg precedent, is a criminal trial based on adversarial elements, with very strong roots in common law systems. Nevertheless, the combination of both the *increased international corpus of human rights provisions*, protecting the right of individuals to a fair trial (the right to confront witnesses, to obtain evidence, to remain silent) and a trend towards the abandonment of the biased approach of 'victor's justice' (impartiality and independence of the judges, strongest protection for the presumption of innocence) have made international criminal procedure much more balanced. Moreover, it would be tempting to add that States, while drafting the Statute and the Rules of the ICC, had in mind the application of those provisions to their citizens (and in particular to their military personnel) and therefore were eager to provide for all necessary safeguards.

Furthermore, the situation has improved with respect to the position of victims. In Nuremberg and Tokyo victims had no particular status, there was no special counselling activity, nor any special organ entrusted with the task of supporting victims, nor were there provisions on restitution or compensation. A first step forward in this respect was made in the system of the UN *ad hoc* Tribunals. The interests of victims are specifically mentioned in the Statute. Moreover a special unit has been created to assist and counsel victims. Additionally there are express provisions on restitution and compensation. Even if there is no enforceable right deriving from international decisions, it has explicitly been provided that the national judge before whom the victim can file a request for compensation must take into account the Tribunals' findings. With the ICC Statute additional steps have been taken. First of all, the right has been proclaimed for victims or associations of victims to submit information to the Prosecutor. Moreover, there is the possibility for the victims to be heard by the Pre-Trial Chamber in the course of hearings to examine the request by the Prosecutor for authorization to open an investigation. Besides, provision has been made, to a certain extent, for the right of victims to participate in the proceedings. This right was the result of both strong pressures from victim groups during the 'Rome Conference' and the ICTY and ICTR systems were criticized for not allowing such participation. Lastly, there are in the ICC Statute extensive provisions on the right of victims to protection, and the need for the interests of victims to be weighed against the rights of the defendants.

The condition of individuals in the international criminal justice system has undoubtedly improved. There has been progress in both directions: the rights of defendants, on the one hand, and the rights of victims, on the other. This process has certainly not exhausted its potential for change.

It should be noted that the prevailing adversarial inspiration has positively influenced the modes of protection of the rights of the accused. This implies that, even if there may still be a need to amend the Rules, amendments must always respect the rights of defendants.

A worrying area, which may justify some restraints on the adversarial model, is that individuals may be left without protection with regard to their defence counsel's inability to act or misconduct. In this respect the decision delivered by the ICTY against one of Tadić's lawyers is very instructive. Mr Vujin, a lawyer from Belgrade and head of the Yugoslav Bar, worked for several months on the Tadić defence team. In the end it was discovered that he had acted against the interests of the accused[89] and, whilst in the opinion of the Chamber he did not alter the outcome of the trial, this may have made it more difficult for the defendant to exercise his rights effectively.[90] This episode is enlightening and poses the question whether an international criminal trial can ever really be a proceeding in which two parties confront each other on an equal footing. It is submitted here (and this idea will be explored more accurately in next chapter) that international authorities are under a specific obligation to protect the rights of the accused. Both the judges and the Registrar should monitor the enjoyment by defendants of their rights. Additionally, the Prosecutor must be made responsible for co-operating in ensuring respect for individual rights.[91]

Another example, which shows the limits of a purely adversarial approach and the need for overall control of the proceedings by judicial organs, is the issue of guilty pleas and the saga of the first Erdemović guilty plea. Erdemović was a soldier who had participated in the massacre of Srebrenica in July 1995. After having been transferred to the Tribunal he co-operated with the office of the Prosecutor. Charged with both crimes against humanity and war crimes he

---

[89] Apparently, Mr Vujin had tried to persuade some witnesses not to testify or to lie under oath to the detriment of the defendant's position. See Appeals Chamber Judgment, on Allegations of Contempt, *Vujin in Tadić* (IT–94–1-R77), 31 January 2000 and 27 February 2001.

[90] On 18 June 2001, Duško Tadić filed a motion for review, on the ground that he was unfaithfully represented by one of the members of his defence team. On 30 July 2002, however, the ICTY Appeals Chamber dismissed the motion; see Decision on Motion for Review, Tadić (IT–94–1–R), 30 July 2002. On the trial phase of the Tadić case see M. Scharf, *Balkan Justice: The Story Behind the First International War Crimes Trial since Nuremberg* (Durham: Carolina Academic Press, 1997).

[91] Another event that could have had worrying effects on the Tadić case, but was luckily discovered in time, is the false testimony of Dragan Opačić who was supposed to be a key eye witness against the accused and turned out to be totally unreliable. On this issue see M. Wladimiroff, 'Rights of Suspects and Accused', in G. McDonald and O. Swaak-Goldman (eds.), *Substantive and Procedural Aspects of International Criminal Law* (The Hague: Kluwer, 2000), i 417–450, at 441.

decided to enter a guilty plea to the crimes against humanity charges. Subsequently, the Appeals Chamber found that the procedure followed for the plea was incorrect and quashed it because the accused was not well informed.[92] From the Appeals Chamber decision one may infer that both the Trial Chamber, and—more importantly—Erdemović's defence attorney misled or did not correctly guide the accused.[93] This was largely due to the fact that the attorney came from Yugoslavia and was not familiar with the 'guilty plea' procedure. Subsequently, the Rules of Procedure of the Tribunal were amended to provide for appropriate safeguards and guidance for the Chamber to verify the validity of a plea. There was no malice or bad faith in the attitude of Erdemović's lawyer and the mistake, if any, was entirely due to his scant knowledge of common law procedures. However, even if in the end the plea had been annulled and a new trial ordered, the misinterpretation of guilty plea proceedings may have damaged the accused substantially.

The abovementioned episodes show how the transposition of a purely adversarial model in international criminal proceedings can lead to some unfairness. It is not possible to leave it only to defendants to protect their interests in an international context. In other words, it is clear that there should be a sort of control over the exercise of defence rights and, to a certain extent, also on the activity of defence attorneys: control, it goes without saying, designed not to hamper or interfere with the action of defence counsel, but rather to ensure that the defence is effective and duly safeguarding the rights and interests of the accused. Indeed, international criminal trials show several complexities that should be taken into account. These may be, for example, the need for State co-operation, which for an individual may be impossible to obtain, or the risk that 'witness syndicates' or hostile governmental authorities try to instrumentalize proceedings. To avoid such deviations leading to substantial unfairness in the outcome of the proceedings, the Prosecutor must play a more impartial role than it usually does in traditional adversarial trials and the Chambers cannot limit themselves to being silent arbiters.

Finally, the most important element that has characterized the law-making activity of the *ad hoc* Tribunals in the last four years (1998–2002) is the attempt to settle the problem of the length of trials. It may be contended that in certain respects it would be preferable not to continue along the lines of a modification of the adversarial paradigm. Certainly, length and, as a consequence, potential ineffectiveness constitute the main weakness of adversarial proceedings. Recent amendments to the system of the *ad hoc* Tribunals

---

[92] On Erdemović's guilty plea procedure see S. Yee, 'The *Erdemović* Sentencing Judgement: A Questionable Milestone for the International Criminal Tribunal for the Former Yugoslavia', in 26 *GeorgiaJICL* (1997), at 263, and S. Linton, 'Reviewing the Case of Drazen Erdemović: Unchartered Waters at the International Criminal Tribunal for the Former Yugoslavia', in 12 *LJIL* (1999), 251–270.

[93] See Appeals Chamber Judgment, *Erdemović* (IT–96–22-A), 7 October 1997.

have tried to address these concerns. Elements such as the introduction of the Pre-Trial Judge (including more incisive powers of control over the pre-trial phase), the extension of the opportunity to proceed by depositions and the broader admission of written evidence will play a very important role in ensuring a more expeditious and hopefully fairer administration of justice. Nonetheless, adversarial principles should not be put aside too easily and the desire to ensure efficiency should never negatively affect and curtail the rights of defendants. Usually, a trial conducted following the adversarial style offers a better guarantee to the accused that his case will be more carefully examined and evidence cautiously tested.

True, the adversarial inspiration of the trial before *ad hoc* Tribunals has led to very long pre-trial and trial phases, which may violate both the right of the accused to a speedy trial and the interests of justice (and of victims) that trials be prompt and effective. On the other hand, however, the desire to ensure speedy trials can under no circumstances be taken as a justification for reducing the rights of defendants. It would be dangerous to surrender to the temptation of thinking that greater effectiveness may justify fewer guarantees. The judges of the *ad hoc* Tribunals have amended the Rules to try to address this issue and have introduced innovations to accelerate proceedings. Additionally, in November 2000 and August 2002 the Security Council authorized the appointment of a new category of judges, called *ad litem* judges, that will assist the Tribunals in conducting trials.[94]

It is too early to measure in its entirety the effectiveness of this amendment process. At this stage, it can be noted that the amendments adopted, characterized by an overall non-adversarial tendency, have ensured the more effective handling of pre-trial matters and the reduction of hearings devoted to testimonies on issues other than facts pertaining to the individual responsibility of the defendant. These elements seek to temper the adversarial character of international criminal trials with inquisitorial inputs. This amendment process has generally been coupled with great care fully to respect the rights of individuals. Nonetheless, an appeal for caution must be made, as there may be areas of concern, such as the very broad admission of written evidence[95] or the provisions authorizing the judge who confirms the indictment to sit as a member of the Chamber for trial or appeal proceedings.

[94] A pool of 27 judges was appointed by the General Assembly, pursuant to Security Council Res. 1329 (2000), 30 November 2000. Some of these judges were assigned to the Tribunal by the Secretary General in June 2001, sworn in on 29 September 2001, and started exercising their functions. In this respect cf. Ascensio and Maison, note 3 above, at 290–291. However, I disagree with these authors in so far as they tend to equate the *ad litem* judges under res. 1329 (2000) with those that were authorized under res. 1126 (1997) to complete the 'Celebici' trial, although their mandate had expired. On 14 August 2002 the Security Council adopted a similar resolution for the ICTR, UNSC Res. 1431 (2002).

[95] Cf. in this respect, P. Wald, 'To Establish Incredible Events by Credible Evidence: the Use of Affidavit Testimony in Yugoslavia War Crimes Tribunal Proceedings', in 42 *HILJ* (2001), 535–553, at 551–553.

2

The Rights of Persons During Investigations

I. THE INITIATION OF INVESTIGATIONS AND THE POWERS OF THE INVESTIGATIVE AUTHORITY

1. *The power of the Prosecutor to initiate investigations* proprio motu

(a) General

It is generally assumed that international criminal proceedings may make a substantial contribution to the fight against massive human rights violations.[1] Naturally, the effectiveness of resorting to such instruments to address very serious human rights violations depends largely on the scope of jurisdiction of international judicial institutions and on the powers attributed to organs responsible for investigation and prosecution of international crimes.

In the last decade there has been an increasing demand for international criminal justice. This has led to the adoption of the Statute establishing the International Criminal Court. The creation of the *ad hoc* Tribunals, the projects for a Tribunal to judge the Khmer Rouge regime,[2] the Special Court for Sierra Leone,[3] the investigations into the atrocities committed in East Timor,[4] the opening of some investigations at a national level, such as the Pinochet 'saga' in the United Kingdom and Spain,[5] the Hissène Habré case in Senegal,[6] the Ghaddafi case in France,[7] the case in Belgium[8] involving the

---

[1] This contention has, however, been criticized by several authors to different degrees. Cf. J. Alvarez, 'Rush to Closure: Lessons from the Tadić Judgement', in 96 *Mich. LR* (1998), 2031–2112, and 'Crimes of State—Crimes of Hate: Lessons from Rwanda', in 24 *YJIL* (1999), 365–483. See also G. Rana, '. . . And justice for all: Normative Descriptive Frameworks for the Implementation of Tribunals to Try Human Rights Violators', in 30 *Vand. JTL* (1997), 349–378; A. D'Amato, 'Peace vs. Accountability in Bosnia', in 88 *AJIL* (1994) at 500 ff., F. Forsythe, 'Politics and the International Criminal Tribunal for the Former Yugoslavia', in 5 *CLF* (1994) 401–422. For a more balanced view cf. D. Wippman, 'Atrocities, Deterrence, and the Limits of International Justice', in 23 *FJIL* (1999) at 473 ff. *Contra* the authors cited in note 10 below.

[2] Cf. S. Linton, 'Cambodia, East Timor and Sierra Leone: Experiments in International Justice', in 12 *CLF* (2001), 185–246.

[3] See M. Frulli, 'The Special Court for Sierra Leone: Some Preliminary Comments', in 11 *EJIL* (2000), 857–869; and R. Cryer, 'A "Special Court" for Sierra Leone, in 50 *ICLQ* (2001), 435–466.

[4] Cf. X. Tracol, 'Justice pour le Timor oriental', in 56 *RSCDPC* (2001), 291–306.

[5] On the various aspects of the Pinochet case see D. Woodhouse (ed.), *The Pinochet Case A Legal and Constitutional Analysis* (Oxford: Hart Publishing, 2000). See also A. Bianchi, 'Immunity versus Human Rights: the Pinochet Case', in 10 *EJIL* (1999), 237–277.

[6] Cf. the dossier 'Affaire Hissène Habré', in 12 *African Journal of International and Comparative Law* (2000), 815–820.

[7] See A. Cassese, *International Law* (Oxford: OUP, 2001), at 260.

[8] On this issue a case had been brought by Congo before the International Court of Justice, see <www.icj-cij.org>, 'Decisions'; see the Judgment of the Court (*Congo* v. *Belgium*), 14 February 2001.

Minister of Foreign Affairs of the Congo are all indications of a growing interest in international criminal justice.[9] These elements certainly evidence a trend based on the belief that criminal justice has a role to play *vis-à-vis* serious human rights violations.[10]

Leaving aside the problem of the powers and the instruments available for investigations and prosecutions at a national level,[11] the focus of this analysis will be restricted to international criminal courts. It is submitted that in order to try to evaluate the impact that the activity of international authorities responsible for investigating and prosecuting international crimes may have, it is necessary to see how they operate. In particular, it seems logical to examine the mechanisms that trigger international investigations and the role, if any, played by the victims in this process (besides answering the question whether victims should have a role in determining the opening of an investigation). This will be done by trying to compare the proceedings against the major war criminals of the Second World War with the system of the UN *ad hoc* Tribunals, and, finally, the procedural system of the ICC.

Moreover, it should be made clear that, in the unique context of international criminal justice, the Prosecutor of the *ad hoc* Tribunals and, in future, of the permanent Court must play a fundamental role in ensuring the protection of the rights of persons under investigation or prosecution. This is a distinctive trait of the international Prosecutor[12] and will be discussed in sub-sections (c) and (d) below.

(b) The Nuremberg and Tokyo Tribunals

At Nuremberg there were four Chief Prosecutors, representing the four Allied Powers (one for each of the Signatories), each of them responsible for a section of the Indictment. It cannot really be contended that the investigative authori-

---

[9] For a general view of progresses and current developments in international criminal law cases both at the national and international levels cf. <**www.diplomatiejudiciaire.com**>.

[10] In general on the need for justice and accountability see S. Ratner and J. Abrams, *Accountability for Human Rights Atrocities in International Law: Beyond the Nuremberg Legacy* (2nd edn., Oxford: OUP, 2001); M. Osiel, *Mass Atrocities, Collective Memory and the Law* (New Brunswick, NJ: Transaction Publ., 1997); C.S. Nino, *Radical Evil on Trial* (New Haven, Conn.: Yale UP, 1995); and D. Orentlicher, 'Settling Accounts: The Duty to Prosecute Human Rights Violations of a Prior Regime', in 100 *YLJ* (1991) 2537. See also P. Akhavan, 'Beyond Impunity: Can International Criminal Justice Prevent Future Atrocities?', in 95 *AJIL* (2001), 7–31. Moreover, the protection of human rights may be strengthened by the cumulative effect of human rights monitoring bodies (and human rights law) and the ICC (and international humanitarian law). In this respect see F. Pocar, 'The Rome Statute of the International Criminal Court and Human Rights', in M. Politi and G. Nesi (eds.), *The Rome Statute of the International Criminal Court—A Challenge to Impunity* (Aldershot: Ashgate, 2001), 67–74.

[11] On this issue cf. A. Cassese and M. Delmas Marty (eds.), *Juridictions Nationales et Crimes Internationaux* (Paris: PUF, 2002).

[12] On the role and functions of the international Prosecutor, see L. Arbour *et al.* (eds.), *The Prosecutor of a Permanent International Criminal Court* (Freiburg im Bresgau: Edition Iuscrim, 2000).

ties were international.[13] On the contrary, investigations were essentially within the purview of separate authorities of each of the four Allied Powers. In particular, national contingents of the occupation armies conducted searches for evidence and analysis of the elements discovered. Investigative methods and activities were mainly based on mechanisms particular to the various national military justice systems and the exercise of criminal jurisdiction over enemies. The issue of the Indictment, however, can be properly considered an international act, since the Prosecutors acted jointly.[14]

In this respect it should be recalled that Article 14 of the Nuremberg Charter specifically established the activities that ought to be conducted by the four Chief Prosecutors acting as a committee. On the other hand, Article 15 of the Charter indicated the tasks that they had to accomplish individually. This last category comprised crucial activities such as: (a) the conduct of investigation, collection and production of evidence; (b) the preparation of relevant portions of the indictment; and (c) the preliminary examination of necessary witnesses and defendants. These powers, attributed to the Prosecutors acting in their individual capacity, seem to confirm that the action of investigation was conducted at the level of national contingents. A further element that shows the prevalence of the national dimension is the concluding sentence of Article 15, where it is established that 'no witness or defendant detained by one of the Signatories can be taken out of the possession of that Signatory without its assent'. This provision reveals beyond any doubt that investigations at Nuremberg were still firmly based on the exercise by the Allies of their power as occupying countries.

It should be admitted, however, that there was an international element even in the pre-trial phase. As mentioned above, prosecution itself—defined as the decision concretely to trigger the jurisdiction of the Tribunals (i.e. the request to put somebody on trial for certain charges)—had to be decided collectively by the four Chief Prosecutors acting together as a Committee pursuant to Article 14 of the Nuremberg Charter. To a certain extent it can be argued that the committee operated in this area as an international organ. This is confirmed by the fact that decisions on the choice of the defendants and of the offences to be charged could be taken by majority vote.

Compared with the Nuremberg mechanism, the system established for the Tokyo trial was slightly different. Article 8 of the IMTFE Charter provided that there would be only one Chief Counsel, who could have several adjuncts.

---

[13] Despite the creation of the UN War Crimes Commission, this agency was not able to play an international role in proceedings before the International Military Tribunal (IMT). In this respect see M.C. Bassiouni, 'International Criminal Investigations and Prosecutions: From Versailles to Rwanda', in M.C. Bassiouni (ed.), *International Criminal Law* (2nd edn., Ardsley, NY: Transnational, 1999), iii, 'Enforcement', at 39. See also A. Cassese, *International Criminal Law* (Oxford: OUP, 2003) at 374.

[14] See B. Smith, *The Road to Nuremberg* (New York: Basic Books, 1981) and A. Tusa and J. Tusa, *The Nuremberg Trial* (London: BBC Books, 1995), 92–115.

In particular pursuant to paragraph (B) of Article 8, it was specified that 'any United Nation with which Japan has been at war may appoint an Associate Counsel to assist the Chief of Counsel'. However, it was the Chief Counsel— appointed by the Supreme Commander for the Far East—who was responsible for investigation and prosecution. The Associate Counsel co-operated with him and assisted him but always acted, at least formally, under his authority.

American authorities played a dominant role in the post-war trials in Europe, both in the investigation phase and in trial proceedings. Additionally, the USA dominated even more the Tribunal for the Far East.[15] At the Tokyo trial, although there was more variety among the judges, the Chief Prosecutor was American and representatives from other countries were admitted only as deputies. The methods and forms of investigation and prosecution were very similar to those already experienced in Nuremberg. However they were even more under the control of the United States.[16]

There is no reason to deny that the post-war trials were deeply affected by the paradigm of victor's justice.[17] They did contain some international elements, but still not in the form of truly supranational proceedings.[18] These trials can be seen as the joint exercise by the Allies of their jurisdiction over captured enemies and the application of their power to administer justice over German and Japanese territories that were under their control.[19] However, it must be noted that many other States in 1945 adhered to the Charter of Nuremberg[20] and that the UN General Assembly subsequently endorsed the

---

[15] A. Cassese note 13 above at 379, and M.C. Bassiouni, 'From Versailles to Rwanda', in M.C. Bassiouni (ed.), *International Criminal Law* (2nd edn., Ardsley, NY: Transnational, 1999), iii, at 40. See also P. Piccigallo, *The Japanese on Trial* (Austin, Tex.: University of Texas Press, 1979), 34–48, and 145.

[16] See E. Wallach, 'The Procedural and Evidentiary Rules of the Post-World War II War Crimes Trials: Did They Provide an Outline For International Legal Procedure?', in 37 *CJTL* (1999), at 864 ff.

[17] Cf. Judge Pal's dissenting opinion appended to the Tokyo Judgment, reprinted in B.V.A. Röling and F. Rüter (eds.), *The Tokyo Judgment (The I.M.T.F.E.), 29 April 1946–12 November 1948* (Amsterdam: Amsterdam University Press, 1977) ii, at 1037. On the dissenting opinion of the Indian Judge, see recently, L. Varadarajan, 'From Tokyo to The Hague: A Reassessment of Radhabinodh Pal's Dissenting Opinion at the Tokyo Trials on its Golden Jubilee', in 38 *IJIL* (1998), 233–247, at 241.

[18] On the controversial characterization of the Nuremberg Tribunal as an international body see R. Woetzel, *The Nuremberg Trials in International Law* (2nd edn., London: Stevens and Sons, 1962), at 40–49 and 55–57.

[19] Cf. G. Schwarzenberger, 'The Judgement of Nuremberg', in 21 *Tul. LR* (1947), 328. See also G. Sperduti, 'Crimini internazionali', in *Enciclopedia del Diritto* (Milan: Giuffrè, 1962), xi, at 340–341, and 'L'individu et le droit international', in 90 *Rec. des Cours* (1956-II) 732–849, at 785. For a more precise characterization of the status of Germany see H. Kelsen, 'The Legal Status of Germany According to the Declaration of Berlin', in 39 *AJIL* (1945), 518–526, clarifying (at 518) that it was not belligerent occupation *stricto sensu*.

[20] Pursuant to Article 5 of the London Agreement 'any Government of the United Nations may adhere to this agreement by notice given through the diplomatic channel to the Government of the United Kingdom, who shall inform the other signatory and adhering Governments of each such adherence'. Between 10 September and 22 December 1945 the following States ratified the

principles of the Charter and the Judgment of the IMT.[21] In any event, even if those trials were seen as the joint exercise by the Allied Powers of criminal jurisdiction over captured enemies, this would not diminish the widespread international recognition of their achievements, which paved the way for the creation of a system of individual accountability for international crimes.

Finally, referring to the sources that could determine the opening of investigations, it does not seem that either at Nuremberg or Tokyo victims had any role to play in activating the proceedings. This was probably due to the high level of criminals prosecuted and consequently on the number of victims affected (naturally a very large number). Moreover, there were absolutely no provisions on this issue in the Charters or the Rules of Procedure of the two Tribunals.

(c) UN *ad hoc* Tribunals

Fifty years later, in the system of the UN *ad hoc* Tribunals, the situation is different in many respects. Of course, these are still *ad hoc* tribunals and the restricted scope of their jurisdiction limits the width of investigations and the effectiveness that these may have in the protection of human rights. Additionally, the *ex post facto* creation of the Tribunals undermines the possibility that they may effectively operate as a deterrent to the commission of atrocities.[22]

In the system of the *ad hoc* Tribunals 'the Prosecutor shall initiate investigations *ex-officio* or on the basis of information obtained from any source, particularly from Governments, United Nations organs, intergovernmental and non-governmental organizations. The Prosecutor shall assess the information received or obtained and decide whether there is sufficient basis to proceed' (Article 18 ICTY St., Article 17 ICTR St.). In this context, one may opine that victims (or more likely an organization of victims) could contact the Office of the Prosecutor to submit general or even specific information on crimes within the jurisdiction of the Tribunals. However, there is absolutely

London Agreement: Australia, Belgium Czechoslovakia, Denmark, Greece, Ethiopia, Haiti, Honduras, India, Luxembourg, The Netherlands, New Zealand, Norway, Panama, Paraguay, Poland, Uruguay, Venezuela, Yugoslavia.

[21] See UNGA Res. 1/95 (1948), by which the General Assembly 'affirms the principles recognized by the Charter of the Nuremberg Tribunal and the judgement of the Tribunal'. In this respect see Woetzel, note 18 above, at 57, where he concludes that 'the United Nations resolution and the latter codification in addition to the fact that the twenty-three nations, representing the quasi-totality of civilised states, subscribed the London Charter, indicates that the IMT had clearly the sanction of the international community, and can be considered an international court'.

[22] In this respect it must be highlighted that the ICTY was already operational when the massacres of Srebrenica took place. Therefore, to a certain extent this event nullifies arguments linked to the power of deterrence of the Tribunals. See the comments made by G. Gaja, 'Il rischio di un ruolo "complementare" del Tribunale penale internazionale' in P. Lamberti Zanardi and G. Venturini (eds.), *Crimini di guerra e competenza delle giurisdizioni nazionali* (Milan: Giuffrè, 1998), at 89.

no mechanism for them to force or even pressurize the Prosecutor to investigate or to prosecute. Additionally, there is not even a mechanism for inform-
ing victims of why the Prosecutor has eventually decided not to investigate or
not to prosecute (or the basis for the decision to subsequently withdraw an
indictment).

(d) The International Criminal Court

The International Criminal Court (ICC) system is a trifle more complex than
its predecessors: first, because of the broader scope of its jurisdiction and its
permanent character; secondly, because the Prosecutor has been vested with
the power to open investigations *proprio motu*, also following submissions
made by non-governmental organizations, which probably will include
human rights non-governmental organizations (NGOs), or associations of
victims, or even (although it seems more unlikely) individual victims.

The perspective of creating a permanent judicial institution, with general
jurisdiction, necessarily implied a more cautious approach on the part of
States. Originally, in the ILC draft no mention was made of a power for the
Prosecutor to open an investigation *proprio motu*.[23] The so-called trigger
mechanisms were only Security Council and State referral. Subsequently, on
the initiative of national delegations—and under the pressure of international
NGOs—a proposal was submitted to the preparatory committee to allow the
Prosecutor to open an investigation on his or her own initiative. Thus, the
proposal was included as an option in the draft Statute that was presented to
the Rome Conference. In Rome, at the UN Diplomatic Conference, the confrontation on the issue of the *proprio motu* power of the Prosecutor was one
of the points of highest tension between delegations.[24]

Eventually, the global compromise found in the entire text of the Statute
designed a mechanism that recognizes the power of the Prosecutor to open an
investigation on the basis of information collected from various sources
(Articles 13.c and 15 ICC St.). This power, however, is subject to review by a
judicial organ of the Court (the Pre-Trial Chamber), which should protect the
international community against frivolous investigations and inappropriate
resort to international criminal justice.[25]

[23] It seems surprising that a Commission composed of international lawyers, sitting in their
own capacity (thus not representing their governments) and entrusted with the specific task of
codifying, but also progressively developing, international law, submitted a project that excluded
the *proprio motu* power of the Prosecutor, while States concluded that it was worth assigning such
power to the Prosecutor. On the ILC Draft Statute see J. Crawford, 'The ILC adopts a Statute
for an International Criminal Court', in 89 *AJIL* (1995) 404–416, and 'The ILC's Draft Statute
for an International Criminal Court', in 88 *AJIL* (1994), 140–152, at 148.
[24] Cf. P. Kirsch and J. Holmes, 'The Rome Conference on an International Criminal Court:
The Negotiating Process', in 93 *AJIL* (1999), at 2.
[25] Cf. the statement of the Head of the Brazilian delegations, 16 June 1998, at <**www.un.org/
icc/speeches/616bra.htm.**>.

It seems correct to argue that information provided by victims should be included among the sources that may induce the Prosecutor to open an investigation. To be more precise, it should be noted that the Statute does not specifically refer to victims or to individuals in general. Article 15, paragraph 1, of the ICC Statute (ICC St.) recognizes the general power of the Prosecutor 'to initiate investigations *proprio motu* on the basis of information on crimes within the jurisdiction of the Court'. There is no specific indication of the source of this initial information, but information provided by individuals may also be considered as falling within the scope of the rule. Moreover, Article 15, paragraph 2, ICC St., states that the Prosecutor may 'seek additional information from any reliable source that he or she deems appropriate'. This provision seems to reinforce the belief that victims may furnish information to the Prosecutor.

Furthermore, other provisions contained in the Statute have contributed to strengthening consideration for victims in international criminal proceedings. Article 15, paragraph 6, ICC St., for example, provides that, should the Prosecutor decide not to proceed with the investigation, he or she shall inform those who have furnished relevant information. This is a notable difference from the system of the *ad hoc* Tribunals. Naturally, it also implies a sort of accountability of the Prosecutor to the source providing information, even if it is extremely unclear what may be the outcome of this sort of control. Even more obscure remain the legal implications of the violation of such duty to report on the outcome of the communication received. It should also be noted that such a duty disappears when we move to the decision on whether or not to prosecute (Art. 54 ICC St.). In this case the Prosecutor has a duty to report to the Security Council or to the State, where investigations are opened pursuant to a referral. On the other hand, there is only a general duty to report to the Pre-Trial Chamber in cases of investigations *proprio motu*, but no mention is made of the source that has provided the initial information.[26]

Finally, it is interesting to note that victims can make representations according to the provisions of Article 15.3 ICC Statute, even at the pre-investigative stage, before the Pre-Trial Chamber. They can thus influence (albeit only to a limited extent) the process of determination on whether it is appropriate or not to launch an investigation.

---

[26] In addition, Article 53 entrusts the Pre-Trial Chamber with broad powers of review of a decision of the Prosecutor not to proceed. In particular, Article 53.3 provides that a decision of the Prosecutor that an investigation or a prosecution is not in the interests of justice shall be effective only if confirmed by the Pre-Trial Chamber.

2. Judicial scrutiny over the discretion of the Prosecutor both in the interest of the international community and to protect the rights of suspects

One of the keys that led to the acceptance in the ICC Statute of the *proprio motu* power of the Prosecutor to start an investigation was the proposal to submit the opening of the investigation to the control of the Pre-Trial Chamber.[27]

The adoption of such a mechanism of judicial supervision over the discretion of the Prosecutor, however, was not entirely new. In the system of the UN Tribunals a similar, albeit not identical, mechanism was envisaged for verifying whether the elements collected by the Prosecutor were of such a nature that would justify the indictment of a person.[28] Building upon that experience, when in the course of negotiations on the ICC Statute in New York, it emerged that many States were not ready to accept a Prosecutor with the *proprio motu* power to open investigations, some delegations suggested subjecting this power to judicial control. Thus, the basis for a compromise was devised.

There is, however, an important difference between the system of the *ad hoc* Tribunals and the ICC system. In the latter judicial supervision is exercised both prior to the opening of investigations and subsequently for the confirmation of charges. On the contrary, in the system of the *ad hoc* Tribunals judicial organs intervene only after investigations have been conducted and a case against one or more individuals has already been prepared. In other words, in the ICC system a judge already intervenes at the pre-investigative stage to determine whether there are grounds for an investigation to be opened. In contrast, in the procedure of the *ad hoc* Tribunals this intervention occurs prior to prosecution but after investigation has been entirely or, at least, largely completed.

Article 19 of the Statute of the ICTY (and Article 18 ICTR St.) regulates the procedure for the review of the indictment. In particular, it establishes that if the judge is satisfied that a *prima facie* case exists the indictment must be confirmed, whereas if the supporting material does not contain sufficient grounds the indictment must be dismissed.[29] Rule 47 of the Rules of Procedure and Evidence (RPE) further details the procedure to be followed for the review of an indictment.

---

[27] On the role and functions of the Pre-Trial Chamber generally see M. Marchesiello, 'Proceedings before the Pre-Trial Chamber', in A. Cassese, P. Gaeta, and J. Jones (eds.), *The Rome Statute of the International Criminal Court: A Commentary* (Oxford: OUP, 2002), ii, 1231–1246.

[28] See Article 19 ICTY St. and Article 18 ICTR St.

[29] On the standard to be applied by the reviewing judge see D. Hunt, 'The Meaning of a "*prima facie* Case" for the Purposes of Confirmation', in R. May *et al.* (eds.), *Essays on ICTY Procedure and Evidence—In Honour of Gabrielle Kirk McDonald* (The Hague: Kluwer, 2001), at 137–149.

The mechanism for review of the indictment aims at determining whether there is sufficient evidence to move from the investigative phase to trial. The reviewing judge can either confirm or dismiss the indictment, but he or she can also adjourn the review. In the course of the hearing for review of the indictment the judge can interact positively with the Prosecutor, asking for clarifications or for additional evidence, or even indicating charges on which the grounds presented are insufficient or other charges that could be moved in view of the material submitted.[30] Furthermore, it seems possible that the confirming judge may suggest different classifications of the crimes charged.

The solution adopted in the ICC Statute is much more based on a non-adversarial model. The Pre-Trial Chamber not only plays the role of scrutiny over the Prosecutor after the investigation is finished, but is also involved in the investigative process. This participation of the Pre-Trial Chamber in the investigative phase is limited, not merely to the authorization to open the investigation. On the contrary, there is a continuous role for the Pre-Trial Chamber that has the power to issue and the task of issuing all necessary orders and warrants that may be required for the purpose of the investigation (Article 57, paragraph 3 (a), ICC St.). The Pre-Trial Chamber also intervenes to take measures of protection for witnesses and victims. It is always the Pre-Trial Chamber that has the power to authorize the Prosecutor to take specific investigative steps within the territory of a State Party (Article 57, paragraph 3(d)). It is again the Pre-Trial Chamber that issues a warrant of arrest or a summons to appear, under Article 58 ICC St., in the name of the person subject to an investigation, to obtain his or her appearance before the Court. Finally, it is the same Pre-Trial Chamber that holds the hearing for the confirmation of the charges on which the Prosecutor intends to seek trial (Article 61 ICC St.). At this hearing, contrary to what happens before the *ad hoc* Tribunals, the presence of the suspect is required, and the person may object to the charges, challenge the evidence presented by the Prosecutor, and even present evidence. The ICC mechanism is similar to proceedings known to Anglo-Saxon systems, such as the procedure before the *grand jury* or the committal proceedings.[31]

In the system of the ICC St., the Pre-Trial Chamber has a considerable role. It should be added that this move towards a more active role for the Judges in the pre-trial phase is reflected in various amendments to the Rules of Procedure and Evidence of the ICTY. Rule 65-*ter* ICTY-RPE, for example,

---

[30] The issue of whether the reviewing judge has this power may be open to debate. Nonetheless, while there are few doubts about the existence of such a power, its scope and its effects are more contentious. It seems reasonable to conclude that the only effect of such a power is a suggestion for the Prosecutor.

[31] Cf. C. Emmins, *A Practical Approach to Criminal Procedure* (3rd edn., London: Financial Training Publications, 1985), at 23.

provides for the appointment among the members of the competent Trial Chamber of a Pre-Trial Judge, whose role it is to regulate the exchanges between the parties and ensure that the pre-trial phase proceeds expeditiously[32]. Naturally, the main difference is that the involvement of the Judges in the system of the *ad hoc* Tribunals follows the confirmation of the indictment, while in the ICC system the Pre-Trial Chamber is involved in the procedure from the outset.

The solution found in the ICC implies the involvement of judicial authorities in the investigative phase. Awareness of the unsettled status of the situations in which the Court is likely to intervene made it appropriate to add an element of judicial supervision in the pre-trial phase. This element was not necessary for the *ad hoc* Tribunals because in that case the Security Council had already made the evaluation as to the political impact of criminal investigations and prosecutions, when the decisions to create the Tribunals were taken.

However, in spite of the differences between the system of the *ad hoc* Tribunals and the ICC Statute, it is certainly interesting to note that there has been a consistent trend towards a sort of expansion of the role of the judiciary, even in the investigative phase. This is an innovation in international criminal procedure that may represent a tribute to civil law systems. It was presented as such by the French Minister of Foreign Affairs, who explained that '*[l]a France a demandé que l'on trouve des solutions originales pour que cette nouvelle juridiction s'inspire autant de la tradition juridique romano-germanique que de la "*common law*". Ainsi la création d'une formation des juges qui participera à l'instruction des dossiers dès la phase préliminaire, aux côtés du Procureur, suggérée par notre pays, est désormais admise*'.[33] Nonetheless, it is submitted that such an increased role for the judges is more than a mere tribute to civil law. It is one of the distinctive features of international criminal justice and, although it came from the inevitable confrontation between different legal cultures, it embodies a *sui generis* combination that better responds to the needs of international trials.[34]

The criteria to be followed by the Chamber in exercising its power of supervision over the opening of an investigation tend to follow two main directions that ought to be mentioned. The first—explicitly desired by States—is linked to the safeguarding of the international community against frivolous investigations.[35] The second—which derives from the interpretation of the ICC

---

[32] Rule 65-*ter* was adopted at the Eighteenth Plenary Session, 9–10 July 1998 (IT/32/Rev.13).

[33] Statement of Hubert Vedrine, French Minister of Foreign Affairs, at the Plenary Assembly of the Diplomatic Conference, 17 June 1998, **www.un.org/law/icc/speeches/617fra.htm**.

[34] It is interesting to note that such an expansion of the role of judges is not a specific feature of international criminal proceedings: cf. S. Doran and J. Jackson (eds.), *The Judicial Role in Criminal Proceedings* (Oxford: Hart Publishing, 2000).

[35] Supervision by the Pre-Trial Chamber also protects the overall integrity of the judicial process.

Statute in a human rights perspective—concerns the protection of the rights of individuals. In drafting the Statute, delegations probably wanted more to address the former problem than the latter. However, nothing in the interpretation of the provisions of the Statute seems to prevent a reading of the powers of the Pre-Trial Chamber as a guarantee for individual rights.

The Pre-Trial Chamber's power to supervise the Prosecutor's action originates from the need to reassure States, which were against the attribution to the Prosecutor of the power to investigate on his or her own initiative. This issue raised the problem of the relationship between justice and politics. States feared that untimely investigations by the Prosecutor might endanger international relations. This fear was also addressed by recognizing the power of the Security Council to request suspension of the proceedings. It is submitted, however, that the Court should always tend to implement the decisions of the Security Council respecting the rights of individuals involved in the proceedings. In this respect, it would have been desirable to have an express provision in the Statute. However, absent such a specific provision it would be important to clarify the consequences of the decision of the Security Council to request suspension, *vis-à-vis* the rights of individuals in the proceedings before the Court.

From the point of view of the rights of individuals involved in the proceedings it seems that the role of the Pre-Trial Chamber could be of great relevance in guaranteeing their rights in the pre-trial phase from the opening of the investigation. The power of the Pre-Trial Chamber to determine whether there are grounds for proceeding with the investigation do not seem to be limited to those cases in which the Prosecutor operates *proprio motu*. Nothing in the provisions seems to limit this power to such a case. On the contrary, it seems appropriate to extend such scrutiny to all cases, irrespective of the trigger mechanism adopted. This interpretation is justifiable if one considers that, in the language of the Statute, the Security Council or States parties will normally refer to the Prosecutor not specific cases but 'situations' more broadly. Subsequently, the decision to investigate a specific case will always be made by the Prosecutor. Therefore, it would be desirable also in the case of investigations triggered by a deferral of the Security Council or by a State that the decision to open a specific investigation be submitted to the evaluation of the Pre-Trial Chamber. Arguably such an interpretation should be followed in order fully to respect the principle of equal treatment of individuals before the Court. This is particularly true if the control of the Pre-Trial Chamber is intended to avoid the pursuit of investigations which are not supported by substantial evidentiary indices, and which may only cause prejudice to the individual and the interests of justice.

Furthermore, it can be argued that a duty of the judges to protect the rights of persons during the investigations phase also exists in the system of the *ad hoc* Tribunals. This duty is imposed on the reviewing judge in the phase of the confirmation and the issue of any orders in the initial phase of the proceedings. Subsequently, it is incumbent on the Pre-trial Judge envisaged in Rule 65-*ter* ICTY RPE to protect the rights of the accused. It should be emphasized that there is no express provision imposing such a duty on the single judge. However, it seems correct to suggest that the general duty imposed on the Chambers by the provisions contained in Articles 20 St. ICTY and 19 St. ICTR to protect and preserve the rights of the accused naturally extends to the Reviewing and Pre-trial Judges.

In conclusion, the role of judicial organs in the investigative phase, and generally in the pre-trial phase, of international criminal proceedings has expanded. There was no such role at Nuremberg and Tokyo. A limited power, particularly in closing the purely investigative phase, was recognized before the *ad hoc* Tribunals. However, the judges of the *ad hoc* Tribunals were also entrusted with a number of powers that ought to be exercised to guarantee individual rights. Finally, with reference to the system of the ICC, the role of the Pre-Trial Chamber is arguably crucial in ensuring equality of treatment and full respect for the rights of individuals in proceedings before the Court. The expansion of the power of supervision of judicial organs over the Prosecutor is certainly linked to the need to find a balance between common law and civil law procedural conceptions. The compromise found in the form of control by the judges over some parts of the investigative activity is one of the elements of this compromise. Another very important element is the progressive move towards clarifying the status of the Prosecutor, in what may be called an '*organe de justice*', that is an official whose position is assisted by a number of legal guarantees that tend to preserve its impartiality and independence. In other words, the Prosecutor is becoming more and more an *impartial* party to the proceedings.[36]

3. The role of the International Prosecutor not simply as a party to the proceedings but as an organ of justice: the duty to search for exculpatory evidence and fully to respect the rights of suspects

The institutional profile of international prosecutors has moved from a very partial dimension, deeply grounded both in a victor's justice paradigm and in the choice of an adversarial type of criminal procedure, to a more impartial

---

[36] Cordero has harshly criticized such a description of the Prosecutor, as '*parte imparziale*': see F. Cordero *Ideologie del Processo Penale* (Rome: Università della Sapienza, 1997), at 7. However, it seems that such criticisms are not entirely justified. The definition of impartial party certainly describes with great accuracy how prosecutorial organs are perceived by public opinion. It also expresses in a formula the ambiguity of an organ which has to exercise the activity of a party with impartiality. In other words in the exercise of its functions the Office of the Prosecutor is a party to the proceedings but in terms of its structure and mandate it must be an impartial agency. The ambiguity of the organ is thus reflected in that definition, which, however, does nothing more than describing the ambiguity of reality.

character. Of course authorities conducting international investigations and prosecutions have always aimed at being perceived as organs of justice and not as a mere party to the proceedings.[37] This was clearly recognized by the Trial Chamber of the ICTY in a decision in *Kupreškić*, where the Chamber held that 'the Prosecutor of the Tribunal is not, or not only, a Party to adversarial proceedings, but is . . . an organ of international criminal justice whose object is not simply to secure a conviction but to present the case for the Prosecution, which includes not only inculpatory, but also exculpatory evidence, in order to assist the Chamber to discover the truth in a judicial setting'.[38] Nonetheless, until the adoption of the norms provided for by the ICC Statute no appropriate legal framework supported this aspiration.

In this respect the experience of Nuremberg and Tokyo, notwithstanding its historic relevance, cannot really be taken as a precedent. In those trials, to a certain extent, even the organs responsible for judgment and sentencing have been accused of not really being *super partes*. Moreover, referring to the investigative stage it was said above that this was essentially within the competence of national contingents.

The situation is different in the system of the *ad hoc* Tribunals. The Prosecutor of the UN Tribunals is responsible for investigations and prosecutions. The Statutes of the Tribunals require the intervention of a judge only after the investigation has been initiated and an indictment has been prepared. The Prosecutor is the *dominus* of the investigative phase and is the organ that decides on the 'opportunity' (appropriateness) for prosecutions. The reviewing judge cannot decide on the appropriateness of prosecution or the gravity of the offences charged, etc. The decision to confirm or dismiss the indictment must be taken only on the basis of a determination that a *prima facie* case exists. Thus, it is for the Prosecutor to decide on the appropriateness of a prosecution. This is in line with the notion of the organs of investigation and prosecution in an adversarial system. Moreover in the system of the *ad hoc* Tribunals there is no duty on the Prosecutor to seek exculpatory evidence. Rule 68 RPE establishes the duty to 'disclose to the defence the existence of evidence known to the Prosecutor which in any way tends to suggest the innocence or mitigate the guilt of the accused or may affect the credibility of prosecution evidence'. This, however, does not imply any duty to search for such evidence.[39] Furthermore, there is no express provision either in the Statutes or in the Rules of the Tribunals that clearly states the duty of

---

[37] Cf. Robert Jackson, Opening declaration of the case for the Prosecution, 21 November 1945, Nuremberg.

[38] Cf. Trial Chamber Decision on Communication between the Parties and their Witnesses, *Kupreškić and others* (IT–95–16–PT), 21 September 1998, at 3 para. (ii).

[39] In this respect I submit that the judges of the *ad hoc* Tribunals may consider adopting an amendment to the RPEs in order to supplement the duty to disclose exculpatory evidence with a specific duty to search for such evidence. This may be of some assistance in solving a number of problems relating to non-compliance by the Prosecution with its obligations under Rule 68.

the Prosecutor fully to respect the rights of individuals. Moreover, rules on impartiality and disqualification do not cover the role of the Prosecutor. Therefore, it can be concluded that the normative framework of the *ad hoc* Tribunals depicts an international Prosecutor more deeply grounded in an adversarial logic.[40]

The shift in perspective occurred with the drafting of the ICC Statute. Contrary to previous experiences, in the system of the ICC the Prosecutor has a number of features of impartiality guaranteed by appropriate statutory norms. In the ICC Statute there has been a departure from the notion of the Prosecutor as a mere party to the proceedings and a stronger characterization of the Prosecutor as an *organ of justice*. This is not only true as a matter of perception, but is essentially reflected in the provisions adopted in the Statute. The provisions of Article 54, paragraph 1 (a) ICC St., which impose on the Prosecutor a duty to seek exculpatory evidence; the rules on disqualification (Article 42 ICC St.); and the right to appeal and seek revision in the interest of the accused (Articles 81 and 84 ICC St.) are all elements that indicate a clearer awareness of the need for an impartial characterization for the Prosecutor of an international criminal court. Moreover, the objective character of investigations in the ICC system is guaranteed by the continuing presence of the Pre-Trial Chamber that has been entrusted with a number of powers to be exercised in this phase of the proceedings.

The reasons that require an impartial and objective character for the investigative phase are closely linked to the essential features of international criminal proceedings. First, this necessity derives from the complexity of the cases that the Court is likely to have to try. Such cases, although aiming at demonstrating the individual responsibility of certain persons, often require the collection of evidence on the more complex global context in which individual crimes have been committed. Secondly, the 'political' character of the cases may lead to serious difficulties in obtaining the co-operation of State authorities (or in certain cases *de facto* authorities governing certain territories). This could be an insurmountable obstacle for

---

[40] See in this respect the separate opinion of Judge Shahabuddeen, *Barayagwiza*, (ICTR–97–19-AR72), 31 March 2000, where, although he emphasizes the impartial nature of the Prosecutor of the ICTR, he notes that the Prosecutor is still a party: '[t]he Prosecutor of the ICTR is not required to be neutral in a case; *she is a party. But she is not of course a partisan.* This is why, for example, the Rules of the Tribunal require the Prosecutor to disclose to the defence all exculpatory material. The implications of that requirement suggest that, while a prosecution must be conducted vigorously, there is room for the injunction that prosecuting counsel "ought to bear themselves rather in the character of ministers of justice assisting in the administration of justice". The prosecution takes the position that it would not prosecute without itself believing in guilt. The point of importance is that an assertion by the prosecution of its belief in guilt is not relevant to the proof. Judicial traditions vary and the Tribunal must seek to benefit from all of them. Taking due account of that circumstance, I nevertheless consider that the system of the Statute under which the Tribunal is functioning will support a distinction between an affirmation of guilt and an affirmation of preparedness to prove guilt' (emphasis added).

the defence. Thirdly, there is the very high risk of unfair actions by national authorities to limit the chain of responsibility to the person charged, etc. Finally, the costs of defence investigations may be so high that even wealthy persons would find it very difficult to bear them.

These are only some of the main traits of international investigations which require, at least at this stage of development of the system, a truly unbiased role for the Prosecutor, under the supervision of a judicial organ of the Court. This does not of course mean that the role of the defence should be undermined or diminished in any way. On the contrary, it should be assumed that all the safeguards of an adversarial trial must be granted to the accused. Furthermore, however, there should be an awareness of the need for a strong commitment on the part of investigative and prosecutorial organs to the discovery of the truth, also in the interests of the suspect.

In the ICC system the Prosecutor is explicitly bound by respect for human rights. Pursuant to Article 54, paragraph 1 (c), ICC St. the Prosecutor must 'fully respect the rights of persons arising under this Statute'. It may be contended that the provision should have been wider and should not have been limited to the rights arising under the Statute. However, it should be noted that a reading of this rule jointly with Article 21 ICC St., on applicable law, may clarify the scope of the protection. The provisions of Article 21 refer to the Court in general. These naturally also include the Prosecutor and the Office of the Prosecutor. In Article 21 is made clear that the Court is bound by 'principles and rules of international law' (Article 21, paragraph 1 (b)) and furthermore that the interpretation of law must be 'consistent with internationally recognized human rights' (Article 21, paragraph 3). A wider reading of these provisions imposes a duty on the Prosecutor of the ICC fully to respect the rights of individuals, even those which may not be specifically provided for in the Statute, but are part of internationally recognized human rights.[41]

4. Conclusion

The unique nature of international crimes inevitably highlights the tormented relationship between politics and criminal justice. The interplay between criminal justice and politics is naturally well known even at the national level. It is, however, more evident in international criminal proceedings, given the classes of crimes within the jurisdiction of international Tribunals and the Court.

In particular, in drafting the ICC Statute it appeared necessary to preserve the integrity of proceedings without turning a blind eye to their political

---

[41] K. Gallant, 'Individual Human Rights in a New International Organization: The Rome Statute of the International Criminal Court', in M.C. Bassiouni (ed.), *International Criminal Law* (2nd edn., Ardsley, NY: Transnational, 1999), iii, 693–723.

dimension. This objective has been pursued by submitting the political element implicit in these proceedings to constant monitoring through the combined action of both political and judicial organs. The former has been crafted in the form of the power of the Security Council to request the suspension of proceedings in order to protect international peace and security.[42] The latter has been realized by entrusting the Pre-Trial Chamber with the duty to safeguard the interests of a correct administration of justice. In other words, the ICC Statute has created a judiciously structured mechanism of checks and balances, by which States decided, on the one hand, to attribute to the Security Council the power to request the suspension of proceedings.[43] However, in this respect it is important to emphasize that it will always be for the Court to determine the concrete modalities for the enforcement of such decisions. On the other hand, it was admitted that the power of the Prosecutor of the Court to initiate an investigation *proprio motu* had to be conditioned with the approval of the Pre-Trial Chamber. Moreover, as discussed above, the role of the Pre-Trial Chamber in this respect must be construed in a more general way so as to furnish appropriate protection to individual rights.

Furthermore, it should be reaffirmed that the Prosecutor also has a precise duty to operate in the interests of the persons under investigation. One aspect affected by the intrinsic political nature of international criminal trials is that the accused may run the risk of becoming a sort of 'scapegoat'. This is why the greatest attention should be paid, by the organs of prosecution, to thoroughly protecting and respecting the rights of persons under investigation. This will certainly help in trying to avoid the excessive criminalization of certain individuals and the loss of a more global picture. The involvement of judicial organs at the pre-trial stage can probably contribute to ensure fairness also during the initial phases of the proceeding.

However, it is the individual that can best defend his, or her, own interests. Therefore, the greatest care must be given to his rights. First, there is a set of rights attributed to individuals for the phase of investigations and pre-trial proceedings (see below in this chapter, section II, on the rights of the suspect). Secondly, additional protection is afforded to individuals in view of and in the course of trial proceedings (see Chapter 3 below, on the protection of the rights of the accused).

---

[42] On the relationship between the Security Council and the ICC see V. Gowlland-Debbas, 'The Role of the Security Council in the New International Criminal Court from a Systemic Perspective' in L. Boisson de Chazournes and V. Gowland Debbas (eds.), *The International Legal System in Quest of Equity and Universality, Liber Amicorum G. Abi-Saab* (The Hague: Nijhoff, 2001), 629–650; L. Condorelli and S. Villalpando, 'Relationship of the Court with the United Nations', in Cassese *et al.* (eds.), i, note 27 above, 627–655.

[43] It is questionable what the effects of this provision are and whether it can be argued that the Security Council does not have such a power under the UN Charter. In other words the norm of the ICC is simply the recognition of an existing power, admitting that the Security Council has this power.

On the possibilities for victims to determine the opening of an investigation, it can certainly be affirmed that there has been progress. Since Nuremberg and Tokyo, where victims had no possibility of initiating investigations or prosecutions, and the Statutes of the *ad hoc* Tribunals, where victims have a very limited role, mainly as witnesses, a clear attempt has been made in the ICC to strengthen the position of victims. It must be admitted that ICC solutions represent an improvement in the recognition of a procedural status for victims (or association(s) of victims), as they are afforded an opportunity to interact with the organs of international prosecution. However, the significance of the International Criminal Court system as a means of satisfying the demands of justice coming from victims of international crimes will mainly depend upon the way in which the Prosecutor exercises the *proprio motu* powers.

II. THE RIGHTS OF SUSPECTS IN INTERNATIONAL CRIMINAL PROCEEDINGS

1. General

It is well known that the Charters and the Rules of Procedure of the two International Military Tribunals created by the Allies after the Second World War[44] did not contain concrete due process safeguards for the investigation phase. Norms protecting the rights of persons in the preliminary phase of those criminal proceedings were almost entirely lacking. The terse provisions of the Charters did not explicitly attribute any rights to persons during investigation. The investigative phase was entirely outside the scope of the Charters. Nevertheless, it can be noted that the Nuremberg Charter recognized some rights to defendants during preliminary examination.[45] According to these provisions the defendant had the right 'to give any explanation relevant to the charges made against him' (Article 16.b) and the right to have the examination conducted in a language he understood or to have appropriate translation (Article 16.c). The International Military Tribunal for the Far East (IMTFE) Charter did not even contain such or similar provisions.

It is quite clear that real protection of the rights of persons during investigation did not exist. Moreover, even in the trial phase the level of protection was at a minimum and most criticisms have targeted the unfair administration

---

[44] The Nuremberg International Military Tribunal (IMT) was established by the Charter of London on 8 August 1945, while the International Military Tribunal for the Far East (IMTFE) was established pursuant to a decision of the Supreme Commander of the Allied Powers.

[45] The status of 'defendant', however, would already have been determined at that stage as the Indictment had already been issued.

of the rules.[46] There are, however, at least two reasons that can explain the relative unfairness of the Nuremberg and Tokyo trials, and can partially justify it. First, there certainly was a strong element of hostility, which derived from the conflict and appears inevitable between parties to a conflict.[47] This also led to that suspicion of a lack of impartiality summarized in the well-known formula that defines the Nuremberg and Tokyo trials as 'victor's justice'.[48] It seems, however, that under the circumstances prevailing at that time defendants received fair treatment.[49] Although these considerations, certainly, do not justify the flaws in the Nuremberg and Tokyo trials, they do explain them.

Secondly, there are reasons that partially justify the absence of detailed provisions on the protection of the rights of defendants. In this respect, it must be noted that most international standards relating to the protection of fundamental rights in the administration of criminal justice had not yet been the object of international law-making.[50] This factor grants stronger legitimacy to the Nuremberg and Tokyo proceedings and may, to a certain extent, justify some of the flaws contained in the provisions on the rights of persons during investigation.

When, after the Second World War, human rights started to be laid down in international legal instruments some protection was also afforded to persons under investigation. The first step of this process was certainly the adoption of the Universal Declaration of Human Rights (UDHR) in 1948. The rights provided for by the UDHR that are more relevant to a person under

---

[46] Cf., e.g., R. Minear, *Victor's Justice: The Tokyo War Crimes Trial* (Princeton, NJ: Princeton University Press, 1971), at 122–124.

[47] The 'victor's justice' paradigm has been overcome—at least to a large extent—with the creation of the UN *ad hoc* Tribunals. The ICC has been created along those lines so as to offer a credible model of impartiality for supranational justice. Some criticisms have been moved to the ICTY, which has been considered as not thoroughly impartial and independent; in particular, after the decision not to investigate the alleged crimes committed during NATO's bombing against FRY. In this respect see P. Benvenuti, 'The ICTY Prosecutor and the Review of the NATO Bombing Campaign against the Federal Republic of Yugoslavia', in 12 *EJIL* (2001), 503–539; and N. Ronzitti, 'Is the *Non Liquet* of the Final Report by the Committee Established to Review the Nato Bombing Campaign against the Federal Republic of Yugoslavia Acceptable?', in 82 *IRRC* (2000), 1017–1027.

[48] In this respect it can also be noted that negotiations behind the establishment of the Nuremberg Tribunal confirm that the idea to punish adequately Nazi criminals for their crimes was shared among the Allies. It was, however, very clear that many government officials of the Allied Powers were not totally in favour (and some were even totally against) the creation of a tribunal and the conduct of fair trials. There were many eminent figures that would have preferred to execute sentences without trial or to hold trials only for the limited purpose of identification of the culprits. For a long period of time the Soviets held the position that trials should be conducted only for the very limited purpose of identification. See D. Irving, *Nuremberg: The Last Battle* (London: Focal Point, 1996), at 35.

[49] It is very difficult to deny that under those circumstances it was difficult to conduct a fairer trial.

[50] In this respect it has also been clarified that in 1945, even the US Supreme Court had not yet thoroughly developed its jurisprudence on fair trial safeguards: see D.M. Amman, 'Harmonic Convergence?', in 75 *ILJ* (2000), 820.

criminal investigation are the right to liberty (Article 3), the right to non-discrimination (Article 7), the right to have access to a tribunal for redress of violations of the rights protected (Article 8) and the protection against arbitrary arrest or detention (Article 9). The provisions of the UDHR on the rights of accused persons are rather terse. They were, however, the cornerstones for the subsequent codification of the more detailed norms of the International Covenant on Civil and Political Rights (ICCPR).[51]

The ICCPR contains several rules protecting individual rights, which may be applicable during a criminal investigation. There are both general guarantees, not necessarily drafted with criminal proceedings in mind, such as the protection from acts of torture provided for by Article 7,[52] and more specific rights strictly connected to criminal investigations. In this latter category, there are rights of a more general nature, such as the right to liberty (Article 9.1) and other rights, which are more closely linked to the criminal process. These are the right of the person arrested to be informed of the charges against him or her (Article 9.2) or the right to be promptly brought before a judge (Articles 9.3 and 9.4).

Provisions with a content very similar to that of those mentioned above are also contained in the European Convention on Human Rights (ECHR). Article 3 of the ECHR lays down a general prohibition against torture, which is certainly applicable to persons during an investigation. Article 5 provides for the right to liberty and security with a whole set of more specific guarantees. Further, the ECHR contains a set of principles protecting the right to a fair trial, which to a certain extent can also be applicable to the investigative phase.[53] The American Convention on Human Rights (ACHR) contains rules similar to those of the texts discussed above. There is a general prohibition on torture and there are also specific provisions on the right to humane treatment.[54] Analogous provisions are also contained in the 1989 Convention on the Rights of the Child, in Article 40, relating to juvenile criminal justice.

All these international rules were drafted with municipal law in mind and impose obligations on States, requiring that the national criminal procedure system of each State comply with international guarantees. However, it was logical to extend these guarantees to international trials. This extension has

---

[51] As stated by an eminent scholar referring to Article 10 UDHR, 'here more than elsewhere, guidance as to the meaning of the right must be obtained from parallel provisions in subsequent international human rights instruments': R. Lillich, 'Civil Rights', in T. Meron (ed.), *Human Rights in International Law* (Oxford: Clarendon Press, 1984), 115–170, at 140. It is submitted that the same reasoning may also apply to other provisions in the UDHR, such as the rule on the right to liberty.

[52] Cf. Article 7 ICCPR which states: ' [n]o one shall be subjected to torture or to cruel, inhuman or degrading treatment or punishment'.

[53] For example the right to legal assistance or the right to the free assistance of an interpreter, cf. Article 6.3 ECHR.

[54] Cf. Article 5 ACHR.

been realized by the express decision of the Security Council and the UN Diplomatic Conference to ensure the highest standards of fairness in international criminal proceedings.[55]

Most of the rules contained in international instruments are specifically designed to protect the person accused in the perspective of a trial. Certainly, in the investigation phase it is not yet clear whether there will be a trial or not. However, it is submitted that persons under investigation must benefit from all those rights established for the accused which may be applicable to their situation.[56] Two main reasons support this interpretation. First, it seems illogical to reduce the rights of a person against whom no charges have yet been formulated, while these rights would be recognized to him or her if he or she were accused. Secondly, the status of suspect paves the way for that of accused. Thus, it seems logical to argue that if an individual is granted a certain right when he or she becomes an accused it would be puzzling to allow for the infringement of such a right just before he comes under the protection of a specific norm. This may render the subsequent protection vain.[57]

In this section the provisions of the ICC Statute will be taken as a starting point. These provisions represent the most advanced text on the protection of pre-trial rights of persons during international criminal investigations.[58] No such provisions were contained in the Nuremberg and Tokyo Charters, nor are present, at least certainly in such a detailed form, in the ICTY and ICTR Statutes or RPEs. It is indisputable that, in the ICC Statute, there has been a clear attempt to improve the protection of rights relating to the administration of criminal justice. This development is based on the assumption that this is one of the parameters that will be examined in evaluating the fairness of the proceedings before the ICC. However, it is also due to the fact that, for the first time in history, these rules were adopted by States clearly having in mind that one day these rights might be applicable in proceedings instituted against their own citizens. Therefore, it seems appropriate to discuss the more relevant issues concerning the rights of suspects by explicitly referring to the provisions of the ICC Statute and specifically focusing on them.

---

[55] Cf. Articles 21, 55, and 64 ICC St. and Articles 21 ICTY St. and 20 ICTR St. See A. Cassese, 'Opinion: The International Criminal Tribunal for the Former Yugoslavia and Human Rights', in *EHRLR* (1997), 329 at 331, and Chapter 1 above, Section III.

[56] In some national systems this extension to the suspect of the rights of the accused is provided for by law: see e.g. Italy: Article 61 Code of Criminal Procedure.

[57] This is an opinion which may be found both in common law and civil law systems: see e.g. the US Supreme Court decisions in *Escobedo* v. *Illinois*, 378 US 484, 490–491 (1964); in *Miranda* v. *Arizona*, 384 US 446 (1966); in *US* v. *Wade*, 388 US 236–237 (1967), and, for continental systems, the decisions of the Italian Constitutional Court (Corte Costituzionale) Decision 5 July 1968, no. 86, published in *Giurisprudenza Costituzionale* (1968), 1441–1445 and 3 December 1969, no. 348, *Giurisprudenza Costituzionale* (1968), 2262.

[58] See D. Scheffer, 'Staying the Course with the International Criminal Court', in 35 *Cor.ILJ* (2002), 47–100, at 72 and 95, where he clarifies that the provisions of the ICC Statute for the protection of due process rights are satisfactory even from the perspective of the USA.

2. *The status of suspect*

In the early stages of international criminal proceedings, the authorities entrusted with the task of investigating crimes are the protagonists. These organs, which in the system of international criminal Tribunals and in the ICC fall under the authority of the Prosecutor,[59] formulate hypotheses on the genesis of the crime, on the possible perpetrators, and, in general, offer a potential reconstruction of the truth. In this endeavour investigators identify when the criminal act was committed, how, and by how many persons, etc. Finally, the investigation process comes to a conclusion about the guilt of one or more specific individuals. Naturally, this process is not instantaneous and depends upon many factors affecting the quality of the investigation itself. One of these is that investigations are consistent with individual rights. These rights must not be seen (or used) as shields for the suspect, but must be respected because they represent part of the rules for the discovery of the truth.[60]

In this phase investigative organs are obliged to undertake research in relation to certain persons and may even need to question them. At this stage a person involved in the investigation is not yet an accused and may not even be 'a suspect', at least *stricto sensu*.[61] The status of accused is a more specific position triggered, in the ICC system as well as in the system of the *ad hoc* Tribunals, only when a judge has confirmed the Prosecutor's case.[62]

It may very well happen that investigators identify a certain number of persons who they consider to be potentially involved in the crime. Hence, investigators will have to evaluate individually the respective positions of each of these persons. In the course of this process these persons must be granted appropriate protection from unjustified intrusions into their lives or other forms of unfair treatment, especially in the case of questioning.

Provisions contained in the international instruments mentioned above and their interpretation by the various supervisory bodies produced a set of

[59] Cf. Article 42.1 ICC Statute. In international criminal justice the Chief Prosecutor is ultimately responsible for both investigations and prosecutions.

[60] There is a parallel between the legal process and the scientific discovery. Just as in science precise rules ought to be followed to reveal the truth.

[61] There certainly are many problems with the definition of this term. The drafters of the ICC Statute did not want to use the word 'suspect'. Although one may be tempted to agree with this decision, which avoids premature criminalization and prevents a number of problems about the determination of the moment when a person becomes a suspect, it is undeniable that in all likelihood this term will be resorted to in practice, despite the fact that it has not been used in the Statute. This will happen in the absence of a better formula accompanied by a precise determination of the status of a person under investigation in the various steps of the proceedings. In other words it is suggested that by avoiding the use of the word 'suspect' the drafters did not really solve possible problems linked to its definition, but, on the contrary, may have created even more uncertainty. In this respect see S. De Gurmendi, 'International Criminal Law Procedures—The Process of Negotiations', 217–227, at 223 note 13 and H. Friman, 'Rights of Persons Suspected or Accused of a Crime', 247–262, at 248–250, both in R. Lee (ed.), *The International Criminal Court—The Making of the Rome Statute, Issues, Negotiations, Results* (The Hague: Kluwer, 1999).

[62] The organ entrusted with this task is the Pre-Trial Chamber, under Article 61 ICC Statute.

principles that can be considered representative of a core of international law safeguards relating to the protection of human rights in the administration of criminal justice. Naturally, as mentioned above, these provisions were created to impose obligations on States concerning domestic prosecutions. However, when in 1993 the Security Council established the ICTY, the text adopted for the rights of the accused (Article 21 ICTY Statute) reproduced almost *verbatim* Article 14 of the ICCPR. This 'parallelism' has also been reinforced by the opinion of the Secretary General of the UN, who explicitly affirmed that '[it] is *axiomatic* that the International Tribunal must fully respect internationally recognized standards regarding the rights of the accused at all stages of its proceedings. In the view of the Secretary General, such internationally recognized standards are, in particular, contained in Article 14 of the International Covenant on Civil and Political Rights'.[63] Whether the same protection must be afforded to a person before he or she assumes the status of accused cannot really be discussed. It is logical to assume, as explained above, that, in general, protection for those who are not yet accused may be wider but certainly not narrower. However, the crucial question is to determine the status that triggers the rights and how they actually operate.

Both Articles 18.3 of the ICTY Statute and 17.3 of the ICTR Statute confer on the suspect a number of rights.[64] In particular these provisions recognize the right of the suspect to be assisted by counsel of his or her own choice. At the same time, they also provide for legal assistance at the expense of the United Nations for indigents and for the necessary translation or interpretation.

An important flaw in these provisions is linked to the fact that it seems that the suspect is entitled to these rights only 'if questioned', while some of the rights considered, such as the right to legal assistance may be needed independently of any questioning. Another significant problem is that the determination of the status of suspect is left quite vague, as there is no express definition in the Statute.[65] The judges tried to address this problem in the RPE but left it mainly to prosecutorial discretion to determine when to trigger the rights granted to the suspect.[66] According to the definition given in Rule 2 RPE, a suspect is 'a person concerning whom the Prosecutor possesses reliable information, which tends to show that he may have committed a crime over which the Tribunal has jurisdiction'. This definition is not specific, does not ensure uniformity of application, and assigns a crucial role to the Prosecutor. Naturally, this is the organ which, better than any other, can decide when a person becomes a suspect. However, the real problem is that there is no

---

[63] Cf. UN doc. SG Rep. S/25704, 3 May 1993 paragraph 106 (emphasis added).

[64] Contrary to what has been done in the ICC Statute, in the Statutes of the UN Tribunals there is an explicit use of the term 'suspect' Article 18 (Art. 17 ICTR).

[65] Cf. note 61 above.

[66] This element, linked to the absence of specific sanctions, creates the risk of abuses, which, albeit not deliberate, may not only infringe fundamental rights of persons, but may undermine the credibility of the entire institution.

guidance on the determination of what can be considered 'reliable information' which tends to show that a person may have committed a crime within the jurisdiction of the Tribunal. This makes the determination by the Prosecutor totally discretionary. It would have been better to trigger the rights of the suspect from a precise moment, such as for example the need to question the person, or the need to issue a request for assistance in the investigation process to national authorities. In any case it seems more appropriate to impose the formalization of this status either through the formal keeping of a record or through the issue of a specific document.[67] The Prosecutor, albeit impartial and acting only in the interests of justice and in the pursuit of the truth, is still a party to the proceedings. Therefore it may be inappropriate to grant him or her such wide discretion. This element acquires even more importance, given the circumstance that in the ICTY and ICTR systems there is no specific mechanism for sanctioning procedural violations apart from the general provision contained in Rule 5. This norm establishes that 'the Trial Chamber shall grant relief if it finds that the alleged non-compliance is proved and that it has caused material prejudice to that party' (paragraph A), but it leaves it to the Chamber to determine the appropriate relief (paragraph C). This naturally does not have any effect of deterrence on the Prosecutor to avoid procedural violations, nor does it help to ensure equality of treatment. It ultimately encumbers the Trial Chamber with a burden which may prove too heavy, such as for example determining that owing to the violation of the due process rules a case must be dismissed with prejudice for the Prosecution.[68]

As regards what actually constitutes the rights of suspects, the RPEs have supplemented the Statute with a view to implementing those rights provided for by the Statute. They specify the rights granted to a suspect who is to be questioned by the Prosecutor. Moreover, it is established that the Prosecutor must inform the suspect of his or her rights. Furthermore, in addition to those rights included in Article 18 of the Statute, Rule 42.A (iii) RPE also recognizes the right to silence. Finally, Rule 43 establishes the procedure to be followed in the course of questioning, providing for the requirement of video and audio recording.

It is submitted that the current normative framework of the *ad hoc* Tribunals poses two basic problems. First, the status of a person who is to be questioned is unclear. This may cause problems both in terms of his/her rights and as to the correctness of the investigation.[69] Secondly, the fact that these

---

[67] Such as e.g. the '*registro delle notize di reato*' and the so-called '*informazione di garanzia*', cf. (Italy) Articles 335, 369 and 369-*bis* of the Code of Criminal Procedure. These are, respectively, a record containing all information relating to facts or acts that may constitute an offence, and a specific notice issued to an individual that he or she is under investigation.

[68] Cf. ICTR Appeals Chamber, 3 November 1999, *Barayagwiza* (ICTR–97–19–AR72).

[69] Particularly if one thinks of the right to translation. If this right is not exercised in due time the comprehension of the questioning may not be accurate and, thus, the result of the investigation may be affected.

rights are limited to questioning may leave other situations unprotected, such as for example the seizure of blood samples or other evidence. There is no doubt that these rights can be extended by means of interpretation but it is uncertain whether this would really ensure adequate protection. It would, no doubt, be preferable to add an express provision to this effect.

An example of the ill-functioning of the system, in terms of uncertainty about the status of persons, is the case of General Djukić and Colonel Krsmanović.[70] These two high-ranking officers in the Serbian Army were arrested in February 1996 by Bosnian authorities.[71] The arrest led to growing tension in the relationships between Bosnian Serbs and Bosnian Muslims who had just started building the peace process. The conflict, which had just ceased after four years of war with the conclusion of the Dayton Agreement, seemed to be about to erupt again when the Tribunal requested Bosnia to transfer the two officers to the Tribunal. They were transferred to the Tribunal under Rule 90-*bis* RPE as detained witnesses.[72] After their arrival at the UN Detention Unit, they were questioned. Subsequently General Djukić was charged with crimes within the jurisdiction of the Tribunal. Leaving aside

---

[70] On the legal issues raised by this case see P. De Waart, 'From "Kidnapped" Witness to Released Accused "for Humanitarian Reasons": The Case of the Late General Djordje Djukić', in 9 *LJIL* (1996) at 453.

[71] Following this incident the so-called 'Rules of the Road' were established. These Rules established a power of supervision by the Tribunal over arrests, either by the Bosnian authorities or by the Bosnian Serbs, of individuals accused of crimes within the competence of the ICTY. The activities under the Rules of the Road are performed by a section of the Office of the Prosecutor. See in this respect the ICTY *Eighth Annual Report* (2001), UN doc. A/56/352, 17 September 2001, paras. 201–204.

[72] Rule 90-*bis* RPEs, Transfer of a Detained Witness, reads as follows:

'(A) Any detained person whose personal appearance as a witness has been requested by the Tribunal shall be transferred temporarily to the detention unit of the Tribunal, conditional on the person's return within the period decided by the Tribunal.

(B) The transfer order shall be issued by a Judge or Trial Chamber only after prior verification that the following conditions have been met: (i) the presence of the detained witness is not required for any criminal proceedings in progress in the territory of the requested State during the period the witness is required by the Tribunal; (ii) transfer of the witness does not extend the period of detention as foreseen by the requested State.

(C) The Registrar shall transmit the order of transfer to the national authorities of the State on whose territory, or under whose jurisdiction or control, the witness is detained. Transfer shall be arranged by the national authorities concerned in liaison with the host country and the Registrar.

(D) The Registrar shall ensure the proper conduct of the transfer, including the supervision of the witness in the detention unit of the Tribunal; the Registrar shall remain abreast of any changes which might occur regarding the conditions of detention provided for by the requested State and which may possibly affect the length of the detention of the witness in the detention unit and, as promptly as possible, shall inform the relevant Judge or Chamber.

(E) On expiration of the period decided by the Tribunal for the temporary transfer, the detained witness shall be remanded to the authorities of the requested State, unless the State, within that period, has transmitted an order of release of the witness, which shall take effect immediately.

(F) If, by the end of the period decided by the Tribunal, the presence of the detained witness continues to be necessary, a Judge or Chamber may extend the period on the same conditions as stated in Sub-rule (B).

the specifics of this case,[73] this example illustrates how a series of problems may arise. It is unclear, for example, what the status of these two detainees was when they arrived at the Tribunal and when they were questioned. If they were considered suspects, they should have been transferred under a different rule and following a different procedure (Rule 40-*bis* of both RPEs). If, on the contrary, they were witnesses, on what basis were they questioned and from what rights did they benefit?

This case was very sensitive and had complex political implications, particularly because of the special period in which it took place: the Dayton Peace Agreements had just started to be implemented. However, this kind of political element will, in all likelihood, be a common feature of international criminal proceedings. This is an additional reason for suggesting that it would be appropriate to have more precise rules and a lesser degree of discretionary powers in triggering pre-trial guarantees.

The same problem may also arise before the International Criminal Court (ICC). The ICC Statute identifies three distinct positions. First, a person may be involved in the proceedings assuming a generic status of 'person in respect of an investigation'. Secondly, there is the more specific position of 'person concerning whom there are reasons to believe that he or she has committed a crime within the jurisdiction of the Court'. Finally, there is the status of accused that is triggered after confirmation of the charges pursuant to Article 61 of the ICC Statute. The resulting normative framework in this respect is rather different from what was contained in the draft Statute and has excluded any precise definition of the various statuses at the different stages. In the ICC system, as it appears from the Statute, there are no precise definitions. Although it would have been logical to think that they would be included in the Rules of Procedure, no such provisions have been adopted.[74] In any case it would have been preferable to have them in the Statute, at least referring to the status of persons in the various stages of the proceedings. This is so because, in particular, different individual rights are triggered by different statuses and there is little guidance in the Statute on the precise determination of the moment from which these rights operate.

The draft Statute presented to the Rome Conference contained most of the provisions on the protection of the rights of suspects which are now included in the Statute. These draft provisions were contained in Article 54 of the Draft Statute, together with the general normative framework regulating the initiation and conduct of investigations. In particular, paragraphs 10 to 13 of that Article laid down the rights of the 'suspected person'. However, although similar in terms of their content, these rules were quite different in their structure.

---

[73] The *Djukić* case (IT–96–20-T) was terminated in summer 1996 by the premature demise of the accused.

[74] Cf. Rules of Procedure and Evidence, UN doc. PCNICC/2000/Rev.1/Add.1.

The draft text focused on the 'person suspected of a crime' and established that this person was entitled to a whole set of rights. During the Conference, delegations progressively agreed to differentiate and expand the situations to be protected. First of all, it was decided to avoid using the terms 'suspect' or 'suspected'[75] in order to avoid any kind of premature evaluation of the guilt of the person under investigation and given the difficulties in finding agreement on such definitions. Secondly, it was agreed to identify two steps in organizing the protection of individual rights during the investigative phase.[76] On the one hand, it was decided to recognize a core of rights to any person in respect of an investigation, independently of the existence of grounds indicating his or her guilt. On the other hand, the text adopted provides for additional protection for individuals, where there are grounds for believing that they have committed a crime and are about to be questioned.

Article 55 ICC St. aims at furnishing appropriate protection to the individuals through the granting of a set of rights which operate at the stage of investigation.[77] These rights are conferred both at the initial phase (Article 55.1 ICC St.), when there are still no grounds for believing that a person is responsible for the crime under investigation. They are also recognized at a subsequent stage, when 'there are grounds to believe that a person has committed a crime within the jurisdiction of the Court' and that person is about to be questioned by investigative authorities[78] (Article 55.2 ICC St.).

In the process of (re-)drafting these norms some specific provisions contained in the draft Statute were not included in this Article. However, substantially, most of the rights therein are directly or indirectly contained in other rules of the Statute.[79] The only rule which does not seem to be reflected anywhere in the Statute is the rule suggesting that the suspect should be 'entitled to collect all evidence that he [or she] deems necessary for his [or her] defence'.[80] This rule would have imposed on the Pre-Trial Chamber the specific obligation to co-operate with him or her in the investigative phase (even before the confirmation of charges against that person).

---

[75] Cf. Article 54-c, para. 1, in UN doc. A/CONF.183/C.1/WGPM/L.1, 18 June 1998, at 4. See De Gurmendi, note 61 above.

[76] Cf. *ibidem*, Article 54-*ter*, para. 2.

[77] See in this respect, C.K. Hall, 'Article 55', in O. Triffterer (ed.), *Commentary on the Rome Statute of the International Criminal Court* (Baden-Baden: Nomos, 1999), 727–734.

[78] These provisions include national authorities when questioning is conducted upon the request of the Prosecutor under Part 9 of the Statute.

[79] Such as, e.g. Article 54, which now contains the obligation for the Prosecutor to collect exculpating as well as incriminating evidence.

[80] Cf. ICC Draft Statute Article 54(13).

3. General rights of a person in respect of an investigation (the right not to incriminate oneself, the right not to be subjected to any form of coercion, and the right to an interpreter)

The Statute of the ICC provides for general rights for persons in respect of an investigation of the Court. Article 55, paragraph 1 letter a), ICC St. refers to the right of a person 'not to be compelled to incriminate himself or herself or to confess guilt'. The various aspects of what may be broadly defined as 'the right to silence' will be discussed in more detail in connection with the analysis of the right of the suspect to remain silent and of the accused not to be compelled to testify (cf. sub-section 7 below and Chapter 3, section I.2). It is submitted that all these rights derive from the wide protection offered to individuals in respect of criminal investigations in the sense that the innocence of any individual is presumed, thus there is absolutely no duty on him or her to co-operate. Furthermore, in the preliminary phase the individual is protected against any attempt to force him or her to 'incriminate himself or herself or to confess guilt'. This protection is very broad and covers every form of compulsion, certainly beyond the prohibition of acts of torture or other similar forms of physical or moral violence (which are specifically forbidden by Article 55, paragraph 1, letter b). The scope of this rule is broad enough to include use of *agents provocateurs*, or other sorts of tricks by investigators indirectly to obtain information against the person with his or her assistance. This is an important achievement in terms of human rights protection, but it may nonetheless create some problems for investigators.

Article 55, paragraph 1 letter b) ICC St. states that a person 'shall not be subjected to any form of coercion, duress or threat, to torture or to any other form of cruel, inhuman or degrading treatment or punishment'. The impact of this rule is twofold. On the one hand it has symbolic value as a restatement of the general principle—in accordance with universally recognized rules of international law—that everyone has the right not to be subjected to torture or other forms of inhumane treatment. On the other hand, it also aims at protecting the individual from illegitimate acts by the authorities conducting investigations under the ICC Statute, including national authorities. Finally, it may be maintained that the rule also covers treatment of individuals in pretrial detention, upon order of both national or international authorities, for crimes investigated by the Court.

Moving to rights more specifically linked to the organization of proceedings before the Court, Article 55, paragraph 1 letter c), ICC St. establishes that when during an investigation a person is questioned in a language he or she does not understand, that person is entitled to the assistance of a competent interpreter and such translations as are necessary to meet the requirements of fairness. The right to appropriate translations and interpretation is essential at all stages of the proceedings, and as such the furnishing of such a service must be read as a continuing duty imposed on the Court.

It is submitted that this rule was specifically drafted with a view to the possible passage of that person from the generic status of a person questioned during an investigation to a person against whom 'there are grounds to believe that he or she has committed a crime'. In general it would have been logical to consider that it is also in the interest of the Prosecution to have adequate interpretation and translation. In this case, instead, the emphasis is on the 'person questioned' because the outcome of the questioning could prejudice that person (this is also the reason there is a general right not to incriminate oneself, see section 7 below). In this respect, it might be suggested that the Rules of Procedure should have organized more clearly the transition from the situation when somebody is questioned under Article 55.1 to the status recognized under Article 55.2.[81]

The right to have the assistance of an interpreter introduces the more general problem of languages. This issue, which may seem of little importance, has several interesting facets that deserve some attention.

First, there is the problem of the determination of the language of translation and the standards for such determination. Solutions adopted before international tribunals vary from 'a language the accused understands'[82] to 'the language of the accused'[83] to 'a translation that meets the requirements of fairness'.[84]

In the system of the *ad hoc* Tribunals, the Trial Chambers of the ICTY have interpreted the notion of 'a language the accused understands' on several occasions. It has been affirmed that the language of the interpretation must always be a language that the accused understands. It is not, however, necessary that he recognizes it as 'his own language'.[85] In *Djukić* and in *Delalić and others*, the defendants raised objections on the ground that they were being given the translation in Croatian, while their language was Serbian in the first case and Bosnian in the second. The Chambers of the Tribunals, having heard

---

[81] In this respect the RPE provide for audio and video recording of questioning under Article 55.2.

[82] Articles 18. and 21.4 (a) and (f) ICTY St. (Articles 17 and 20.4(a) and (f) ICTR St.); Article 55.1 (b).

[83] Rules 3 and 44 RPE.   [84] Article 67.1 (f) ICC St. and Rule 144 ICC RPE.

[85] Cf. Trial Chamber Decision on Defence application for forwarding documents in the language of the accused, *Delalić and others* (IT–96–21-T), 25 September 1996. By this decision the Chamber set out the criteria for determining the language in which evidence should be made available to the defendant. The Chamber held that the documents covered by the norm are all the materials that were submitted to the judge for the confirmation of the indictment, irrespective of whether these were or were not going to be introduced as evidence. Moreover, all other evidence submitted by either party at trial must be in one of the working languages of the Tribunal and in the language of the accused.

the Registrar (who as administrator of the Tribunal is responsible for providing translation and interpretation services), decided to reject the motion on the basis of a specialist linguistic opinion. It concluded that the language of the interpretation, although not the language of the accused, was certainly easy for the accused to understand.[86] The situation may be slightly different in the ICC Statute, as Article 55 lays down the right to an interpretation that would meet the requirements of fairness. It could be argued that it would have been better to adopt a more precise wording without leaving too much to the future interpretation of this provision by the judges.

In this respect, however, some problematic examples can be thought of: for example, would it be fair to question a suspect from Morocco in French? Or a French Swiss person in German? Or a person who speaks only a dialect or a minority language in the formal language of his or her country (for example, would it be fair to question an Italian from the Alto Adige whose mother tongue is German, and with little knowledge of Italian, in Italian)? The ICC St. requires that translation meet the requirements of fairness, both at the pre-trial stage (Article 55, paragraph 1 letter c) and also at trial (Article 67, paragraph 1 letter f). As mentioned above, this expression is rather vague, in that it does not offer guidance on its actual meaning. Nevertheless this may be an advantage because it may allow the judges to find solutions which can best combine the interests of justice and individual rights in difficult cases such as those referred to above.

Secondly, there is the problem of relationships between the working languages and the language of the suspect. This aspect also relates to the language spoken by Defence Counsel. In the *ad hoc* Tribunals this should in principle be one of the working languages. Originally, the Rules of Procedure and the Directive on the Assignment of Defence Counsel implied that, to be assigned, a lawyer was required to have a good knowledge of one of the working languages of the Tribunal. However, the developments that occurred in *Erdemović* led to the amendment of Rule 3 RPE ICTY and of the Directive to provide for the possibility, in exceptional circumstances, of lawyers being assigned to the case who do not speak either of the working languages. The Chambers of the ICTY have dealt with the issue of legal assistance and representation. In the late spring of 1996 the accused, Mr Erdemović, was transferred to the Tribunal and wanted the assignment of the lawyer who had already been working on his case when he was detained in Serbia. This attorney, however, spoke neither French nor English, the Tribunal's working languages. Rules 3 and 45 of the RPE, at that time, expressly stated that the assigned counsel must speak one of the Tribunal's languages. By an order of the presiding judge of the Trial Chamber, the request for the assignment of

---

[86] Decision on the Language of Translation, *Djukić* (IT–96–20-PT), 2 June 1996.

that lawyer was granted,[87] and subsequently the Rules were amended to allow, in particular situations, for the assignment of lawyers who do not speak either of the two working languages.[88]

Another issue raised in respect of the language of translations is whether the accused has a right to receive all documents from Prosecution in a language he or she understands. In *Naletilić* and *Martinović*, the Trial Chamber specified that the guarantees provided in Article 21.4(a) do not extend to all documents, but only to evidence that forms the basis of the determination by the Chamber of the charges against the accused. Therefore, while all evidence and exhibits must be in a language that the accused understands, other documents do not need to be translated, provided that they are in one of the working languages.[89]

It is worth mentioning the enormous care taken by the Tribunals to improve their translation services. As stated by the President of the ICTY in his *Third Annual Report to the United Nations:* '[a]s the Tribunal has grown, so have the size and importance of the Conference and Language Services Section. The Section is responsible for both interpretation and translation services for the Registry, the Office of the Prosecutor, the Chambers and defence counsel. Simultaneous interpretation is provided not only from and into English and French, the official working languages of the Tribunal, but also from and into Bosnian/Croatian/Serbian. In addition, simultaneous interpretation of other languages is provided as required.'[90] This is an issue that will require even greater care in the system of the ICC, as the Court will have to deal with many more languages. It must be kept in mind that translation and interpretation in legal language may be more complex. Nevertheless specific training may be very useful. It is suggested that specific courses regarding Court procedure should be devised for translators and interpreters that will work for the Court.

---

[87] Order of the presiding judge of the Trial Chamber, *Erdemović* (IT–96–22-T), 28 May 1996, specifying that an exceptional situation existed so that counsel who did not speak any of the working languages of the Tribunal could be assigned.

[88] See in this respect J. Jones, *The Practice of the International Criminal Tribunals for the Former Yugoslavia and Rwanda* (Irvington on Hudson, NY: Transnational, 1998), on Rule 3, at 131–134, and Rule 45, at 176–179.

[89] Decision on Defence Motion Concerning the Translation of All Documents, *Naletilić and Martinović* (IT–98–34-T), 18 October 2001.

[90] *Third Annual Report of the ICTY to the United Nations*, UN doc. A/51/292, 16 August 1996, para. 134. Cf. also para. 135, which states: '[t]his Section translates all kinds of written material and audio and videotapes from and into the official languages of the Tribunal, as well as Bosnian/Croatian/Serbian, German, Dutch and occasionally other languages. The material ranges from witness statements to the official documents of the Tribunal. In order to meet the requirements of such a significant workload sufficiently, the Section now numbers more than 25 full-time staff members and calls on the services of about 100 contractors'. See also *Seventh Annual Report*, UN doc. A/55/273, 7 August 2000, paras. 241–243 and *Eighth Annual Report*, note 71 above, para. 275. See also *ICTR Seventh Annual Report*, UN doc. A/57/163, 2 July 2002, para. 111.

Lastly, it seems important to mention the differences in language that go beyond the plain meaning of the terms. Legal language is a technical language where every word has a variety of meanings, which remain implicit in an unspoken code of communication. It is certainly not possible to address this issue in the context of this study; however, it may well be of some interest for further research. At this stage it may be suggested that this aspect should be taken into account in the training and recruiting of translators and interpreters. Moreover, the difficulties arising out of language both in its legal and ordinary dimensions reinforce the need for greater vigilance by the Court.

4. The right to legal assistance

The right to legal assistance is another of those fundamental safeguards that ought to be triggered from the very beginning of international criminal proceedings.[91] This right is crucial, particularly in criminal proceedings where the freedom of the individual is at stake. The importance of this right becomes even greater with specific regard to international criminal trials because of the complexity of the applicable law and due to the difficulties which are linked to possible investigations that, in the adversarial system, the defence should conduct on its own.[92]

The right to legal assistance is not always triggered and organized in the same way. For example, the Statutes of the *ad hoc* Tribunals provides for a right of the suspect to legal assistance, which is very wide when the suspect is questioned (Article 18, paragraph 3, ICTY St. and Article 17, paragraph 3, ICTR St.). This right seems to be somewhat reduced in the subsequent trial phase. The provisions of the Statutes of the *ad hoc* Tribunals state that '[if] questioned, the suspect shall be entitled to be assisted by counsel of his own choice, including the right to have legal assistance assigned to him without payment by him in any such case if he does not have sufficient means to pay for it'. Further, Article 21.4 (d) ICTY St. and Article 20.4 (d) ICTR St. state that the accused has the rights 'to defend himself in person or through legal assistance of his own choosing; to be informed, if he does not have legal assistance, of this right; and to have legal assistance assigned to him, in any case where the interests of justice so require, and without payment by him in any such case if he does not have sufficient means to pay for it'.

It is interesting to note that the right of an indigent person to have legal assistance assigned is not subject to any condition in the investigative phase

---

[91] Cf. ECourtHR, *Murray* v. *UK*, 8 February 1996, **www.echr.coe.int/Eng/Judgments.htm**, para 66. On the right to legal assistance in the *ad hoc* Tribunal system see M. Wladimiroff, 'The Assignment of Defence Counsel Before the International Criminal Tribunal for Rwanda', in 12 *LJIL* (1999), 957.

[92] See M. Wladimiroff, 'Rights of Suspects and Accused', in G. McDonald and O. Swaak-Goldman (eds.), *Substantive and Procedural Aspects of International Criminal Law* (The Hague: Kluwer, 2000), i, 416–450, at 424–426.

(although limited to questioning). Instead, in the trial phase this right is subject to the limitation of being necessary in the interests of justice.

It is uncertain whether the right to counsel triggered by questioning continues to have effect in the pre-trial phase even beyond the actual moment of questioning, or whether it is limited to that specific stage. It would be unfair to impose limitations strictly linked to the formal time frame of the questioning itself. Nonetheless, it is clear that the right to counsel has limitations that may be intrinsically linked to the nature of the proceedings. Before the ICC, for example, it does not seem possible that counsel for the person who is the object of a request to open an investigation already be present at the hearing for authorization by the Pre-Trial Chamber, as these hearings were intended as *ex parte* proceedings.

In this respect a case brought before the ICTY can be instructive. In the course of the Rule 61 proceeding against Karadžić and Mladić, the Trial Chamber decided that a lawyer designated by Karadžić to intervene on his behalf in the hearings was not entitled to participate in the proceedings.[93] It has been argued that the Trial Chamber had denied the right of the accused to legal assistance and that therefore Article 21.4(d) was violated.[94] This criticism, however, does not seem to be consistent with the rationale behind the Rule 61 proceedings, which are intended to be a reaction against the non-execution of arrest warrants and the refusal of accused persons to appear before the Tribunal. These proceedings are essentially *ex parte* hearings, where the presence of the accused is not required (should the accused be present there would be no need to hold Rule 61 proceedings), nor is the presence of his lawyers. The right to legal assistance is derived from the participation of the accused in the proceedings (including the pre-trial phase) and emerges only in so far as adversarial proceedings are instituted.[95]

Another interesting facet of the right to assignment of counsel is the determination of professional competence required to appear before the Court. The formal requirements provided for in the draft Rules of the ICC are competence in criminal law and procedure, and experience in criminal proceedings. Moreover, it is required that counsel must have an excellent knowledge of one of the working languages of the Court.[96] Control over the existence of these requirements is exercised by the Registrar, who is also responsible for maintaining a list of lawyers to be assigned as defence counsel to indigent persons (suspect or accused).

---

[93] Cf. Decision Partially Rejecting the Request Submitted by Mr Igor Pantelić, Counsel for Radovan Karadzić, *Karadzić and Mladić* (IT–95–18-R61), 27 June 1996.

[94] In this respect see A.M. La Rosa, 'Réflexions sur l'apport du Tribunal pénal international pour l'ex-Yougoslavie au droit à un procès équitable', in 101 *RGDIP* (1997), at 960.

[95] Equally an individual has no right, under the *ad hoc* Tribunal Statutes, to be present at the confirmation hearing.

[96] Cf. Rule 22.1, Rules of Procedure for the ICC (UN doc. PCNICC/2000/1/ Add.1, 2 November 2000).

As regards the determination of the fact that a person is lacking the means to remunerate counsel, it should be noted that often this is a very difficult endeavour, because of the difficulties in finding financial documents in territories which have been, or are, scenes of armed conflict.[97] The Registrar is the competent organ, but—at least in the system of the *ad hoc* Tribunals—the suspect has a recognized right to seek review before the Trial Chamber.[98]

It is important to mention that the interpretation that has been given to date by the Tribunal of the right to legal aid goes beyond what is required by international standards because 'the choice of a lawyer under a free legal aid system ultimately rests with the state, and the accused cannot insist that the state pay the lawyer he selects'.[99] On the contrary, the practice of the Tribunal shows that although this is not established as a principle, defendants so far have been allowed to choose the counsel they want to have assigned.[100]

[97] Lastly, a Trial Chamber of the ICTY also discussed the issue of the assignment of Defence Counsel and in particular the criteria for determining whether an accused is indigent or not (Order on the motion for assignment of counsel, *Dokmanović* (IT–95–13a-PT), 30 September 1997). The Registrar had decided that the accused, Mr Dokmanović, was not indigent and therefore would himself have to pay his defence counsel. The accused impugned the decision before the Trial Chamber, as provided for in the Rules and in the Directive on the assignment of Defence Counsel, seeking revision of the Registrar's decision. The Chamber concluded that the task of ascertaining the indigence of the accused was assigned, under the system of the Tribunal, to the Registrar. However, it concluded that in the case at issue the determination had not been made in accordance with the Rules, and therefore decided that the defendant was entitled *rebus sic stantibus* to have the Tribunal pay for his Defence Counsel, pending a new examination of his financial situation by the Registrar. This case—which in itself might be of little or no importance at all—shows the commitment the Tribunal feels to ensuring that the accused is in the best possible position to conduct his trial.

[98] Cf. Dokmanović Order, note 97 above, 30 September 1997.

[99] Cf. H.N.A. Noor Muhammad, 'Due Process of Law for Persons Accused of Crime', in L. Henkin (ed.), *The International Bill of Human Rights: The Covenant on Civil and Political Rights* (New York: Columbia University Press, 1981), at 153.

[100] Reference is made to the *Erdemović* case mentioned above, cf. note 87 above, and to the decision of the Trial Chamber in *Dokmanović* (30/09/1997), and also to a decision in *Delalić*, where the lawyer previously working as a chosen counsel paid by the accused was subsequently assigned to him as a result of changes in the economic conditions of the accused (he became indigent). As one can easily imagine, the costs of an international trial are very high, and therefore this practice by the ICTY deserves great attention and seems a step forward in the protection of fundamental rights. In general on the right to legal assistance and legal aid in the ICTY system see S. Beresford, 'The International Criminal Tribunal for the Former Yugoslavia and the Right to Legal Aid and Assistance', in 2 *Int. JHR* (1998), 49–65, at 61.

In this respect the position of the ICTR seems more controversial. On different occasions, the Chambers of the ICTR have had to deal with this issue. In the Akayesu case the Trial Chamber faced two subsequent requests of the accused for substitution of the assigned Counsel. In the first decision, the Trial Chamber opted (albeit not declaring it) for choosing the counsel that the accused wished to have assigned. In the second case, it referred the matter to the Registrar, emphasising that it was within the competence of the Registrar to choose the lawyer to be assigned. In *Nzirorera*, 3 October 2001, the Trial Chamber denied the motion of the accused for withdrawal of his defence counsel, although the accused manifested a 'profound and irreconcilable disagreement' with him. In reality it seems that in this case the Chamber took such an approach to punish a 'fee-splitting' request made by the accused to his Counsel. On this issue see Statement by the Registrar on Allegations of Fee Splitting between a Detainee of the ICTR and his Defence Counsel, ICTR/INFO–9–3–06.EN, 29 October 2001. See also ICTR/INFO-9-3-13.EN, 5 November 2002, and for the ICTY Press Release CC/PIS/686-e, 8 July 2002.

It is interesting to note that such practice has been consolidated. A first indication to this effect was an amendment to the RPE ICTY, which allowed the Registrar to assign, upon request of an indigent person, 'counsel who speaks the language of the suspect or the accused but does not speak either of the two working languages of the Tribunal'.[101] The amendment was introduced because of what had happened in the *Erdemović* case, mentioned above, when the Trial Chamber decided to authorize assignment of a lawyer who did not meet the requirement of speaking one of the working languages of the Tribunal.[102] This decision was justified because of the previous relationship of confidence that the lawyer had established with the accused. Subsequently, this move towards a right of the accused to give indications of who should be appointed as defence counsel has been confirmed by the choice made in the Rules of the ICC.[103] It is interesting to note that the Chambers of the ICTR expressed more balanced views in this respect. First, in *Ntakirutimana* it was noted that the rules on assignment of counsel for indigent persons could not be 'interpreted as giving the indigent accused the absolute right to be assigned the legal representation of his or her own choice', but the Chamber added that 'mindful to ensure that the indigent accused receives the most efficient defence possible in the context of a fair trial . . . an indigent accused should be offered the possibility of designating the counsel of his or her choice from the list drawn up by the Registrar . . ., the Registrar having to take into consideration the wishes of the accused'.[104] Secondly, in the *Nyiramasuhuko and Ntahobali* case it was added that the Registrar could take into consideration other factors, such as the resources of the Tribunal, competence, geographical distribution, and balancing the principal legal systems of the

---

[101] Cf. Rule 45 (B) RPE ICTY, originally introduced as Rule 45 (A) (ii) at the 11th Plenary Session 24 June 1996 IT/33/Rev.9, subsequently became Rule 45 (B).

[102] Cf. Trial Chamber Order on the appointment of defence counsel, *Erdemović* (IT–96–22-PT), 28 May 1996.

[103] Cf. ICC RPE, Rule 21 Assignment of legal assistance:

'1. Subject to article 55, paragraph 2 (c), and article 67, paragraph 1 (d), criteria and procedures for assignment of legal assistance shall be established in the Regulations, based on a proposal by the Registrar, following consultations with any independent representative body of counsel or legal associations, as referred to in rule 20, sub-rule 3.

2. The Registrar shall create and maintain a list of counsel who meet the criteria set forth in rule 22 and the Regulations. The person shall freely choose his or her counsel from this list or other counsel who meets the required criteria and is willing to be included in the list.

3. A person may seek from the Presidency a review of a decision to refuse a request for assignment of counsel. The decision of the Presidency shall be final. If a request is refused, a further request may be made by a person to the Registrar, upon showing a change in circumstances.

4. A person choosing to represent himself or herself shall so notify the Registrar in writing at the first opportunity.

5. Where a person claims to have insufficient means to pay for legal assistance and this is subsequently found not to be so, the Chamber dealing with the case at that time may make an order of contribution to recover the cost of providing counsel.'

[104] This interpretation has been reaffirmed by the Registrar of the ICTR, Mr Adama Dieng, cf. ICTR Press Release 2 October 2001.

world.[105] Naturally, these considerations go beyond the interest of the accused and involve a more global assessment of good administration of justice.

The importance of the regulation of this aspect of legal aid is due to the fact that experience shows that most individuals appearing before the *ad hoc* Tribunals have assigned counsel.[106]

One may wonder whether indigence is the only circumstance in which the assignment of defence counsel by the Tribunal is needed. In this respect, the situation in the early stages of the *Milošević* case is certainly very instructive. It is well known that the former President of FRY did not recognize the Tribunal and thus refused both to defend himself in person and to appoint defence counsel.[107] The Trial Chamber could have assigned him a lawyer, on the basis that this was necessary, in the interests of justice, to ensure a proper administration of justice.[108] On the contrary, the Chamber adopted an innovative solution: it decided that it could not impose a lawyer on the accused, and it instructed the Registrar to appoint *amici curiae* to assist the Chamber in ensuring a fair trial.[109] This solution is not entirely persuasive for three main reasons: first, because it is unclear why the judges, who are the ultimate guardians of justice, would need assistance for ensuring a fair trial; secondly, there is some ambiguity in that the Chamber requested the Registrar to

---

[105] Cf. ICTR, 13 March 1998.

[106] It is interesting to note that the vast majority of defendants before the ICTY have assigned counsel. Cf., e.g., *Third Annual Report of the President of the ICTY to the UN General Assembly and Security Council* (1996), UN doc. A/51/292, 16 August 1996: '[t]he list of assigned counsel continues to lengthen, with 66 lawyers from 13 countries. Counsel assigned by the Tribunal to date are as follows: for Duško Tadić, Professor Wladimiroff and Mr Orie, as well as a consultant, Mr Kay, two investigators and one researcher; for Djordje Djukić, Mr Vujin and Mr Fila; for Aleksa Krsmanović, Professor Sjocrona, then Mr Pantelic; for Radoslav Kremenovic, Mr Guberina; for Zdravko Mucić, Mr Rhodes, QC, then Mr Tapuskovic; for Goran Lajić, Mr Fila; for Drazen Erdemović, Mr Babic; for Hazim Delić, Mr Karabdić; and for Esad Landzo, Mr Brakovic. (par. 107) Non-assigned (private) counsel are as follows: for Tihofil Blaškić, Mr Hodak; and for Zejnil Delalić, Ms. Residović' (para. 108). Subsequently the list has naturally changed, but the proportion is still the same. In this respect see also the Comments by Amnesty International on the ILC Draft for a Permanent Criminal Court, which tend to suggest that a system like the programme of free legal assistance established by the Tribunal should be provided for in the framework of the ICC.

[107] Subsequently, however, it appeared that Mr Milošević changed his mind and started to defend himself in person, including by cross-examining witnesses.

[108] Article 21.4 (d) ICTY St. (20 ICTR St.) provides that the accused has the right 'to have legal assistance assigned to him, in any case where the interests of justice so require, and without payment by him in any such case if he does not have sufficient means to pay for it'. This means that these are two distinct rights: on the one hand the right to the assignment of legal assistance, on the other the right to free assistance.

[109] Cf. Order for the appointment of *amici curiae*, *Milošević* (IT–99–37-PT), 30 August 2001. The Chamber instructed the Registrar to appoint a team of experts to assist the Chamber in ensuring a fair trial. The Registrar appointed three lawyers: Mr Wladimiroff (former Defence Counsel for Duško Tadić), Mr Steven Kay (who was a member of Tadić's Defence Team) and Mr Tapuškovic (who assisted Mucić). On 10 October 2002, however, the Trial Chamber ordered the Registrar to revoke the appointment of Mr Wladimiroff as *amicus curiae* for in two interviews to the press he had made statements that gave rise to a reasonable perception of bias on his part.

appoint *amici curiae*. This is the normal procedure for the assignment of defence counsel,[110] while *amicus curiae* should be designed by the Chamber itself.[111] Thirdly, criminal trials by definition consist of a debate between two parties before an impartial arbiter. This is not something at the disposal of parties: it is in the very nature of a trial. Therefore, although the defendant is not obliged actively to participate in the proceedings,[112] the essence of the trial requires that the charges must be examined through confrontation between two adverse parties. The *amicus curiae* does not fulfil these requirements, as it can be hardly considered 'a Party'.[113]

Defence counsel assigned to the accused against his or her will nonetheless should have the power to indicate to the court possible flaws in the indictment, or to point to exculpatory materials. They should even be under a duty, whenever appropriate, to request the Chamber to allow the production of evidence (including calling witnesses) in the interest of the accused. Naturally, considering the unique features of proceedings brought before international criminal courts, investigations without the co-operation of the defendant could turn out to be very difficult.[114] Moreover, when an accused does not want to be defended it may be inappropriate to impose on him assigned defence counsel. Finally, in particular when the accused is accused of crimes committed while discharging public functions, there may be concerns for the security of attorneys assigned to his case, should they decide to conduct investigations.

Notwithstanding the difficulties arising out of such a scenario, the co-operation of an accused should never be considered a condition for the trial to proceed. In consideration of the main features of the procedural systems of international tribunals, which require a trial with two opposing parties, the Chamber must try to ensure the adversarial character of debates. Assigning a lawyer to the accused when the interests of justice so require may be the best way to reconcile the interests of justice with the right of the accused to a fair trial. Consequently, it would have been more effective for the purpose of ensuring a fair and expeditious trial to assign legal assistance to the accused, already at the pre-trial stage, in order to ensure the two parties' confrontation.[114a]

---

[110] Rule 45 RPE.

[111] Rule 74 RPE: '[a] Chamber may, if it considers it desirable for the proper determination of the case, invite or grant leave to a State, organization or person to appear before it and make submissions on any issue specified by the Chamber'.

[112] On the basis of the presumption of innocence it is for the Prosecution to prove guilt. The accused can simply await the verdict. There is no obligation requiring the actual participation of the defendant.

[113] For a different opinion see W. Schabas, 'Article 67', in Triffterer (ed.), note 77 above, at 857, para. 30.

[114] The Tribunal has no police force of its own and must rely on State co-operation, which however is essentially based on the carrying out of specific requests. An investigation may need a general activity of collection of information that is difficult to perform in normal conditions and would be nearly impossible in cases where the accused refused any defence.

[114a] See Rule 45-*quater* ICTR RPE adopted at the 12th Plenary Session (July 2002).

In any case, it seems that beyond its formal characterization, the solution chosen by the Chamber in *Milošević* is less innovative than it may appear. Substantially, although the Chamber formally referred to the 'appointment of *amici curiae*', one may consider that it intended to request the 'assignment of Defence Counsel';[115] this is confirmed by the circumstance that it instructed the Registrar to appoint the *amici curiae*.

It has been suggested that an international defence office, with a separate budget and autonomous resources available for all indigent defendants, should be created, and this office could start conducting investigations in the interests of suspects even before they were formally charged.[116] This solution is not necessarily appropriate. The role that such a proposal would like to assign to an international defence office should be played—in accordance with the interpretation suggested above—by the Prosecutor of the ICC and the Pre-Trial Chamber at the stage of investigations. One may wonder whether there are sufficient reasons to duplicate institutions.[117] The preliminary phase in *Milošević*, however, although the accused has subsequently decided to defend himself in person, may give some additional strength to this idea.

---

[115] Many consequences a different characterization of the team of experts appointed for Milošević may lead to many different consequences and a few questions arise: should *amici curiae* receive all supporting materials, witness statements, lists of witnesses, and exhibits? Do the Rules and the Code of Professional Conduct bind them? To respond to these doubts the Trial Chamber in a subsequent order of 19 September 2001 imposed a number of specific duties onto the team of lawyers.

[116] In this respect see K. Gallant, 'The Role and Powers of Defense Counsel in the Rome Statute of the International Criminal Court', in 34 *IL* (2000), at 42. For the time being steps have been taken for the creation of an international bar association (or an association of defence counsel appearing before *ad hoc* Tribunals), see Press Release CC/PIS/688-e, 19 July 2002.

[117] It should also be added that the Rules for the ICC impose a precise duty on the Registrar to assist the Defence. Cf. Rule 20, Responsibilities of the Registrar relating to the rights of the defence:

'1. In accordance with article 43, paragraph 1, the Registrar shall organize the staff of the Registry in a manner that promotes the rights of the defence, consistent with the principle of fair trial as defined in the Statute. For that purpose, the Registrar shall, *inter alia*:

(a) Facilitate the protection of confidentiality, as defined in article 67 (1) (b) of the Statute;

(b) Provide support, assistance, and information to all defence counsel appearing before the Court;

(c) Assist arrested persons, persons to whom article 55 (2) of the Statute applies and the accused in obtaining legal advice and the assistance of legal counsel;

(d) Advise the Prosecutor and the Chambers of the Court, as needed, on relevant defence-related issues;

(e) Provide the defence with adequate facilities as may be necessary, for the direct performance of the duty of the defence;

(f) Facilitate the dissemination of information and case law of the Court to defence counsel.

2. The Registrar shall carry out the functions stipulated in paragraph 1, including the financial administration of the Registry, in such a manner as to ensure the professional independence of defence counsel.

3. For such purposes as the management of legal assistance in accordance with rule 21 and the development of a code of professional conduct in accordance with rule 8, the Registrar shall consult, as appropriate, with any independent representative body of counsel or legal associations, including any such body the establishment of which may be facilitated by the Assembly of States Parties'.

Article 55, paragraph 2, of the ICC Statute specifies that the person about to be questioned has, in addition to the right to legal assistance, the right to be questioned in the presence of counsel, unless he or she voluntarily waives this right. In this respect it seems appropriate to suggest the inclusion in the Rules of Procedure of provisions clarifying how this right should operate. Provisions should be made aimed at recognizing the right of the person questioned to request, if appropriate, suspension of the questioning and attendance of counsel at any stage, whenever he or she may deem it necessary.[118] One may think, for example, of the case where suspects have initially agreed to be questioned without counsel and subsequently change their mind.

Finally, in the current system the decision on the need to assign a lawyer to the suspect is substantially left to the Prosecutor. It is submitted that this solution is not appropriate. It hardly seems fair to leave it to the Prosecutor to determine whether or not it is in the interests of justice to assign defence counsel to a person under investigation. In general, it is correct to leave the role of supervision, organization, and assignment of defence counsel to the Registrar, as in the ICTY and ICTR systems. However, it seems inappropriate to leave it to the Registrar to determine whether or not it is in the interests of justice to assign a lawyer to a suspect. This would amount to attributing a very broad discretionary power to an organ that is essentially administrative in nature and serves both the Chambers and the Prosecution. Tensions among the organs of the Court might ensue. Thus, it would be more appropriate for the Pre-Trial Chamber to decide on the existence of the interests of justice in such cases. Another option could be to specify in detail, in the Rules of Procedure, the situations in which it may be considered that it is in the interests of justice to assign defence counsel to an indigent suspect, removing this concept from the sphere of discretion.

5. The right not to be subjected to arbitrary arrest or detention (including the right to compensation for unlawful arrest or detention)

From a brief overview of the provisions contained in the most relevant international human rights texts it appears that most of the safeguards provided for in the preliminary phase are directly or indirectly linked to the issue of personal liberty. Moreover, it is certain that in the context of a criminal investigation, when a person is in custody, i.e. in provisional detention, his or her rights are more at risk than when this person is free. It is essential in this phase, too, that equality between the parties be preserved and keeping the defendant in detention makes him more vulnerable. This is why the ICCPR explicitly states that '[it] shall not be the general rule that persons awaiting

---

[118] Cf. Pre-Trial Rights in the Rules of Procedure and Evidence, Lawyers Committee for Human Rights, February 1999, at <**www.lchr.org/icc/papv2n3.htm**>.

trial shall be detained in custody'.[119] On the other hand, provisional detention and deprivation of liberty may become very important, particularly in the phase of investigation, in order to prevent a suspect from attempting to destroy relevant evidence, including threatening witnesses.

It is well known that at Nuremberg and Tokyo the Allies held defendants in custody before the issue of the indictment. Most of the defendants had been arrested even before the final decision to establish an international tribunal had been taken and were detained by national authorities. Detention was the general rule and there were no exceptions. Moreover, there were no options to argue for provisional release, or at least there was no express provision to this effect in the Rules.[120]

The reasons behind the adoption of this solution were clearly linked to the unique character of those jurisdictions. The Nuremberg and Tokyo Tribunals were international military organs created by the victorious powers to judge persons allegedly responsible for the most heinous crimes. Naturally, the combination of the gravity of the crimes, the international character of the proceedings, and the post-conflict situation created a solid set of reasons for trying to prevent any attempt at escape.

Furthermore, the same reasons behind the lack of international legal standards on fundamental rights at the time, including protection for persons under investigation, also holds true in respect of the right to personal liberty. At the time of the Nuremberg trial the values behind the protection of this right—which is now considered as one of the most fundamental tenets of human rights law, to be preserved in all phases of the administration of criminal justice—were probably not shared by the whole international community. At any rate they had not yet been laid down in international rules.

With the adoption of the UDHR the right to personal liberty had been affirmed and considered as a fundamental right.[121] Subsequently, this right was further specified in the ICCPR[122] and in the regional conventions elaborated in

---

[119] Along the same lines see the General Comment no. 8 by the Human Rights Committee on Article 9.3 ICCPR, 27 July 1982.

[120] Only one of the defendants, Gustav Krupp von Bohlen und Halbach, was not detained in prison, since he was ill; thus his trial was postponed indefinitely. Mr Krupp died in 1950.

[121] The UDHR states that 'no one shall be subjected to arbitrary arrest, detention or exile' (Article 9) and recognizes a general right to judicial review by the competent national authorities for violations of rights granted to a person by the constitution or by law (Article 8).

[122] The ICCPR is more specific in that, apart from recognizing the right to liberty and security, it also limits the reasons for which deprivations may occur. These may be justified on 'such grounds and in accordance with such procedure as are established by law' (Article 9.1). Then it further establishes that 'anyone who is arrested shall be informed, at the time of arrest, of the reasons for his arrest and shall be promptly informed of any charges against him' (Article 9.2). It also assigns to the person deprived of his/her liberty the right to take proceedings before a court to obtain a decision on the lawfulness of the detention and to obtain release if the detention is unlawful (Article 9.4). Moreover, the ICCPR comprises other general guarantees for the position of the person involved in a criminal proceeding. First, it establishes—as previously mentioned—the principle according to which detention shall not be the general rule for persons awaiting trial

Europe and in America.[123] Moreover, most national systems, in accordance with the content of the obligations imposed by international norms, recognize this right.[124]

There are traits common to the various international texts. On the one hand, there is the general recognition of the exceptional character of provisional detention. On the other hand, deprivation of liberty must not be arbitrary, in that it may be imposed only on selected and specified grounds. Furthermore, there are additional rights linked to the fact of being in detention.[125] As regards the core of these rights, it seems reasonable to agree with those who, referring comparatively to an ensemble of international texts, submit that there '[is] strong evidence that [common elements] express a rule of general international law. These elements may be defined as: (a) the right in criminal cases of a detained person to be brought promptly before a judge and (b) the right of anyone deprived of liberty to challenge the lawfulness of detention and to be released if the detention is found to be unlawful.'[126]

The Statutes of the *ad hoc* Tribunals do not include any express provisions allowing the Prosecutor to request the arrest of a person under investigation. The judges, however, when drafting the RPE were confronted with the need to provide the Prosecutor with appropriate tools for investigation. It is well known that during an investigation it may become necessary to adopt conservative measures in order to preserve evidence or to prevent the suspect from escaping, which include requests for arrest and detention of suspects. The judges, aware of this problem, initially adopted Rule 40, which—under the title of 'Provisional Measures'—empowers the Prosecutor to request a State: (i) to arrest the suspect provisionally; (ii) to seize physical evidence; and

(Article 9.3). Secondly, it recognizes the right of those arrested to be brought promptly before a judge for trial within reasonable time or to be released (Article 9.3). Finally, it also adds specific guarantees for the treatment of persons in detention and for granting different detention regimes in different situations (Article 10). Cf. Articles 9 and 10 ICCPR.

[123] Cf. Article 7 ACHR, Article 5 ECHR. The ECHR and the ACHR contain rights analogous to those recognized in the Covenant. The European text is much more specific as regards the lawfulness of the detention and it lists in Article 5.1 from a) to f) a series of cases in which arrest and detention may be lawful. On the provisions of Article 5 of the ECHR, see S. Trechsel, S., 'Liberty and Security of Person, in R.S.J. MacDonald *et al.* (eds.), *The European System for the Protection of Human Rights* (Dordrecht: Nijhoff, 1993), at 277. Additionally the ACHR specifically refers to the conditions established by the constitution of the State Party concerned or by a law (Article 7.2).

[124] Cf. M.C. Bassiouni, 'Human Rights in the Context of Criminal Justice: Identifying International Procedural Protections and Equivalent Protections in National Constitutions', in 3 *DJICL*, (1993), at 240.

[125] In this respect, it has been contended that the RPE of the Tribunals lack provisions relating to the rights of persons in pre-trial detention: see L. Sunga, *The Emerging System of International Criminal Law* (The Hague: Kluwer, 1997), at 320. Nonetheless, it must be recognized that these rights have been protected to a very large extent by the regulations concerning the administration of the UN Detention Units: see *ICTY Basic Documents* (1998).

[126] N. Rodley, *The Treatment of Prisoners Under International Law* (2nd edn., Oxford: Clarendon Press, 1999), at 340.

(iii) to take all necessary measures to prevent the escape of a suspect, or injury or intimidation of witnesses, or the destruction of evidence. According to this Rule, States shall comply with these requests pursuant to Article 29 of the ICTY Statute.[127] Subsequently, however, it became clear that it was necessary to adopt more specific provisions containing a more detailed procedure on provisional detention. Therefore the judges adopted an amendment to the RPE and introduced Rule 40-*bis*, on the 'transfer and provisional detention of suspects'.

The procedure laid down in Rule 40-*bis* provides for two sets of guarantees: on the one hand, it establishes the conditions for the issue of an order for detention of a suspect; on the other hand, it provides adequate safeguards for the detained suspect. First of all, it is established that the issue of an order for transfer and detention under this rule is conditioned by a requirement that the Prosecutor demonstrate the existence of 'a reliable and consistent body of material which tends to show that the suspect may have committed the crime' (Rule 40-*bis*(B)(ii) RPE). Furthermore, provisional detention must be 'a necessary measure to prevent the escape of the suspect, injury or intimidation of a victim or destruction of evidence, or to be otherwise necessary for the conduct of investigation' (subparagraph (B)(iii)). Then the Rule specifies the safeguards for the suspect. First, Rule 40-*bis* subparagraph (C) clarifies that the order for transfer and detention must state the grounds for making the order, the initial time limit for the provisional detention, and a statement of the rights of the suspect. Secondly, subparagraph (D) stipulates that the detention 'shall be ordered for a period not exceeding thirty days', then that this period can be extended for thirty more days 'if warranted by the needs of the investigation', and finally that only under exceptional circumstances can the detention be further extended for thirty more days, but 'in no case it can exceed ninety days'. Thirdly, subparagraph (F) recognizes the right of the suspect to be assisted by counsel and to be brought, without delay, before a judge, who shall ensure that the rights of the suspect are respected. Lastly, subparagraph (G) provides that the suspect at any time during detention may file applications relating to the detention or to release to a Trial Chamber or a judge. This amendment of the Rules filled the *lacunae* in the previous norms and offers a model that may be considered as satisfactory in terms of protection of the rights of the suspect.

---

[127] In this respect many doubts may be raised as to the legitimacy of this Rule. It seems to imply that the Prosecutor may directly request a State to arrest a person or to seize evidence. This drafting does not correspond to Article 29, wherein it is made very clear that States shall comply with the orders issued by a Trial Chamber. Therefore the norm inserted in Rule 40 which requires States to comply with the request of the Prosecutor is *ultra vires*. Moreover there is absolutely no reason why the Prosecutor should not ask the Trial Chamber (or a single judge acting in the name of the entire Chamber) to issue a request to that State. This would also ensure more protection to individual rights. This part of the rule remained unchanged in spite of the introduction of Rule 40-*bis*.

Naturally, there is still room for abuse;[128] for example, there are no specific guarantees that the transfer from the State of custody to the Tribunal will be effected without delay,[129] and the period of time spent in detention in the State is not calculated in the overall period of ninety days.

The abovementioned provisions of Rule 40-*bis* apply to individuals prior to confirmation of charges, while, after confirmation of the indictment, accused persons are detained on remand pursuant to Rule 65. The general practice in the *ad hoc* Tribunal system shows that once the indictment is confirmed defendants are normally held in pre-trial detention.[130] The consistent practice of the two Tribunals is that the judge confirming the indictment at the same time issues one or more arrest warrants addressed to relevant State authorities requesting the arrest and transfer of the accused. Pursuant to such an order the indicted person should be arrested and transferred to the custody of the Tribunal. Thereafter, the accused is detained at the UN Detention Units (either in The Hague or in Arusha) and may be released only under the conditions set out in Rule 65 RPE.

In this respect, it is interesting to note the evolution of the rules on provisional release in the ICTY system.[131] Originally, Rule 65 was extremely restrictive and provided for provisional release only in exceptional circumstances, which the accused had to prove. Subsequently, also in consideration of the enhanced co-operation by relevant State authorities in the region of the former Yugoslavia, the judges amended the Rules deleting the requirement that exceptional circumstances had to be shown.[132] The amendment brought the Rules more into line with human rights standards; nonetheless, it still remains true that liberty is the exception while detention is the rule.[133]

With regard to the execution of arrest warrants by the Tribunals two issues need to be discussed. First, one may wonder what requirements make an arrest lawful under the Statutes and the Rules of the *ad hoc* Tribunals. Secondly, one may ask what would be the consequences of the violation of the rights of the

---

[128] In this respect it should be noted that the issue of the legality of arrest procedures has been raised a number of times in relation to recent arrests. Cf. e.g. M. Scharf, 'The Prosecutor v. Dokmanović: Irregular Rendition and the ICTY', in 11 *LJIL* (1998), at 369.

[129] Recently in a decision by the Appeals Chamber of the ICTR it has emerged that problems and delays in the transfer may unduly affect the individual: cf. Decision of 3 November 1999, note 68 above.

[130] Rule 40-*bis* has rarely been applied by the ICTY, while the ICTR has so far resorted to this provision more frequently.

[131] So far the ICTR has not yet amended Rule 65 of its RPE.

[132] The amendment was adopted at the 21st Plenary Session in November 1999, Rev. 17.

[133] On the evolution of the Rules on provisional release see P. Wald and J. Martinez, 'Provisional Release at the ICTY: A Work in Progress', in May and others (eds.), *Essays on ICTY Procedure and Evidence in Honour of Gabrielle Kirk McDonald* (The Hague: Kluwer, 2001), 231–246. For more detailed consideration of this issue see Chapter 3 below, section I.3 on the effects of the presumption of innocence.

accused.[134] On the first issue, the Rules of Procedure and Evidence specify the requirements for the Tribunal's arrest warrants and the rules for their transmission to national or international authorities (Rules 55 and 59-*bis*).[135] In both cases the Rules require that upon arrest the accused must be informed of the rights provided for in Article 21 ICTY St. The procedure for arrest is not regulated in detail, since such specific regulation is left to each national system. Turning to the second issue, there is no certainty that arrests by State authorities will be conducted in compliance with internationally recognized standards. Thus, the question of what would happen in such cases remains open. Does a violation of the rights of the defendant at the stage of arrest imply that the Tribunals forfeit their jurisdiction? In at least three cases the issue was

---

[134] In this respect see S. Lamb 'The Power of Arrest of the International Criminal Tribunal for the former Yugoslavia', in 70 *BYIL* (2000), 165–244, by the same author see also, 'Illegal Arrest and the Jurisdiction of the ICTY', in May *et al.* (eds.), note 133 above, 27–43. For a broader analysis of the issue of abduction contrary to international law and its consequences see S. Wilske, *Die völkerrechtswidrige Entführung und ihre Rechtsfolgen* (Berlin: Duncker and Humblot, 2000).

[135] Rule 55, Execution of Arrest Warrants, provides that:
'(A) A warrant of arrest shall be signed by a Judge. It shall include an order for the prompt transfer of the accused to the Tribunal upon the arrest of the accused. (B) The original warrant shall be retained by the Registrar, who shall prepare certified copies bearing the seal of the Tribunal. (C) Each certified copy shall be accompanied by a copy of the indictment certified in accordance with Rule 47 (G) and a statement of the rights of the accused set forth in Article 21 of the Statute, and in Rules 42 and 43 *mutatis mutandis*. If the accused does not understand either of the official languages of the Tribunal and if the language understood by the accused is known to the Registrar, each certified copy of the warrant of arrest shall also be accompanied by a translation of the statement of the rights of the accused in that language. (D) Subject to any order of a Judge or Chamber, the Registrar may transmit a certified copy of a warrant of arrest to the person or authorities to which it is addressed, including the national authorities of a State in whose territory or under whose jurisdiction the accused resides, or was last known to be, or is believed by the Registrar to be likely to be found. (E) The Registrar shall instruct the person or authorities to which a warrant is transmitted that at the time of arrest the indictment and the statement of the rights of the accused be read to the accused in a language that he or she understands and that the accused be cautioned in that language that the accused has the right to remain silent, and that any statement he or she makes shall be recorded and may be used in evidence. (F) Notwithstanding Sub-rule (E), if at the time of arrest the accused is served with, or with a translation of, the indictment and the statement of rights of the accused in a language that the accused understands and is able to read, these need not be read to the accused at the time of arrest. (G) When an arrest warrant issued by the Tribunal is executed by the authorities of a State, or an appropriate authority or international body, a member of the Office of the Prosecutor may be present as from the time of the arrest.'
Rule 59 *bis* Transmission of Arrest Warrants: (A) Notwithstanding Rules 55 to 59, on the order of a Judge, the Registrar shall transmit to an appropriate authority or international body or the Prosecutor a copy of a warrant for the arrest of an accused, on such terms as the Judge may determine, together with an order for the prompt transfer of the accused to the Tribunal in the event that the accused be taken into custody by that authority or international body or the Prosecutor. (B) At the time of being taken into custody an accused shall be informed immediately, in a language the accused understands, of the charges against him or her and of the fact that he or she is being transferred to the Tribunal. Upon such transfer, the indictment and a statement of the rights of the accused shall be read to the accused and the accused shall be cautioned in such a language. (C) Notwithstanding Sub-rule (B), the indictment and statement of rights of the accused need not be read to the accused if the accused is served with these, or with a translation of these, in a language the accused understands and is able to read.

explicitly raised before the ICTY. In *Dokmanović*, the defendant claimed that he had been surreptitiously arrested by the UN Transitional Administration for Eastern Slavonia (UNTAES). The Trial Chamber, however, dismissed the objections and held that the arrest was lawful and the rights of the accused had not been violated.[136] In *Todorović*, the accused claimed that he had been kidnapped by Stabilization Force (SFOR) troops on the territory of the FRY. The accused raised issues ranging from the infringement of individual rights to the violation of the sovereignty of the Federal Republic of Yugoslavia. Eventually, however, all motions by Todorović, challenging the legality of his arrest, were withdrawn as a result of an agreement with the Prosecutor and his entering a guilty plea on 13 December 2000.[137] The same issue was raised in *Nikolić*, but also in this case the Trial Chamber rejected the motion.[137a]

In all instances the defendants sought the dismissal of their cases on the grounds that their rights had been violated. Their submissions were incorrect and inappropriate for two main reasons. First, none of those alleged violations was really imputable to the Tribunal, unless one proved that the order of the Tribunal implied the need to resort to unlawful methods. Secondly, from a procedural viewpoint, the accused was at most entitled to release and/or, where applicable, exclusion of the evidence collected in violation of fundamental rights; instead, he had no right to dismissal of the proceedings.[138] Additionally, these kinds of violations should also be redressed through compensation.[139] Of course, the problem would be far more serious if one could prove a consistent pattern of violations of the rights of individuals by State or international authorities performing arrests at the request of *ad hoc* Tribunals.[140] In this case it could be argued that the Tribunals should react vigorously, for example by adopting a specific rule providing for the quashing of proceedings based on arrests inconsistent with individual rights.[141]

[136] See Decision on the Motion for Release, *Dokmanović* (IT–95–13a-PT), 22 October 1997. On the Dokmanović case see also L.C. Green, 'Erdemović, Tadić, Dokmanović: Jurisdiction and Early Practice of the Yugoslav War Crimes Tribunal', in 27 *Isr. YHR* (1997) 313–364, at 362–364, where the author criticizes the decision of the Trial Chamber.

[137] For more details on the *Todorović* case see ICTY *Eight Annual Report*, UN doc. A/56/352 17 September 2001, paras. 141–144.

[137a] Decision on Defence Motion Challenging the Exercise of Jurisdiction by the Tribunal, *Nikolić* (IT–95–2–PT), 2 October 2002.

[138] This would be in line with normal remedies under international law: see F. A. Mann, 'Reflections on the Prosecution of Persons Abducted in breach of International Law', in Y. Dinstein (ed.), *International Law at a Time of Perplexity* (Dordrecht: Nijhoff, 1989), at 411.

[139] This was also the solution adopted by the Tribunal in *Barayagwiza* when the organs of the Tribunal bore a certain degree of responsibility for the violations of the rights of the accused. For a more detailed discussion of this case see Chapter 4 below.

[140] G. Abi-Saab, 'Droits de l'homme et juridictions pénales internationales: Convergences et tensions', in R.-J. Dupuy, *Mélanges Valticos—Droit et Justice* (Paris: Pedone, 1999), discusses the *Dokmanović* case, warning on the risks of a consistent pattern of illegal arrests, at 252.

[141] In this case the Tribunal would be making a policy choice, in that it would try to prevent violations by clearly indicating that the effect of such violations would be counterproductive in that it would make not only the arrest vain, but also the entire proceedings.

On the issue of personal liberty, criticism may be directed at the ICC Statute. In spite of the generally very advanced model in terms of protection of individual rights, the protection of the right to liberty is not sufficiently developed. Although the Statute does not contain provisions contrary to international human rights standards in respect of detention on remand, it does not explicitly recognize the right to personal liberty and leaves unclear, for lack of specific norms, the conditions of provisional detention. The reasons justifying arrest and detention may be inferred from Article 58, paragraph 1, ICC St.,[142] but in the interests of achieving greater clarity the Statute should have been more detailed with a specific article devoted to the issue.

It can be maintained that the right to liberty and provisional detention are certainly areas where the evolution from the Nuremberg model towards more developed forms of international criminal justice has been less remarkable.[143]

Article 55, paragraph 1 letter d), of the ICC Statute provides that '[a] person shall not be subjected to arbitrary arrest or detention; and shall not be deprived of his or her liberty except on such grounds and in accordance with such procedures as are established in the Statute'. This rule is based on generally recognized international norms in respect of deprivation of personal liberty in criminal proceedings. Nevertheless, its main defect lies in being too faithful to the other international texts. In particular, this fidelity becomes a defect when the ICC norm refers to other rules of the Statute without explicitly specifying which rules ('on such grounds and in accordance with such procedures as are established in the Statute'). While this kind of drafting was necessary in international instruments concerning inter-State judicial cooperation (the drafters could not have been aware of the content of national laws on arrest and detention), the same reasoning does not apply to the Statute. Hence, it is not appropriate to refer to the criteria set forth in the Statute, without referring either to the criteria themselves or to the Article(s) in which they are spelled out. As it stands, this provision is not precise and it is therefore necessary to look at other rules of the Statute to identify the precise regulation to be applied to such cases. The grounds for arrest and

---

[142] Article 58, para. 1, ICC St. reads: '[a]t any time after the initiation of an investigation, the Pre-Trial Chamber shall, on the application of the Prosecutor, issue a warrant of arrest of a person if, having examined the application and the evidence or other information submitted by the Prosecutor, it is satisfied that: (a) There are *reasonable grounds to believe* that the *person has committed a crime* within the jurisdiction of the Court; and (b) The arrest of the person appears necessary: (i) To *ensure* the person's *appearance* at trial, (ii) To ensure that the person *does not obstruct or endanger the investigation* or the court proceedings, or (iii) Where applicable, to *prevent* the person from *continuing with the commission of that crime* or a related crime which is within the jurisdiction of the Court and which arises out of the same circumstances' (emphasis added).

[143] Naturally, this can be explained by the peculiar nature of these tribunals, the absence of enforcement agents, difficulties in securing the presence of defendants, and so on. This, however, in spite of its being a serious problem should not be a justification for not complying with internationally recognized standards to be applied in the administration of criminal justice.

guarantees for persons arrested are provided for elsewhere in the Statute. For example, Article 58 specifies that the arrest warrant must contain concise information for the arrested person concerning the reasons for the arrest and the crimes allegedly committed. The grounds on which the Pre-Trial Chamber may issue a warrant of arrest are also laid down in Article 58. There must be reasons for believing that the person has committed crimes.[144] The arrest must be necessary to ensure the attendance of that person at trial, to prevent obstruction of investigations, and, where applicable, to prevent the commission of other related crimes. These criteria, in conformity with international standards, must be construed as exhaustive and cannot be extended by means of interpretation.

This system of reference to other provisions reinforces the suggestion that there is a precise need to extend the right to legal assistance to all instances of arrest. Therefore, the right to legal assistance, including free assistance for indigents provided for by Article 55.2(c), should also be applicable to situations under Article 55.1(d). Moreover, recent decisions of both the ICTR and the ICTY show that there are problems due to the absence of clear and specific provisions regulating decisions of the Chambers on issues relating to the lawfulness of detention or arrest.[145] Thus, it is confirmed that the need for appropriate legal advice is very strong from the earliest stages of the proceedings.

Finally, it must be emphasized that there is an additional right which has been inserted into the Statute of the ICC. This is the right to compensation for unlawful arrest or detention. Article 85, paragraph 1, ICC St. provides that '[a]nyone who has been the victim of unlawful arrest or detention shall have an enforceable right to compensation'. This is an improvement when compared with the system of the *ad hoc* Tribunals, in which no such protection was afforded to individuals. In *Lajić*, for example, an individual was arrested and transferred to the ICTY. Subsequently, after a couple of weeks it turned out that there had been an error as to that person's identity and the person erroneously arrested was released.[146] Lajić wanted to ask for compensation but the proceedings were never started. Actually, it seems that under the rules of the ICTY it was not possible to file such a request and that the UN—in application of the agreements on privileges and immunities of the United Nations—would have been immune

---

[144] This is a requirement which already puts the warrant outside the scope of Article 55.1, because, if there are reasons to believe that the person has committed the crime, then he or she is also entitled to all the other rights provided for by para. 2.

[145] The judges progressively articulated the solution through the Tribunal's case law in the *Dokmanović, Todorović, Brdjanin* and *Talić* cases, at the ICTY, and *Barayagwiza* and *Semanza* cases, at the ICTR, all mentioned elsewhere.

[146] See Order for the Withdrawal of the Charges Against the Person Named Goran Lajić and for His Release, *Lajić* (IT–95–8-PT), 17 June 1996. It is shameful that this person remained in detention for more than two months (he was arrested by German authorities on 18 March 1996 and released by the Tribunal on 17 June 1996).

from the legal process in The Netherlands. This was at least the official position of the UN Office for Legal Affairs, but, as the person who had wrongfully been detained did not pursue his claim, it was never presented before a court.

The ICC Statute provisions on compensation for unlawful arrest certainly need to be supplemented and spelled out in the Rules of Procedure. The Rules clarify the procedure to be followed, including provisions specifying whether or not the request for compensation must be discussed within the proceedings on the lawfulness of the detention or must be separate. In this respect the Rules have opted for a separation of the proceedings on determination of unlawfulness and the decision on compensation (Rule 173.2 ICC Rules). Moreover, these provisions offered guidance on the criteria that the judges had to follow in specifically determining forms and amounts of compensation. On the question of determining the amount of the compensation, the Rules require the competent Chamber to 'take into consideration the consequences which the grave and manifest miscarriage of justice has had for the personal, family, social and professional situation of the person filing the request'. The term 'grave and manifest miscarriage of justice' should not be read in the narrow sense of referring only to Article 85, paragraph 3, ICC St. and Rule 173.2 (c) of the ICC RPE, but also more generally to all cases of compensation provided for in Article 85 and Rule 173.2. Finally, it would have been preferable to attribute competence to decide on compensation to the same Chamber that determined the unlawfulness of the arrest or detention. It does not seem appropriate to burden the system of the Court with several micro-proceedings unrelated to the main object of its jurisdiction.

In the *ad hoc* Tribunals systems there are no specific provisions for *habeas corpus* motions or for compensation for unlawful arrest or detention.[147] However, the practice of Chambers has shown that the judges are willing to admit such motions, irrespective of the lack of express provisions, in accordance with international human rights law.[148] Furthermore, as regards the right of compensation the Appeals Chamber of the Tribunal held that where the rights of the accused were violated he or she had to receive compensation.[149] Hence, only through practice did such a fundamental principle find its way into the Tribunal system. However, it is submitted that a right to compensation for violation of human rights by the Tribunals should be specifically provided for through an amendment to the Rules.[150]

---

[147] See in this respect Wladimiroff, note 92 above, at 450 note 118.

[148] Cf. Appeals Chamber Judgment, *Barayagwiza* (ICTR–97–19-AR72), 3 November 1999, para. 88, and Trial Chamber Decision on petition for a writ of Habeas Corpus on Behalf of Radoslav Brdjanin, *Brdjanin and Talić* (IT–99–36PT), 8 December 1999, paras. 3 and 7.

[149] Cf. Appeals Chamber Review Judgment, *Barayagwiza* (ICTR–97–19-AR72), 31 March 2000, and *Semanza* (ICTR–97–20-A), 31 May 2000, the disposition of the decision.

[150] Such an amendment would justify assigning specific budgetary resources to this end. The President of the ICTR submitted a proposal to the UN Secretary General for the amendment of the Tribunal's Statute, see *ICTR Seventh Annual Report* note 90 above, para. 92.

6. The right to be informed of the reasons for arrest

The right to be informed of the reasons for arrest is part of the due process guarantees and completes the right to personal liberty. It is laid down in both the UDHR and the ICCPR. Moreover it is also recognized by regional human rights conventions.[151]

The norms of the *ad hoc* Tribunals provide for prompt information on the reasons for arrest. In general it is required that at the moment of execution of the arrest warrant the accused must be informed of the cause for his or her arrest. Usually, persons arrested pursuant to a warrant issued by the Tribunal receive a copy of the indictment, so they are immediately informed of the reason for the arrest. It is uncertain what happens with those who spontaneously surrender. It seems that they are provided with the indictment at the moment of placement in detention. The same requirements are also required under Rule 40-*bis*.

The *ad hoc* Tribunals' Appeals Chamber held that 'international standards require that a suspect who is arrested be informed promptly of the reasons for his arrest and the charges against him. The right to be promptly informed . . . serves two functions. First, it counterbalances the interest of the prosecuting authority in seeking continued detention of the suspect. In this respect the suspect needs to be promptly informed of the charges . . . in order to challenge his detention. . . . Second, the right to be promptly informed gives the suspect the information he requires in order to prepare his defence.'[152]

Often there is confusion between the right to be informed of the reasons for arrest and pre-trial detention and the right to receive all details and to be sufficiently informed to prepare a defence. The latter is a distinct right, which in the system of the *ad hoc* Tribunals, and also in the ICC procedure, will be fulfilled through the process of discovery. The difference is important, because of course the detail of information received is not the same. A concise statement may be sufficient for the purpose of satisfying the right to be informed of the reasons for arrest, whilst it would certainly be insufficient as regards the information on the charges. It seems that the Appeals Chamber in the case mentioned above erred in merging the two concepts. However, in that case both issues were at stake, because the suspect had subsequently become an accused and had not been duly informed of the charges against him for the purpose of the preparation of his defence.

In the system of the ICC the right to be informed of the reasons for arrest is not specifically provided for in any rule. Arguably, however, this right can be inferred from the provisions of Article 58 ICC St. on the execution of an

---

[151] Cf. the ECHR, ACHR, and the other conventions mentioned above at Chapter I, Section II.

[152] Cf. Decision of Appeals Chamber, 3 November 1999, *Barayagwiza*, note 148 above, para. 80.

arrest warrant issued by the Court. It is true that the provision does not state that the accused has a right to be informed. It provides, however, for the requirements of the arrest warrant, and among them it specifies the need for a reference to the crimes for which the arrest is sought and a concise statement of the facts that would constitute those crimes. Naturally this is not equivalent to a specific provision on the right to be informed of the reasons for the arrest; it nonetheless represents the content of that right.

Moreover, it must be remembered that the fact that Article 85 of the ICC Statute provides for a right to compensation for unlawful arrest necessarily implies the existence of a right to challenge the lawfulness of arrest. It is also well known that to challenge the lawfulness of an act it is necessary to know what are the reasons for that act, as recognized by the ICTR Appeals Chamber decision quoted above. Therefore, it can be argued that the right to be informed of the charges must also be recognized as a sort of corollary to the right to challenge the lawfulness of arrest and detention. This right certainly exists in the system of the ICC because the right to obtain compensation for unlawful arrest or detention is provided for.

7. *The right not to be compelled to incriminate oneself or to confess guilt, and to remain silent*

The multifaceted dimension of the right to remain silent depends on the status of individuals to whom the right is granted and on the phase of the proceedings in which the right is triggered.[153] Different names are given to the various aspects of the right to remain silent. Sometimes it is called a right to silence or privilege against self-incrimination, sometimes a right not to confess guilt, but in any event the core substance appears to be the same. Coming from the Anglo-Saxon tradition this right can be given either a narrow or a wide interpretation.[154] In the earlier stages of the investigation and pre-trial proceedings it consists of a general right not to be compelled to incriminate oneself or to confess guilt, which includes the prohibition of any form of pressure (either physical or psychological) on the person. Subsequently, however, when the Prosecutor thinks there are grounds for believing that the person has committed a crime within the jurisdiction of the Court and when that person is being questioned, this right becomes a right to remain silent. At the trial stage it means that the accused can refuse to testify, but on a wider reading it may even imply that the accused has a sort of *right to lie* (provided of course that he or she does not take the oath as a witness).[155]

---

[153] Cf. sub-section 3 above.

[154] On the right to silence see A. Ashworth, *The Criminal Process—An Evaluative Study* (Oxford: OUP, 1994), at 112–118.

[155] Cf. M. Ayat, 'Le silence prend la parole: la percée du droit de se taire en droit international pénal', in *RDIDC* (2001), at 237, where the author writes '*relevons que durant tout le procès pénal*

The various aspects of this right have been thoroughly recognized in the ICC Statute. First, Article 55, paragraph 1, ICC. St. establishes that this right shall be granted to any person during an investigation. Article 55, paragraph 1, of the ICC Statute contains several guarantees which are given to a person in respect of an investigation. Pursuant to this provision 'a person shall not be compelled to incriminate himself or herself, or to confess guilt'. In the interpretation of this provision it is, first of all, necessary to establish the difference between incriminating oneself and confessing guilt. It may be suggested that, in this context, the former means providing the prosecution with elements of evidence that, objectively considered, can lead to incrimination[156] whilst the latter can be construed from a subjective perspective, and probably means that a person must not be compelled to confess—a dimension that refers mainly to the reconstruction of the facts and to an admission of guilt from the point of view of that person.

Secondly, it is important to identify the consequences of this rule and the actions it forbids. It could be argued that the rule excludes all forms of pre-trial pressure, including threats or unfair tactics (such as, for example, saying to the person questioned that somebody else has already confessed, etc.). The person cannot be pressured into renouncing his or her right not to incriminate himself or herself, or to confess guilt, in any way. This holds true independently of the provisions on 'admission of guilt' (Article 65 of the ICC Statute), because the provision admitting them has a different objective and purpose. In the first place that rule provides for the possibility for the accused to plead guilty only once a charge has been formulated. Moreover, at least in theory, the guilty plea process should take place spontaneously (i.e. without plea-bargaining).[157] Furthermore, it must be noted that this provision extends the guarantee to individuals heard by the Prosecutor as mere witnesses. In this respect it should be specified in the Rules of Procedure that when a person heard by the Prosecutor as a witness exercises his or her right under Article 55, paragraph 1, there should be some form of guarantee that the Prosecutor will not use any information derived from the questioning against that person. Otherwise there is a risk that the Prosecutor may be tempted to try to circumvent the unwillingness of the person to testify on certain elements.

---

l'accusé ne dépose jamais sous serment. On lui accorde ainsi le droit de ne pas s'accuser, voire, à la limite, un droit au mensonge'. More generally, on the right to silence in common law see S. Easton, *The Right to Silence* (Aldershot: Avebury, 1991); and on the implications of such a right in civil law systems cf. V. Grevi, '*Nemo tenetur se detegere. Interrogatorio dell'imputato e diritto al silenzio nel processo penale*' (Milan: Giuffrè, 1972).

[156] In this respect it is interesting to note that the text originally contained in the Draft Statute read as follows: 'a person suspected of a crime under this Statute shall have the right . . . *not to be compelled to testify* or to confess guilt' (emphasis added).

[157] Although in this respect, a recent amendment to the ICTY RPE explicitly recognizes the existence of plea agreements between the parties: see Rule 62-*ter* on the Plea Agreement.

A distinct right is laid down in paragraph 2 of Article 55 of the ICC Statute. This is the right of the suspect to remain silent, without his silence being taken into account in the determination of guilt or innocence. The second part of the sentence adds a precise meaning to this additional right. This is a different right from that provided for in paragraph 1. That provision aims at precisely focusing on the conduct of the questioning and, also, implies that the person under investigation can refuse to answer the questions of the investigators (while it is clear that, if heard as a witness, he or she would be in principle under the obligation to answer, excluding the guarantees provided for by Article 55, paragraph 1, i.e. self-incrimination). In this sense, it seems that this provision introduces an element linked to the principle of the presumption of innocence. This principle was not expressly drafted referring to the suspect; however it must be regarded as applicable to all stages of the proceedings.[158] It seems that the rationale behind the presumption of innocence also applies to the right to silence and its implications in this phase. It is submitted that these provisions must be taken into account, above all, by the Pre-Trial Chamber when deciding on pre-trial detention and on the confirmation of the charges. Moreover, even if to a lesser degree, it also imposes a rule of conduct on investigators and prosecutors, who should never interpret the silence of a suspect as an indication in respect of his or her guilt or innocence.

The right of the suspect to remain silent is subsequently reinforced and extended to the trial phase as a right of the accused listed in the minimum guarantees. This right is also recognized when an indictment has been confirmed and thus the person has assumed the status of 'accused' (Article 67.1.g ICC St.). This rule has been drafted using both paragraphs 1 and 2 of Article 55 and aims at completing the protection specifying that the judges cannot base a determination of guilt or innocence on the silence of the accused. The addition of the words 'or innocence' is superfluous or even wrong; judges could very well base a finding of innocence on the silence of the accused, because this would not be contrary to the presumption of innocence. Additionally, a correct interpretation of this rule would tend to indicate that the accused cannot testify at his or her trial, also in accordance with Article 67.1.h. This can be inferred from the consideration that the right to remain silent does not apply to witnesses.

All the issues relating to the right to remain silent in the trial phase will be discussed further in Chapter 3, specifically devoted to the rights of the accused, and Chapter 6, where the rights of witnesses, including the privilege against self-incrimination, will be discussed.

---

[158] Article 66.1 states that '[e]veryone shall be presumed innocent until proved guilty'. On this issue cf. Chapter 3 below on the rights of the accused.

8. Conclusion

Certainly, between Nuremberg (1945) and Rome (1998) considerable improvements have been made in ensuring the protection of individual rights in the administration of international criminal justice. Through the ICTY and ICTR Statutes international human rights standards were imposed on international organs and there was a move towards abandoning the victor's justice paradigm. In establishing the ICC, further efforts were made to satisfy the requirements of providing high standards for the rights of persons during investigations and to ensure that the Court would operate independently and impartially.[159]

The system protecting individual rights in criminal proceedings before the ICC is built in a pyramidal way. Article 55, paragraph 1 ICC St.,[160] which contains the provisions on the rights of persons during investigations, represents the first step: those rights are granted to anybody during an investigation by the organs of the ICC, or by other bodies acting at the request of the ICC. This implies that *any person*, irrespective of the future status he or she will have in the proceedings (if any), including a potential witness, is entitled to those guarantees. Then, paragraph 2 provides for an additional set of rights for those persons in respect of whom there are grounds to believe that they have committed crimes within the jurisdiction of the Court and are about to be questioned. This second step aims more specifically at protecting individual situations with a view to the trial. In this respect it might have been appropriate to keep the provision contained in the draft Statute, which established an automatic exclusionary rule for all those elements of evidence collected in violation of the rights of persons in this phase. Naturally, the same protection may be granted through a broad interpretation of the general rule contained in Article 69.7 on the exclusion of evidence obtained in violation of the Statute or internationally recognized human rights.[161] Unfortunately, this Rule lays down two further requirements: (a) that the violation casts substantial doubt on the reliability of the evidence; or (b) the admission of it would damage the integrity of the proceedings. However, the admission of

---

[159] For example, the fact that judges cannot be reappointed for a second term is a sign in this direction: cf. Article 36.

[160] Article 55, para. 1, ICC St. reads: '[i]n respect of an investigation under this Statute, a person: (a) Shall not be compelled to incriminate himself or herself or to confess guilt; (b) Shall not be subjected to any form of coercion, duress or threat, to torture or to any other form of cruel, inhuman or degrading treatment or punishment; (c) Shall, if questioned in a language other than a language the person fully understands and speaks, have, free of any cost, the assistance of a competent interpreter and such translations as are necessary to meet the requirements of fairness; and (d) Shall not be subjected to arbitrary arrest or detention, and shall not be deprived of his or her liberty except on such grounds and in accordance with such procedures as are established in this Statute'.

[161] Article 69.7 ICC St.

evidence obtained through the violation of human rights should be *per se* considered damaging to the integrity of the proceedings. Therefore, the Rule should be interpreted accordingly and the judges should not give too much weight to the additional conditions.

In general, Article 55 grants adequate protection to persons during an investigation by the ICC. However, specific provisions on other rights such as, for example, the right to privacy would not have been superfluous.[162] Naturally, this provision has been further specified and implemented through the Rules of Procedure and Evidence, namely in terms of details about the concrete implementation of the rights protected. For example, the procedure and requirements for the assignment of legal assistance, at the expense of the Court, to suspects who are indigent have been clarified (Rule 21). Moreover, the Rules also require that a record of questioning must be made, even in the form of audio and video recording (Rules 111 and 112). Furthermore, specific mechanisms for the implementation of the right of the suspect to obtain evidence in his or her favour prior to trial were adopted (Rule 116).

On the other hand some defects could not really be cured by the Rules. For example, it would have been more correct explicitly to extend to this phase the presumption of innocence as well as the principles of equality of arms and of non-discrimination. Nevertheless, such an extension may be achieved by the interpreter in accordance with the general principles referred to in Article 21 and pursuant to the general idea of extending to the suspect those rights of the accused that are not intrinsically limited to trial proceedings.

Generally speaking, it would have been beneficial to add, in the context of Article 55, express reference to international standards protecting the rights of persons in respect of an investigation, both for the sake of clarity (very important in this phase in which the person can be without legal assistance) and to create a safety net for the interpreter. Of course, it could be argued that it is possible to construe other norms of the Statute in this sense, such as those contained in Article 21 on applicable law.[163] In particular, it can be contended that the reference in Article 21.1 (b) to international norms and standards also covers the rights of persons during an investigation. However, it should be noted that Article 21 establishes a sort of hierarchy of the various sources of law. In this hierarchy the Statute and the Rules of the Court are bound to prevail over other provisions. Therefore there may not be the chance to refer to the provisions of general international law or human rights law.

Furthermore, one ought to emphasize the novelty of the structure of Article 55. This Article, by introducing the idea of general protection of the 'rights of persons during an investigation', represents a commendable

---

[162] See the extensive study by G. Edwards, 'International Human Rights Law Challenges to the New International Criminal Court: the Search and Seizure Right to Privacy', in 26 *YJIL* (2001), 323–412; cf. Gallant, note 41 above, 720.

[163] Article 21.3 ICC St.; see Edwards, note 162 above, at 368.

attempt to increase the level of protection of the rights of individuals involved in criminal proceedings. Moreover, whilst some elements in its conception may not be entirely satisfactory,[164] the adoption of such a provision in an international instrument may also result in an important contribution to the enhancement of human rights standards in criminal proceedings at the national level.

Only one minor criticism may be made of the adoption of such new logic: it has made the text less clear. This may be considered a drawback, since, for reasons of fairness, it would be preferable, when referring to rights of individuals in the context of criminal proceedings, to use the clearest possible language. This would enable the persons involved immediately and easily to identify their rights, and know exactly what implications of them are.

---

[164] The absence of the right to produce and obtain evidence at the pre-trial stage, the absence of protection against violations of the privacy (e.g. in case of monitoring of telephone calls or mail), etc.: see the authors cited in note 162 above.

3

The Rights of the Accused in Trial Proceedings

I. THE PRESUMPTION OF INNOCENCE

1. General

The presumption of innocence is one of the cornerstones of modern criminal procedure and as such has been enshrined in Article 11 of the Universal Declaration of Human Rights (UDHR)[1] and Article 14, paragraph 2, of the International Covenant on Civil and Political Rights (ICCPR).[2] Furthermore, similar or identical provisions are contained in a number of other international human rights treaties,[3] as well as the Statutes of UN *ad hoc* Tribunals[4] and the International Criminal Court (ICC) Statute.[5] Moreover, the presumption of innocence is constitutionally protected in many countries, although, in this respect, it is important to distinguish two tendencies. Whilst the majority of States recognize the presumption of innocence as such, a smaller group of States has adopted the principle that the accused must not be presumed guilty.[6] It has been affirmed that this standard is more restrictive and slightly less demanding in terms of human rights protection than the full recognition of the presumption of innocence.[7] In the Statutes of the UN *ad hoc* Tribunals and the ICC, however, the broader

---

[1] This rule states that '[e]veryone charged with a penal offence has the right to be presumed innocent until proved guilty according to law in a public trial'.

[2] Article 14, para. 2, ICCPR provides that '[e]veryone charged with a criminal offence shall have the right to be presumed innocent until proved guilty according to law'.

[3] Cf. ECHR, Article 6.2; American Declaration of the Rights and Duties of Man, Article XXVI: '[e]very accused person is presumed to be innocent until proved guilty'; ACHR, Article 8, paragraph 2: '[e]very person accused of a criminal offence has the right to be presumed innocent so long as his guilt has not been proven according to law'; African Charter, Article 7, para. 1 letter b.: '[e]very individual shall have the right to have his cause heard. This comprises: . . . (b) the right to be presumed innocent until proved guilty by a competent court or tribunal'; Arab Charter on Human Right Article 7: '[t]he accused is presumed innocent until proven guilty in a lawful trial where defence rights are guaranteed'; the Convention on the Rights of the Child, Article 40, para. 2 letter (b)(i): '[e]very child alleged as or accused of having infringed the penal law has at least the following guarantees: (i) to be presumed innocent until proven guilty according to law'.

[4] Cf. Statute of the ICTY, Article 21, para. 3, and Statute of the ICTR, Article 20, para. 3: 'the accused shall be presumed innocent until proved guilty according to the provisions of the present Statute'.

[5] Cf. Article 66 ICC St., Presumption of Innocence.

[6] This is the case, e.g., of the Italian Constitution, cf. Article 27.

[7] Cf. in this respect, see M.C. Bassiouni, 'Human Rights in the Context of Criminal Justice: Identifying International Procedural Protections and Equivalent Protections in National Constitutions', in 3 *DJCIL* (1993), 235 at 265–267.

formula was adopted to ensure the highest standards of protection for fundamental rights.

Although the Nuremberg and Tokyo Charters did not explicitly recognize the presumption of innocence, it may be argued that it was accepted *de facto*.[8] Indeed Justice Robert Jackson, the US Prosecutor at the International Military Tribunal (IMT), conceded that 'we accept that [the defendants] must be given a presumption of innocence'.[9] However, the fact that these Tribunals aimed at granting a fair trial cannot be equated with the explicit recognition of the presumption of innocence as a right of defendant.[10]

There are two interdependent issues that emerge in respect of the presumption of innocence. First, it is necessary to try to evaluate the implications of this right. Secondly, one ought to pinpoint the precise moment at which the general protection of the right is triggered.

On the second point, it appears that in international criminal procedure, if one adopts an excessively strict interpretation of the texts, one may infer that the right to be presumed innocent is triggered only when the person is accused (i.e. formally charged). This interpretation may seem justified by the fact that the provision on the presumption of innocence is placed among the rights of the accused, as provided for in Articles 21 and 20 of the *ad hoc* Tribunals' Statutes and Article 66 of the ICC Statute (ICC St.) (in Part Six, on Trial Proceedings). Hence, it may be tempting to maintain that the presumption of innocence does not apply to the investigative phase. On the contrary, it is argued here that the scope of the principle is very broad and covers all situations, even prior to the formulation of charges, irrespective of where the provisions on the presumption of innocence are placed in the Statutes of the *ad hoc* Tribunals and the ICC.

To my mind, the presumption of innocence influences all stages of criminal proceedings and the concepts of 'persons accused' or 'against whom criminal charges have been moved' should not be read as technically binding. Moreover, it may be suggested that if this is a right that is granted to the accused it should *a fortiori* be granted to a suspect.[11] The presumption of innocence should indeed be even stronger in respect of a person against whom not even a *prima facie* case has been confirmed. First, it would be totally illogical for the judge reviewing the charges to presume that the suspect is guilty.

---

[8] Nonetheless, one may consider that even specific components of the presumption of innocence, such as e.g. the privilege against self-incrimination, were absent.

[9] See Opening Address for the United States at IMT, in Nazi Conspiracy and Aggression (Washington, DC: US Gov. Printing Office, 1946), i, at 117.

[10] *Contra* cf. R. May and M. Wierda, 'Trends in International Criminal Evidence: Nuremberg, Tokyo, The Hague and Arusha', in 37 *CJTL* (1999), 725–765, at 753–754.

[11] Cf. in this respect C. Van den Wyngaert, 'Criminal Procedure in Belgium' in C. Van den Wyngaert (ed.), *Criminal Procedure Systems in the European Community* (London: Butterworths, 1993), at 15. The same opinion is shared by C. Safferling, *Towards an International Criminal Procedure* (Oxford: OUP, 2001), at 67.

Secondly, if the presumption of innocence were not applicable before the confirmation of charges, irreparable prejudice could be done to the rights of the individual prior to confirmation (for example, through a campaign depicting the suspect as a criminal or by the adoption of asset-freezing measures). Thus, any subsequent protection would prove ineffective.

The reasons for limiting the enjoyment of this right may be connected to the narrow idea that the presumption of innocence only determines the assignment of the burden of proof on the prosecution. Certainly, this is its most important effect. However, it is submitted that the establishment of a rule on the burden of proof cannot be considered the only consequence of the principle.

In general, there are three main consequences of the presumption of innocence. First, there is the general consequence that it should affect the overall *treatment of the individual*, both within the proceedings and externally. Secondly, there is the more specific effect of imposing the *burden of proof on the Prosecutor*. Finally, the third effect relates to the establishment of a certain *standard of proof* and the procedure that must be followed in the determination of guilt.[12]

These effects, which are now reflected in the provisions of the ICC Statute, were not explicitly laid down in previous provisions on the presumption of innocence. Here we will concentrate on the provisions of the ICC Statute, discussing them in the light of the *ad hoc* Tribunals' rules and practice.

2. *The right of the accused to be presumed innocent as a general rule for the treatment of individuals; guilty plea procedure and the right of the accused to remain silent*

The presumption of innocence has implications that relate to the treatment of the accused by the judicial organs of the Court, by Court and Registry officials, by detention personnel, etc. It should also have an external influence, for example on the media: the image that is transmitted to the public should take into account that the person against whom criminal charges have been preferred has not yet been found guilty.[13] The risk of excessive 'mediatization'

[12] Cf., e.g., J. Kokott, *The Burden of Proof in Comparative and International Human Rights Law: Civil and Common Law Approaches with Special Reference to the American and German Legal Systems* (The Hague: Kluwer, 1998).

[13] A criticism that can be made in this respect to the policy of the Tribunals relates to the greater effort deployed in operating a widespread diffusion of documents relating to the charges against accused persons. The fact, for example, that the Internet home page of the ICTY contains all the indictments and some opening or final statements by the prosecution, but does not have motions coming from the defence, must be criticized. Naturally this could be due to the unwillingness of the Defence to provide the Tribunal's press and information office with documents, but efforts towards the creation of an effective equilibrium between the parties should be made. It must, however, be recalled that the Directive for the Registry requires the filing of motions both on paper and in electronic format.

of this kind of trial has also been examined, though in a different context, by the Trial Chamber in *Tadić*.[14] In its closing arguments the Defence had challenged the declarations of numerous witnesses on the ground that their perception of reality had been influenced and distorted by the media coverage of the trial, which had caused contamination of the evidence. The Chamber, whilst admitting the influence of the media on the trial and on witnesses, stated that media coverage is a common feature in modern criminal trials.[15] Nevertheless, as in many national criminal cases, newspaper titles in which defendants are called 'war criminals' or descriptions of the accused as the 'Butcher of Omarska' (or in the French version '*le Bourreau d'Omarska*') are violations of the presumption of innocence. Naturally, these violations do not contribute to fostering a balanced perception of criminal justice by the public. Later on it can prove difficult to redress such violations.

Generally the duties connected to the presumption of innocence are limited to public authorities, at least in the usual interpretation given, for example, by the European Court of Human Rights (ECourtHR).[16] Nevertheless, this reading is closely linked to the scope of the Convention. In the system of the European Convention (ECHR), a State can be found in violation of the presumption of innocence only if the violation is imputable to public authorities. On the contrary, the scope of the protection offered by the presumption of innocence to the individual is wider and should include violations of the presumption by other persons, including NGOs and the international media.[17] At a national level this is ensured by rules preserving the right to privacy and by specific provisions dealing with attacks on personal reputation. Additionally, at a national level a person complaining about the violation of his or her rights by another person or the media may submit a claim to a court and seek compensation. However, resorting to such instruments may prove very difficult, if not impossible, for persons charged before international tribunals. First, there is the problem of identifying the country in which to bring the claim and the applicable law. Secondly, bringing such a claim would certainly involve expenses, which the defendant, who may already be facing the huge costs of an international trial, would, in all likelihood, be unable to bear. Thirdly, in international criminal procedure defendants are often held in custody pending trial. This would make it more difficult for them to file a

[14] Cf. ICTY, Trial Chamber Judgment, *Tadić* (IT–94–1–T), 7 May 1997.

[15] The Trial Chamber stated that 'in all trials, the potential impact of pre-trial media overage is a fact that must be taken into account in considering the reliability of witnesses, and where this aspect was raised in cross examination of witnesses, it has been taken into account in the evaluation of their testimony' (Cf. Tadić proceedings on trial, IT–94–1–T, at 17487 Case File—para. 544).

[16] Cf., e.g., the ECourtHR in *Minelli* v. *Switzerland*, judgment of 25 March 1983, (Series A–62) **www.echr.coe.int/Eng/Judgments.htm**.

[17] At the national level there are solutions to address this problem, e.g. the accused can sue the media if unjustified and prejudicial allegations against him are published. This is more difficult at the international level.

civil claim against newspapers or TV channels which published or broadcast news contrary to the presumption of innocence.[18] All these difficulties suggest that it is very important to insist on respect for the presumption of innocence by third parties (in particular, the international media). It is clear that with respect to these violations there is little to be done by international organs *ex post*. The Tribunals and the Court, however, should do their best to try to prevent media or non-governmental organization (NGO) campaigns against individuals involved in international criminal proceedings.[19] This is particularly true for the Prosecutor and members of his or her Office, in the light of his or her specific duty to respect the fundamental rights of the accused (Article 54 ICC St.).

In the Rules of the *ad hoc* Tribunals there are two surprising provisions, which seem to be in conflict with the presumption of innocence. First is Rule 93 on 'evidence of a consistent pattern of conduct'. This Rule states that such evidence 'may be admissible in the interests of justice'. This means that evidence not necessarily connected to the crimes with which the accused is charged will be presented to his or her detriment. Whilst paragraph (B) further specifies that 'acts tending to show such a pattern of conduct shall be disclosed by the Prosecutor to the defence pursuant to Rule 66', thus enabling the accused to challenge such evidence at trial, this in no way eliminates the detrimental effects of this Rule.[20] Naturally, the admission of this evidence as a matter of principle does not preclude its rejection on a case-by-case basis by the Trial Chamber. However, the inclusion of such provision in the Rules of Procedure and Evidence (RPE) appears to be in conflict with the presumption of innocence, or, at the very least, it restricts its scope.

The other striking provision of the *ad hoc* Tribunals RPEs is Rule 99(B). This Rule establishes that even if acquitted the defendant—pending the time limit for the filing of an appeal by the Prosecution[21]—may, upon order of the

---

[18] In this respect it is interesting to note how human rights standards provided for by international human rights texts, such as the ECHR, may even weaken the protection afforded to individuals by some national systems: J.R. Spencer, 'English Criminal Procedure and the Human Rights Act 1998', in 33 *Isr. LR* (1999), at 670, clarifies how the impact of the ECHR on the pretrial phase concerns in the media and publicity has resulted in a reduction of the protection previously provided for accused persons under British law. In particular, he quotes the well-known *Sunday Times* v. *UK* case, 26 April 1979 (Series A–30): see **www.echr.coe.int/Eng/Judgments.htm**, where the Court considered freedom of expression as prevailing.

[19] This is certainly a role that could be played by the Press and Information Office of the Tribunal. In this respect it may be interesting to look at the decision of the EcourtHR in *Allenet de Ribemont* (Series A–308), of 10 February 1995, **www.echr.coe.int/Eng/Judgments.htm**, which makes specific reference to Press conferences as the place where usually the presumption of innocence is violated.

[20] It is a mere application of normal rules on discovery.

[21] The possibility for the Prosecution to appeal against an acquittal sounds at the very least a bit odd to common lawyers; however, it is a common feature in some continental systems, though not in every system (e.g. not in France). It is submitted that in international criminal procedure this possibility should at least be strictly limited to an appeal on issues of law but not on the merits. See Chapter 4 below.

Trial Chamber, be made to remain in detention on remand. This does not seem to accord with the presumption of innocence.[22] It could correctly be argued that such a provision is motivated by the same concerns that have justified reversing the general principle related to the issue of detention on remand pending trial. The horrific nature of the crimes[23] and the enormous difficulties of the Tribunal in apprehending indicted persons may have justified the system of generalized detention of defendants. Nevertheless, even admitting the 'correctness' of this approach, it seems necessary to organize a much more detailed procedure coupled with very stringent time limits, at least for the case of an accused acquitted by a Trial Chamber. However, it is important to note that, so far in the practice of the Tribunals, defendants acquitted by Trial Chambers have normally been released pending appeal.[24]

The presumption of innocence, as a general rule for the treatment of individuals appearing before the Tribunals (and in the future before the Court), is also the implicit source of a number of other guarantees. For example, Rule 62(iii) RPEs, on the procedure to be followed in the case of a *guilty plea*, dictates that should an accused refuse to enter a plea the Chamber must enter a plea of not guilty on his behalf. It is quite clear that the refusal of the accused to declare either his innocence or his guilt cannot be interpreted as an admission of guilt, but, on the contrary, must be regarded as a plea of not guilty, and that the Chamber must act accordingly.

In the ICC Statute the procedure detailed in the guilty plea provisions rests on the fundamental principle of the presumption of innocence. Therefore a plea that does not meet the requirements provided for in Article 65 ICC St. cannot be entered. It may be argued, however, that this is due to the overriding duty of the Chambers to ascertain the truth, even beyond the allegation made by the parties. The rules of the ICC Statute on the proceedings on admission of guilt are much more detailed than the corresponding provisions of the *ad hoc* Tribunals' system. The special procedure on admission of guilt provided for by the ICC Statute, which represents an attempt to adapt the traditional rules on guilty pleas to the specific demands of international criminal justice, merits closer attention.

---

[22] In particular, in the case of an acquittal, innocence has been confirmed by a Trial Chamber Moreover this rule may create problems concerning the legality and arbitrariness of the prolonged detention, pending the time limit for the Prosecutor to file an appeal.

[23] Cf. Rule 65 RPE ICTY. When adopting the Rules the judges decided to deviate from the internationally recognized standards. However the difference was only formal and not substantial, because the case of people accused before the ICTY in general falls within the scope of the categories for which orders for detention on remand can be issued. Nonetheless, this rule has subsequently been amended.

[24] In *Baglishema* the International Criminal Tribunal for Rwanda (ICTR) provisionally released the defendant to France and requested the French authorities to keep a close eye on him as he was authorized to reside there pending appeal proceedings. On 3 July 2002 the Appeals Chamber confirmed the acquittal: Appeals Chamber Judgment, *Baglishema* (ICTR–95–1/A), 3 July 2002.

Under national laws 'guilty plea' procedures generally aim at reducing the number of trials, and their main purpose is to reduce the overall burden for the judicial system. International criminal justice, however, is not an ordinary means for prosecuting serious violations of humanitarian law and human rights law. In principle, therefore, it should not be overloaded with cases.[25] Furthermore, the other main features of the guilty plea procedure do not seem to respond entirely to the needs of international criminal trials. First, in the case of a guilty plea there is generally no determination of judicial truth nor is there any presentation of evidence. This contradicts the pedagogical mission of the Tribunals (and the ICC) and may cause prejudice to the interests of victims.[26] Secondly, guilty pleas usually lead to sentence discounts,[27] whereas often the crimes under the jurisdiction of the *ad hoc* Tribunals or the ICC deserve harsh penalties.[28]

Nonetheless, although the introduction of guilty plea procedures in international criminal proceedings is not totally persuasive,[29] there are some convincing reasons for supporting it. First, guilty plea procedures may be a useful tool in the hands of the Prosecutor for the purpose of other investigations.[30] Secondly, in some cases (for example, in the case of an accused who bears minor responsibility, either for his or her level in the hierarchy or for the crimes committed) it may be in the public interest to shorten international

[25] See *contra*, explaining why guilty plea procedures may fulfil a public interest also before international tribunals, the Separate and Dissenting Opinion on Appeal by Judge Cassese, *Erdemović* (IT–96–22–A): 'the draftsmen intended to enable the accused . . . to avoid a possible lengthy trial for the benefit of the accused himself, the international community (international criminal proceedings are expensive) . . . Thus by pleading guilty the accused undoubtedly contributes to a public advantage' at 3.

[26] It is precisely to meet these concerns that Article 65, para. 4, of the ICC Statute entitles the Trial Chamber to ask the Prosecutor to present evidence, including witnesses, where the interests of justice, and in particular the interests of victims, so require.

[27] Recently, see R. Henham, 'Truth in Plea-Bargaining: Anglo-American Approaches to the Use of Guilty Plea Discounts at the Sentencing Stage', in 29 *An.-Am. LR* (2000), 1–38.

[28] The proceedings in *Kambanda* are extremely instructive in this respect. The former Prime Minister of Rwanda pleaded guilty to charges of genocide and started co-operating with the Prosecutor. However, notwithstanding his plea, the Trial Chamber imposed a sentence of life imprisonment on him. Although Kambanda appealed against his sentence, the Appeals Chamber eventually upheld it. This case shows that guilty plea procedure may not be appropriate for high-level criminality, where no sentence discount is really possible. See Trial Chamber Judgment, *Kambanda* (ICTR–97–23–S), 4 September 1998, paras. 35–37 and the Appeals Chamber Judgment, 19 October 2000, paras. 114–126.

[29] The crucial question is whether it is appropriate to allow plea-bargaining and plea agreements between the parties in the case of crimes of extreme gravity, such as those under the jurisdiction of the Tribunal. A recent amendment to the ICTY RPE shows that in a certain sense this practice is recognized and admitted by the Tribunal. See Rule 62-*ter* adopted at 23rd Plenary Session, 12–14 December 2001 (it entered into force on 28 December).

[30] The *Erdemović* case is paradigmatic in this respect. The accused entered a guilty plea and subsequently testified against Karadzić and Mladić in the Rule 61 hearing on the Srebrenica case. On the other hand, the plea agreement in *Todorović* is less persuasive, in that it is unclear what interests were protected by the acceptance of the guilty plea, and thus it is difficult to evaluate whether these deserved protection.

criminal proceedings, particularly in the light of the very high costs involved. Finally, the defendant may have a specific interest in avoiding trial, in particular on account of the psychological impact and public discredit involved in a criminal trial.

In respect of guilty plea procedures, the provisions of the ICC Statute strike a reasonable balance between competing interests,[31] by conferring on Trial Chambers the power to request the presentation of evidence (including witness testimonies), and eventually to accept the plea. This solution ensures both the advantages of guilty plea procedures and respect for the interests of justice and the victims. Finally, it seems that these rules ensure stronger protection of the presumption of innocence, reducing the risks that an innocent person be tempted to enter a plea of guilt for unclear reasons.

Other rules inspired by the presumption of innocence are those on the *right*, both of the suspect and of the accused, but also of witnesses, *to remain silent*. The right of an accused to remain silent is very wide and, as mentioned above, already arises at the investigative stage. The right to remain silent is also protected by Rules 42 and 63 of both RPEs, dealing with the questioning of suspects and the accused. In both cases, the Rules aim to protect the individual (in the case of a suspect, protection is afforded in view of trial) against any possible use that may subsequently be made by the Prosecution of his or her statements. In the pre-trial as well as in the trial phase, these provisions substantially aim at protecting the right of the accused to refuse to answer questions, because he or she is presumed innocent and, hence, has no duty to contribute to the proceedings.[32]

Finally, in Rule 90, paragraph (F) of both RPE the privilege against self-incrimination is specifically set out with regard to witnesses, who are entitled to 'object to making any statement which might tend to incriminate' them. Again, according to Rule 90 (F) 'the Chamber may however compel the witness to answer the question. Testimony compelled in this way must not be used as evidence in a subsequent prosecution against the witness for any offence other than perjury.' This last sentence indicates that the privilege against self-incrimination operates in this case as an 'exclusionary rule' rather than as a provision allowing the person to refuse to answer. In other words, should the witness subsequently be indicted by the Prosecutor and become an accused, it will not be possible for the Court to admit into evidence the incriminatory declaration he or she may have made under Rule 90 (F). Clearly this

---

[31] On the provisions of the ICC Statute see F. Guariglia, 'Proceedings on an Admission of Guilt (Article 65)', in O. Triffterer (ed.), *Commentary on the Rome Statute of the International Criminal Court, Observers' Notes, Article by Article* (Baden-Baden: Nomos, 1999), 823–831.

[32] It has been clearly pointed out that '[the] right to silence is based on two principles: (1) the privilege against self-incrimination and (2) the rule that in criminal trials the prosecution bears the burden of proof': R. May, *Criminal Evidence* (2nd edn., London: Sweet and Maxwell, 1990), at 274–279. On the right to silence see also Chapter 2, Section II.7 above.

rule amounts to a further application of the right to silence which, active at different stages, ultimately manifests its effects at the trial stage.[33]

3. *The* onus probandi *on the Prosecution, including the prohibition of reversal of the onus and the issue of pre-trial detention*

As mentioned above, the most relevant effect of the presumption of innocence is to impose on the Prosecution the duty to prove the guilt of the accused.[34] There are no specific rules in the *ad hoc* Tribunals' system that specify that the duty to prove guilt lies on the Prosecutor. However, it seems logical to assume that this was considered as an implicit consequence of the presumption of innocence and, as such, was taken for granted by the draftsmen. Certainly, it cannot be said that the Statutes or the Rules of the ICTY and ICTR are in breach of the presumption of innocence for not having explicitly stated that the *onus probandi* is on the Prosecution.

It was primarily in the light of the presumption of innocence that a Trial Chamber of the ICTY took into consideration a motion of no case to answer, filed by the Defence in *Tadić*. This motion was lodged at the end of the presentation of the prosecution case and substantially sought acquittal, claiming that the defendant at that stage had no case to answer, as the Prosecution had not proved his guilt (beyond reasonable doubt). The motion was rejected on the merits, but the fact that it was examined at all evinces great concern for the rights of the accused and, in particular, for the presumption of innocence. The Chamber could have dismissed the motion on the ground that, at that time, a ruling of no case to answer was not specifically provided for in the Rules. The concern of the Chamber regarding this issue shows a real attempt to guarantee the highest possible standards. Subsequently, another motion of the same type was filed in *Celebici*. Also in this case the Trial Chamber agreed to examine the motion but rejected it on the merits. As a consequence of these decisions an amendment was introduced into the RPE to the effect that a specific rule would allow the filing of motions for acquittal.[35] The new rule goes even further, conferring on the Trial Chamber the power to issue *proprio motu* a judgment of acquittal after the close of the Prosecution case (Rule 98-*bis* RPE ICTY). The rationale behind this rule is clear. It is in the interests of both the accused and justice that whenever the Prosecutor does not succeed in proving the guilt of the accused, it is unnecessary for the Defence case to be

---

[33] On the right to silence for witnesses cf. Chapter 6, Section II below.

[34] Today, this is so both in inquisitorial and accusatorial systems, see e.g. G. Stefani, G. Levasseur, and B. Bouloc, *Procédure Pénale* (14th edn., Paris: Dalloz, 1990), at 34–35 and J. Smith, 'Criminal Procedure in England and Wales', in Van Den Wyngaert (ed.), note 11 above, at 82.

[35] The amendment was adopted at the 18th Plenary Session in July 1999, IT/32/Rev.13 RPE.

heard. It is reasonable to believe that this rule and this approach were inspired by the intention to provide stronger protection for the presumption of innocence.

Several motions under the new Rule have been brought before the Chambers, and in some cases motions were granted, at least on certain counts.[36] Indeed, in *Jelisić* the Trial Chamber, acting *proprio motu*, acquitted the accused on the charges of genocide on the basis of Rule 98-*bis*, paragraph (B).[37]

In *Blaškić* the Defence submitted a motion for the withdrawal of certain charges but did not want to have it considered under Rule 98-*bis* RPE. Rather, on the basis of the precedents in *Tadić* and *Celebici*, it submitted it as a motion under Rule 54 RPE. However, the Defence, in *Blaškić*, did not want to rely on Rule 98-*bis* because this rule requires a precisely determined standard for acquittal: '[the] Trial Chamber shall order the entry of judgement of acquittal . . . if it finds that the *evidence is insufficient to sustain a conviction* on that or those charges'.[38] Regarding the legal basis of the Motion the Trial Chamber pointed out that 'it is appropriate to note that those decisions [the above mentioned precedent] were taken specifically because the current Rule 98-*bis* did not exist and that, to remedy the fact that the Rules stated nothing in that respect, the Judges based their decision on the general procedural scope established in Rule 54'.[39] The Trial Chamber however held that, even basing its decision on Rule 54, the standard required by the Rules for acquittal after the presentation of the Prosecution case were contained in the provisions of Rule 98-*bis,* i.e. evidence presented by the Prosecution must be insufficient to justify conviction for all or part of the counts concerned.

Furthermore, in *Kupreškić*, the Trial Chamber denied a motion for acquittal.[40] In this case, one of the accused presented such a motion *after the close of the defence case*. The Trial Chamber held that 'Rule 98-*bis* is only concerned with the situation that *after the Prosecutor has closed her case* the evidence [presented] so far [was] deemed to be insufficient to support a conviction

---

[36] This rule has been invoked by the Defence in many cases: see, e.g., Judgment on Defence Motion to Acquit, *Sikirica and others* (IT–95–8–T), 3 September 2001, in which the Trial Chamber granted the motion and acquitted two co-accused on the counts of genocide and complicity in genocide. See also Decision on Defence Motions for Acquittal, *Kvocka and others* (IT–98–30/1–T), 15 December 2000 and Decision on Defence Motions for Judgment of Acquittal, *Kordić and Čerkez* (IT–95–14/2–T), 6 April 2000. The ICTR also adopted a similar rule in June 1998 at the fifth Plenary Session. Such a rule was applied for the first time in *Semanza* (ICTR–97–20–T), 27 September 2001.

[37] Cf. ICTY Trial Chamber Judgment, *Jelisić* (IT–95–10–T), 14 December 1999. The test applied by the Trial Chamber, however, was rejected by the Appeals Chamber, which, although it criticized the approach adopted by the Trial Chamber, eventually upheld the sentence imposed.

[38] Emphasis added.

[39] Decision on Defence Motion to Dismiss, *Blaškić* (IT–95–14–T), 3 September 1998.

[40] ICTY Trial Chamber Decision, *Kupreškić and others* (IT–95–16–T), 28 July 1999. Another motion for acquittal had already been previously denied on 8 January 1999, cf. Decision on Motion of the Accused Vlatko Kupreškić to the Trial Chamber to Order the Entry of a Judgment of Acquittal Pursuant to Rule 98-*bis* of the Rules of Procedure and Evidence.

regardless of any exculpatory evidence the Defence may adduce'.[41] The Chamber considered that in the motion before it the Defence was in effect asking for a 'final part judgement with regard to one of the six accused without a formal severance of his trial'.[42] In particular, the Trial Chamber noted that the Prosecution had already indicated that it reserved the right to call rebuttal witnesses with regard to the accused. Therefore it concluded that it was not certain that all the relevant evidence had been heard.[43] The Trial Chamber was, thus, probably correct in denying the motion, since it had been presented after the defence case had been closed. The Chamber, however, did not clarify why it did not apply Rule 98-*bis* by analogy. In the case of motions for acquittal filed after the close of the defence case, the situation is largely different from that envisaged by Rule 98-*bis*. This Rule refers to cases in which the Prosecutor is not able, in the course of the Prosecution case, to present sufficient evidence to prove the guilt of the accused. After presentation of the defence case, judges are provided with additional elements that can be challenged by the Prosecution with rebuttal evidence. In its final judgment the Chamber must then assess the whole of the evidence presented. Thus a decision on a motion for acquittal at this stage of the proceedings is neither necessary nor appropriate. Indeed, in all likelihood, it is not even possible, as this would amount to calling the judgment by another name.

As regards the test to be applied by the Chamber, acting either *proprio motu* or on a motion by the accused, the standard set by the Appeals Chamber is that 'evidence must be insufficient for any reasonable trier of fact to find that guilt has been proved beyond reasonable doubt'.[44] By applying this test the Appeals Chamber reversed the Trial Chamber's judgment in *Jelisić*. According to the Appeals Chamber Judgment, the Trial Chamber had erred, in that the test it applied to determine whether or not there was sufficient evidence to sustain a conviction was not correct. The Trial Chamber had concluded that in light of the evidence presented it would not have come to a finding of guilt. On the other hand, the Appeals Chamber held that the correct test to be applied was to consider the evidence presented in light of whether any reasonable trier of fact *could* (and not would) convict on the basis of the evidence presented.[45] This approach, however, seems too much inspired by concepts intrinsically related to systems where verdicts are given by a jury (the trier of fact) and which are usually delivered without a detailed

[41] See ICTY Trial Chamber Decision, *Kupreškić and others* (IT–95–16–T), 28 July 1999, para. 3 (emphasis added).

[42] *Ibidem.*   [43] *Ibidem.*

[44] Cf. Appeals Chamber Judgment, *Jelisić* (IT–95–10–A), 5 July 2001, para. 37. The test had already been applied on several occasions by the Chambers of the Tribunal, cf. *Kunarac et al.* (IT–96–23–T), Decision on motion for acquittal, 3 July 2000, para. 3, and *Kvocka et al.* (IT–98–30/1–T), Decision on defence motions for acquittal, 15 December 2000, para. 12.

[45] Cf. Appeals Chamber Judgment, *Jelisić*, note 44 above, paras. 30–40. See also Trial Chamber Decision, *Galić* (IT–98–29–PT), 3 October 2002, paras. 7–12.

analysis of the reasons governing the assessment of evidence. In international criminal proceedings, conducted before professional judges who provide detailed reasons for their verdicts, there is no reason to be so restrictive.[46] It would, thus, seem more reasonable to follow the less restrictive approach suggested by Judge Pocar in his dissenting opinion.[47]

It should be noted that, in respect of the presumption of innocence, the rules of the ICC Statute are to be considered as a model. Article 66, paragraph 2, ICC St. explicitly clarifies that it is the Prosecutor who has to prove that the accused is guilty.[48] In the ICC Statute the protection of the presumption of innocence is definitely more clearly organized and the provisions of the Statute take into account the multifaceted aspects of the presumption described above (at 1). Article 66, paragraph 1, ICC St. states that '*[e]very-one* shall be presumed innocent until proved guilty'. The use of the term 'everyone' reinforces the belief that this is a right attributed to any person, not just to the accused.[49] In this respect, however, it might have been inappropriate to place this principle in the section on trial proceedings. Furthermore, paragraph 2 of Article 66 ICC St. clearly states that the 'onus is on the Prosecutor to prove the guilt of the accused'.

The impact of the presumption of innocence on evidentiary matters has received further protection through Article 67.1(i) ICC St., which states that no reversal of the burden of proof is admissible. This is a major breakthrough because in the system of the *ad hoc* Tribunals there are reversals that virtually require a *probatio diabolica*. Instances of this are: proof that the confession was forced (Rule 92 RPEs) or the burden being placed on the accused to prove that circumstances exist that may justify provisional release established in Rule 65 of both RPEs.

---

[46] I would add that more consideration should be given to the presumption of innocence. At this stage of the proceedings the accused is still presumed innocent and the Prosecutor has already discharged his or her duty to prove guilt beyond reasonable doubt. Now, if we apply the test suggested by the Appeals Chamber, i.e. whether any reasonable trier of fact could find guilt beyond reasonable doubt, we simply require that a hypothetical trier have no reasonable doubts about guilt. In so doing it seems to me that one impinges upon the presumption of innocence *in concreto*. We should rather require that *no* reasonable *trier* of fact *could acquit*. In other words, if there is even a single possibility of 'reasonable doubt' about the guilt of the accused, then a verdict of not guilty should be entered. There is no reason why this 'reasonable doubt' cannot be the doubt of the judges of the Trial Chamber before which the evidence has been concretely presented. It is difficult to understand why one should look, for the test to be applied, for a hypothetical trier of fact that, in theory, could convict. This would be particularly unclear at a stage where only incriminating evidence has been presented and has proved insufficient for those who are the triers of fact in that given case. It would seem more reasonable to take into account that three (or at least two) triers of fact have reasonable doubts. The only reason for reversing an acquittal decided according to this test should be that the doubts of the actual triers of fact (the three judges of the Trial Chamber) were unreasonable, which does not seem to have been the case in *Jelisić*, or at least it was not discussed. The solution adopted by the ICTY seems too rigidly grounded on the common law approach.

[47] Cf. Judge Pocar's Partial Dissenting Opinion, para. 6.

[48] The Rule states that '[t]he onus is on the Prosecutor to prove the guilt of the accused'.

[49] See sub-section I.1 and note 11 above.

Rule 92 of both RPEs provides that 'a confession by the accused given during questioning by the Prosecutor shall . . . be presumed to have been free and voluntary unless the contrary is proved'. It has been correctly suggested that such a provision establishes an inversion of the burden of the proof that may cause prejudice to the accused.[50] It may be extremely difficult for an accused person, who is usually placed in detention, to prove the illegality of the methods by which a confession was obtained. Moreover, it seems somewhat strange, in a system that provides for the possibility of guilty pleas, and which allows for the accused to testify, to add such a rigorous rule on confessions. It is suggested that if the will to confess disappears at the trial stage, the accused should be granted every chance of denying his confession at any stage.

Turning to Rule 65, it may be noted that originally this Rule stated that an accused could be released only 'in exceptional circumstances'. Clearly the onus of proving the exceptional character of any circumstances justifying release rested on the accused.[51] In the ICTY RPE this Rule was modified at the 21st Plenary Session of November 1999 and the reference to exceptional circumstances was removed (the ICTR has not yet amended Rule 65 of its RPE). The amendment, however, although reducing the contrast with international human rights law and the prohibition of reversal of the onus of proof,[52] still leaves it to the accused to prove that 'he will appear for trial and . . . will not pose a danger to any victim, witness or other person'.[53] Moreover, the amendment does not increase certainty about the outcome of the procedure. Release remains at the complete discretion of the Chamber even if all the conditions set out above are fulfilled.[54] Nevertheless, it would, of course, be

---

[50] Cf. J.L. Falvey, 'UN Justice or Military Justice: Which is the Oxymoron? An Analysis of the Rules of Procedure and Evidence of the International Criminal Tribunal for the Former Yugoslavia', in 19 *FJIL* (1995), at 475.

[51] Cf. Decision rejecting the application to withdraw the indictment and order for provisional release, *Djukić* (IT–96–20–PT), 24 April 1996; order on provisional release, *Blaškić* (IT–95–14–T), 20 December 1996, it was clearly stated that illness was the only exceptional circumstance that could be accepted. Not even the fact that the accused surrendered spontaneously was considered sufficient to allow for provisional release.

[52] This, in any event, is not specifically provided for in the system of the *ad hoc* Tribunals as it is in Article 66 of the ICC Statute.

[53] *Contra* Judge Robinson who, in a passionate dissenting opinion, regretfully denouncing the prevailing culture of detention at ICTY (para. 22), concludes that the burden must rest on the Prosecution to prove that the conditions under Rule 65 (B) are not satisfied. Judge Robinson also affirmed that the Trial Chamber does not retain any discretion, since 'the Rule does not have . . . a catch-all provision allowing a Chamber to reject an application for provisional release for any other reason if it is in the interest of justice to do so' (para. 28).

[54] See in this respect the Order on Miodrag Jokić's Motion for Provisional Release, *Jokić* (IT–01–42–PT), 20 February 2002 and the Order on Motion for Provisional Release, *Ademi* (IT–01–46–PT), 20 February 2002. In both these case the Trial Chamber clearly held that '[even] if these requirements are met, this Trial Chamber does not believe that it is obliged to release the accused. In this regard, it agrees with the interpretation that a Trial Chamber will still retain discretion not to grant provisional release even if it is satisfied that the accused will appear for trial and will not pose danger to any victim, witness or other person.'

more difficult for the Chamber to refuse provisional release once the conditions of Rule 65 are met.[55]

If the positive impact of an amendment can be measured from its practical effects, it should be noted that just a few months after the Rule was amended, the Tribunal for the first time released two accused, for other than medical reasons.[56] These were two accused (Tadić and Zarić) in the case against *Simić and others*.[57] In particular, the Trial Chamber specifically relied on the amendment to Rule 65. The Chamber held that 'Rule 65(B), as amended, no longer requires an accused to demonstrate exceptional circumstances before release may be ordered'. Moreover, in responding to the argument made by the Prosecution that the amendment was *ultra vires*, since it did not take into account that the Tribunal has no police force and is under the duty to protect witnesses, the Chamber noted that the amendment was 'wholly consistent with the internationally recognised standards regarding the rights of the accused which the International Tribunal is obliged to respect'. In arriving at this decision, consideration was given to the fact that the accused had 'voluntarily surrendered to the custody of the International Tribunal'. Furthermore, the Chamber considered that the accused had provided (both on their own behalf and through the Government of the *Republika Srpska*) the necessary guarantees. Finally, one of the reasons that induced the Trial Chamber to release the defendants was that they had been held in detention, awaiting trial, for more than two years, and there was no prospect of an early date being fixed for the commencement of trial.[58]

Although detention pending trial remains the general rule,[59] the practice of the Tribunal regarding Rule 65 has changed and a number of defendants have

---

[55] Although it seems that this was done in *Kordić and Cerkez*, Order on Application by Dario Kordić for Provisional Release Pursuant to Rule 65, (IT–95–14/2–T), 17 December 1999. Nonetheless, one must note that in that case the motion for release was filed at an advanced stage of the proceedings, after the presentation of the Prosecution case. The Trial Chamber considered that 'it would have been inappropriate to grant provisional release during trial because [. . .] [it could have disrupted] the remaining course of the trial'.

[56] The ICTY released Djukić and Kovacević for medical reasons. After the amendment to the Rule was adopted the Tribunal released two other accused, cf. Decision on Miroslav Tadić's Application for Provisional Release, *Simić and others* (IT–95–9–PT), 4 April 2000 and Decision on Simo Zarić's Application for Provisional Release, *Simić and others* (IT–95–9–PT), 4 April 2000. On the history of Rule 65 see P. Wald and J. Martinez, 'Provisional Release at the ICTY: A Work in Progress', in R. May *et al.* (eds.), *Essays on ICTY Procedure and Evidence in Honour of Gabrielle Kirk McDonald* (The Hague: Kluwer, 2001), at 231–246.

[57] Subsequently in summer 2001 the two defendants returned to The Hague for their trial.

[58] Wald and Martinez, note 56 above, at 242.

[59] See Trial Chamber, Decision on Momčilo Krajišnik's Notice of Motion for Provisional Release, 8 October 2001, *Krajišnik and Plavšić* (IT–00–39 and 40–PT), in which the Trial Chamber held that 'provisional release continues to be the exception' (para. 12). More recently, in *Jokić*, Order on Miodrag Jokić's Motion for Provisional Release, (IT–01–42–PT), 20 February 2002, the Trial Chamber held that '[it] does not believe that recourse to a so-called "rule-exception" system provides it with assistance in reaching a decision' (para. 18).

been released,[60] including the former Prime Minister of *Republika Srpska*, Ms Biljiana Plavsic.[61] Generally speaking, importance is attached to the fact that defendants have voluntarily surrendered and to guarantees offered by the State where the accused, if released, must reside.[62]

4. The right of the accused that guilt must be proved in accordance with law and beyond reasonable doubt

The third effect of the presumption of innocence is related to the standard of proof and the procedure to be followed by judges in determining whether or not the accused is guilty.

As regards the method of proving guilt, it appears that the rules impose the precise need to prove guilt in accordance with law and require that legal methods must be followed to establish 'guilt or innocence'. This does not only mean that any 'crystal ball' method is banned—it also implies that legal argumentative and interpretative techniques must be adopted by the Prosecution to demonstrate guilt and by the judges to give reasons for their decision. Moreover, the provision implies that respect for procedural rules has overriding importance in international criminal trials.

The provisions of the *ad hoc* Tribunals simply state that '[the] accused shall be presumed innocent until proved guilty according to the provisions of the present Statute' (Article 21 ICTY St. and Article 20 ICTR St.). This not only implies that the prosecution must demonstrate guilt and that this cannot be presumed or inferred from circumstances, but also indicates that guilt must be proved following principles established in the Statute. Unfortunately the Statutes do not say much about how proof of guilt must be reached.

In the common law world it is usually required that guilt be proved beyond reasonable doubt,[63] while the civil law approach hinges on the so-called

---

[60] See, e.g., Decision on Request for Pre-Trial Provisional Release, *Halilović* (IT–01–48–PT), 13 December 2001 and the three Decisions Granting Provisional Release to Enver Hadzihasanović, Mehmed Alagić and Amir Kubura, *Hadzihasanović et al.* (IT–01–47–PT), 19 December 2001.

[61] See Decision on Biljana Plavšić's Application for Provisional Release, *Krajišnik and Plavšić* (IT–00–39 and 40–PT), 5 September 2001.

[62] See also the orders for Provisional Release of Rahim Ademi and Miodrag Jokić, note 52 above, part IV Disposition, at 15–19 and the dicision in *Blagojević and others* (IT–02–60–AR72), 3 October 2002, where the Appeals Chamber—reversing the Trial Chamber decision—held that the guarantees offered by *Republika Srpska* should be taken into account despite the fact that it is not a 'State' under public international law.

[63] On this principle see J. Newman, 'Beyond "Reasonable Doubt"', in 68 *NYULR* (1993), 979. See also *Woolmington* v. *DPP* [1935] AC 462, (1935) 25 Cr. App. R. 72 for England and Wales, and the US Supreme Court pronouncement in *Victor* v. *Nebraska*, 511 US 1 (1994).

[64] This difference, however, could be interpreted as nothing more than a linguistic variance, since the *intime* conviction is more a rule regarding the evaluation of evidence in respect of the guilt of the accused. In any event the real control mechanism over the decision is granted by the reasoning of the judgment. The reasoning behind the judgment of guilt or innocence is made public and, therefore, will be subject to the scrutiny of the whole international community. The

principle of the '*intime conviction du juge*'.[64] The Statutes of the *ad hoc* Tribunals did not set forth any specific test. Subsequently, however, the judges in adopting the Rules of Procedure and Evidence decided to adopt the common law standard.[65] Hence, the test laid down in Rule 87(A) RPEs is that guilt must be proved beyond reasonable doubt.

Article 66, paragraph 1, of the ICC Statute establishes that guilt must be proven 'in accordance with the *applicable law*'. This represents a notable improvement on the text contained in the Statutes of the *ad hoc* Tribunals. The reference to 'applicable law' in the ICC Statute is certainly wider than the general reference to 'the Statute' contained in the provisions of the *ad hoc* Tribunals. It is clear that the approach adopted in the ICC provision covers the rules of procedure and any other norms applicable before the Court pursuant to Article 21 of the ICC Statute. Moreover, this reference is considerably more accurate than that of the *ad hoc* Tribunals. As mentioned above, the Statutes of the *ad hoc* Tribunals do not contain procedural rules implementing the principle.

Furthermore, paragraph 3 of Article 66 ICC St. spells out the *standard of proof* that must be reached, which is that the judges must be convinced of the guilt of the accused *beyond reasonable doubt.* The issue of a test for judgment is certainly controversial.[66] The rule does not imply that *any doubt* must be interpreted to the advantage of the accused, and may thus indicate that the judges must reach a determination of guilt in accordance with reasoning essentially based on a probabilistic analysis of the evidence submitted at trial. Only a 'doubt' that renders the commission of the crime by the accused unlikely, according to an assessment based on the evaluation of probabilities, can thus be 'reasonable doubt'. The determination of guilt must thus be well grounded not only from a legal perspective but also from a logical point of

reasons on which the determination of the judges on guilt or innocence is grounded are therefore subject to verification on the basis of logical arguments.

The verdict of the jury is not motivated and therefore there is no way to control how the determination on the guilt of the accused was reached. In the system of international criminal justice there is an obligation to state the reasoning behind conviction. Therefore it is submitted that in the end the standard beyond reasonable doubt is implicit in every case where judges must give reasons for their findings of guilt. Cf. in this regard, J. Hatchard, B. Huber, and R. Vogler (eds.), *Comparative Criminal Procedure* (London: British Institute of International and Comparative Law, 1996), at 30; *contra* G. Fletcher, *Basic Concepts of Criminal Law* (New York: OUP, 1998), at 16–17.

[65] On the application of this rule in the system of the *ad hoc* Tribunals see R. Pruitt, 'Guilt by Majority in the ICTY: Does This Meet the Standard of Proof Beyond Reasonable Doubt?', in 10 *LJIL* (1997) 557–578, expressing doubts on the compliance of the Tribunal with the rule to prove guilt beyond reasonable doubt, in that the Rules allow for convictions by a majority of the judges (2 to 1 in Trial Chambers, or 3 to 2 in the Appeals Chamber); and K. Carter, 'Proof Beyond a Reasonable Doubt? Collecting Evidence for the International Criminal Tribunal for the Former Yugoslavia', in 31 *CYIL* (1993), 235–263.

[66] On the attempts to define the notion of 'beyond reasonable doubt' see R. May, note 32 above, at 56–58, in particular where the author concludes that 'the expression is therefore better left to speak for itself, undefined' (at 57): a wise conclusion that it is impossible to disagree with.

view. It should be added that the refusal of jury trials and the admission of separate or dissenting opinions increase the need for stringent reasoning.[67]

The Appeals Chamber of the ICTY, in its judgement in *Aleksovski*,[68] discussed the issue of the standard of proof, dealing with a ground of appeal by the accused based on the alleged failure of the Trial Chamber to apply the 'beyond reasonable doubt' standard of proof. The Defence submitted that the Trial Chamber erred in considering that the Prosecutor had proved the objective elements of the crime beyond reasonable doubt (the crime charged was offences to personal dignity, under Article 3 ICTY St.). This submission was essentially supported by the argument that the evidence presented by the prosecution consisted only of witness statements, and that there was no medical report or expert evidence on the mistreatments allegedly committed in the prison of which the accused was the director. Moreover, the Trial Chamber had dismissed the testimony of a witness who had testified that he had seen those mistreatments, finding that this witness was unreliable. Therefore, the Defence submitted that, as the Chamber had itself determined that the witness testimony was unreliable, it had to conclude that there were doubts about the guilt of the accused. The Prosecution, on the other hand, contended that it was perfectly admissible to rely only upon oral evidence and that 'the need for medical or other scientifically objective evidence at trial'[69] had been rejected in the judgment at first instance. The Appeals Chamber concluded that the Trial Chamber had not erred: first, because even 'the testimony of a single witness on a material fact does not require, as a matter of law, any corroboration';[70] secondly, because Trial Chambers have wide discretion in admitting evidence and in evaluating its probative value, depending on the circumstances of each single case.[71] In the end the Appeals Chamber held that '[it] may overturn the Trial Chamber's finding of fact only where the evidence relied on could not have been accepted by any reasonable tribunal or where the evaluation of the evidence is wholly erroneous'.[72]

In conclusion, arguably proof of guilt in accordance with law and beyond reasonable doubt means that the judge must reach a finding based on the *highest probability* that a certain sequence of acts led to the commission of the crime by the accused. It is precisely the assessment of this probability that is influenced by the reasonable doubt standard as opposed to the '*intime conviction*', which does not mean that the judge can rely on a balance of probabilities, but rather that guilt is affirmed by excluding all other reasonable possibilities. The transparency of this process is ensured by the duty to render a reasoned decision.[73]

---

[67] It is, however, interesting to note that in the system of the *ad hoc* Tribunals dissent has so far focused only on issues of law.

[68] Cf. Appeals Chamber Judgment, *Aleksovski*, (IT–95–14/1–A), 24 March 2000.

[69] *Ibidem*, para. 58.   [70] *Ibidem*, para. 62.   [71] *Ibidem*, paras. 63 and 64.

[72] *Ibidem*, para. 64.   [73] Rule 88 of both RPEs.

It is generally argued that the *'intime conviction'* standard furnishes fewer guarantees to the accused. However, it is here submitted that this difference should not be over-estimated, particularly in light of the obligation imposed on the judges to render reasoned decisions. The determination of guilt should be based in both cases on a reasoned appraisal of the evidence that must be adequately discussed in the decision. Furthermore, the determination of guilt should be reached through a trial conducted in accordance with the rules of procedure and subsequently affirmed by applying legal rules and juridical interpretative techniques.

II. THE RIGHT TO BE JUDGED BY AN INDEPENDENT AND IMPARTIAL TRIBUNAL

1. General

The right to be judged by an independent and impartial tribunal is derived directly from international human rights provisions. Article 10 UDHR, Article 6 ECHR, and Article 14 ICCPR all provide for this right. Moreover, the UN Basic Principles on the Independence of the Judiciary have restated this principle. Furthermore, this is a requirement commonly found in many national constitutions.[74] The independence and impartiality of the judiciary are a basic principle of the *rule of law*.[75]

Independence and impartiality, whilst two distinct concepts, are usually combined into a formula that merges them together as a unique safeguard. There are, however, two distinct aspects of this right. First, there is the right to be tried by independent and impartial judges *in abstracto*, with regard to the organization and structure of the Tribunals or the Court. This aspect influences the protection of independence from external authorities, the method of selection of the judges, etc. Secondly, the requirement of an independent and impartial judge applies *in concreto*. In particular, the independence and impartiality of judges must be specifically ensured in the course of every single proceeding. In this respect, reference should be made to provisions on disqualification and rules on the composition of the different Chambers at the various stages of proceedings.[76]

[74] Cf. Bassiouni, note 7 above, at 235. The author, however, classifies this specific right as one of the elements of a fair trial (at 270).

[75] Cf. International Commission of Jurists (ICJ), *Universal Aspects of Judicial Independence*, *Yearbook of the Centre for the Independence of Judges and Lawyers*, January 2000, and in particular C. Amerasinghe, 'Judicial Independence—An Enduring, Widespread Social Value', at 13.

[76] The ECourt HR has usually referred to this distinction between the two aspects of the character of independence and impartiality as *objective* and *subjective*. It is submitted, however, that these categories are to a certain extent misleading for the purpose of this study, which is not to evaluate the conformity of a single case to a system of protection of human rights but to assess the structure of the system in general. See *Hauschildt* v. *Denmark*, 24 May 1989 (Series A–154), **www.echr.coe.int/Eng/Judgments.htm**, para. 46.

In international criminal trials, at least initially, the independence and impartiality of judges were not strongly protected. At Nuremberg, for example, the four judges (and four alternates) were all nationals of the four allied countries. Moreover, it is interesting to note that the Russian Judge (Mr Nikithcenko), as well as the French alternate (Mr Falco), had been involved in the preparation and drafting of the indictment just before being appointed judges. In Tokyo, the situation was slightly different as there were eleven judges, including two from newly independent countries (India and the Philippines); thus, there was a greater variety of experience and possibly more impartiality. The judges, however, were all 'appointed by the Supreme Commander for the Allied Powers from the names submitted by the Signatories to the Instrument of Surrender, India and the Commonwealth of the Philippines' (Article 2, IMTFE Charter), and even the President of the Tribunal was appointed by the Supreme Commander. Furthermore, neither the Charters nor the Rules of the two Tribunals contained provisions on disqualification. It is clear that although the judges sitting on these trials were independent and impartial persons of high moral standing, the Tribunals, globally considered, could hardly be classified as independent and impartial. It is also certain that the right of the accused to an independent and impartial tribunal (or to a hearing conducted impartially) was not provided for in the normative framework of these Tribunals.

2. *The independence and impartiality of the judges* in abstracto

Provisions on the independence and impartiality of the judges in the Statutes of the *ad hoc* tribunals and in the ICC Statute are not designed to attribute rights to the accused. However, it can be contended that objective independence and impartiality of judicial organs, which can be defined as a structural guarantee,[77] may be protected *de facto* by simply providing for general norms that require independence and impartiality in the appointment of judges.

In the Statutes of the *ad hoc* Tribunals, Article 11 ICTY St. and Article 10 ICTR St. provide that Chambers must be composed of fourteen[78] independent judges, Article 13 ICTY St. (Article 12 ICTR St.), further specifying that 'the judges shall be persons of high moral character, impartiality and integrity'. This seems to confirm that although there is no express provision conferring on the accused the right to be judged by an independent and impartial tribunal, judges are nonetheless characterized by independence and impartiality.

[77] Cf. M. Chiavario, *Processo e Garanzie della Persona* (3rd edn., Milan: Giuffrè, 1984), ii, at 43–87.

[78] Originally, there were 11 judges at the ICTY and 6 at the ICTR (plus the 5 judges of the Appeals Chamber of the ICTY that serves as Appeals Chamber also for the ICTR). Subsequently the Security Council added 3 more judges to each Tribunal. Finally, in November 2000 and August 2002 the Security Council adopted provisions for the appointment of *ad litem* judges.

The independence of the *ad hoc* Tribunals is broad, but of course intrinsically limited by their having been created by the Security Council.[79] The decision on jurisdiction of 2 October 1995 in *Tadić*,[80] however, showed great independence, in that it affirmed a power, albeit limited, of judicial review over the acts of the Council. The same holds true for the Rwanda Tribunal, which adopted the same reading in a decision on a preliminary motion on jurisdiction in *Kanyabashi*.[81] Naturally, there are financial limitations on the independence of the Tribunals linked to the approval of their budgets by the UN General Assembly. These restraints may adversely affect the Tribunals' independence, especially in that they may have an influence on the ability of the Tribunals to conduct effective trials. These are, however, inevitable limitations essentially linked to the creation of those Tribunals within the UN system.[82]

In the system of the *ad hoc* Tribunals the short mandate of the judges (only four years) and the fact that they can be re-elected for a second (or even a third or fourth) term can, in theory, diminish the guarantee of independence.[83] In this respect the solution found in the ICC St. seems more appropriate in ensuring the greatest degree of independence. Pursuant to Article 36, paragraph 9 letter a, ICC St. judges are only elected for a single mandate of nine years. It was decided that, only at the first election, one third of the judges would be subsequently selected to serve for nine years, one third for six years and one third for only a three-year period (Article 36, paragraph 9 letter b). The latter judges are also eligible for re-election for a full term (Article 36, paragraph 9 letter c).

Additionally, the overall impartiality of the Court is ensured by the requirement that judges must come from different geographical areas of the world and the principal legal systems.[84] Furthermore, privileges and immunities for the Tribunals and the Court, including the judges and other personnel, add a final guarantee of the independent character of the Tribunals and the Court as a whole.

Impartiality, as often stated by the ECourtHR, should not only be effectively protected, but it must also be seen and perceived to be such.[85] The ICTY

---

[79] See T. Van Boven, 'Autonomy and Independence of United Nations Judicial Institutions: A Comparative Note', in K. Wellens (ed.), *International Law: Theory and Practice* (The Hague: Kluwer, 1998), 679–688, at 687.

[80] Cf. Appeals Chamber Decision on Defence Motion of Lack of Jurisdiction, *Tadić* (IT–94–1–AR72), 2 October 1995.

[81] Cf. Trial Chamber Decision on the Defence Motion on Jurisdiction, *Kanyabashi* (ICTR–96–15–PT), 18 June 1997.

[82] It should, however, be noted that the General Assembly progressively increased the budgets of the two *ad hoc* Tribunals, which are now working in satisfactory conditions.

[83] Cf. M.C. Bassiouni and P. Manikas, *The Law of International Criminal Tribunal for the Former Yugoslavia* (Irvington on Hudson, NY: Transnational, 1996), at 806.

[84] Article 37, ICC St.

[85] Cf. ECourtHR, *Delcourt* v. *Belgium*, 17 January 1970 (Series A–11), para. 31; see also *De Cubber* v. *Belgium*, 26 October 1984 (Series A–86), both at **www.echr.coe.int/Eng/Judgments.htm**.

has often been blamed for an alleged bias against the Serbs, and various statements made by the Presidents of the Tribunal on the lack of co-operation by the authorities in Belgrade have been criticized.[86] Nevertheless, it should be said that non-compliance with the Tribunal's orders preceded presidential statements, and these pursued the single goal of recalling the primacy of the Tribunal and the duty of national authorities to comply with its orders. In addition, one should note that the President of the Tribunal, in the framework on international tribunals, plays a non-judicial role, exercising both administrative and diplomatic function as well as judicial ones. Moreover, investigations and prosecutions have also been conducted against Croats and Muslims. Thus the allegation of an anti-Serb bias that has been directed towards the Tribunal seems essentially to be the fruit of misconception or even propaganda against international criminal justice.

In the ICC Statute, Article 40 is devoted to the issue of the independence of the judges.[87] Paragraph 1 states the general rule that judges must be independent in the performance of their functions. The other paragraphs of this Article specify in detail what rules should be followed. Judges must refrain from engaging 'in any activity which is likely to interfere with their judicial function or to affect confidence in their independence',[88] and must serve on a full-time basis and not engage in other occupations of a professional nature.[89]

In the ICC and in the system of the *ad hoc* Tribunals, the requisite of independence is not established as a right of the accused. It is more an attribution that must characterize the judges. However, it can be persuasively argued that in substance this does not affect the right of the accused to be tried by an impartial and independent tribunal. In particular, this right is granted through the abovementioned norms that provide for the nomination of independent and impartial judges.

Recently, the Appeals Chamber of the ICTR, in a decision delivered in *Barayagwiza*,[90] stated that due to very serious breaches of the rights of the accused, the case against him had to be dismissed and the accused released.[91] Subsequently, the Prosecutor filed a motion for revision (it is highly questionable that revision is possible against this kind of decision). The Appeals Chamber, having considered the new elements brought by the Prosecution, overturned its previous decision.[92] This whole affair was very sensitive from

[86] See G. Robertson, *Crimes Against Humanity—The Struggle for Global Justice* (London: Penguin Books, 2000), 300.

[87] Generally on this issue see J. Deschênes, 'Article 40 Independence of the Judges', in Triffterer, note 31 above, 619–624.

[88] Article 40.2 ICC St.   [89] Article 40.3 ICC St.

[90] On this case see Chapter 4 below.

[91] Appeals Chamber Decision, *Barayagwiza* (ICTR–97–19), 3 November 1999.

[92] Appeals Chamber Decision on the motion of the Prosecutor for Review or Reconsideration, *Barayagwiza* (ICTR–97–19), 31 March 2000.

the political point of view. One could be tempted to argue that the application for revision by the Prosecutor and the subsequent decision of the Tribunal overturning its previous opinion were due to pressure by the Rwandan government and very delicate political circumstances. Appended to this decision was a declaration by Judge Nieto-Navia discussing the issue of the independence of the Tribunal,[93] which was dramatically at risk in this case. A person suspected of being one of the architects of the Rwandan genocide could be released due to the violation of several of his rights by various organs of the Tribunal.[94] On the one hand, the credibility of the Tribunal *vis-à-vis* the Rwandan people and the international community was endangered. On the other hand, very serious violations of the rights of the accused had occurred. The lack of any sanction in respect of these violations would have negatively affected the perception of fairness of the proceedings before the Tribunal. This case dramatically highlighted the tensions behind the administration of international criminal justice. However, it cannot be said that independence as such was fundamentally at stake. That is to say, even admitting that the Tribunal made a mistake in reversing its decision to dismiss the case and release the accused, this was done principally to fulfil its mission, rather than to satisfy external political pressures.

In conclusion, it can be stated that, in general, there should be no problem in terms of the protection of the right of the accused to an independent and impartial tribunal in respect of external pressures. Nevertheless, problems may arise concerning the non-structural dimensions of the right to an independent and impartial tribunal and, in particular, the enforcement of this right in respect of individual cases.

3. Independence and impartiality of judges in respect of an individual case

The guarantees, classified above as structural, contribute to the independence and impartiality of the judges in respect of each individual case. However, in this respect, there are further measures that reinforce their independence and impartiality.

A reference to impartiality in the proceedings is made in Article 67 ICC St., whereby 'the accused shall be entitled . . . to a fair hearing conducted impartially'. Such a reference is not even provided for by the Statutes of the *ad hoc* Tribunals, in which, as mentioned above, the consideration of impartiality and integrity is only required for the election of the judges.

The formula adopted by the Statutes of the *ad hoc* Tribunals satisfies the requirement to guarantee a structurally independent and impartial tribunal.

---

[93] See Declaration of Judge Nieto Navia, 31 March 2000.

[94] It seems that in this case the Chambers, the Registry, and the Office of the Prosecutor are all responsible, although to different degrees, for not having protected the rights of the defendant satisfactorily.

Nonetheless, it is questionable whether this solution is satisfactory in terms of the protection of the right of the accused to have independent and impartial judges at his or her trial. This second aspect of the right of the accused was not sufficiently ensured in the Statutes of the *ad hoc* Tribunals. For this purpose, the judges, when drafting the Rules of Procedure and Evidence, provided the accused with reinforced safeguards through appropriate rules on disqualification, affording a more adequate protection of the right of the accused to be tried by independent and impartial judges. Rule 15, paragraph (A), of both RPEs establishes that '[a] Judge may not sit on a trial or appeal in any case in which the Judge has a personal interest or concerning which the Judge has or has had any association which might affect his or her impartiality'. In such circumstances the judge shall himself decide to withdraw. In any event the defendant or the Prosecutor can always apply for the disqualification of a judge. This matter is then decided by the Bureau, which makes a decision whether the judge should be disqualified or not, after having considered the facts of the case under examination. In addition to these provisions, Rule 15 originally contained mandatory rules for the disqualification of the confirming judge from subsequent stages of a case. For example, it established that the judge who confirms the indictment must not be a member of the Trial Chamber or the Appeals Chamber in that case (Rule 15 C). Nor can a judge sit on the appeal of a case in which he or she sat at trial (Rule 15 D). Recently (at the 21st Plenary Session of November 1999), Rule 15 RPE ICTY was amended and the system was largely subverted. Now Rule 15 (C) establishes that 'the Judge of the Trial Chamber who reviews an indictment against an accused, pursuant to Article 19 of the Statute and Rules 47 or 61, *shall not be disqualified* for sitting as a member of the Trial Chamber for the trial of that accused'. Moreover, the new rule allows the confirming judge to sit as a member of the Appeals Chamber, or as a member of a bench of three judges appointed pursuant to Rule 65 (D), 72 (B)(ii), 73 (B) or 77 (J).

This amendment was probably due to the fact that the Tribunal was faced with too many pending cases and not enough judges. However, there may also be some doubts about its conformity with the principle of impartiality,[95] since it may be contended that the reviewing judge has already decided that there are grounds for believing that an accused has committed certain crimes. If the meaning of *prima facie* case is that 'there is a credible case which would (if not contradicted by the Defence) be a sufficient basis to convict the accused on the charges',[96] the judge who has confirmed the indictment is certainly convinced of this. This implies that the defence will have to make an additional effort to

---

[95] Cf. ECourtHR, *Hauschildt* v. *Denmark* (Sereis A–154), 24 May 1989, **www.echr.coe.int/ Eng/Judgments.htm**, *De Cubber*, note 85 above.

[96] Cf. J. Jones, *The Practice of the International Criminal Tribunals for the Former Yugoslavia and Rwanda* (Irvington on Hudson, NY: Transnational, 1998), at 96, quoting the Draft Statute for an International Criminal Court of the International Law Commission.

persuade such a judge that the Prosecutor's case is not convincing, and it can, thus, hardly be said that this judge will be seen at the outset of the trial as an impartial organ. In other words, the confirming judge may be unlikely to vote in favour of a motion for acquittal pursuant to Rule 98-*bis* RPE ICTY after the close of the prosecution case (in many ways the confirming judge has already endorsed the Prosecutor's conclusions as outlined in the indictment). Finally, it seems that the participation of the confirming judge in the trial of the accused could be challenged as to its congruity with the presumption of innocence. The defence is, to a certain extent, obliged to bring evidence to convince the confirming judge of the innocence of the accused.[97] However, consideration must be given to the notion that, first, the *prima facie* standard adopted for confirmation of an indictment is not totally equivalent to proof of guilt beyond reasonable doubt.[98] Secondly, the grounds submitted by the Prosecutor to the confirming judge are only documentary sources (witness statements, pictures, videotapes, reports, etc.) and no witness is heard. Therefore, the confirming judge does not really examine evidence *stricto sensu*. Thirdly, the Rules even prior to this amendment already allowed the Trial Chamber before which the trial was to be conducted to confirm modifications of the indictment pursuant to Rule 50 RPE. These modifications of the indictment could include the confirmation of new charges. Therefore, such a power was already granted to the entire Chamber. The fact that the single judge who confirms the indictment is not disqualified from being a member of the Trial Chamber in a case he or she has confirmed is, thus, in line with Rule 50 RPE.

Nonetheless, it should be emphasized that the ICC Statute has explicitly excluded such a possibility by providing that 'under no circumstances shall a judge who has participated in the pre-trial phase of a case be eligible to sit on the Trial Chamber hearing that case'.[99] Arguably, it would be inappropriate for the Presidents of the *ad hoc* Tribunals to allow reviewing judges to sit on the Trial Chamber in cases they have confirmed. Furthermore, the emergency situation with which the Tribunal was confronted when the amendment was

---

[97] This reasoning is in line with the jurisprudence of the ECourtHR. The Court has held on various occasions that it cannot be affirmed in general that *ipso facto* a judge who has been involved in a case and also issued procedural decisions, and subsequently becomes a member of the Trial Chamber that hears the case, is not impartial. However, the Court found violations of Article 6.1 ECHR (impartiality of the judge) when the procedural decisions taken by such a judge involved considerations of the guilt of the defendant. Cf. *Hauschildt* v. *Denmark* (Series A–154), 24 May 1989, **www.echr.coe.int/Eng/Judgments.htm**. in particular para. 52 which explains that the judge had issued procedural decisions implying that 'the judge has to be convinced that there is a very high degree of clarity as to the question of guilt. Thus the difference between the issue the judge has to settle when applying this section [the Court is referring to a section of the Danish code of criminal procedure] and the issue he will have to settle when giving judgement at the trial becomes tenuous'.

[98] In respect of the standard for confirmation of the indictment see D. Hunt, 'The Meaning of a "prima facie Case" for the Purposes of Confirmation', in May *et al.* (eds.), note 56 above, at 137–149.

[99] Cf. Article 39.4 of the ICC Statute.

adopted is now less dramatic, considering the appointment by the Security Council of a pool of twenty-seven *ad litem* judges on which the Tribunal may rely to ensure expeditious trials.

A mechanism for disqualification, similar to that originally established for the *ad hoc* Tribunals, has also been adopted in the ICC Statute. Article 41 ICC St. provides that 'a judge shall not participate in any case in which his or her impartiality might be reasonably doubted on any ground'. The provision further specifies a number of other situations in which there is an automatic basis for disqualification. These include all instances of previous involvement of the judge in the case, including any involvement at national level.[100] Additionally, the rule leaves it to the RPE to add other grounds for disqualification.[101] Nonetheless, even if there is a reference to a sort of catalogue of reasons for disqualification, nothing prevents an accused or the Prosecutor from seeking disqualification on any other ground irrespective of its inclusion in the catalogue contained in the RPE.[102]

In the *ad hoc* Tribunals, in *Delalić and others* and in *Furundžija*, defendants invoked the provisions on disqualification, claiming that some of the judges were not impartial. In *Delalić and others*, the matter at issue was that Judge Odio-Benito had been elected Vice-President of Costa Rica. The defendants considered that such a political role was incompatible with the requirements set out in the Statute and the Rules. However, no specific rule existed on this point, and so the Bureau was called upon to decide the matter. In its decision it concluded that provided that Judge Odio-Benito declared that she would not take up office as Vice-President before the end of the trial, her role as Vice-President *in pectore* did not affect her independence and impartiality.[103]

In *Furundžija*, the defendant pleaded the lack of impartiality of a judge as a ground for appeal. The defendant claimed that Judge Mumba lacked independence and impartiality in that, in the past, she had been associated with the UN Commission on the Status of Women (UNCSW). The appellant submitted that because of Judge Mumba's personal interest in the campaigns of the Commission, i.e of her links as a former member of the Commission with three *amici curiae* and one of the members of the prosecution team, she should be disqualified from sitting as a judge of the Trial Chamber. The Appeals Chamber held that the test to be applied in these cases was twofold. On the

---

[100] See J. Deschênes, 'Article 41 Excusing and Disqualification of Judges', in Triffterer (ed.), note 31 above, 425–426.

[101] See Rules 33–35, dealing with excusing and disqualification of judges, the Prosecutor, and the Deputy, Draft Rules of Procedure and Evidence for the ICC, UN doc. PCNICC/2000/INF3/Add.1, 12 July 2000.

[102] In particular, Rule 34 contains a non-exhaustive listing of the grounds for disqualification.

[103] Decision of the Bureau on Motion on Judicial Independence, *Delalić and others* (IT–96–21–T), 4 September 1998. For reasonable criticisms of such a Decision see Deschênes, note 100 above, at 424, where the author also points out that no provision on this issue has been provided for in the system of the ICC, notwithstanding its original inclusion in the ILC Draft.

one hand, a judge cannot be considered impartial where it is shown that an actual bias exists.[104] On the other, a judge must also be disqualified where there is an appearance of bias. This appearance of bias results when 'a Judge is a party to the case, or has a financial or proprietary interest in the outcome of a case, or if the Judge's decision will lead to the promotion of a cause in which he or she is involved, together with one of the parties'.[105] In this case, disqualification from the case is automatic. Moreover, there should be disqualification when 'the circumstances would lead a reasonable observer, properly informed, to reasonably apprehend bias'.[106] This notion must be interpreted referring to 'whether the reaction of the hypothetical fair-minded observer (with sufficient knowledge of the actual circumstances to make a reasonable judgement) would be that [the Judge in question] . . . might not bring an impartial and unprejudiced mind'.[107]

As regards the power of the parties to request disqualification, it is submitted that given the characterization of the Prosecutor as an impartial organ exercising its functions in the interest of justice, where the Prosecutor has information suggesting that a judge may be biased, the Prosecutor is entitled to seek disqualification in the interest of the accused, provided, of course, that the accused does not disagree.

The reviewing judge in the *ad hoc* Tribunals should not, and the judges of the Pre-Trial Chamber in the ICC cannot, be members of the panel that will sit on the case at trial or in appeal proceedings. This is certainly a major guarantee of impartiality, since it bars judges who have already expressed their views on the case from pronouncing again on the same case.

With regard to impartiality, some doubts can be expressed regarding two innovations adopted in the procedure before the ICTY: the Pre-trial Judge, provided for by Rule 65-*ter* and the 'dossier approach' adopted by Trial Chambers in some cases pending before the Tribunal.[108] The Pre-trial Judge, who is a judge of the Trial Chamber to which the case has been assigned, is entrusted with the task of co-ordinating the exchanges between the parties in the pre-trial phase. He or she sets appropriate deadlines should the Prosecutor request time for further investigations. The Pre-trial Judge also records the agreement and disagreement between the parties on points of fact and law, and may order the presentation of written submissions. Since this cluster of powers and tasks may, in a certain sense, lead to the judge being heavily involved in the case prior to the opening of the debates, it could be argued that this involvement might subsequently prejudice his or her impartiality at trial.

---

[104] Appeals Chamber Judgment, *Furundžija* (IT–95–17/1–A), 21 July 2000, para. 189.
[105] *Ibidem.*   [106] *Ibidem.*
[107] Decision on Application by Momir Talić for the Disqualification and Withdrawal of a Judge, *Brdjanin and Talić* (IT–99–36–PT), 18 May 2000, para. 15.
[108] Cf., e.g., the admission of the Tuliča report into evidence in *Kordić* and *Čerkez*, or the admission of pre-trial witness statements in *Dokmanović*, on which see notes 136 and 137 below.

A similar reasoning can also be applied to the so-called 'dossier approach'.[109] On some occasions the judges of the Trial Chamber have asked the parties to submit documents and the witnesses' statements to the court, before hearing the witnesses. This documentary approach to evidence is very similar to the approach of the reviewing judge to the case. It might be suggested that the same reasons that can be suggested to preclude the reviewing judge from being a member of the Trial Chamber in the cases he or she has reviewed should also apply here. In other words, the judges of the Trial Chamber should be prevented from receiving documents that form part of the supporting material, before their presentation as evidence in court. This reasoning, however, is not correct. The reasons for not allowing the reviewing judge to sit in the Trial Chamber are linked to the idea that he or she has already expressed an opinion on the supporting material in the decision of confirmation of the indictment. It would, thus, be improper to have a judge who has already pronounced on the matter on the panel that will decide the case. In other words, the reviewing judge is not excluded from the Trial Chamber because of the knowledge he or she has of the case. It is, rather, the fact that he or she has already decided on those grounds that makes the reviewing judge unsuitable for sitting at trial.

A final note should be added concerning the system adopted at the *ad hoc* Tribunals pursuant to which the judges rotate from the Trial Chambers to the Appeals Chamber. Such rotation makes the impartiality of the appellate body far less effective.[110] Of course, this does not affect the individual case, because in respect of a single case the same judge can never sit both at trial and in appeal proceedings. It does, however, influence impartiality (intended as an unprejudiced approach) on points of law, as there may be the risk of not establishing authoritative precedents, but rather occasional decisions linked to varying majorities due to rotation in the composition of the Chambers.

III. THE RIGHT TO A 'FAIR AND EXPEDITIOUS TRIAL'

1. The right to a fair trial as a general guarantee and the principle of equality of arms

The right to a fair trial is a fundamental feature of modern systems of criminal procedure. The need to ensure a fair trial was also enshrined in the Charters of the Nuremberg and Tokyo Tribunals.[111] Section IV of the Nuremberg

---

[109] On this approach see also notes 199 and 200 below.

[110] Cf. on this issue Chapter 4, section II below, on appeal proceedings.

[111] Robert Jackson was implicitly referring to the principles of fair trial, when he uttered the famous statement: '[we] must never forget that the record on which we judge these defendants today is the record on which history will judge us tomorrow. To pass these defendants a poisoned chalice is to put it to our lips as well. We must summon such detachment and intellectual integrity

Charter, as mentioned above, was entitled 'Fair Trial for Defendants'. This section contained only one Article, Article 16, which listed the safeguards necessary to ensure a fair trial to the accused. It included the right to receive the indictment and all the other documents accompanying it in a language spoken by the accused. Additionally, it established that the indictment had to be handed to the accused a reasonable time before the trial. Defendants also had the right to conduct their own defence or to have the assistance of Counsel (paragraph d), and the right to present evidence at the trial in support of their defence (including the right to cross-examine witnesses) (paragraph e). Other provisions in the Charter had the indirect effect of protecting the right of the accused to have a fair trial. It appears, however, that these norms should not be construed as attributing rights to the accused but more as imposing duties on the Tribunal. Under Article 17, for example, the Tribunal was given powers such as the authority to summon witnesses, to order the production of documents or other sorts of evidentiary materials, or to appoint court officers for the purpose of collecting evidence. However, it has been contended that these powers did not help to achieve the goal of ensuring a fair trial to defendants, since they were not really exercised in favour of the Defence.[112]

The rules of procedure adopted by the Tribunal did not substantially alter the situation. The right to assistance of counsel and the right to have the documents and the proceedings translated into a language understood by the accused were reaffirmed and the conditions for their implementation specified (rule 2, IMT rules). Moreover, consistently with the provisions of Article 17 of the Charter, Rule 4 entitled the defence to file an application with the General Secretary of the Tribunal to obtain the attendance of witnesses or the production of documents. It would have been possible to achieve this goal through the assistance of the governments of the Signatories or those of the adhering States. It should, however, be pointed out that the norm provided for witnesses to be summoned only 'if possible' and therefore attributed to States a wide margin of appreciation that did not seem to be subject to any control by the Tribunal.[113]

to our task that this trial will commend itself to posterity as fulfilling humanity's aspirations to do justice': cf. Robert Jackson, Opening Speech, 21 November 1945, Nuremberg, Nazi Conspiracy and Aggression, note 9 above, at 116.

[112] Cf., e.g., the allegations reported by D. Irving, *Nuremberg: The Last Battle* (London: Focal Point, 1996), at 173–177, and M. Marrus, *The Nuremberg War Crimes Trials 1945–46: A Documentary History* (Boston, Mass.: Bedford Books, 1997), at 247.

[113] The issue of the co-operation of States with international criminal tribunals has been the object of a specific decision of the Appeals Chamber of the ICTY, in a matter brought to the attention of the Tribunal by the Republic of Croatia, which did not want to comply fully with an order of a judge of the Tribunal (perhaps improperly entitled 'subpoena'). In this decision the Appeals Chamber—reversing the decision of the Trial Chamber—affirmed several important principles concerning the obligation of States to co-operate with the International Tribunal and possible remedies against non-co-operation. See Appeals Chamber Decision on the Request of the Republic of Croatia for Review of the Decision of Trial Chamber II of 18 July 1997, *Blaškić* (IT–95–14–AR108bis), 29 October 1997.

The Charter for the Tokyo Tribunal (IMTFE Charter) solemnly stated that the Tribunal was created for the 'just and prompt trial and punishment of the major war criminals in the Far East' (Article 1 IMTFE Charter). Section III of the Charter dealt with the issue of fair trial, and specified the requirements for a fair trial. This Section included the obligation to furnish the accused, in adequate time for defence,[114] with the indictment and all relevant documents in a language he understood and with appropriate interpretation during the trial. Furthermore, the right of representation by Counsel was also recognized. Article 9 letter d established that an accused had the right to examine any witnesses; this right was, however, subject to such reasonable restrictions as determined by the Tribunal.[115]

This illustrates, in general, the protection afforded by the Charters of the International Military Tribunals to the right of the accused to a 'fair trial'. It might be questioned whether such protection was sufficient. However, what matters here is that it emerges that there was an intention to protect this right. Naturally there were flaws, in particular concerning the lack of provisions on disqualification, of a detailed procedure for discovery, and for collection and disclosure of exculpatory evidence. Moreover, there was an additional defect in the absence of express provisions on the presumption of innocence; also, there was no right against self-incrimination. These elements support the idea already expressed above that these trials were not 'fair trials' in the understanding of contemporary international law. However, the main criticisms concerned the unfair administration of the rules.[116]

The Statutes of the *ad hoc* Tribunals recognize the right of the accused to 'a fair hearing' (Article 21 ICTY St. and Article 20 ICTR St.). The right to a fair trial is a general concept encompassing several more specific rights.[117] Nevertheless, its formulation as a separate right may have the positive effect of functioning as a safety net.[118] This would imply that, in a given situation, even if there are no express provisions to regulate it, the interpreter should prefer the solution that ensures the actual realization of a fair trial. In a sense,

---

[114] This period was further specified by the Rules of Procedure, adopted on 25 April 1946, which stated that each accused should receive the indictment, the charter, and any other documents lodged with the indictment, so that copies could be taken, not less than 14 days before the Tribunal began.

[115] It will be further shown how under the Statutes of the UN international tribunals the restrictions on the examination of witnesses need to be defined in detail and that the interests protected need to be accurately identified.

[116] Cf. R. Minear, *Victor's Justice—The Tokyo War Crimes Trial* (Princeton, NJ: Princeton University Press, 1971), at 19.

[117] Cf. Article 21 ICTY St., Article 20 ICTR St., and Article 67 ICC St. In general, on the right to a fair trial cf. D. Harris, 'The Right to a Fair Trial in Criminal Proceedings as a Human Right', in 16 *ICLQ* (1967), 352 and other authors cited in Chapter 1 notes 9, 12, and 13 above.

[118] For example, interpreting the ECHR, the Court has often used this as a general concept: cf. *Delcourt* v. *Belgium*, 17 January 1970 (Series A–11).

overall fairness is also the yardstick against which the decisions of international criminal tribunals and Court must be measured.

The right to a fair trial implies the principle of *equality of arms*.[119] This principle assumes enormous importance in proceedings based on the adversarial approach.[120] In this respect, however, one should recall that the system of the *ad hoc* Tribunals has progressively undergone a number of changes.[121] Initially, the model adopted hinged very strongly on an adversarial perspective. Subsequently, the Chambers, first, and, thereafter, the judges in plenary session modified the system by introducing a more proactive role for the judicial organs of the Tribunal. This role is also intended to compensate for some of the flaws of the system, which may be too onerous for the Defence. In this respect, the activity of the Registrar in support of defendants has proved very important. For example, resources have been made available to the Defence for investigations. The Chambers have also adopted various orders to summon witnesses, to order the production of evidence, and to grant safe-conducts and to allow testimony by videoconference. These instruments, however, may not always prove sufficient actually to achieve 'equality of arms', and challenges in this respect have been brought before the Chambers of the Tribunal.

The first ground of appeal for the Defence in *Tadić* addressed the issue of whether the inequality of arms had led to a denial of a fair trial. The argument of the Defence was that the Trial Chamber had failed appropriately to support the Defence in obtaining evidence in *Republika Srpska*. The contention of the Defence was that the balance between the parties was too much in favour of the Prosecution and the support of the Trial Chamber for the defence case had been insufficient to overcome these difficulties. In its judgment, the Appeals Chamber explained that the dimension of the duty of the Trial Chamber to enact the principle of equality could not extend beyond the issue of the relevant orders to assist the Defence in the preparation of its case. That is to say, the principle of equality of arms is procedural and does not cover acts that are outside the control of the Tribunal. In particular, the Chamber held that '"equality of arms" implies that each party must be afforded a reasonable opportunity to present his case—including his evidence—under conditions that do not place him at a substantial disadvantage vis-à-vis his opponent. . . . There is nothing in the ECHR case law that

---

[119] In this respect see, e.g., the judgment of the ECourtHR in *Ruiz-Mateos* v. *Spain*, 23 June 1993 (Series A–262), paras. 63–68, or in *Bendedau* v. *France*, 24 February 1994 (Series A–284A), both at **www.echr.coe.int/Eng/Judgments.htm**.

[120] Cf. A. Ashworth, *The Criminal Process: An Evaluative Study* (Oxford: OUP, 1994), at 66, where the author states that '[this] is a principle that has emerged from the jurisprudence of the European Court of Human Rights. It is not stated explicitly in the Convention itself, although we have seen that Article 6 (1) requires trials to be "fair". The principle is that defendants should have the same access to documents, to records and to other evidence as the Prosecution.' Cf. also the report of the ECommHR in *Öfner and Hopfinger* v. *Austria* (1962), 6 *Yearbook* 676.

[121] See D. Mundis, 'From "Common Law" Towards "Civil law": The Evolution of the ICTY Rule of Procedure and Evidence', in 14 *LJIL* (2001), 367–382.

suggests that the principle is applicable to conditions, outside the control of a court, that prevented a party from securing the attendance of certain witnesses. All the cases considered applications that the judicial body had the power to grant'.[122]

The Chamber added:

> The Appeals Chamber is of the view that under the Statute of the International Tribunal the principle of equality of arms must be given a more liberal interpretation than that normally upheld with regard to proceedings before domestic courts. This principle means that the Prosecution and the Defence must be equal before the Trial Chamber. It follows that the Chamber must provide every practicable facility it is capable of granting under the Rules and Statute when faced with a request by a party for assistance in presenting its case. The Trial Chambers are mindful of the difficulties encountered by the parties in tracing and gaining access to evidence in the territory of the former Yugoslavia where some States have not been forthcoming in comply-ing with their legal obligation to co-operate with the Tribunal. Provisions under the Statute and the Rules exist to alleviate the difficulties faced by the parties so that each side may have equal access to witnesses. The Chambers are empowered to issue such orders, summonses, subpoenas, warrants and transfer orders as may be necessary for the purposes of an investigation or for the preparation or conduct of the trial.[123]

On the other hand, the principle of equality of arms has been invoked on various occasions by the Prosecution, arguing that there should be a sort of symmetry between the rights of the accused and the recognition of certain powers of the prosecution.[124] The Trial Chamber must ensure the fairness of the trial also with a view to preserving the prerogatives of the prosecution. However, it is certainly incorrect to argue that there is a right of the prosecution that corresponds to the right of the accused to a fair hearing in full equality.[125] This is a right specifically attributed to the defendant and not to *any party* to the proceedings.[126] Therefore, the interpretation given by various Chambers of the ICTY, inspired by the notion of a general symmetry between the rights of the two parties, cannot be fully shared.[127] In this sense, the abovementioned passage of the *Tadić* Appeals Chamber judgment does not seem fully convincing.

---

[122] Appeals Chamber Judgment, *Tadić* (IT–94–1–A), 15 July 1999, paras. 48–49.

[123] *Ibidem*, para. 52.

[124] Cf. R. May and M. Wierda, note 10 above, at 760.

[125] This seems also to be the idea expressed by the ICTY Trial Chamber: Decision on Prosecution Motion for Clarification in respect of the Application of Rules 65-*ter*, 66(B) and 67 (C), (IT–00–39&40–PT) *Kraijšnik and Plavšić* 1 August 2001.

[126] May and Wierda show persuasively that '[the] principle of equality of arms is used to provide a safeguard for the accused': note 124 above, at 757.

[127] It has been correctly noted, referring to disclosure obligations in the ICC, that there is no perfect symmetry between the Prosecution and the Defence: cf. M. Shaw, 'The International Criminal Court—Some Procedural and Evidential Issues', in 3 *JACL* (1998), 65–96, at 77.

Naturally, the right to a fair trial is recognized in the Statute of the ICC. Article 67 establishes that 'the accused shall be entitled . . . to a fair hearing'. It is premature to say what problems the Court will have to face in the actual administration of this right. Nevertheless, the right to a fair trial is one of the fundamental principles for the functioning of the Court. A discussion of the problems encountered by the *ad hoc* Tribunals may, thus, be instructive from the perspective of the establishment of the Court, because many of the problems faced by the Tribunals are also likely to emerge before the Court. It is, however, clear that in some respects, compared to the provisions of the *ad hoc* Tribunal, the ICC Statute is likely to ensure better protection for the right to a fair trial.

2. *Problems of effectiveness and expeditiousness of trials: the influence of the model adopted and the right of the accused to be tried without undue delay*

One of the main problems that the Tribunals have to face is the length of the proceedings. While in the first three years the ICTY did not carry out any judicial activity, the problem that the Tribunal now has to face is that it has more defendants in custody than it can realistically try. With the first trials running and its increased workload, the Tribunal faced the problem of limited resources for handling the new situation. The Security Council amended the Statute of the ICTY to add three more judges composing a new Trial Chamber. New courtrooms were built and additional staff hired.[128]

The difficulties and length of proceedings, however, were due not only to the limited structural capacity of the Tribunal; there was also a problem linked to the type of procedure adopted before the Tribunal.

The impression is that, in the context of international criminal justice, the characteristics of adversarial proceedings lead to very long trials with no real increased benefit for the rights of accused persons, who, in the system of the *ad hoc* Tribunals, are generally detained during trial.[129] It is well known that, in general, in the adversarial system only a minority of cases (10 per cent) are dealt with according to the normal trial procedure,[130] since cases are usually concluded through alternative proceedings, such as guilty plea procedures.[131] Additionally, it should be noted that normally in common law adversarial

---

[128] Cf. Fourth Annual Report (UNGA 52/375), 18 September 1997, Fifth Annual Report (UNGA 53/219), 10 August 1998, Sixth Annual Report (UNGA 54/187), 25 August 1999.

[129] This is one of the traits that represent an important deviation from most adversarial systems.

[130] See, e.g., Hatchard, Huber and Vogler (eds.), note 64 above, at 224–225. Cf. also C. Emmins, *A Practical Approach to Criminal Procedure* (3rd edn., London: Financial Training Publications, 1985), at 147.

[131] Up to October 2002, there were 7 cases of guilty plea before the ICTY (Erdemović, Jelisić, Todorović, Dosen, Kolundžija, Sikirica, and Simić) and 3 before the ICTR (Kambanda, Serushago, Ruggiu).

proceedings there is the possibility for defendants to be released on bail. This right does not really exist before the Tribunals and provisional release has been granted only exceptionally in a few cases. It should, then, be recognized that in this respect many problems were caused by the host country's fierce opposition to an accused being released on bail in its territory. This is an element that should be addressed in the future in the relationship between the Tribunals and the host country.[132] Moreover, it should be made very clear to the Netherlands, especially with a view to the actual establishment of the permanent Court, that it is a part of the duties of the host country to have an open attitude towards the possibility of releasing the accused on its territory.[133] In addition, it may be suggested that the opportunity for release of defendants pending trial should be taken into account and possibly explicitly mentioned in the Headquarters Agreement between the Court and the host State. The unwillingness of the host country to assume the responsibility of the accused's security does not seem to be a valid justification for withholding release to an accused who would otherwise be entitled to it. This solution is inconsistent with the rights of the accused to the extent that the refusal is unconditional.

The other side of the duty of the Chamber to ensure an expeditious trial is the right of the accused to be tried without undue delay, which amounts to a right to have an expeditious trial,[134] and to which the Chambers of the Tribunals have shown an increasing commitment. In this respect, it seems important to discuss some particularly significant decisions and orders of the Chambers of the Tribunals. Finally, attention should be devoted to various amendments to the Rules of Procedure and Evidence aimed at accelerating the procedure, which are, in a sense, the result of the abovementioned jurisprudence.

In particular, it is interesting to analyse the impact of a decision of a Trial Chamber on a request by the Prosecutor to amend an indictment and various decisions and orders imposing an obligation on the parties to transmit certain documents to the Trial Chamber. Moreover, reference should be made to the *Barayagwiza* case before the ICTR.[135]

In *Kovacević*, the Trial Chamber on 5 March 1998 issued a decision denying a request by the Prosecutor for leave to amend the indictment. This decision

---

[132] On the early relationship between the ICTY and The Netherlands, see J. Schutte, 'Legal and Practical Implications, from the Perspective of the Host Country, Relating to the Establishment of the International Tribunal for the Former Yugoslavia', in 5 *CLF* (1994), 423–450.

[133] A recent amendment to the Rules, adopted at the 23rd Plenary Session in December 2001, provides that the Chamber must always hear the views of the State in which the accused is authorized (and obliged) to reside if provisionally released pending trial.

[134] Decision Trial Chamber, *Kovacević* (IT–97–24–PT), 5 March 1998.

[135] Cf. the Appeals Chamber Decision of 3 November 1999 and the Decision by which it was reversed on 31 March 2000.

was taken on the ground, *inter alia*, that the Chamber had to ensure respect for the right of the accused to be tried without undue delay. In the case at issue the accused had already been in detention for seven months awaiting trial and, moreover, the indictment against him had been confirmed months before his arrest. Furthermore, the Prosecution had already announced its decision to request leave to amend the indictment almost twelve months before it actually did so. Therefore, the Chamber deplored 'the delay in filing this request and trusts that no Trial Chamber in the future will be faced so late with an application of this kind'. The Chamber refused to grant the Prosecutor's request to amend the indictment on the grounds that it would have led to a further postponement of the trial and would have thus infringed upon the right to be tried without undue delay. Subsequently, the Appeals Chamber, rather surprisingly, reversed the decision of the Trial Chamber and allowed the amendment of the indictment.[136]

In order to ensure the effectiveness and expediency of the proceedings the Trial Chamber in *Dokmanović* issued an order for transmission to the Chamber of witness statements before the opening of trial proceedings.[137] The aim of the order was to enable the judges to determine the relevant issues and thus to avoid wasting as much time as possible. In *Kordić* and *Čerkez* a similar approach was taken with reference to the admission of the so-called 'Tulica dossier'.[138] Moreover, again in *Blaškić* the Chamber decided not to hear certain witnesses on the ground that a sufficient number of witnesses had already been heard on the same topic.[139] Another indication in this direction was the admission into evidence of transcripts of other proceedings.[140]

These decisions and orders progressively contributed to a modification of the system. It may be questioned whether this approach, reflected in the various amendments to the RPE, was appropriate in that it deviated radically from the original adversarial model. In this respect, however, two important elements must be considered. First, although predominant in the Statute, the adversarial model was not compelling. Secondly, the judges were faced with a particularly difficult situation that, given the absence of any reform, could have jeopardized the entire mission of the Tribunal.[141] These two aspects

---

[136] Oral decision delivered on 29 May 1998 and written decision on 2 July 1998. In this respect S. Murphy, 'Progress and Jurisprudence of the International Criminal Tribunal for the former Yugoslavia', in 93 *AJIL* (1999), 57–97, at 73.

[137] Cf. Order of Trial Chamber, *Dokmanović* (IT–95–13a–PT), 28 November 1997.

[138] Cf. Trial Chamber Decision, *Kordić* and *Čerkez* (IT–95–14/2–T), on the Prosecution application to admit the Tulića Report and Dossier into evidence, 28 July 1999.

[139] *Ibidem.*

[140] Appeals Chamber Decision on Prosecutor's Appeal on Admissibility of Evidence, *Aleksovski* (IT–95–14/1–A), 16 February 1999.

[141] In an interview given to the newspaper *Libération*, Judge Jorda affirmed that if all the persons against whom a warrant of arrest had been issued had been arrested or had surrendered, the Tribunal would have been overwhelmed with cases and would thus have found itself in a very difficult situation: *Libération*, 5 July 1999.

allowed for a progressive departure from the original model and led to the adoption of innovative solutions, not necessarily derived from any particular system, constituting an interesting attempt to reconcile fairness and effectiveness.[142]

The administration of justice requires time. However, a balance must be found between the time necessary to conduct the proceedings and the sacrifices imposed on the persons charged. The *right to be tried without undue delay* is certainly *distinct* from the right contained in the provisions on detention on remand to be *tried within a reasonable time*.[143] It is submitted, however, that within the context of the ICTY (and the ICTR) it is more difficult to specify the difference between these two rights. So far the Chambers have dealt with these issues separately. The Chambers of the Tribunal have decided to focus attention on the concept of *reasonable time* when referring to a request for provisional release, and they have adopted the limit of *undue delay* when dealing with preliminary matters arising after the initial appearance.[144]

In an order dated 20 December 1996, the Trial Chamber in *Blaškić* rejected a motion brought by the accused for provisional release, holding that the period of eight months could not be considered beyond the limits of what 'reasonable time' meant.[145] This is particularly the case when the accused is in privileged conditions of detention, as was the case for Blaškić.[146] The Chamber also affirmed that, in the system of the Tribunal, there is a certain degree of similarity between the requirements of the right to be tried without undue delay and the right to be tried within a reasonable time. The latter is generally granted to persons accused in criminal proceedings and kept in detention on remand.[147]

It is important to keep in mind the relationship between expeditiousness and fair trial. Article 67, paragraph 1 ICC St. guarantees the accused a fair hearing in the same way as does Article 21, paragraph 2 ICTY Statute (Article 20.2 ICTR St.). Similarly, both Statutes provide for the right of the accused

[142] Combining various aspects of the different systems may be risky in that the balance found may not be appropriate.

[143] See e.g. Article 9.3 ICCPR.

[144] It should, however, be noted that given the practice of almost automatic pre-trial detention in the *ad hoc* Tribunals' system the difference tends to fade and implies the need for trial 'within a reasonable time', since the accused is normally in custody.

[145] Even longer periods have not been considered unreasonable: e.g., in *Krajišnik*, the Trial Chamber held that 'in the instant case the length of detention, although long [18 months], does not exceed the periods which the European Court of Human Rights has found reasonable': Decision on Momčilo Krajišnik's Notice of Motion for Provisional Release, Decision on Momčilo Krajišnik's Notice of Motion for Provisional Release, *Krajišnik and Plavšić* (IT–00–39 and 40–PT), 8 October 2001, para. 22.

[146] Pursuant to an order of the President on modification of the conditions of detention, *Blaškić* (IT–95–14–T), 2 April 1996.

[147] Cf. Trial Chamber Order denying a motion for provisional release, *Blaškić* (IT–95–14–T), 20 December 1996, and also Article 9 ICCPR and Article 5 ECHR, which establish the right for a detained accused to be tried within a reasonable time.

to be tried without undue delay. However, the most important rule relating to expeditiousness is Article 66, paragraph 3, ICC St., which obliges the competent Chamber to 'confer with the parties and adopt such procedures as are necessary to facilitate the fair and expeditious conduct of the proceedings'. This is a rule that seems to be reflected in some of the amendments to the ICTY RPE, such as the duties of the Pre-trial Judge and the organization of the pre-trial conference.

The efforts of the judges to ensure expeditious proceedings have been reflected in amendments to the RPE. The most relevant amendments in this respect have been the adoption of the rules on the Status Conference (Rule 65-*bis* RPE ICTY) and the Pre-Trial Conferences (Rule 73-*bis* RPE ICTY), including the Pre-Defence Conference (Rule 73-*ter* RPE ICTY). Additionally, great importance has been attached to the introduction of the Pre-trial Judge (Rule 65-*ter* RPE ICTY), the admission of written evidence (Rule 92-*bis* RPE ICTY), the power of the Trial Chamber to obtain a series of documents related to the presentation of evidence, and to decide not to hear certain witnesses (Rule 73 RPE ICTY).

These amendments to the RPE have certainly brought about a modification of the procedural system before the Tribunals (although most changes have so far affected only the ICTY). The original adversarial trial has now been largely modified. The possibility for judges to receive the supporting material or summaries of witness statements is a departure from the abstract dimension of the model. The idea of the 'virginity' of the judge (in the sense that he or she should have no knowledge of the facts of the case, other than those put before him or her in open court), which is essential to purely adversarial proceedings, is subverted by his or her previous knowledge of the declarations made by witnesses to the prosecution during the pre-trial phase, given that the oral presentation of evidence (principle of orality) is impaired by the communication of the content of those statements. Moreover, the possibility for the judge who reviewed the indictment to be a member of the Trial Chamber definitely places the ICTY procedural system outside the scope of an adversarial procedural model. This, however, does not automatically imply that the procedure currently adopted, as it has been reshaped by the most recent amendments, is less appropriate in terms of the protection of the rights of the accused, or less fair. On the contrary, it has been stated at the outset that international criminal proceedings are conducted in a context that does not necessarily adapt itself to the rigid requirements of a procedural model. In this respect, it must be restated that the adversarial/non-adversarial dichotomy should not become prescriptive. Nonetheless, independently of the departure from the abstract model, the participation of the confirming judge in the Trial or Appeals Chamber in a case he or she has confirmed is potentially contrary to the principles of impartiality and the presumption of innocence. Although, as mentioned above, there are some arguments that may attenuate conflict between recent amendments and such principles, it would seem appropriate for the Tribunals to refrain from including confirming judges in panels for trial or appeal.

The situation is certainly different in the ICC Statute. In this context States took a lengthy period of time over confronting views and drafting much more detailed Rules. Thus the model adopted in the ICC Statute is to a large extent more complete and stringent. However, it is still questionable whether the combination found in the ICC Statute is more coherent and will ensure speedier trials.[147a]

ICTY judges have progressively adjusted the system of the *ad hoc* Tribunals to the needs of international criminal justice. They have tried to combine with great sensitivity the various needs of these international trials with the rights of the accused and the interests of justice. This has been a particularly arduous endeavour, as it does not fall precisely within the scope of judicial competence. In this respect it must certainly be conceded that if the power of drafting the Rules attributed to the judges may, on the one hand, enable them to address difficult issues more effectively, on the other hand, it has allowed for repeated (and largely unjustified) criticism.

3. The right of the accused to be informed of the charges and the question of cumulative or alternative charges

One of the key elements of a fair trial is to provide the accused with all necessary information to prepare his or her defence.[148] There are two aspects to this right: one is addressed through disclosure (and will be discussed below in the next section), and the other is linked to the presentation of charges made by the Prosecutor in the indictment. The way in which charges are presented is a fundamental basis for the accused to prepare his or her defence.

It is argued that the exercise of this right may be seriously impaired by the practice of the prosecution of charging the accused cumulatively with more crimes under the Statute in respect of the same act or transaction. The Chambers of the Tribunal have dealt with this issue on many occasions and have constantly held that such an approach is generally admissible, provided that the crimes charged contain an element of differentiation.

First, it is necessary to clarify that there are no specific provisions dealing with this matter in the Statutes and in the Rules of Procedure. Therefore, the Chambers have had to base their judgments on general principles of international criminal law and on the principles common to the major legal systems (as well as on principles of legal logic).

[147a] However, it is interesting to note that in the ICC system the Trial Chamber may be entitled to consult the record of the confirmation proceedings held before the Pre-Trial Chamber, which includes the materials in support of the indictment, see Chapter 1 above note 88[a].

[148] Cf. ECourtHR, *Bendedoun* v. *France*, 24 February 1994 (Series A–284), **www.echr.coe.int/ Eng/Judgments.htm**, para. 53.

In *Akayesu*, a Trial Chamber of the ICTR held that there are three instances in which cumulative charges may be justified:[149] first, where offences charged have different elements; secondly, where the provisions creating the offences protect different interests; thirdly, where it is necessary to record a conviction for both offences in order fully to describe what the accused did. In *Tadić*, a Trial Chamber of the ICTY had taken a practical approach and expressed the view that the matter had only theoretical relevance.[150] The important thing was to address the problem, and the most appropriate means of doing so was to take into account the various norms violated by the conduct of the accused at the sentencing stage. As a conclusion, the Chamber took the view that concurrent sentences had to be imposed for offences cumulatively charged.[151] Such a solution may not be intrinsically unfair for the accused, but it does not conform to the idea of a rigorous application of the law, and of legal certainty about the outcome of trial. Moreover, it had the disadvantage of not offering precise guidelines regarding the law on this matter.

These were the precedents before the *ad hoc* Tribunals when a Trial Chamber, in *Kupreškić*, had to deal with the question of cumulative charges. In its judgment the Trial Chamber discussed the matter thoroughly and reached important conclusions. The *Kupreškić* judgment has the undeniable merit of trying to suggest a *principled way of addressing this question*.

The Trial Chamber identified two main implications of the problem of cumulative charges: from the viewpoint of substantive law and that of procedural law. Naturally, there is an additional aspect that specifically concerns sentencing[152] as an autonomous stage (this issue will be further addressed in Chapter 5 on sentencing issues).

Referring to substantive law, the Trial Chamber identified two main hypotheses: first, when 'various elements of a general criminal transaction . . . infringe different provisions',[153] such as cases in which 'there exist distinct offences; that is, an accumulation of separate acts, each violative of a different provision';[154] secondly, when 'one and the same act or transaction simultaneously' violates more rules.[155] The Trial Chamber first, identified some general principles of law resulting both from common law and civil law and subsequently suggested a solution according to which a single act can be

---

[149] Cf. ICTR Trial Chamber, Judgment, *Akayesu* (ICTR–96–4–T), 2 September 1998.

[150] Cf. ICTY Trial Chamber Decision on the form of the indictment, *Tadić* (IT–94–1–PT), 14 November 1995. In the light of the case law of the Tribunals, this is probably true. Nonetheless, it seems interesting to try to explore this matter further.

[151] It is interesting to note that the same practical approach has been taken in *Delalić et al.*, (IT–96–21–PT), 15 November 1996 (on a motion by Delić) and in *Furundžija* (IT–95–17/1–PT), 29 April 1998.

[152] The Trial Chamber Judgment, *Kupreškić* (IT–95–16–T), 14 January 2000, classifies the issues for discussion only under the first two headings: substance and procedure (para. 670). However, it is here submitted that the sentencing approach deserves separate standing.

[153] *Ibidem*, para. 678 (a).   [154] *Ibidem*, para. 678 (c).   [155] *Ibidem*, para. 679.

charged cumulatively under two different headings (for example, crimes against humanity and war crimes) provided that two requirements are met. These are that (a) the offences charged contain different elements; and (b) the offences protect different values. In contrast to the approach taken by the Chamber in *Akayesu*, the Trial Chamber considered that cumulative charging could be justified only when the two requirements were *jointly* met. Furthermore, the third criterion adopted in *Akayesu*, i.e. the need to record a conviction for both crimes, was considered by the Chamber as used, in general, only *ad abundantiam* in conjunction with the other two.

More recently, however, the Appeals Chamber rejected the approach suggested in *Kupreškić* by the Trial Chamber. First, in *Delalić and others*,[156] and subsequently in *Jelisić*[157] and in *Kupreškić* itself,[158] the Appeals Chamber held that there is no need to look at the values protected by the provisions incriminating certain acts or conduct. In *Celebici*, the Appeals Chamber articulated a two-pronged test to be applied, holding that 'reasons of fairness to the accused and the consideration that only distinct crimes may justify multiple convictions, lead to the conclusion that multiple criminal convictions entered under different statutory provisions but based on the same conduct are permissible only if each statutory provision involved has a materially distinct element not contained in the other'. One element is materially distinct from the other if it requires proof of a fact not required by the other. Where this test is not satisfied, the Chamber must decide in relation to which offence it will enter a conviction. This should be done on the basis of the principle that the conviction under the more specific provision should be upheld. Thus, if two provisions regulate a set of facts, one of which contains an additional materially distinct element, then a conviction should be entered only under that provision. The Appeals Chamber, however, rejected the idea that importance should be given to the values protected by the incriminating provisions, in order to determine which offence is more specific (among those cumulatively charged). Therefore, notwithstanding the undeniable merit of suggesting a principled approach, the Trial Chamber judgment in *Kupreškić* can no longer be considered as a point of reference.

Nonetheless, on the issue of procedural law, the Trial Chamber had correctly identified two fundamental principles that should guide the decision on cumulative charges.[159] The Chamber considered that these principles were the rights of the accused and the need to ensure that the Prosecutor is in a position to exercise fully his or her mandate to prosecute very serious crimes of international concern. The Chamber suggested that the prosecution might adopt the approach of making *cumulative charges* 'whenever it contends that

---

[156] Appeals Chamber Judgment, *Delalić et al.* (IT–96–21–A), 20 February 2001.
[157] Appeals Chamber Judgment, *Jelisić* (IT–95–10–A), 5 July 2001.
[158] Appeals Chamber Judgment, *Kupreškić et al.* (IT–96–16–A), 23 October 2001.
[159] Trial Chamber Judgment paras. 583 ff.

the facts charged *violate simultaneously* two or *more provisions* of the Statute'. On the other hand, it also stated that the Prosecutor should formulate charges in the *alternative* 'whenever an offence appears to be in breach of more than one provision, *depending on the elements* of the crime the Prosecution *is able to prove*'.[160] In this respect, the Appeals Chamber disagreed with the approach of the Trial Chamber and held that cumulative charging on the basis of the same acts 'is to be allowed in light of the fact that, prior to the presentation of all of the evidence, it is not possible to determine to a certainty which of the charges brought against an accused will be proven'.[161] Actually there is no substantial difference between the two approaches, in so far as the Prosecutor is entitled to present charges for both crimes. However, the suggestion that alternative charging should be preferred to cumulative charging was, from a theoretical perspective, more logical.

To sum up, there are three perspectives on the issue of cumulative charges (substantive law, procedural law, and sentencing). The multifaceted nature of this issue makes the solution of the various problems less dramatic from the point of view of the rights of the accused. In effect, the protection of the rights of the accused can be found at each of the various stages of the procedure.[162]

There is a final aspect of cumulative charging that ought to be mentioned, which does not relate to the offences *per se*, but to the various forms the participation of an accused in a crime may take. In this respect, it seems rather inappropriate to allow the Prosecutor to charge an accused under both Article 7.1 ICTY St. (direct participation) and Article 7.3 ICTY St. (forms of superior responsibility). The reason is that the accused should be in a position to understand what is the form of contribution to the crimes he is charged with and thus be able to organize his defence accordingly.[163] Indeed, there may be cases where formulating a defence against charges of direct perpetration may be in conflict with a defence trying to show that there is no superior responsibility.[164]

---

[160] Trial Chamber Judgment, para. 590 (*emphasis added*).

[161] Cf. *Delalić et al.* Appeals Chamber Judgment, para. 400. With all due respect it seems that this approach is not fair to the defendant, who is exposed to conviction for whatever the prosecution is able to prove. On the other hand, it seems that a correct approach would be to ask the prosecution specifically to identify the charges on which a conviction is sought. In other words the issues to be proved should be precisely set out before evidence is offered. In this respect, both the Delalić and the Kupreškić approaches are not satisfactory.

[162] The main disadvantage of this practical solution from the point of view of the rights of the accused is that facing multiple charges presenting overlapping elements may adversely affect the preparation of his defence or his right of appeal.

[163] In this respect it seems that even alternative charging does not ensure adequate protection, in that the accused will have to prepare his defence both on direct participation and superior responsibility, two forms of participation that seem intrinsically incompatible (either one planned, ordered, or committed, or one failed to prevent).

[164] For example, a defendant who is charged with direct participation in a crime may focus on trying to show that he was not at the scene of the crime when the offence was committed. This line of defence, however, would not be effective in rebutting charges on the grounds of superior

Broadly speaking, the general approach adopted by the Tribunal is to allow cumulative charges and to solve problems, if any, of duplication at the sentencing stage. In this respect, however, it should be noted that the attitude of the Chambers was not uniform. For example, the Appeals Chamber in *Tadić* found the accused guilty of crimes cumulatively charged.[165] Whilst in *Erdemović*, where the accused had been charged in respect of the same transaction with both war crimes and crimes against humanity, the accused was given the choice of pleading to one of the two charges, and he in fact pleaded guilty to crimes against humanity. In that case the Appeals Chamber held that the first guilty plea of the accused should be considered void, since he had not been duly informed of the increased gravity of crimes against humanity as opposed to war crimes. It is logical to deduce that the rationale behind this decision was to consider that the accused could not be guilty of both, but had to choose whether he would enter a guilty plea to crimes against humanity or war crimes. When he entered a plea for the second time, Erdemović pleaded guilty to the war crime charge and a sentence was passed only for this crime.

The right of the accused to be informed in detail of the charges so that he or she can prepare his or her case is not, however, thoroughly protected by the approach that defers everything to the sentencing stage. It does not seem that the ICC Statute offers a more definite solution to this issue. There is a provision that suggests the approach of treating the matter as a mere sentencing issue. This interpretation seems justified by the rules of Article 78 of the ICC Statute which, although they refer to multiple convictions, do not specify whether for the same or different conduct. Nothing more specific on this issue has been provided for in the RPE. We must therefore await further judicial practice, in the hope that it will shed some light on the matter.

4. *The right to have adequate time and facilities*

(a) The right to have adequate time

In general, upon arrest, persons accused before the Tribunals receive a copy of the indictment, the review of indictment, and a statement of the rights of the accused in a language they understand.[166] Subsequently, they are transferred to the UN Detention Units (either in Arusha, for the ICTR, or The Hague, for the ICTY) to prepare for their initial appearance, which takes place before the Trial Chamber to which the case is assigned (Rule 62 of both

responsibility. Allowing the Prosecutor to bring charges on both grounds may be prejudicial both to the rights of the accused and to the interest of justice, in that it results in longer trials with presentation of presumably irrelevant evidence on at least one of the grounds.

[165] This was the approach followed by the Appeals Chamber in *Tadić*, 15 July 1999 (IT–94–1–A), paras. 233 ff.

[166] According to Rule 55 RPE ICTY each certified copy of the arrest warrant 'shall be accompanied by a copy of the indictment . . . and a statement of the rights of the accused'.

RPEs). It seems clear that, at least from the moment of his (or her) arrival at the UN Detention Unit, the accused must receive adequate facilities and time for the preparation of his or her case. These facilities must be initially directed to the preparation of the initial appearance, the hearing during which the accused will be asked to enter a plea. The rights provided for in Article 21, paragraph 4(b), correspond to continuing duties which are implicitly imposed on the Tribunal as a whole, even if naturally the main duty to assist the accused falls on the Registrar and his or her staff.

Concerning the issue of adequate time for the preparation of the defence, it is clear that this provision must be read in correlation with the right of the accused to be tried without undue delay and that it is the duty of the Trial Chambers to ensure expeditious trials. The time for the preparation of the defence cannot be indefinite. Judges must always try to balance the need for the accused to have time to prepare his defence with his right to be tried without undue delay. Moreover, they must take into account that the duty of the Trial Chambers is to ensure an expeditious trial. This duty is closely linked to the need to respect the right of the accused to be tried without undue delay, and is reinforced by paragraph 1 of Article 20 of the ICTY Statute (Article 19 ICTR St.), which imposes a general duty on the Chambers. Thus, it might be difficult for the Chamber to take a decision in the case of a conflict between a claim by an accused to have more time to prepare (and therefore a request to postpone the trial) and the general interests of justice. An expeditious trial is not only in the interests of the accused. The provision on expedition, contained in Article 20 ICTY St. (Article 19 ICTR St.) mentioned above, should not be construed as a provision granting rights to the accused, but rather as a norm that imposes a duty on the Trial Chamber in the public interest. Hence, the Chamber should also take into account other elements that may suggest accelerating the proceedings to satisfy the concern of the international community that justice be done. It is obvious that such a decision should be taken having cautious regard to the circumstances of each case and to the reasons time is needed by the accused. In addition, the procedural behaviour of the parties could help to determine whether a postponement would be appropriate. To date, however, the Tribunals have never had to face the problem in these terms.

(b) The right to have adequate facilities

The right of the accused to have facilities for the preparation of his defence includes the right to communicate with counsel. The judges, when drafting the Rules of Procedure, preferred to leave the details to the subordinate regulations of the Tribunal contained in the Rules on Detention, in the Regulations concerning mail, in the Directive on the Assignment of Defence Counsel, and in the Directive for the Registry. These texts contain a number of provisions giving shape to the right to have facilities and regarding the right to communicate with counsel. For example, in the Directive on the Assignment of Defence Counsel, rules have been included to provide for office space for Defence Counsel;[167] moreover, the Tribunal has made the Tribunal's library and reference resources available to Defence Counsel.[168] Presumably the same entitlements would have to be extended to an accused deciding to defend himself in person without the assistance of counsel. In addition, since many defence lawyers are not permanently resident in Arusha or in The Hague, adequate means of communicating and corresponding with them have been furnished.[169] Finally, the right to communicate with counsel has been protected and action has been taken to make communication possible even on the premises of the Tribunal, so as to give the accused the possibility of discussing any relevant matter with his or her Defence Counsel during breaks in the hearings.[170]

This right is provided for in the ICC Statute; however, neither the Statute nor the Rules of Procedure furnish any more details. It is clear that the extent to which the right is protected will inevitably depend on the functioning of the Court when it becomes operational. In general, it seems that this should be the approach to this issue. It is, however, important to state that the right to receive adequate time and facilities depends upon the actual circumstances of each case and its implementation has to be evaluated on a case by case basis.

5. *The right to be present at trial (the issue of trial* in absentia*)*

The essential difficulty with the issue of *in absentia* trials is basically due to a problem of fundamental choices. It is often contended that they are by their very nature a violation of the right of the accused to be present, thus leading their opponents to claim that they are intrinsically unfair. It is argued here

---

[167] See, e.g., Third Annual Report of the President of the ICTY to the UN: 'Facilities for defence counsel have improved over the last year. Two rooms adjacent to the courtroom have been allocated exclusively to defence counsel and are equipped with a computer, printer, fax machine and telephones' (at 112), **<www.un.org/icty/thir96tc.htm>**.

[168] As a result of financial and logistical constraints, 'the library of the Tribunal became operational only in late 1995. Prior to that, jurists at the Tribunal made use of the other international law libraries in The Hague. The library serves as a documentation and research centre for the different organs of the Tribunal *as well as for defence counsel*' (emphasis added) (para. 145), cf. Third Annual Report of the President of the ICTY to the UN, on Internet at **<www.un.org/icty/thir96tc.htm>**.

[169] Lockers have, therefore, been assigned to counsel for service of documents upon them when they are in The Hague, and for the filing of documents by counsel with the court. When counsel are not in The Hague, the usual means of communication is by facsimile; however, the quality of facsimile transmission in the former Yugoslavia is often poor, and this method of communication remains problematic.

[170] Office space has been provided for Defence Counsel 'to speak with their client during breaks in the hearings, as an alternative to interviewing him or her in the cells in the basement': Third Annual Report, note 168 above, 112.

that such an approach to the question is wrong. Provided that the accused has all the necessary guarantees to be able to exercise his or her right to be present and intervene at trial, it is unjustified to consider trials *in absentia* as a violation of the rights of the accused. As a matter of principle, it cannot be excluded that the accused may well prefer to be tried *in absentia* as part of an intentional strategy of defence. This seems particularly reasonable in a system that often requires that the accused be detained pending trial.

On the contrary, it is submitted that acceptance of trials *in absentia* is a policy choice that has more to do with the general objectives of international criminal justice than with the rights of the accused. It may certainly be reasonable for other purposes to exclude *in absentia* proceedings. For example, one might think that it is undesirable to disclose evidence in open court, or that there can be no real investigation of the truth without the contribution of the accused in person, or that it is pointless to hold a trial if the person cannot ultimately be sentenced. All these are reasonable (albeit not necessarily acceptable) arguments for excluding *in absentia* proceedings. However, one thing should be made clear: the argument that trials *in absentia* would violate the rights of the accused is not compelling.[171]

In his report to the Security Council on the establishment of the Tribunal for the Former Yugoslavia, the UN Secretary-General affirmed that the accused must be present.[172] The Report did not state that the accused 'has the right to be present' but that he 'shall be present'. As a consequence, in the Rules of Procedure and Evidence of the UN Tribunals trials *in absentia* have been excluded. It seems, however, that they are not forbidden because they are contrary to the rights of the accused, but rather because it has been considered that they would be *inappropriate* in the light of the effectiveness of prosecuting the crimes under the Tribunal's jurisdiction.

An interesting indication in this direction emerged in the decision of the Appeals Chamber on the issue of the Subpoena to the Republic of Croatia. In this decision not only was the legality of trials *in absentia* accepted in general, but the possibility of holding them was clearly foreseen in the case of persons refusing to comply with orders of the Tribunal in violation of Rule 77 RPE. The Appeals Chamber held that 'if the subpoenaed individual who failed to deliver the documents or appear in court also fails to attend contempt proceedings, *in absentia* proceedings should not be ruled out', and further continued, '[t]he Appeals Chamber finds that, generally speaking, it would not be appropriate to hold *in absentia* proceedings against a person falling under the

---

[171] Professor Abi-Saab noted that '*le droit de l'accusé d'être présent à son procès ne lui donne pas le droit d'entraver la justice*': G. Abi-Saab, 'Droits de l'homme et juridictions, pénales internationales—Convergences et tensions', in R.-J. Dupuy, *Mélanges en l'honneur de Nicolas Valticos—Droit et Justice* (Paris: Pedone, 1999), at 250. See also A. Cassese, *International Criminal Law* (Oxford: OUP, 2003) at 396.

[172] Report of the UN Secretary General to the Security Council pursuant to para. 2 of Resolution 808 (1993) S/25704, para. 101.

primary jurisdiction of the International Tribunal (i.e., persons accused of crimes provided for in Articles 2–5 of the Statute). Indeed, even when the accused has clearly waived his right to be tried in his presence (Article 21, paragraph 4(d) of the Statute), it would prove extremely difficult or even impossible for an international criminal court to determine the innocence or guilt of that accused. By contrast, *in absentia* proceedings may be exceptionally warranted, in cases involving contempt of the International Tribunal, where a person charged fails to appear in court, thus obstructing the administration of justice . . . If such *in absentia* proceedings were to be instituted, all the fundamental rights pertaining to a fair trial would need to be safeguarded. Among other things, although the individual's absence would have to be regarded under certain circumstances as a waiver of his right to be tried in his presence, he should be offered the choice of a counsel.'[173]

Moreover, the fact that trials *in absentia* are not *per se* a violation of the right of the accused to be present has been confirmed by the Expert Group mandated by the General Assembly to review the activity of the Tribunals.[174] In particular, the Report of the Expert Group suggests that trials *in absentia* should be considered as an option to resort to, at least under specific circumstances.[175]

In the system of the Tribunals a sort of limitation on the right to be present can be found in the proceedings under Rule 61 of both RPEs, intended as a possible reaction to the non-execution of the arrest warrants issued against the defendants. These proceedings pursue various objectives. First, they seek to allow the voice of the victims to be heard. Secondly, they aim at public exposure of the evidence collected by the Prosecutor so as to illustrate to the public the magnitude of the crimes attributed to the accused and, if possible, prompt the indicted person to turn up to defend him- or herself. Thirdly, there is the clear intention to put some pressure on the relevant national or international authorities to apprehend the accused. After a 'Rule 61 hearing' the indicted person can no longer be considered as not being informed of the indictment issued against him or her. In particular, he or she could be (but this is only a possible interpretation) considered to have waived his right to be present so that a trial *in absentia* could be reasonably undertaken.[176] The different philosophy behind the two traditional models of criminal trial (adversarial

---

[173] Decision of the Appeals Chamber on the Subpoena, 29 October 1997, at 1863 of the Case file (para. 59). It is important to note that the Trial Chamber did not say that trials *in absentia* are forbidden under the Statute or that they are contrary to human rights; in reality it affirmed that they are not appropriate, which is quite a different issue.

[174] See Report of the Expert Group, UN doc. A/54/634, 22 November 1999, at 25.

[175] In particular, this is provided for in the case of provisionally released defendants who do not return to the Tribunal to attend trial.

[176] Cf. M. Niang, 'Le Tribunal Pénal International pour le Rwanda: Et si la Contumace Était Possible!', in 103 *RGDIP* (1999), at 379, 401–403; E. David, 'Le Tribunal International Pénal pour l'ex Yougoslavie', in 25 *RBDI* (1992), 564–597, at 589.

and inquisitorial)[177] here stands out clearly. If the purpose of the trial is to punish the offender then there is no point in proceeding in his or her absence. If, on the contrary, the final goal of the proceedings is to ascertain the truth, then the trial can be held in the absence of the defendant, provided that he or she has been duly informed of the proceedings. This is particularly so when there are good reasons to believe that he or she is voluntarily refusing to appear before the court.

Non-execution of arrest warrants has also been fairly common, particularly in the early stages of activity of the ICTY. However, the issue of a detained accused refusing to participate in the hearings has emerged, apparently, only once. In spring 1998, in *Celebici*, one of the four co-accused refused for two days to be transferred from the Detention Unit to the seat of the Tribunal to participate in his trial on the grounds that he was not feeling well.[178] The interesting thing is that his lawyers clearly stated that the accused was not waiving his right to be present. The accused in question was eventually brought to the Tribunal to attend the hearings; however, this episode indicates the limits of a narrow reading of the right to be present.

Another interesting situation in this respect is the preliminary phase in *Milošević*. In the early stages of the proceedings, the former Serbian President did not recognize the Tribunal as a legitimate institution and thus refused either to appoint a lawyer or to defend himself in person (cf. Chapter 2, Section II.4 above).[179] Notwithstanding the efforts of the Chamber to ensure

---

[177] See in general F. Tulkens, 'La Procédure Pénale en Europe', in M. Delmas-Marty (ed.), *Les Procédures Pénales d'Europe* (*Allemagne, Angleterre et Pays de Galles, Belgique, France, Italie*) (Paris: PUF, 1995).

[178] The accused Zdravko Mucić temporarily broke the monotony of the Celebici trial with his refusal to appear before the court. At the same time, as his defenders specified, the accused '[had] not waived his right to be tried only in his [own] presence'. To make the confusion worse, Mucić's attorneys, Zeljko Olujić and Michael Greaves, offered two different explanations for their client's conduct. First, Olujić claimed that Mucić had remained in the Detention Unit so that he could get in touch with his private investigator who is looking for additional defence evidence on the ground. But Greaves went on to quote 'severe lung problems and hyperventilation' as the reason for his client's absence. Prosecutor Grant Niemann maintained that the accused 'should be brought in this courtroom', while Olujić opposed it, pointing out that 'any forcible attempt to bring him here . . . would violate his basic rights and his [wish] to be absent'. Judge Saad Saood Jan asked the lawyers in the defence and prosecution teams to report on what is done in such situations in their respective countries: the United Kingdom, the United States, Italy, Australia, and Bosnia. It turned out that there are ways everywhere to bring the accused to court forcibly if it is established that the accused has no reason for such conduct. Subsequently, the Presiding Judge, H.E. Judge Karibi Whyte, interrupted the hearing and ordered that the accused be brought before the court within 45 minutes 'by whichever method one can bring him'. The trial resumed in the presence of Mucić, who was feeling his head and back all the time, in order to demonstrate to the judges that he was not feeling well. But they just ignored him, which apparently irritated Mucić even further. In the afternoon, Greaves suggested that his client could go on a hunger strike (Mucić had gone on a hunger strike on the eve of his trial): cf. Tribunal Update 63, Institute for War and Peace, 18–25 April 1998. The same thing seems to have occurred, in the first months of 2002, in the *Barayagwiza* case before the ICTR when the accused refused to attend the hearings.

[179] On this issue cf. Chapter 2, Section II.4 above on the right to legal assistance.

a fair trial, with the appointment of a team of experts as *amici curiae*, this case shows the limits of a rigid approach to the presence of the accused. In *Milošević*, the accused was formally present in the pre-trial stage, but was it really possible to consider that he was participating in his trial? What then would be the difference between a trial *in absentia* and a trial where the accused refused any defence? It is well known that subsequently the situation in the case at issue changed and Mr Milošević decided actively to defend himself, including by cross-examining witnesses. However, the case is indicative of what may occur if an accused refuses to participate in the proceedings.[180]

In the draft Statute for a Permanent Criminal Court prepared by the International Law Commission in 1994, specific provisions were drafted to deal with the case of defendants refusing to participate in the proceedings against them.[181] There are different sets of solutions, from allowing trials *in absentia* to requiring at all costs the presence of the accused, irrespective of his (or her) will to participate. It is, however, clear that a reasonable yardstick should be identified so as to determine when the behaviour of the accused tends to obstruct justice.

In the negotiations for the ICC Statute, the debate was reopened.[182] The issue of trials *in absentia* is one of the key divisions between most civil law countries and common law systems. The outcome is a mechanism that does not admit by way of principle a trial '*par contumace*'. However, it does allow, under very specific circumstances and to a limited extent, that proceedings can take place in the absence of the accused (Articles 61 and 63 ICC St.).

In conclusion, it can be said that it may be undesirable to conduct international trials *in absentia*. The reasons, however, are not linked to a better protection of the rights of the accused, but rather to the protection of victims and witnesses and to the interests of the effective administration of justice.

IV. RULES OF EVIDENCE AND RIGHTS OF THE ACCUSED—SOME PROBLEMATICAL ISSUES

1. The right to confront witnesses and obtain their attendance

(a) General

Pursuant to Article 21.4(e) of the ICTY Statute (Article 20.4 (e) ICTR St.) and Article 67.1 (e) ICC St., the accused has the right 'to examine, or have

---

[180] Apparently this has occurred also in a case before the ICTR, where an accused (Barayagwiza) refused to attend the hearings, causing serious problems to the Trial Chamber in the conduct of the proceedings.

[181] Cf. Article 37 of the Draft Statute CDI 1994.

[182] On the issue of trials *in absentia* in the ICC Statute see D. Brown, 'The International Criminal Court and Trials *in Absentia*', in 24 *BJIL* (1999), 763–796.

examined, the witnesses against him and to obtain the attendance and examination of witnesses on his behalf under the same conditions of witnesses
against him'. The substance of this right is twofold: on the one hand, it confers on the accused the power to examine the witnesses against him, including
the right to challenge their testimony. On the other hand, it imposes a positive duty on the Tribunal and the Court to assist the accused in obtaining the
attendance of witnesses for his defence. The two facets of this right produced
intense debate and questions that were rigorously dealt with by the Chambers
of the *ad hoc* Tribunals. It seems more interesting to refer to these decisions
rather than discuss the issues in abstract. Three main groups of issues can be
identified. First, there is the problem of compatibility between the right to
cross-examination and *anonymity*, as a measure of protection for witnesses.
Secondly, it is interesting to reflect upon the relationship between the rules on
admission of evidence and *hearsay evidence* (and other indirect evidence such
as affidavits). Thirdly, it is important to mention the *measures* adopted by the
Tribunals to enforce the right of the accused *to obtain the attendance of witnesses*.

(b) Anonymity

In the Statute of the *ad hoc* Tribunals, as well as in the ICC Statute, principles
of fairness and publicity of the hearings are established, with a limitation concerning the protection of victims and witnesses. In the summer of 1995, a
Trial Chamber of the ICTY delivered, in *Tadić*, a significant decision on a
motion by the Prosecutor requesting the adoption of protective measures for
witnesses.[183] The motion sought two sets of protective measures. The first
aimed at non-disclosure to the public and the media of the identity of certain
witnesses (which included the possibility of testifying behind closed doors).
The second aimed, albeit for only three of those witnesses, at the extension of
the measure of non-disclosure so as to include the defendant and his lawyers.
This is what has been generally defined as 'anonymity'.[184]

The members of the Trial Chamber decided unanimously to grant the first
set of protective measures sought, but did not find the same agreement on the
'anonymity' of witnesses. Concerning the issue of non-disclosure to the public and the media, the Trial Chamber stressed the importance of publicity as
a cornerstone of the exercise of judicial activities. However, it stated that the
Tribunal had the duty under the Statute to ensure the protection of witnesses.
Moreover, it added that in this framework the duty to strike a balance

---

[183] Trial Chamber Decision on Protective Measures, *Tadić* (IT–94–1–T), 10 August 1995.

[184] On confidentiality and witness anonymity as measures for the protection of witnesses both
under national law and regional human rights law see C. Chinkin, 'The Protection of Victims and
Witnesses', in G. McDonald and O. Swaak-Goldman (eds.), *Substantive and Procedural Aspects
of International Criminal Law* (The Hague: Kluwer, 2000), i, 453–478, at 459–469.

between the rights of the accused and the need to protect the victims and witnesses was assigned to the Chambers.

The Chamber instead split on the issue of anonymity. The majority, whilst admitting that the testimonies of anonymous witnesses restrict the defendant's right to cross-examination, decided that under exceptional and specific circumstances anonymity could be admitted as the sole effective measure the Tribunal could adopt to protect those witnesses. Moreover, the concession of anonymity was accompanied by a number of guidelines on the questioning of these witnesses as well on the requirement of an investigation into the reliability of the witnesses to be transmitted to the Chamber. Additionally, it was required that supplementary information should be furnished to the judges. Finally, the Chamber reserved its right subsequently to exclude the evidence furnished by anonymous witnesses to the guilt of the accused pursuant to Rule 89(D) of both RPEs, if its probative value was substantially outweighed by its unfairness to the defendant.[185]

Judge Stephen—who appended his dissenting opinion—concluded, on the contrary, that such a protective measure infringed upon the right of the accused to a fair trial, mainly because it radically undermined his capacity effectively to cross-examine the witnesses. Article 22 of the Statute (Article 21 ICTR St.) states that measures for the protection of witnesses 'shall include, but shall not be limited to, the conduct of "in camera" proceedings and the protection of the victim's identity'. In his reading of this provision, however, the Australian judge ruled out that such protective measures could be adopted when they might prejudice the right of the accused to a fair trial. In particular, Article 21.2 ICTY St. (Article 20 ICTR St.) states that the accused has the right to a 'fair and public hearing, subject to Article 22 of the Statute'. Judge Stephen suggested that this rule should be read as meaning that limitations may be imposed upon the public character of the hearing but not upon its fairness. The latter should by no means be subject to any restriction, and anonymity would diminish the fairness of the proceedings.[186]

Judge Stephen laid down in a masterly way the essential elements of the problem in his dissenting opinion: if the defendant is supposed effectively to cross-examine the witness, he needs to know who the person he is facing is.[187]

---

[185] It should, however be noted that the declarations of the anonymous witness may—at this stage of the procedure—have already produced their prejudicial effects.

[186] Cf. Judge Stephen's Dissenting Opinion, 10 August 1995, at 3.

[187] It has been argued that the system of the Tribunal does not provide for a right of confrontation in the sense that this is guaranteed by the Sixth Amendment of the US Constitution: cf. M. Leigh, 'The Yugoslav Tribunal: Use of Unnamed Witnesses Against Accused', in 90 *AJIL* (1996), at 236; *contra* C. Chinkin, 'Due Process and Witness Anonymity', in 91 *AJIL* (1997), at 75, with a final reply by M. Leigh, 'Witness Anonymity is Inconsistent with Due Process', *ibidem*, at 80. Nevertheless it could be pointed out that the substantial right effectively to examine the witnesses against him provides the accused with a protection which does not seem inferior to the right of confrontation under the US Constitution, considering also that the Tribunal has the specific duty to ensure the protection of witnesses.

In general, this hardly seems disputable. However, there may be some exceptions. It could, for example, be imagined that a person has simply been an eyewitness to a crime and has no other possible connection with the accused.[188] A pertinent observation has been made to the effect that the fact of accepting anonymity, together with the interpretation of the rules in the sense that corroboration is never necessary,[189] could lead to the conviction of an accused on the sole basis of anonymous testimony, which seems utterly unfair.[190]

The European Court of Human Rights—which had admitted anonymity in previous decisions[191]—ruled against it in a subsequent case.[192] The Court 'recalled that a conviction should not be based either solely or to a decisive extent on anonymous statements'.[193]

It is difficult to find a solution to the problem of anonymous witnesses that combines the need to protect witnesses with the overriding duty of the Chambers to ensure full respect for the rights of the accused. In this respect, it may be recalled that Defence Counsel in *Blaškić*, although on a slightly different issue, made an interesting suggestion. In a motion for disclosure of exculpatory material the Defence suggested the appointment of a sort of ombudsman (an independent arbiter) to go through the files of the Prosecutor and to identify the materials which could be exculpatory.[194] The Chamber deemed this solution unnecessary in this case. However, it is submitted that such a solution could be employed in cases where anonymity is the only available measure to protect witnesses. The Parties may agree to a neutral third party, or the Chamber may instruct a court official, who would be entrusted with the task of investigating the anonymous witness and examining him or her under the control of the Chamber. This officer would have to be accountable to the judges: after all, trust in the impartiality of the judges is at the core of the criminal process.

---

[188] All these cases have been discussed by the ECourtHR, which has considered anonymous witnesses as admissible but only under very exceptional circumstances, cf. notes 191 and 192 below.

[189] This conclusion was reached in the *Tadić* Judgment when discussing the principle of *unus testis nullus testis*, *Tadić* Judgment (IT–94–1–T), 7 May 1997, para. 535.

[190] Cf. A.M. 'Réflexions sur l'apport du Tribunal pénal international pour l'ex-Yougoslavie au droit à un procès équitable', in 101 *RGDIP* (1997), at 969; *Tadić Judgment* (IT–94–1–T), 7 May 1997. On the issue of anonymity the exchange of views between Monroe Leigh and Christine Chinkin, in *AJIL* (1997), note 187 above.

[191] See e.g. *Doorson v. The Netherlands*, 26 March 1996, Reports of Judgments and Decisions 1996–II, in particular paras. 70–73.

[192] Cf. ECHR decision of 23 April 1997, in case note 55/1996, *Hendrik van Mechelen et al. v. The Netherlands*, published in *Revue Universelle des Droits de l'Homme* [1997] at 209–221. The decision was taken by a majority of 6 to 3. For more details on the reasons for division see Judge van Dijk's dissenting opinion. On the issue of anonymity in the context of the ECHR cf. also the eloquent words by M. Chiavario, 'Serious Crime and the Respect for Human Rights in European Democratic Societies: Introductory Report', in *Proceedings of the Council of Europe*, Taormina 14–16 November 1996 (Strasbourg: Council of Europe Publishing, 1997), para. 8.

[193] Cf. the *Hendrik van Mechelen et al. v. The Netherlands* judgment, note 192 above, para. 55.

[194] See Trial Chamber Decision, *Blaškić* (IT–95–14–T), 27 January 1997, para. 51.

Finally, one should emphasize an important point: a single anonymous witness and no other evidence against the accused, even admitting that it might be theoretically sufficient to convict him or her, would hardly satisfy the requirements of a conviction beyond any reasonable doubt. In general, anonymity is not in the interest of justice, because it may reduce the probative value of very important testimonies. Therefore, it is suggested that the Tribunals should try (as in effect they have done so far) to avoid resorting to such a measure, and that they should enhance co-operation with States to grant full protection to witnesses.

(c) Hearsay evidence, depositions, and written evidence (including affidavits)

(i) Hearsay

Several motions were filed before the Trial Chambers of the ICTY questioning the admissibility of hearsay evidence. In the course of the *Tadić*, *Blaškić*, and *Aleksovski* trials, for example, the defence filed motions seeking the exclusion of all hearsay evidence on the ground that this evidence made it impossible for the defendant to examine the witnesses on the content of their declaration. In other words, the accused would be deprived of the right to challenge the primary source of evidence against him. It was, thus, contended that hearsay is intrinsically untrustworthy and that it must therefore be excluded. To support this thesis the Defence in *Tadić* relied on the US Federal Rules of Criminal Procedure, which contain detailed exclusionary rules on what evidence can be admitted. The Statutes and both the RPEs of the Tribunals, although inspired by the American adversarial model, do not contain strict exclusionary rules. On the contrary, the Rules have established the principle that '*a Chamber may admit any relevant evidence which it deems to have probative value*' (Rule 85.C RPE), provided that it is not irrelevant or illegally obtained (Rule 95 RPE). Therefore, the Trial Chamber in *Tadić* concluded that in the system of the Tribunal hearsay evidence could be admitted without any problem. It justified the difference between the procedure before the Tribunal and the traditional approach taken in common law systems, by referring to the absence of the jury.

Exclusionary rules of evidence have been drafted to protect the jurors, who are not familiar with legal and evidentiary technicalities.[195] In contrast, the Tribunal is composed of professional and experienced judges who are fully aware of the weight they should attribute to each piece of evidence. Leaving the exclusion of evidence to the judges implies that no evidence will in principle be excluded.[196] In international criminal procedure there has been a very

[195] Justice Robert Jackson expressed the same opinion when referring to the absence of detailed exclusionary rules in the Nuremberg Charter and Rules of Procedure.

[196] See Trial Chamber Decision on Defence Motion on Pre–determination of Rules of Evidence, *Bagosora* (ICTR–96–7–PT), 8 July 1998.

liberal approach to evidence (the so-called 'flexibility principle'[197]), which has led to the admission of more or less any evidence. Hence, the evaluation of the probative value of evidence and its exclusion may be carried out in due time at the moment of judgment, when the judges conclude whether it is favourable to the accused or otherwise. Nonetheless, the evaluation of evidence is not exclusion properly speaking; thus, one may share the view that no mandatory rules amount to no exclusionary rules at all.[198]

In *Aleksovski*, the Appeals Chamber held that: '[i]t is well settled in the practice of the Tribunal that hearsay evidence is admissible'.[199] Out-of-court statements are admissible under Rule 89(C), provided that the Chamber considers that they have probative value. This principle was initially affirmed by the Trial Chamber in *Tadić*[200] and subsequently followed by another Trial Chamber in *Blaškić*.[201] As noted by the Appeals Chamber in *Aleksovki*, '[neither] decision was the object of an appeal, nor it is now submitted that they were wrongly decided'.[202] Accordingly, it is possible to conclude that Chambers have broad discretion to admit hearsay evidence.[203] The only obligation incumbent upon them is to give reasons for the admission of such evidence with specific regard to its reliability and the circumstances under which it was gathered.

Finally, in *Kordić* and *Čerkez* the Prosecution sought the admission as evidence of a 'dossier of evidence relating to the attack on the town of Tulica', which contained several documents (including witness statements and transcripts), photographs, and videos.[204] Moreover, the Prosecution asked for the admission of another report prepared by an investigator, which was a summary of information relating to the attack. In particular, the investigator was supposed to give evidence in court and be submitted to cross-examination on the information in the dossier. On the other hand, the persons who had made the statements contained in the dossier would not be called as witnesses and, therefore, their declarations would not be subject to cross-examination. The Prosecutor suggested that the admission of the dossier as hearsay evidence

---

[197] In this respect see G. Boas, 'Admissibility of Evidence under the Rules of Procedure and Evidence of the ICTY: Development of the Flexibility Principle', in May *et al.*, note 56 above, 263–274.

[198] Cf. C. Bradley, 'The Emerging International Consensus as to Criminal Procedure Rules', in 14 *Mich. JIL* (1993), 171–221, at 220.

[199] Appeals Chamber Decision on Prosecutor's Appeal on Admissibility of Evidence, *Aleksovski* (IT–95–14/1–A), 16 February 1999, at para. 15.

[200] Decision on the Defence Motion on Hearsay, *Tadić* (IT–94–1–T), 5 August 1996.

[201] Decision, *Blaškić* (IT–95–14–T), 21 January 1998.

[202] Appeals Chamber Decision, note 199 above, para. 15.

[203] In this respect see P. Robinson, 'Ensuring Fair and Expeditious Trials at the International Criminal Tribunal for the Former Yugoslavia', in 11 *EJIL* (2000), 569–589, at 577–578 and notes 41–46.

[204] Decision on the Prosecution Application to Admit the Tulica Report and Dossier into Evidence, *Kordić and Cerkez* (IT–95–14/2–T), 29 July 1999.

was possible under Rule 89(C). The Defence, on the contrary, objected that its admission would affect the right of the accused to cross-examination. The Chamber eventually refused to admit into evidence the investigator's report on the grounds that it was of little or no probative value, since the investigator 'was not reporting as a contemporary witness of fact, he has only recently collated statements and other materials for the purpose of the Application. He would, in reality, only give evidence that material was or was not in the Dossier.' Moreover, the Chamber refused to admit one transcript for the reason that the witness to whom the transcript related had already given evidence in the case; admission would thus be unnecessarily repetitious. Nonetheless, the Chamber, admitted into evidence the other three court transcripts, as well as all the other items in the 'Tulića Dossier'.[205]

This was the first attempt to adopt a dossier approach, a feature of the civil law system, in the Tribunal. The significance of this approach for expeditiousness is obvious. This advantage, however, needs to be weighed against the risks of infringement of the rights of the accused. Recently, at the plenary session of December 2000, the judges adopted a new Rule 92-*bis*, which provides for proof of facts other than by oral evidence, including written statements by witnesses (on this rule cf. sub-section (iii) below). Arguably, this amendment represents the final step of the progressive shift made by the Tribunals from the original essentially adversarial model to a more balanced procedural system. However, the question of a broader admission of written evidence needs to be observed closely to verify whether the impact of such evidence on the rights of the accused is too detrimental or otherwise unfair.

(b) Depositions

From the point of view of the admission in evidence of 'out-of-court statements', an interesting norm in the Statutes of both *ad hoc* Tribunals allows depositions. In particular, the interpretation and subsequent amendment of this rule experienced in proceedings before the ICTY may prove very instructive.

Rule 71 (A) RPE in its original text provided that 'at the request of either party, a Trial Chamber may, in exceptional circumstances and in the interests of justice, order that a deposition be taken for use at trial, and appoint, for that purpose, a Presiding Officer'.

In order not to interrupt proceedings whenever a judge was was ill, the Chambers of the ICTY resorted to this rule in cases where one of the judges of the Trial Chamber was temporarily unavailable. Decisions to proceed by deposition were, thus, taken in *Kordić* and *Čerkez*[206] and in *Kupreškić*.[207] In

---

[205] Robinson, note 203 above, at 579.

[206] Cf. Trial Chamber Decision on Prosecution Request to Proceed by Deposition, *Kordić* and *Cerkez* (IT–95–14/2–T), 29 November 1999.

[207] Cf. Trial Chamber Decision on Prosecution and Defence Requests to Proceed by Deposition, *Kupreškić et al.* (IT–95–16–T), 11 February 1999.

one of these decisions it was explicitly held that 'the unavailability of one of the members of the Trial Chamber must not prejudice the right of the accused to be tried without undue delay'. Moreover, usually these decisions were taken with the agreement of both parties. The defence of an accused (Papić) in *Kupreškić*, however, filed a motion before the Appeals Chamber against a ruling of the Trial Chamber to proceed by deposition. The Appeals Chamber in deciding on this motion held that the temporary unavailability of a judge could not be considered as an exceptional circumstance within the meaning of Rule 71. The Appeals Chamber maintained that Rule 71 was intended exceptionally to allow the taking of depositions from witnesses that could not come to the seat of the Tribunal. Nevertheless, the Chamber confirmed the possibility of resorting to depositions in other cases, provided that the parties agreed. In this decision the Appeals Chamber gave a very strict interpretation of Rule 71 (A). Moreover, the Trial Chamber in *Kvocka and others* followed this approach.[208] The Chamber, however, held that the 'strict interpretation of Rule 71 advanced by the Appeals Chamber in *Prosecutor v. Kupreškić*, [was] not applicable [in the case before it], since all four accused [had] consented to the use of Rule 71 in these circumstances'.[209] It is interesting to note, however, that two days after this decision of the Trial Chamber, at the 21st Plenary Session (17 November 1999) Rule 71 was amended to broaden its scope.

The Rule now reads 'where it is in the interests of justice to do so, a Trial Chamber may order, *proprio motu* or at the request of a party, that a deposition be taken for use at trial, whether or not the person whose deposition is sought is physically able to appear before the Tribunal to give evidence'. The broadening of this rule may be very useful to speed up proceedings, because it enables parties to use the time before the formal opening of the trial to start hearing witnesses on a variety of issues. In particular, considering the length of the pre-trial stage (from the initial appearance onwards) it is suggested that parties could use depositions at that stage to hear witnesses on general issues.

Depositions as a means of accelerating proceedings are certainly more appropriate than the admission of hearsay evidence, because in the case of depositions the defence is allowed effectively to cross-examine witnesses, which ensures the better protection of the rights of the accused. Moreover, depositions seem more effective than affidavits (cf. (iii) below) in reconciling the interests of justice and the rights of the accused. There are at least two reasons for this proposition: first, the use of depositions is not limited to corroborating other evidence; and secondly, depositions are taken in the presence of both parties who may duly cross-examine the witness. Naturally, depositions

---

[208] Cf. Trial Chamber Decision to proceed by Deposition pursuant to Rule 71, *Kvocka et al.* (IT–95–17–PT), 15 November 1999.
[209] Cf. *ibidem*.

are admitted at trial as documents (or transcripts)[210] and do not have exactly the same impact as live testimony on the judges of the Trial Chambers. They are, however, an interesting attempt to try to shorten the list of witnesses of each party and to ensure, at the same time, adequate levels of protection for the rights of defendants.

(iii) Affidavits and other written evidence

Amendments to the RPE ICTY of the 21st Plenary Session, in November 1999, explicitly introduced the possibility of using affidavits. Affidavits are in principle less trustworthy than depositions because they are taken *ex parte*, without any chance of cross-examination. Moreover, they present the same drawbacks as hearsay evidence, since they are out-of-court statements presented at trial by a witness (who is not the person having declared what is contained in the affidavit) or as documents. When affidavits are submitted, defendants are clearly not confronted with the source of evidence. Additionally, affidavits lack those elements of orality and direct examination that should characterize the presentation of evidence in adversarial trials.

Rule 94-*ter* established that 'to prove a fact in dispute, a party may propose to call a witness and to submit in corroboration of his or her testimony on that fact affidavits or formal statements signed by other witnesses in accordance with the law and procedure of the State in which such affidavits or statements are signed'. This implied that affidavits could be used only to corroborate declarations made by witnesses who appeared at trial. Furthermore, the Rule required that to be admissible such affidavits should have been 'filed prior to the giving of testimony by the witness to be called' and the other party should not object. Additionally, as a final guarantee the Rule provided that 'if the party objects and the Trial Chamber so rules, or if the Trial Chamber so orders, the witnesses shall be called for cross-examination'. In general it can be said that the guarantees offered by this rule on affidavits were satisfactory. Their reliance as a means of corroboration depends largely on the agreement of the other party. Therefore, in the event that the Prosecution uses them the right of the accused to object would always preserved. The only thing that was not very clear in that Rule was by what standard the Trial Chamber would decide on objections. It would have been appropriate to offer some guidance in the Rules so that the parties would know how to argue their objections. Finally, it seems clear that affidavits cannot be used as a general instrument to speed up proceedings because they do not ensure adequate protection for the right of the accused to confront witnesses against him or her. The whole question of affidavits, however, should be re-examined in light of

---

[210] Rule 71 (E) refers to a 'record': '[the] Presiding Officer shall ensure that the deposition is taken in accordance with the Rules and that a record is made of the deposition, including cross-examination, and objections raised by either party for decision by the Trial Chamber. The Presiding Officer shall transmit the record to the Trial Chamber'.

the abovementioned amendment, adopted at the plenary session of December 2000, which introduced a new general rule (Rule 92-*bis*). According to this new text 'a Trial Chamber may admit, in whole or in part, the evidence of a witness in the form of a written statement in lieu of oral testimony which goes to proof of a matter other than the acts and conduct of the accused as charged in the indictment'. Subsequent paragraphs of the rule further clarify the procedure for admission of such evidence.[211] Additionally, these provisions set out the conditions for admission. In particular, such evidence must not be admitted in the case of overriding public interest in presenting evidence orally, or a party objects and demonstrates the unreliability of the source, or there are other factors that require the attendance of the witness. Finally, paragraph D of Rule 92-*bis* provides for the admission of court transcripts of other proceedings before the Tribunal.

This new Rule represents a turning point in the reform undertaken by the judges of the ICTY. It clearly evinces the trend towards broader resort to the admission of written evidence[212] and strengthens the 'dossier approach' already adopted by Trial Chambers in practice. It is important to note that the Rule lays down two main guarantees for the rights of the accused. First, the Rule clearly specifies that such evidence may be admitted only in so far as '[it] goes to proof of a matter *other than the acts and conducts* of the accused *as charged in the indictment*'. This makes the Rule more restrictive than the previous text on affidavits contained in Rule 94-*ter*, recently deleted, which did not limit the admission of such evidence to matters other than the acts referred to in the charges. Secondly, paragraph E requires that 'a party seeking to adduce a written statement or transcript shall give fourteen days notice to the *opposing party*, who *may* within seven days *object*'. It is submitted that this right to object should be interpreted very broadly, particularly in favour of the accused, in accordance with the right to confront witnesses against him or her. For example, an accused should be granted the right to object even beyond the time limit of seven days, whenever a written statement, previously admitted with no objections, turns out to be potentially prejudicial at a later stage of trial.

(c) Summonses, safe-conducts, and testimony by videoconference

The Statutes of the Tribunals (and the Court) grant to the accused not only a *right to call witnesses* but also a right to *obtain their attendance*. This implies

---

[211] Rule 92-*bis*, paras. (B)–(E) ICTY RPE.

[212] A plea for a cautious approach to written evidence has been made by Judge Patricia Wald, 'To Establish Incredible Events by Credible Evidence', in 42 *HILJ* (2001), at 535–553. Judge Wald emphasizes the need for the judges to be cautious in resorting to such evidence, as the credibility of the Tribunal will very much depend on how they use their broad powers to admit written evidence.

a positive duty on the Tribunal to do whatever is necessary to have the witness brought before the Chamber. The ICTY has dealt with this problem on a number of occasions. Naturally, these issues were dealt with for the first time in *Tadić*. In this case, the Trial Chamber had to decide on a Defence motion requesting the Chamber to summon witnesses for the accused and to adopt special measures to obtain their attendance.[213] These persons, according to the Defence, were not willing to testify before the Tribunal in The Hague because they feared that the Prosecutor of the Tribunal would charge them and ask for their arrest. Therefore the Defence asked that four of them be granted safe-conducts and, for the others, who were still refusing to come to The Hague, that they be allowed to testify by videoconference link. Although there were no provisions for safe-conducts or for videoconference link in the Rules,[214] or in the Statute, the Trial Chamber decided to grant the measures on the basis of the general principles of co-operation in criminal matters (for the safe-conducts). Moreover, it added that alternative solutions were justified on the basis of the extraordinary circumstances of a trial concerning facts connected to a conflict that had just finished. However, it could be suggested that the rationale (or at least an important, albeit unspoken, reason) behind the decision was the intention to limit the potential complaints of the defendant about the fairness of his trial.[215] By allowing him to obtain the attendance of any witness who could support his case, the Trial Chamber intended substantially to implement the rights of the accused.[216]

The Trial Chamber, responding to the criticisms made by the Defence of *Duško Tadić* in its closing arguments, restated the importance of the Tribunal's support for the parties in its judgment in *Tadić*: '[a] number of steps have been taken by the International Tribunal to assist the parties. A videoconferencing link from a secure location in the territory of the former Yugoslavia was established so that numerous Defence witnesses otherwise unable or unwilling to give evidence were able to do so . . . Some Defence witnesses, concerned about coming at the seat of the International Tribunal to testify, were granted safe-conduct against arrest or other legal process against them by the prosecutor of the International Tribunal . . . These steps did appear to alleviate the inherent difficulties of the situation.'[217]

---

[213] Cf. Trial Chamber Decision on the Defence Motions to Summon and Protect Defence Witnesses, and on the Giving of Evidence by Video-link, *Tadić* (IT–94–1–T), 26 June 1996.

[214] Since then an amendment has been adopted to include the possibility of witnesses testifying by videoconference link, Rule 71-*bis* RPE (the ICTR has not yet adopted such an amendment). However, so far no provision has been introduced as far as safe-conducts are concerned.

[215] As explained above, one of the grounds on appeal was the violation of the principle of equality of arms.

[216] The co-operation of the Tribunal with the Defence to obtain the attendance of witnesses is essential. It has been mentioned above that at Nuremberg defendants received very little help in their attempt to call witnesses to the stand.

[217] Trial Chamber Judgment, *Tadić* (IT–94–1–T), 7 May 1997, para. 531.

Certainly, the gathering of evidence is one of the most difficult aspects of international criminal trials. It is presumably not easy for the Prosecution to conduct a proper investigation, but it may well be virtually impossible for the Defence to gather exculpatory evidence. This is especially true when the interests of the defendant do not coincide with the interests of the authorities governing the territories in which the evidence (documents or witnesses) is located.[218] This is one of the reasons reinforcing the belief that the Prosecutor should act as an organ of justice and it is the primary duty of Chambers to assist the Defence in collecting evidence.

In *Kupreškić*, the Trial Chamber had to face two different sets of problems.[219] On the one hand, a great number of defence witnesses did not want to appear because they feared being arrested and charged by the Prosecutor. In respect of most of these witnesses the Trial Chamber issued safe-conducts to enable the defence to obtain their attendance. On the other hand, the Trial Chamber was also presented with another problem. The defence wanted to call some witnesses of the opposite ethnic group (Bosnian Muslims, the accused being Croats). These witnesses, however, probably because they feared reprisals by their communities, were not willing to appear to testify 'in favour' of Croats. Therefore, the Chamber summoned these witnesses as 'court witnesses', so that they would appear in court not in favour of one party or the other but—as the Chamber said—as 'witnesses for the truth'.[220]

These orders show once again the commitment of the Chambers of the Tribunal to ensure a fair trial to the accused, by enabling them fully to exercise their rights.

2. The right to make un-sworn oral or written statements

Under the Nuremberg Charter, but not under that of Tokyo, the accused had the right 'to give any explanation relevant to the charges made against him' (Article 16.b). However, from the text itself it remained unclear whether this right implied that an accused could take the stand without taking the oath or whether he could be duly examined and cross-examined. In any case, as a general rule defendants were heard like any other witness.[221] Accordingly, most

---

[218] The case of the subpoena against the Republic of Croatia has shown that the basic structure of the relationships between the International Tribunal and State authorities is based on the principle of co-operation. However, there is very little that can be done when a State refuses to comply with orders given by the Tribunal. It does not seem realistic to believe that the Tribunal would undertake a confrontation with States to obtain the production of evidence for the parties.

[219] Trial Chamber Judgment, *Kupreškić and others* (IT–95–16–T), 14 January 2000, paras. 2–30.

[220] Decision of 21 September 1998.

[221] On the Allies' fear that defendants would take the floor, see M.C. Bassiouni, 'The Nuremberg Legacy', in M.C. Bassiouni (ed.), *International Criminal Law* (2nd edn., Ardsley, NY: Transnational, 1999), iii, at 201–202.

of the defendants who wanted to testify at trial did so under oath and were cross-examined.[222] Furthermore, defendants were authorized to make an unsworn final statement (Article 24.j Nur. Ch.).[223]

In the *ad hoc* Tribunals, originally there were no specific provisions on the possibility for an accused to make unsworn statements. On the contrary, the accused could, in principle, be heard only as a normal witness.[224] There was no other option for an accused to be heard. Subsequently, with an amendment to the Rules, a new provision was introduced into the RPE of the ICTY: Rule 84-*bis* RPE ICTY.[225] This Rule allows the accused, if the Trial Chamber so decides, to make a statement at the beginning of the trial, without being compelled to make a solemn declaration and being cross-examined.[226] One of the purposes of this amendment is that through the statement of the accused at the beginning of the trial, the judges and the Prosecutor may be informed of the position of the accused on particular issues, thereby avoiding any unnecessary production of evidence. Of course, the legal value of such a statement is largely debatable. Can it, properly speaking, be considered as evidence? That is to say, would it be possible for the judges to ground their judgment on elements taken from that statement? Paragraph (B) of Rule 84-*bis* RPE ICTY states that 'the Trial Chamber shall decide on the probative value, if any, of the statement'. The statement, made without a prior solemn declaration, was not subject to cross-examination (or to any other form of questioning), and certainly cannot be considered as equivalent to evidence. Its value is more linked to the management of the trial and to the effort to select relevant issues.[227] Neither can it be considered that the defence will be bound

---

[222] Cf. A.M. Larin, 'The Trial of the Major War Criminals', in G. Ginsburgs and V.N. Kudriavtsev (eds.), *The Nuremberg Trials and International Law* (Dordrecht: Nijhoff, 1990), at 83, where the author explains how '[in] the Charter of the Tribunal . . . a difference [was] drawn between the explanations of the defendants and the testimony of witnesses. That distinction [was] recognized in the procedural legislation of the USSR, as well as of France. The procedure in the United States and Great Britain, however, follows a different route: the defendant who wishes to give evidence is subject to examination as a witness for the defense. It is precisely this formula . . . that was applied by the presiding judge . . . Nineteen defendants were sworn in and questioned as witnesses.' This seems to confirm the unclear drafting of the provisions on the characterization of the 'explanations by defendants'.

[223] See J. Murphy, 'Norms of Criminal Procedure at the International Military Tribunal', in Ginsburgs and Kudriavtsev (eds.), note 222 above, 61–75, at 71.

[224] This occurred in several cases, such as e.g. *Tadić*, *Delalic and others*, *Kunarac, and others*.

[225] This Rule was adopted at the 20th Plenary Session, in July 1999, IT/32/Rev.16.

[226] Rule 84-*bis* ICTY RPE read as follows: '(A) After the opening statements of the parties or, if the defence elects to defer its opening statement pursuant to Rule 84, after the opening statement of the Prosecutor, if any, the accused may, if he or she so wishes, and the Trial Chamber so decides, make a statement under the control of the Trial Chamber. The accused shall not be compelled to make a solemn declaration and shall not be examined about the content of the statement. (B) The Trial Chamber shall decide on the probative value, if any, of the statement.'

[227] This is highlighted by the Report of the Expert Group which considered that 'the rule . . . reflects a worthwhile effort by ICTY to improve case-management': see UN doc. A/54/634, 22 November 1999, and also D. Mundys, 'Improving the Operation and Functioning of the International Criminal Tribunals', in 94 *AJIL* (2000), 759–773, at 767.

by declarations contained in the statement. Moreover, the judges should not draw any adverse inference from the refusal of an accused to make such a statement.[228]

Interestingly the recognition of such a right to the accused is a feature of the ICC Statute. Article 67, paragraph 1, letter h, ICC St. contains a provision enabling the accused 'to make an un-sworn oral or written statement in his or her defence', without explicitly being submitted to examination and cross-examination. It seems correct to argue that it was precisely this rule of the ICC Statute that influenced the amendment of the Rules of Procedure of the ICTY. There are, however, important differences between the two norms. Contrary to the rule of the ICTY that limits the possibility for an accused to make an unsworn statement to the beginning of the trial, in the ICC system arguably such a statement can be made at any time, since there is no express limitation. This would, therefore, enable the accused to be heard at any stage, depending on the circumstances and the course of proceedings. Another difference is that the ICTY provision allows the accused to make such a statement prior to authorization by the Trial Chamber and adds that the statement is made under the control of the Chamber. Moreover, it is questionable whether the statement can be written.

In the ICC system, where the defendant's statement can also be in writing, it is not possible to submit the exercise of such a *right* to the authorization of the Trial Chamber, precisely because it is set out as a right of the accused. This, however, may lead to propagandistic statements of no real use for the management of trial but prejudicial for the interests of justice. Therefore, it seems appropriate to consider that the Trial Chamber must keep control over the declarations of the accused. Naturally, these declarations must not be of an intimidatory nature in relation to the witnesses, or contain any indirect messages, or, worse, insults addressed to victims or their memory, or any other statement made in conflict with the interests of justice. The Trial Chambers of the ICC, even in the absence of specific provisions in the Rules of Procedure, will be able to exercise this power pursuant to their general responsibilities of supervision on the conduct of proceedings.

---

[228] It would have been better to provide it explicitly in the Rules, so that the defendant was more certain that a refusal to make such a statement would have no adverse consequences. Moreover, it would be a precise guideline for judges. In *Delalić and others*, as a result of the Appeals Chamber Judgment, a newly composed Trial Chamber was entrusted with the task of determining the new sentences. The Chamber took into account an unclear passage of the first instance judgment, from which it appeared that the original Trial Chamber had drawn adverse consequences from the unwillingness of an accused (Mucić) to testify, to reduce the sentence imposed. See Sentencing Judgment, *Delalić and others* (IT–96–21–T), 9 October 2001.

3. Disclosure and the rights of defence

(a) The practice of the ICTY

One of the fundamental rules of the adversarial trial is that the Prosecutor must hand over to the defence all the documents and other materials that will be introduced into evidence to prove the guilt of the accused. The Rules of Procedure of the Tribunals establish that, within thirty days of the initial appearance of the accused, the Prosecutor must communicate to the defence a copy of the supporting material and of any prior statement obtained from the accused (Rule 66(A)(i) ICTY RPE). Additionally, the Prosecutor is to communicate 'within the time-limit prescribed by the Trial Chamber, copies of the statements of all witnesses whom the Prosecutor intends to call to testify at trial and . . . of all written statements taken in accordance with Rule 92-*bis*'. Subsequently, communication must be made of copies of the statement of every additional witness as soon as the decision to call such witness is taken (Rule 66, paragraph A ii of both RPEs). The discovery process goes as far as allowing the defence to inspect all books, documents, photographs, and tangible objects in the Prosecutor's custody (Rule 66, paragraph B, of both RPEs). Moreover, Rule 65-*ter* (E) ICTY RPE requires the submission of pre-trial briefs containing a number of details concerning the presentation of evidence and communication of lists of both witnesses and exhibits the prosecution intends to call and offer.[229]

These provisions aim at enabling the accused to be in the best position to organize his case.[230] Only when the disclosure of evidence may prejudice further investigations or be contrary to the public interest or the national security of any State can the Prosecutor be authorized to keep the information confidential beyond the time period described above (Rule 66 (C) of both RPEs). In any event, however, this must be disclosed to the defence before their presentation as evidence at trial.[231] These temporary limitations on disclosure seem to apply only with reference to the materials described in paragraph B of Rule 66. This interpretation would imply that the restrictions on disclosure were not applicable to the supporting material or to the statements of witnesses who were to appear at trial.[232]

---

[229] This further communication, however, may take place after disclosure pursuant to Rules 66 and 68 has taken place.

[230] See Trial Chamber Decision on Prosecution Motion for Clarification in respect of Application of Rules 65-*ter*, 66(B) and 67 (C), *Krajišnik and Plavšić* (IT–00–39&40–PT), 1 August 2001.

[231] Cf. Decision on Motion by Prosecution for Protective Measures, *Brdjanin and Talić* (IT–99–36–PT), 3 July 2000, para. 22.

[232] In this respect, cf. J. Jones, *The Practice of the International Criminal Tribunals for the Former Yugoslavia and Rwanda* (Irvington on Hudson, NY: Transnational, 1998), at 231.

The Trial Chamber, however, may authorize temporary non-disclosure pursuant to Rule 69, on the protection of victims and witnesses.[233] Under this Rule the Trial Chamber may in 'exceptional circumstances' impose restrictions on the disclosure of the identity of witnesses to the defendant. This entails that the Prosecution may be authorized to postpone the disclosure of the identity of witnesses to a later stage in the proceedings, provided that this is done before the commencement of the trial.[234] Although this Rule may be resorted to only in 'exceptional circumstances', the adoption of these protective measures has become almost the norm in proceedings before the Tribunal.[235] The Chambers, however, have clarified, on several occasions, that the balance between the protection of witnesses and the rights of the accused must be struck *in concreto* depending on the circumstances of each individual case.[236]

In *Brdjanin and Talić*, the Trial Chamber denied the Prosecution's request to allow the adoption of a special procedure 'to avoid the need for a witness-by-witness application'.[237] By this procedure the Prosecution sought the authorization to 'take it upon itself to redact the identity of every witness . . . who it deemed to be a vulnerable witness'. The accused could make a 'reasonable request' to the Prosecution for the identity to be revealed. Only if the request were refused could the accused then file an application with the Trial Chamber.[238] The Trial Chamber denied this request on the grounds that it contained 'two basic defects. First it continues to assume that every witness is in fact in danger or risk . . . Secondly, the proposal completely reverses the appropriate onus', which is imposed by the RPE on the Prosecutor, who must prove the need for the protective measures. It is clearly not for the accused to justify the request for disclosure.[239]

---

[233] Rule 69, Protection of Victims and Witnesses:

'(A) In exceptional circumstances, the Prosecutor may apply to a Trial Chamber to order the non-disclosure of the identity of a victim or witness who may be in danger or at risk until such person is brought under the protection of the Tribunal. (B) In the determination of protective measures for victims and witnesses the Trial Chamber may consult the Victims and Witnesses Section. (C) Subject to Rule 75, the identity of the victim or witness shall be disclosed in sufficient time prior to the trial to allow adequate time for preparation of the defence.'

[234] In this respect one should note that no specific time limit is set in the Rules. However, the Trial Chambers have generally considered that disclosure must occur before the trial commences rather than before the witness gives evidence. Cf. Decision on Motion by Prosecution for Protective Measures, *Brdjanin and Talić* (IT–99–36–PT), 3 July 2000, para. 38 and Decision on Prosecution Motion for Provisional Protective Measures Pursuant to Rule 69, *Milošević* (IT–01–52–PT), 19 February 2002, para. 26.

[235] See Decision on Prosecution Motion for Provisional Protective Measures Pursuant to Rule 69, *Milošević* (IT–01–52–PT), 19 February 2002, para. 28.

[236] See Decision on the Prosecutor's Motion Requesting Protective Measures for Witness RPE, *Tadić* (IT–94–1–PT), 31 July 1996, at 4.

[237] Cf. Decision on Motion by Prosecution for Protective Measures, *Brdjanin and Talić* (IT–99–36–PT), 3 July 2000, para. 14.

[238] *Ibidem*, para. 15.　　　　　　　　　　　　[239] *Ibidem*, para. 16.

As the Trial Chamber in *Milošević* has recently noted, although in the system of the Tribunals the protection of victims and witnesses is given greater status than in most national systems of criminal law, in case of persisting conflict between the interests of the protection of witnesses and the rights of the accused, the latter must prevail.[240]

The right to disclosure is very wide and encompasses the duty of the Prosecutor to communicate not only incriminating evidence but also *exculpatory evidence*. Furthermore, Rule 68 establishes that the Prosecutor shall communicate to the defence any evidence that may tend to lessen the credibility of prosecution witnesses.

In *Blaškić*, there was a very long *querelle* between the Defence and the Prosecution on disclosure, and, in particular, on the communication of exculpatory evidence.[241] The Trial Chamber held that the Defence could not ask generically for exculpatory evidence, nor could it seek to conduct a 'fishing expedition' into the Prosecution files. It was held that there should always be at least a *prima facie* showing of relevance and exculpatory character of the materials sought.[242] Moreover, there must be a specific allegation that these elements are in the possession of the Prosecution. The Trial Chamber considered that a lack of evidence cannot under any circumstances be equated with exculpatory evidence; therefore, there is no right of the defence to obtain a declaration from the Prosecution saying that it has no evidence to prove certain charges.

In *Furundžija*, the Prosecution violated its discovery obligation by not communicating to the Defence a document concerning the credibility of one of its witnesses. The Trial Chamber did not defer the opening of the debates, which had already been fixed, but it deplored delays in the transmission of the document. Furthermore, it requested the Chief Prosecutor to open disciplinary proceedings against the attorney responsible for such violation.[243] Moreover, after the trial had ended, the Prosecutor disclosed two documents to the Defence that might have been considered of an exculpatory nature. One was a doctored certificate and the other a witness statement concerning a crucial witness for the Prosecution, witness A, and the psychological treatment this witness had received. Due to the violation of discovery obligations the defence asked the Trial Chamber either to strike the testimony of witness A,

---

[240] See Decision on Prosecution Motion for Provisional Protective Measures Pursuant to Rule 69, *Milošević* (IT–01–52–PT), 19 February 2002, para. 23, where the Trial Chamber held that 'what is clear from the Statute and Rules of the Tribunal is that the rights of the accused are given primary consideration, with the need to protect victims and witnesses being an important but secondary one'.

[241] See the Trial Chamber's Decisions, *Blaškić* (IT–95–14–PT), 27 January 1997, 4 April 1997, 29 April 1998, and 28 September 1998.

[242] Cf. Trial Chamber Decision on the Defence Motion for Discovery, *Blaškić* (IT–95–14–PT), 27 January 1997.

[243] Cf. Formal Complaint by the Trial Chamber, *Furundžija* (IT–95–17/1–T), 5 June 1998.

due to what it considered to be misconduct on the part of the Prosecution (for not having communicated the document), or, in the event of a conviction, to hold a new trial. The Chamber, however, declined to do so and decided to re-open the proceedings, thus giving a new opportunity to the defence to re-cross-examine the witness.[244]

The lack of specific procedural sanctions leaves the defendant substantially unprotected *vis-à-vis* prosecutorial violations of the obligations of discovery. In the above-mentioned case the Chamber decided to report the violation to the Chief Prosecutor and recommended disciplinary sanctions. It did, however, admit the testimony. In reality, the appropriate sanction would probably have been to exclude the testimony, which should not have been taken into any account in the judgment. The determination of sanctions, however, should not be left to the discretion of the judges. Rather, a set of rules specifying sanctions attached to the various procedural violations should be included in both RPEs.

It is interesting to note that, with the introduction of the Pre-trial Judge and with the practice of communicating summaries of previous witness statements (or, in some cases, even the whole file) to the judges of the Trial Chamber, it will certainly be easier for the judges effectively to check that the Prosecutor fulfils his or her duties. In this respect, the Defence in *Blaškić* made an interesting proposal. It suggested appointing an officer of the Court to review the materials in the possession of Prosecution and to assign him or her the task of identifying exculpatory evidence in the Prosecution files.[245] Naturally, this solution was not accepted, since it was not provided for in the Rules and was not in conformity with the type of procedure adopted. It is, however, submitted that such a request by the Defence showed the need for a more active role for the judges in controlling the discovery process. It is clear that the Pre-trial Judge provided for by Rule 65-*ter* RPE ICTY is in a position to play an important role in this respect.

One provision that seems inconsistent with the idea of full disclosure to the accused is Rule 70 of both RPEs. This is a rule that has undergone a number of amendments. Originally it established an exception to the obligation of disclosure only in relation to all internal documents, memoranda, and other written notes used in the Office of the Prosecutor to prepare the case. Subsequently, the rule was amended to include information provided to the Prosecutor by sources that wished to remain confidential.[246] In any case the information provided under Rule 70 could not be 'given in evidence without

---

[244] See Trial Chamber Decision, *Furundžija* (IT–95–17/1–T), 16 July 1998.

[245] See Trial Chamber Decision, *Blaškić* (IT–95–14–PT), 27 January 1997, para. 51.

[246] As Jones explains, this rule, which was added in October 1994, 'was designed to meet a problem encountered by the Prosecutor in the field, namely that his investigations were being hampered by the fact that a number of bodies, in particular certain States and non-governmental organizations, had information . . . which they were reluctant to release. Hence the amendment was introduced to protect the source of such information': cf. Jones, note 232 above, at 248.

prior disclosure to the accused'.[247] Rule 70 was again amended to protect the source of information even in the case of presentation of witnesses at trial. The rule thus introduces a substantially unbalanced situation into the Rules and limits the discovery process. To try to redress the situation, the judges introduced paragraph (F), which provides for a symmetrical right for the defendant to protect his or her sources pursuant to the provisions of paragraphs (C) and (D). The judges added paragraph (G), which warns against abuses of this rule, restating the general power of the Chamber to exclude evidence whenever its probative value is outweighed by the need to ensure a fair trial.

It is very clear that in such cases the Tribunal faces two conflicting interests, and consequently procedural rules must strike the proper balance. It is certainly correct for the international community to decide to protect confidential sources and national (or international) security, but this cannot be done at the expense of the rights of the individual.[248] In other words, it is admissible to withhold documents or other evidence coming from protected sources (and the identity of these sources), but under no circumstances can the accused be convicted on the basis of such evidence. Therefore any material not properly disclosed to the defence must not be admitted into evidence.

(b) Disclosure in the ICC Statute

The ICC Statute does not contain detailed provisions regarding disclosure. Article 61 provides for a general obligation; it has been further implemented in the Rules of Procedure and Evidence. Accordingly, a large section of the RPE (Chapter 4, Section II) deals with this issue and Rules 76 to 84 are devoted to disclosure. The principles upheld in the Rules are based on the recognition of the central importance of the duties of disclosure imposed on the Prosecution. Rule 76 specifies that the Prosecutor must provide the defence with the names of witnesses whom he or she intends to call at trial and with copies of any prior statement by those witnesses. The same must be done in respect of witnesses who may subsequently be called to testify.[249] The statements of witnesses must be made available in a language spoken by the accused.[250] These rules for disclosure are subject to appropriate constraints to

---

[247] *Ibidem.*

[248] In this respect see P. Malanzcuck, 'Protection of National Security Interest (Article 72)', in A. Cassese, P. Gaeta, and J. Jones, *The Rome Statute of the International Criminal Court: A Commentary* (Oxford: OUP, 2002), ii 1371–1386.

[249] Rule 76, para. 2, ii, ICC RPE.

[250] The Chambers of the Tribunal have taken different positions on this issue. In the *Celebici* case, first, the Trial Chamber took the view that the accused had no right to receive the transcripts in his own language. Subsequently, the same Trial Chamber, although composed of different judges, issued a decision taking the opposite view. The Prosecution submitted that the witness statements could be provided in the Tribunal's working languages, while the Defence asserted that the statements had to be in a language accessible to the accused. The Chamber agreed with the Defence and requested that the materials be forwarded to the Defence in the language of the accused.

ensure the protection of victims and witnesses.[251] Inspection by the Defence of books, documents, photographs, and other material is allowed, but limited by provisions that lay down a set of restrictions on disclosure (Rules 76–77 and 81–82).

A limited duty of disclosure is also imposed on the Defence under Rule 79, which specifies that the Defence must notify the Prosecution whenever it intends to plead the existence of an alibi or raise a ground excluding criminal responsibility under Article 31, paragraph 1 of the ICC Statute. Moreover, the Defence must notify both the Trial Chamber and the Prosecutor if it intends to plead a ground excluding criminal responsibility under paragraph 3 of Article 31: in other words, a ground not specifically provided for in the Statute. The Rules reserve the right of the Trial Chamber to impose further disclosure obligations on the Defence. Both the duties of the Prosecutor and those of the Defence are continuing obligations that refer to all additional evidence discovered at any stage of the proceedings.

Restrictions on disclosure are, naturally, included in the Rules. The materials excluded from disclosure are reports, memoranda, and other internal documents of the parties. Disclosure is also restricted whenever it may cause prejudice to ongoing investigations and the Chamber authorizes it. The Prosecutor, however, will not be able to introduce this evidence in Court without first disclosing it to the Defence. Other restrictions on disclosure are granted to protect victims and witnesses and national security interests,[252] but always under the overall supervision of the Chambers, which must ensure that such materials are not admitted into evidence, in the absence of their prior disclosure to the Defence. This is necessary in order to guarantee the right of the accused to challenge the evidence introduced against him or her.

Finally, an important provision contained in the Rules implements the norm of the Statute, providing that in cases of doubt it is for the Court to decide whether evidence is exculpatory or not (Article 67, paragraph 2, ICC St.). Rule 83 of the Rules provides for an *ex parte* hearing, after which the Court may decide on questions put by the Prosecution.

By and large, the provisions of the ICC Statute and the Rules are to a large extent taken from the procedure of the *ad hoc* Tribunals, as both enshrined in the Rules of Procedure and supplemented by the practice of the Chambers. In the ICC provisions there are two main additions. First, the Rules explicitly contain provisions on the duty of the Defence to notify the Chambers and the Prosecutor of the intention to invoke grounds for excluding criminal responsibility.[253] Secondly, a specific obligation has been imposed on the Prosecutor

---

[251] Rules 81 and 82, ICC RPE.

[252] See R. Dixon and H. Duffy, 'Article 72 (Protection of National Security Information)', in Triffterer (ed.), note 31 above, 937–946.

[253] In cases other than 'alibi', which is specifically provided for in the *ad hoc* Tribunals' system, under Rule 67 RPEs.

so that, in the case of doubt, exculpatory evidence must be presented to the Chamber for a ruling.

Finally, it must be noted that, in the ICC Statute, the Prosecutor is under a specific duty to search for exculpatory evidence (Article 54, paragraph 1, ICC St.). This makes it unlikely that the Prosecution may convincingly claim the uncertain exculpatory nature of certain pieces of evidence.[254] On the contrary, the duty to search for such evidence requires that the Prosecution must be perfectly aware of the nature of the materials in its possession. In this respect, it could be suggested that the adoption of an amendment to both *ad hoc* Tribunal RPEs, imposing a specific duty on the Prosecutor, similar to that contained in Article 54 ICC St., could be useful in solving problems relating to the uncertain exculpatory nature of Prosecution evidence.

4. The exclusion of evidence obtained by means contrary to international human rights law

The solution generally found in international criminal procedure is to provide for the exclusion of evidence by judges only in cases in which very serious breaches have occurred, leading to the substantial unreliability of the evidence presented. No rules of this kind were included in the Nuremberg and Tokyo Charters. The rule is present, albeit in slightly different forms, in both the *ad hoc* Tribunals systems and the ICC Statute. In general, in international criminal procedure, there are no mandatory rules on the exclusion of evidence. The approach adopted so far has been to admit any evidence that may have probative value, unless the admission of such evidence is outweighed by the need to ensure a fair trial. This has led to a lack of general norms that would establish the exclusion of certain types of evidence as a matter of principle. Basically, on a case-by-case basis the judges have decided to admit any evidence available and then rule, with great freedom, whether to consider it credible or not, irrespective of any prior evaluation. The tendency has thus been always to admit evidence and, eventually, to avoid using it at a later stage, when appraising the evidence concerning the guilt or innocence of the accused.

In general, rules that exclude evidence may pursue two objectives. On the one hand, they may aim at imposing rules of behaviour on the parties. In this case, they are drafted as sanctions for the violation of the abovementioned rules of behaviour. For example, if the Prosecutor does not communicate to the Defence the name of a witness and his or her statements, the Prosecutor may be deprived of the right to call such witness. This consequence may be

---

[254] For this system to operate satisfactorily, it is important that the Prosecution keeps two separate files: one containing evidence against the accused, the other comprising all exculpatory evidence. In the case of uncertainty about the exculpatory nature of evidence, the relevant document or witness statement or any other material should be placed in both files.

called a 'procedural sanction'; it essentially aims at ensuring respect for the Rules of Procedure. On the other hand, another sector from which the exclusion of evidence may derive is the field of values embodied in the rules of criminal procedure. Exclusionary rules may be linked to the belief that there are certain types of evidence, such as hearsay, which are intrinsically unreliable and therefore unsuitable for the discovery of truth. Other examples, which may make the reasoning clearer are methods such as the lie detector or the 'truth serum', etc. These types of evidence are generally excluded as a matter of principle, on the basis of a negative judgement about their compatibility with the values behind procedural rules. In the systems of international criminal justice, on the contrary, all methods are in principle admitted, unless the judges make a different evaluation. In this respect, it is interesting to note that this interpretation is supported by a decision of the Trial Chamber in *Naletilić and Martinović*.[255] The Chamber had to deal with a motion concerning the request of an accused to be questioned by the Prosecutor by the application of a polygraph, rejected the application because it deemed that polygraph examinations are not a reliable indication of credibility. Specific consideration was given to the fact that under the Rules it is for judges to determine the credibility of witnesses, including the accused. This reasoning, although not entirely persuasive on the ground that the request referred to the use of the polygraph during questioning by the Prosecutor and not to the admission of it as evidence, confirms that in the *ad hoc* Tribunals the admission of evidence is left entirely to the judges.

I submit that the rules of international criminal procedure are too flexible. As mentioned above, there are *no specific sanctions* for violations of the rules of procedure. Thus the judges are left without any guidelines on the principles they should apply. Additionally, there are *no exclusionary rules*. Therefore, in theory any evidence may be submitted to the judges. In the past, judges have never developed general categories pursuant to which a certain kind of evidence might, in principle, be presumed as inadmissible. Thus the general rule is to admit any evidence. Certainly, international criminal procedure contains far fewer formalities and rituals than national criminal procedure. It is, however, questionable whether this is the most appropriate solution. If the interests protected by the rigorous character of the rules of criminal procedure are that justice be done without abuse (or even without the risk of abuse), then it seems highly inappropriate to lower this guarantee at the international level. This is especially so if one considers the political implications which usually lie behind international criminal trials. Moreover, it seems correct to adopt general rules on the exclusion of evidence to ensure equality of treatment to defendants.

---

[255] See Trial Chamber Decision, *Naletilić* and *Martinović* (IT–98–34–PT), 27 November 2000.

It has been argued correctly that no mandatory exclusionary rules means no exclusionary rules.[256] This seems to be the case in international criminal justice. It is submitted that the lack of specific rules both on procedural sanctions and on the exclusion of evidence gives rise to uncertainty. Both exclusionary rules and procedural sanctions are embedded in societal values and policy decisions. These decisions consider the rules of criminal procedure as the method for the discovery of truth in criminal matters. Just as the trustworthiness of scientific discoveries is based on respect for the scientific method, the credibility of the outcome of a criminal trial is based on respect for the rules. Judges have to establish the truth by using a pre-determined method, which is outlined in the rules of procedure. If these rules are not considered as a useful way of attaining truth then they should be amended. It is not possible to decide on a case-by-case basis whether to apply them or not.

It is contended that judges are left with a burden that is disproportionate to their competence. They do not possess societal authority to decide the appropriate sanctions for procedural violations, nor can they determine what evidence should not be admitted as intrinsically unreliable.

In the *ad hoc* Tribunals there are two sets of provisions dealing with this issue. First, there is Rule 89 (C) and (D), providing that 'a Chamber may admit any relevant evidence which it deems to have probative value' and that it may 'exclude evidence if its probative value is substantially outweighed by the need to ensure a fair trial'. Secondly, as regards the exclusion of evidence, Rule 95 stipulates that 'no evidence shall be admissible if obtained by methods which cast substantial doubt on its reliability or if its admission is antithetical to, and would seriously damage, the integrity of the proceedings'. The original text of this rule read 'evidence obtained directly or indirectly by means which constitute a serious violation of internationally protected human rights shall not be admissible'. This text was amended at the Fifth Plenary Session in January 1995 according to a proposal made by the Governments of the United Kingdom and the United States.[257] It seems that the amendment was introduced to broaden the rights of suspects and accused persons.[258] It does not seem that the Chambers of the *ad hoc* Tribunals have ever applied the provisions of Rule 95 RPE. This confirms and reinforces the opinion that the lack of mandatory exclusionary rules amounts to no exclusionary rule at all.

The ICC Statute adopted the original formula of the *ad hoc* Tribunals' Rules of Procedure. Article 69, paragraph 7, ICC St. establishes that 'evidence obtained by means of a violation of this Statute or internationally recognized human rights shall not be admissible'. This rule, however, contains

---

[256] See Bradley, note 198 above.   [257] Cf. Jones, note 96 above, at 311.
[258] Cf. ICTY Second Annual Report, **www.un.org/icty/rappannu-e/1996/index.htm**, para. 26 note 9.

two further qualifications. First, it requires that 'the violation cast substantial doubt on the reliability of the evidence'. Secondly, the 'admission of the evidence would be antithetical to and would seriously damage the integrity of the proceedings'. The overall wording of this rule, thus, implies that the exclusion of evidence will be left *in concreto* to the judges in every single case. Nonetheless, it seems correct to argue that any violation of internationally recognized human rights *ipso facto* meets the requirement that the integrity of the proceedings should not be impaired.[259]

In conclusion, international criminal justice has strengthened the flexible approach to the admission of evidence. This is an approach that may seem useful from the viewpoint of effectiveness of justice. It is argued, however, that such a system does not ensure equality of treatment to defendants. Moreover, it does not increase the expeditiousness of trials. Evidence may be admitted, presented, and discussed in Court, but, in the end, may turn out to be unconvincing. This, naturally, may lead to considerable loss of time, without any real advantage for the enhancement of justice.

[259] Cf. Chapter 2 section B above.

4

The Rights of the Accused to Appeal
and Revision

I. GENERAL—THE RIGHTS OF APPEAL AND REVISION AS A MEANS FOR OBTAINING REDRESS (JUDICIAL AND NON-JUDICIAL REMEDIES)

Originally, in criminal procedure, the right of an accused to file an appeal against conviction or the right to seek review did not exist.[1] Appeal and revision (or review) were not shaped as autonomous rights; rather, they were part of a more general claim for reconsideration of either the judgment or the sentence by the Sovereign.[2] Only subsequently were such rights institutionalized and organized into several proceedings with differing forms.[3] Contemporary forms of review of the judgment on responsibility or the sentencing judgment belong to this broad category. Appeal and revision, as well as pardon and commutation, all emerged as variations of a single original plea for reconsideration of the case by the supreme authority.

In their modern versions these forms of reconsideration may be classified according to the general distinction between judicial and non-judicial remedies. This distinction is based both on the character of the proceedings and on their outcome. As for the character of the proceedings, it can be said that judicial remedies are generally conducted in court, before independent and impartial judges, in the presence of an opposing party, following precise rules of procedure, and their outcome is usually a judgment that affirms, reverses, or revises the impugned decision. In other words, they all imply a pronouncement on guilt or innocence, or on the application of law in the proceedings. On the other hand, non-judicial remedies are generally not afforded by a court, are often summarily organized, and above all do not aim at modifying the judgment that closed the proceedings.

---

[1] In both civil law and common law appellate and review proceedings have been introduced in relatively recent times: cf. W. La Fave, 'Appeal', in S. Kadish (gen. ed.), *Encyclopaedia of Crime and Justice* (New York: The Free Press, 1983), i, 62–67 and R. Orestano, 'Appello, a) Diritto Romano', in *Enciclopedia del Diritto* (Milan: Giuffrè, 1958), ii, 708–714.

[2] Referring to that time it is probably not even totally appropriate to refer to such a possibility as a right. See *ibidem*.

[3] In this respect it may be noted that in *common law* systems the right of appeal has been provided for more recently than in civil law countries. Particularly, '[it] was not until the enactment of the Criminal Appeal Act of 1907 that a modern and satisfactory system of appellate review was available in England': see La Fave, note 1 above, at 62.

Non-judicial remedies are available in the framework of international criminal justice in the form of pardon or commutation of the sentence, and they are both granted by competent state authorities (under the supervision of the Tribunal) during the enforcement phase (see Chapter 5 below).

In this chapter discussion is restricted to the two main forms of judicial remedies provided for in the framework of international criminal procedure: the rights to appeal and to seek review. The first of these remedies is a so-called 'ordinary remedy' against a decision,[4] while the second has an extra-ordinary nature.[5] This aspect of appellate and review proceedings was not properly considered in the procedural system of the *ad hoc* Tribunals. Therefore, the Statutes and the Rules are not very clear on the scope of these proceedings and on their mutual relationship.[6] Additionally, in so far as the right of appeal is concerned, it appears that the idea that trial and appeal are the two phases of a single criminal process[7] was not fully shared (or perceived) by all (or at least by most of) the drafters of the Statute and the Rules of the *ad hoc* Tribunals. Therefore, the resulting procedural system is somehow con-tradictory and appeal proceedings oscillate between really aiming at a second judgment on facts and just amounting to a review on points of law.

The right of appeal (section II below) was lacking in the procedural systems of the Nuremberg and Tokyo Tribunals. Subsequently, it emerged as part of international law on human rights and it has been considered as a rule having 'imperative' character,[8] which, as such, has been inserted into the procedural rules of the *ad hoc* Tribunals and the ICC. However, it does not seem that the notion of imperative rule, adopted by the Appeals Chamber in *Vujin*, may be intended in the sense of Article 53 of the Vienna Convention on the Law of Treaties. It would be very hard to argue that the right of appeal is protected by a rule of *jus cogens*.[9] Nonetheless, it is true that the right of appeal is an essential component of due process guarantees and, as such, it has been inserted into the procedural systems of the *ad hoc* Tribunals and the ICC.

---

[4]   G. Stefani, G. Levasseur, and B. Bouloc, *Procédure Pénale* (14th edn., Paris: Dalloz, 1990), at 937.

[5]   M. Rassat, *Procédure Pénale* (Paris: PUF, 1990), 644–667, and in particular at 660.

[6]   This had been already noted by G. Vassalli, 'Il Tribunale internazionale per i crimini commessi nei territori dell'ex Jugoslavia', in *la Legislazione Penale* (1994), at 355–356.

[7]   See M. Lemonde, 'L'Appel en matière criminelle', in 4 *Justices* (1996), 85–98.

[8]   See Judgment of the Appeals Chamber in the contempt proceedings against one of the defence attorneys of Duško Tadić, Mr. Milan Vujin (IT–94–1–A–AR77), 27 February 2001, fourth 'Considering'. The Judgment reads: '[c]onsidering moreover that Article 14 of the International Covenant reflects an imperative norm of international law to which the Tribunal must adhere'.

[9]   Such a conclusion would have required a more in-depth analysis by the Appeals Chamber. In all likelihood the Chamber somehow over-empasized the importance of the right of appeal, as it deemed inappropriate to dismiss the motion simply because the rules were silent on the matter. Cf. in this respect the dissenting opinion of Judge Wald, notes 10–14. Subsequently Rule 77 was amended (July 2002), and it now contains an express provision on the right to appeal against judgments in contempt by the Appeals Chamber (Rule 77 (K) ICTY RPE).

Appeal proceedings involve both an assessment of the facts of the case as established by the judgment of the Trial Chamber, and scrutiny over the interpretation and application of law.[10] In this respect, one ought to consider that the differences existing between the principles governing appellate proceedings in civil law and common law systems were not clarified in the *ad hoc* Tribunals' Statutes. As mentioned above, in continental systems procedural rules generally provide for a broader scope of appellate review, which includes a re-examination of factual issues. On the other hand, the Anglo-Saxon model is traditionally more restrictive, particularly in so far as review on facts and appeals by the prosecution are concerned. In international criminal procedure the civil law approach has somewhat prevailed,[11] by assigning to the Appeals Chamber a broad scope of review on factual issues and entrusting the Prosecutor with the power to appeal both on errors of facts and law.

As regards the right of review (or revision) it is submitted that the provisions of the ICC Statute should serve as guidelines for interpreting the provisions of the *ad hoc* Tribunals' Statutes. Moreover, the first application of the review procedure by the ICTR, in *Barayagwiza*, raises some concern about the appropriateness of such a precedent, particularly in light of the developments in international criminal procedure as enshrined in the ICC Statute.

The power of the Prosecutor to appeal or seek review seems in conflict with the principle of *ne bis in idem* (or protection against double jeopardy). Arguably, this principle should lead to a limitation of the power of the Prosecutor to appeal or seek review of judgments. Such a power is too broad in the procedural system of the *ad hoc* Tribunals. In particular, since the Prosecutor is under no legal duty to start a case against an accused, but, on the contrary, the Statute and the Rules entrust prosecution organs with very wide discretion as to the choice of cases to be brought for trial. Some improvement in this respect has already been introduced in the Statute of the

---

[10] In civil law countries this is called '*principe de l'effet dévolutif*' or '*principio dell'effetto devolutivo*', cf. Rassat, note 5 above, at 639–640 and F. Cordero, *Procedura Penale* (Milan: Giuffrè, 1998), at 1016–1017.

[11] It is interesting to note, however, that not all civil law systems provide for a right of appeal even in most serious cases. This is, for example, the case in France, where there is no right of appeal against judgments of the *Cour d'Assises*. This is for two main reasons: the Court has a unique composition (professional judges assisted by a jury) and the right to appeal is granted at the preliminary stage against the decision of the *juge d'instruction*. Stefani, Levasseur and Bouloc, note 4 above, describe these reasons as follows: '*[l']impossibilité d'interjeter appel contre un arrêt d'assises s'explique par des considérations particulières à cette juridiction. Elle résulte tout d'abord de la composition de celle-ci . . . et de sa plénitude de juridiction. Elle tient aussi à ce que la Cour d'assises n'est saisie et ne statue qu'après une instruction à deux degrés, faite successivement par le juge d'instruction et par la Chambre d'accusation*', at 30. The same explanation is given by J. Hatchard, B. Huber, and R. Vogler (eds.), *Comparative Criminal Procedure* (London: British Institute of International and Comparative Law, 1996), at 237, where it is said 'the elaborateness of the pre-trial investigation is seen as a justification for limiting the scope of appeals from the *Cour d'assises*'.

ICC, which provides the accused with broader rights than the Prosecution. For example, the right of revision is granted only to the convicted person, while the Prosecutor may seek revision merely on that person's behalf.

II. THE RIGHT OF THE ACCUSED TO APPEAL:
FROM NUREMBERG AND TOKYO TO THE *AD HOC* TRIBUNALS AND THE ICC

1. General

The Nuremberg Charter did not provide for any right of appeal. Article 26 of the Nuremberg Charter clearly stated that the judgment of the Tribunal was final and not subject to review.[12] On the other hand, the Charter of the Tokyo Tribunal contained a rule providing for review of the judgment and sentence by the Supreme Commander for the Allied Powers in Japan (Article 17 of the IMTFE Charter).[13] Hence, all convicted persons filed a request for revision with the Supreme Commander, General MacArthur. These requests raised several issues concerning both the application and interpretation of procedural rules, and also the appropriateness of sentences imposed by the Tribunal. General MacArthur, following diplomatic consultations, decided to uphold the verdicts and sentences of the Tokyo Tribunal. The legal issues raised by the appellants, however, were left unsolved. Thus, subsequently, defendants filed an appeal with the US Supreme Court,[14] which, although it admitted the presentation of such motions, eventually declined jurisdiction on the merits.[15] In any case, it must be said that the procedural systems of the Nuremberg and Tokyo Tribunals did not provide for a right of appeal, certainly not in the current understanding of such a right, or in forms known to national criminal procedural law.

As mentioned above (see Chapter 1, section II above), the human rights doctrine insisted on due process and fair trial guarantees, including the right

---

[12] Nonetheless, a review of sentences by the Control Council was possible, but such a review was linked to the general power of controlling the enforcement of sentences. In this respect, cf. A. Cassese, 'Opinion: The International Criminal Tribunal for the Former Yugoslavia and Human Rights', in 2 *EHRLR* (1997), 329 at 330–331.

[13] Article 17 read as follows: '[t]he record of the trial will be transmitted directly to the Supreme Commander for the Allied Powers for his action thereon. A sentence will be carried out in accordance with the order of the Supreme Commander for the Allied Powers, who may at any time reduce or otherwise alter the sentence except to increase its severity.' This provision included the power of the Supreme Commander to grant pardon or commutation.

[14] It is interesting to note that Justice Robert Jackson, formerly US Prosecutor at the Nuremberg Trial, in his capacity as member of the US Supreme Court voted in favour of hearing preliminary arguments in this matter.

[15] For a thorough examination of this process see R. Minear, *Victor's Justice—The Tokyo War Crimes Trial* (Princeton, NJ: Princeton University Press, 1971), 166–170.

of appeal.[16] This right is specifically protected by various international provisions contained in human rights treaties,[17] and has been included in the provisions of the Statutes of the UN *ad hoc* Tribunals[18] and the ICC Statute.[19] The right of the accused to appeal has been provided for because it is one of the fundamental tenets of modern criminal procedure. The Secretary General clearly set out this view in his report on the establishment of the ICTY[20] and the ICTY Appeals Chamber restated the same view in its decision on jurisdiction in *Tadić*.[21]

2. *The right of appeal as a right protected by international human rights law*

Human rights law made two main conquests regarding the right of appeal. One is the very recognition of this right. The other is that the law must precisely determine the conditions and procedure for the enjoyment of such a right, which no longer depends upon the arbitrary decision of any state official.[22]

Article 14, paragraph 5, of the ICCPR provides that everyone convicted of a crime shall have the right of review of his or her conviction and sentence by a higher tribunal.[23] The same rule is provided for in regional instruments,

---

[16] See in this respect, e.g. H.N.A. Noor Muhammad, 'Due Process of Law for Persons Accused of Crime', in L. Henkin (ed.), *The International Bill of Rights: The Covenant on Civil and Political Rights* (New York: Columbia University Press, 1981), 155–156 and M. Nowak, *UN Covenant on Civil and Political Rights* (Kehl: Engel, 1993), 266–268, at 266.

[17] Article 14.5 ICCPR, Article 2 ECHR Optional Protocol 7, and Article 8.2, ACHR.

[18] The *ad hoc* Tribunal Statutes both provide for the right to appeal by the accused and the Prosecutor. Article 25 ICTY St. and 24 ICTR St. state: '1. The Appeals Chamber shall hear appeals from persons convicted by the Trial Chamber or from the Prosecutor on the following grounds: a) an error on a question of law invalidating the decision; or b) an error of fact which has occasioned a miscarriage of justice. 2. The Appeals Chamber may affirm, reverse or revise the decisions taken by the Trial Chambers.'

[19] The right of appeal as an indispensable condition of the 'due process' model, as embodied in international human rights law, has been reinforced by the adoption of the provisions of Articles 81 and 82 of the ICC Statute on the right of appeal. These Articles, which are far more complete than their equivalent in the *ad hoc* Tribunals system, provide for the right of appeal and organize the procedure to be followed for appellate proceedings, against both judgment and sentence, as well as interlocutory decisions. Moreover, these provisions have been supplemented by Section Eight of the Rules of Procedure and Evidence, which clarifies the procedural framework, including time limits for filing motions and other relevant matters.

[20] The Secretary General's Report, 5/25074, 3 May 1993, states that '[the right of appeal] is a fundamental element of individual civil and political rights and has, *inter alia*, been incorporated in the International Covenant on Civil and Political Rights. For this reason the Secretary General has proposed that there should be an Appeals Chamber' (para. 116).

[21] Cf. ICTY Appeals Chamber decision, *Tadić* (IT–95–1–AR72), 2 October 1995, para. 25.

[22] Cf. section I above.

[23] See in this respect the commentary by M. Bossuyt, *Guide to the 'Travaux Préparatoires' of the International Covenant on Civil and Political Rights* (Dordrecht: Nijhoff, 1987), at 310.

although often in slightly different forms.[24] Two exceptions to the right of appeal are generally allowed: in the case of minor offences or in cases where the trial at first instance is held before the highest court.[25] Additionally, the right of appeal is recognized in many procedural systems at a national level and has been included in the constitutional provisions of a large number of States.[26]

For our purposes, it does not seem necessary to explore in depth the differences among the various provisions as these may be explained referring to the differences existing in the legal systems of countries participating in each treaty-based system.[27] The exceptions contained in the European Convention, for example, are clear indications that national procedural systems have influenced the drafting of those rules.[28]

In short, human rights law leaves a certain degree of flexibility to States in the organization of appellate proceedings in their legal orders.[29] Nonetheless, the right of appeal has been recognized as being a condition for the realization of fair trial and due process,[30] with some exceptions that may justify more restrictive approaches in national systems. Furthermore, it still remains unclear whether, under human rights provisions, the right to appeal is merely

---

[24] See Article 8, para. 2 h), of the American Convention, which provides for a right of appeal before higher tribunals. The ECHR originally did not contain such a right, but subsequently it was added to the European system by Article 2 of Optional Protocol no. 7. This Article establishes that '[e]veryone convicted of a criminal offence by a tribunal shall have the right to have his conviction or sentence reviewed by a higher tribunal'. The explanatory report on Protocol 7 clarifies that there is no need for the right of appeal to be granted in respect of both the judgment and the sentence. It is sufficient that a right of appeal against either the judgment or the sentence be granted. In this respect cf. F. Jacobs and R. White, *The European Convention on Human Rights* (2nd edn., Oxford: Clarendon Press, 1996), at 170. Moreover, the Banjul Charter protects the right of appeal to an extent comparable with those of other international provisions.

[25] Para. 2 of Optional Protocol 7 to the ECHR sets out explicitly the two exceptions to the principle of appeal, but they may be considered implicit in the other texts.

[26] Cf. M.C. Bassiouni, 'Human Rights in the Context of Criminal Justice,: Identifying International Procedural Protections and Equivalent Protections in National Constitutions', in 3 *DJICL* 235, at 287.

[27] In Italy, e.g. when the Head of State or Government or a Member of the Cabinet is tried for offences committed in his or her official functions the trial is conducted before a specially constituted Constitutional Court. In this case no right of appeal is granted. This led Italy to make a reservation to the ICCPR to this effect. On the scope of the reservation an important pronouncement was made by the Human Rights Committee in *Fanali* v. *Italy*, 75/1980.

[28] In the case of the special procedure mentioned above (note 25) Italy needed the exception provided for by para. 2 of Article 2 of Optional Protocol 7 ECHR, in order for the protocol to be compatible with its national law.

[29] France, e.g., when signing the ICCPR declared that the right to review by a higher tribunal could be very well limited just to review on points of law (i.e. before the *Cour de Cassation*). Cf. in this respect, Stefani, Levasseur and Bouloc, note 4 above: '*[la] France a déclaré que l'examen par une juridiction supérieure peut se limiter à un contrôle de l'application de la loi (cas du pourvoi en cassation contre les décisions des Cours d'assises)*', at 27 note 2. This was done because of the absence of a review on facts against the judgment of the *Cour d'assise*.

[30] Noor Muhammad and Nowak, both note 16 above.

directed to obtaining review on points of law, or whether it has a more extensive scope amounting to a re-examination of the facts of the case.[31]

In international criminal procedure, however, the right of appeal has been fully implemented and exceptions, although applicable in theory, have not been admitted.

3. The right of the accused to appeal in the ad hoc Tribunals system

(a) General

The right of appeal guaranteed under international human rights provisions would not perforce have required the creation of an appeals section in the *ad hoc* Tribunals or in the ICC systems. When deciding whether or not to provide for a right of appeal in the framework of the *ad hoc* Tribunals there were arguments both for and against.[32] Some contended that the Tribunals were themselves the highest courts, and thus speaking of review by a higher court would not really make sense.[33] Eventually, however, a literal interpretation of international human rights provisions, and above all the aspiration to offer the best guarantees of a fair trial, induced the drafters to provide for such a right in the Statutes of the Tribunals (and subsequently the ICC).

There were three main reasons militating against a right of appeal. First, the exception of trials held before the highest available court, which is explicitly provided for by the rules of the European Convention, but which may also be considered implicit in the other provisions, would naturally have covered international judicial organs. Secondly, the decisions of international courts are generally not subject to appeal, with a few exceptions such as the decisions of the Court of First Instance of the European Community. Thirdly, earlier international criminal tribunals (Nuremberg and Tokyo) did not provide for a right

---

[31] In this respect, these doubts have been clearly expressed by P. Van Djik, *The Right of the Accused to a Fair Trial under International Law* (Utrecht: 1 SIM Special, 1983), at 49 where the author wonders whether '[the] provision entails that appeal must be open to a court which reviews both the finding of the facts [and] the application of the law, or whether this obligation has also been fulfilled when appeal [is open] to a higher court, whose competence is limited to the latter review'.

[32] No right of appeal was provided for in the first projects for an International Criminal Court, cf. e.g. Article 68 of the Draft of the International Association of Penal Law, on which see V. Pella, 'Towards an International Criminal Court', in 44 *AJIL* (1950), 37–68, at 64: 'there should be, it is thought, no right of appeal from the decisions of an international criminal court save by way of application for revision'. A. Pellet, 'Le Tribunal international poudre aux yeux ou avancée décisive', in 98 *RGDIP* (1994), 7–60, suggested that it may have been more appropriate to hold trials before a larger panel, comprising more judges representing all the components of the international community. The same position had been held by France in the project it submitted for the creation of a Tribunal for the former Yugoslavia: see note 34 below.

[33] Cf., in this respect, the comments made by V. Morris and M. Scharf, *An Insider's Guide to the International Criminal Tribunal for the former Yugoslavia* (Irvington on Hudson, NY: Transnational, 1995), i, at 293–295.

of appeal. Hence, one could have thought that there was no compelling need to provide for a right of appeal in the Statutes of the *ad hoc* Tribunals.[34] These Tribunals, however, were created with the purpose of ensuring the highest standards of protection of fundamental rights.[35] Therefore, the drafters decided to provide for appellate proceedings, thus contributing to the strengthening of fair trial provisions in international criminal procedure.

The Statutes of the *ad hoc* Tribunals contain provisions on the right of appeal against judgments (and albeit implicitly against sentences). The judges, however, when amending the Rules at the fifth Plenary Session (3 February 1995), added the possibility of filing motions for interlocutory appeals. Hence, three main categories of appellate proceedings are now provided for in the system of the *ad hoc* Tribunals: interlocutory appeals, appeals against judgment, and appeals against sentence.

Finally, mention should be made of the decision issued by the Appeals Chamber in *Vujin*, ancillary proceedings on contempt of court in the *Tadić* case. Milan Vujin was one of the attorneys in Duško Tadić's defence team. Allegedly, in the course of the proceedings on appeal in *Tadić*, Vujin had interfered with some of the witnesses; thus he was held in contempt and tried at first instance by the same Appeals Chamber which eventually convicted him.[36] Subsequently, he filed an appeal against this conviction. The Appeals Chamber (although differently composed) heard his appeal.[37] The Chamber held that it ought to admit the motion filed by Mr Vujin, irrespective of the absence of any specific provision to that effect in the Statute or in the Rules, because the right of appeal is one of the most fundamental tenets of due process guarantees.[38] The right of appeal in respect of contempt proceedings was also upheld in *Nobilo*.[39]

---

[34] Actually, some had suggested this option, such as e.g. France in the Report of the Committee of French Jurists to study the establishment of an International Criminal Tribunal to judge the crimes committed in the former Yugoslavia: see *ibidem*, ii, 327–374, at 352 (paras. 138–140).

[35] This has often been emphasized by the Secretary General in his report and echoed by some members of the Security Council in the debates preceding the institution of the Tribunal. This is also the opinion of Cassese, who suggests that international criminal trials aim at being exemplary proceedings, note 12 above: '[the] Tribunal may defend and protect human rights by fully applying the *international human rights standards* relating to the accused, victims and witnesses in criminal trials and setting thereby an exemplary standard for future international criminal trials', at 330. *Contra* see C. Warbrick, 'International Criminal Court and Fair Trial', in 3 *JACL* (1998), 45–64, at 54–55, who argues that human rights provisions do not set out exemplary standards, but simply minimum guarantees.

[36] Appeals Chamber Judgment, Vujin, in *Tadić* (IT–94–1-R77), 31 January 2000.

[37] In this respect it 'was held that the possibility of an appeal to the same judicial organ did not satisfy the guarantee of paragraph 5': see Communication R.15/64, *Salgar de Montejo* v. *Colombia*, A/37/40, at 168 and 173, quoted by Van Dijk, note 31 above, note 264.

[38] See Appeals Chamber Judgment, Vujin, in *Tadić* (IT–94–1-R77–AR72), 27 February 2001.

[39] Cf. Appeals Chamber Judgment, Nobilo, in *Blaškić* (IT–14/1–T-R77), 31 May 2001. As mentioned elsewhere (note 9 above), the Rules were subsequently amended specifically to provide for such a right.

The abovementioned precedents confirm the commitment of UN Tribunals to the fair administration of justice, by offering to the accused, no matter whether in principal or ancillary proceedings, the highest guarantees of due process. As a negative commentary, however, one may note that such proceedings have the counter-effect of implying considerable loss of time, as suggested by Judge Wald and Judge Robinson in their separate and partly dissenting opinions,[40] without being really required by human rights law.

(b) Interlocutory appeals

The Statutes of the *ad hoc* Tribunals do not explicitly mention interlocutory appeals.[41] However, as mentioned above, the judges introduced such a possibility into the Rules. Interlocutory appeals may be filed against decisions of the Trial Chamber on preliminary motions (Rule 72).[42] These are motions aimed at challenging the jurisdiction of the Tribunal, alleging defects in the indictment, seeking severance of counts or separate trial or raising objections based on the refusal to assign defence counsel. Only for one category of preliminary motion, i.e. on jurisdiction, is appeal granted *de jure*, while for all other motions leave must be obtained from a bench of three judges of the Appeals Chamber upon showing that 'good cause' exists.[43] Nonetheless, it must be noted that the amendment adopted in December 2000 provides that the bench must also examine appeals against decisions on jurisdiction, to determine whether the motion really refers to jurisdiction within the accepted meaning of the Rules.[44] Subsequently, the possibility of resorting to interlocutory appeal

[40] Both Judges (Robinson and Wald) expressed the view that such proceedings may globally worsen the efficiency of the Tribunal in fulfilling its mission. See their dissenting opinions, 31 May 2001.

[41] Cf. *contra* M.C. Bassiouni and P. Manikas, *The Law of the International Criminal Tribunal for the former Yugoslavia* (Irvington on Hudson, NY: Transnational, 1996), at 980.

[42] Originally interlocutory appeal was provided for only for motions on jurisdiction; for the text of the RPE prior to the amendments, Rule 72 (B), see UN doc. IT/32/Rev. 6.

[43] In June 1996, interlocutory appeal was extended also to other preliminary motions set forth in Rule 72, but only upon showing before a bench of three judges of the Appeals Chamber that a 'serious cause' existed. Subsequently, this procedure was extended to include application on provisional release and the term serious cause substituted by 'good cause'. For an historical perspective on the amendments to the rules on interlocutory appeals, cf. J. Jones, *The Practice of the International Criminal Tribunals for the former Yugoslavia and Rwanda* (Irvington on Hudson, NY: Transnational, 1998), Rules 72 and 73, 253–271. The Rules on interlocutory appeals were amended again in April 2002. In particular, the possibility of filing an interlocutory appeal other than on jurisdiction has been limited, in that the party must obtain a certification from the Trial Chamber authorizing the party to appeal.

[44] The broad scope of this rule has been limited by the provisions of Rule 72 (D) (1 and 13 December 2000, 23rd Plenary Session; entered into force on 19 January 2001) which explicitly defines what should be intended for a motion challenging jurisdiction. These are motions challenging '[an] indictment on the ground that it does not relate to (i) any of the persons in Articles 1, 6, 7 and 9 of the Statute; (ii) the territories indicated in Articles 1, 8 and 9 of the Statute; (iii) the period indicated in Articles 1, 8 and 9 of the Statute; (iv) any of the violations indicated in Articles 2, 3, 4 and 5 of the Statute'.

was broadened to include other motions.[45] This second category of motions for interlocutory appeal may be heard, but only with leave of the bench, upon satisfying the requirements set out in Rule 73. These requirements are either that the 'impugned decision would cause prejudice to the case of the party that could not be cured by the final disposal of the trial including post-judgment appeal', or that the issue is of 'general importance to proceedings before the Tribunal or international law generally'.[46] However, at the 23rd Extraordinary Plenary Session (April 2001), this Rule was amended to provide specifically that a number of decisions by the Trial Chamber, such as orders and decisions under Rule 71 (depositions) and denials of motions under Rule 98-*bis* (acquittals at the close of Prosecution case), may not be subject to interlocutory appeal (Rule 73(B) ICTY RPE). Moreover, Rule 65 provides for a specific interlocutory appeal motion against decisions denying provisional release, provided that the bench finds that 'good cause' has been shown.[47]

The procedure before a bench of three judges of the Appeals Chamber was introduced by way of amendment to the Rules.[48] It aims at trying to reconcile both the right of the parties to have their motions heard by the Appeals Chamber and the need for effectiveness of the system, as clearly too many interlocutory appeals would seriously obstruct the proceedings and cause delays to the main procedure. Nonetheless, subsequently, a new paragraph (C) was added to Rule 73 of the ICTY RPE. This new rule provides that the Trial Chamber may exclude prior review by the bench by certifying that 'an interlocutory appeal . . . is appropriate for the continuation of the trial'. Where the Trial Chamber issues such certification the party may appeal without leave. Furthermore, rather surprisingly, in April 2002, at another Extraordinary Plenary Session, the judges of the ICTY decided to extend the system of certification to all preliminary decisions except in the case of decision on a preliminary motion on jurisdiction. Therefore, parties may no longer file interlocutory appeals against decisions on preliminary motions, unless the Trial Chamber issues a certification indicating that the decision involves an issue that would significantly affect the proceedings.

The current system of certification does not seem entirely persuasive for two reasons. First, the rule does not seem to fit too well into the procedural

---

[45] This rule was amended at the fourteenth plenary Session in November 1997 and, at that time, the possibility of resorting interlocutory appeal was broadened.

[46] Statistically, the second test has been easier to meet. Globally, less than 25% of the motions are admitted. See in this respect J. Hocking, 'Interlocutory Appeals before the ICTY', in R. May *et al.* (eds.), *Essays on ICTY Procedure and Evidence: In Honour of Gabrielle Kirk McDonald* (The Hague: Kluwer, 2001), at 470.

[47] Rule 65 (D) RPE provides that 'any decision rendered under this Rule shall be subject to appeal in cases where leave is granted by a bench of three judges of the Appeals Chamber, upon good cause being shown'. This Rule was introduced into the ICTY RPE at the 13th Plenary Session in July 1997, (IT/32/Rev.11) and it originally required 'serious' rather than 'good' cause being shown.

[48] In this respect, cf. Jones, note 44 above, Rule 72, 251–262.

system of the Tribunal, in that it shifts onto the Trial Chamber a role, generally played by the bench, which requires a certain detachment from the decision (the certification system is clearly against the principle *nemo iudex in re propria*). In this respect, it should be noted that while decisions by the 'bench' may have led to developing a consistent body of principles on the criteria for the admission of interlocutory appeals, leaving the certification to Trial Chambers increases the potential for diverging approaches. Secondly, the Rules as they stand now seem contrary to the recent effort of the Tribunal towards effectiveness. This 'certification process' burdens the Trial Chamber with re-discussing matters it has already settled for the purpose of deciding whether to issue a 'certification' or not. But what is more disappointing is that the parties, after having obtained such a 'certification', remain free to decide whether or not to file an interlocutory appeal. The Rules should, at least, provide that the party seeking certification loses the right to bring the certified matter before the Appeals Chamber at a later stage. Otherwise, should the party decide that it is not worth filing an interlocutory appeal this certification process simply results in pointless bureaucracy.

Furthermore, in the ICTY system there is another form of interlocutory appeal that concerns States. As a consequence of the proceedings on the issue of a subpoena in *Blaškić*, the judges introduced Rule 108-*bis*. This Rule allows States directly affected by a decision to file an appeal against that decision, where the decision relates to 'issues of general importance relating to the powers of the Tribunal'. The amendment was justified by the consideration that the decisions of Trial Chambers may affect the rights or interests of third parties, which, in specific circumstances, may have an interest in challenging a decision before the Appeals Chamber of the Tribunal. This kind of appeal is closely linked to the place assigned in the *ad hoc* Tribunals system to the Appeals Chamber, which is the authority that must ensure uniformity and certainty with regard to the interpretation of law. Finally, more recently Rule 54-*bis* was added to the Rules in order to provide for a right of appeal for either party against a decision rejecting the application of a party requesting the Chamber to issue an order for a State to produce documents.[49]

To sum up, in the ICTY procedural system there are *five classes of interlocutory appeals*: first, appeals on decision on jurisdiction, which must be heard by the Appeals Chamber because 'the appeal by either party lies as a right';[50] secondly, appeals on provisional release (Rule 65 RPE), subject to approval by the bench, upon showing that a good cause exists; third, appeals on other motions, provided that a certification by the Trial Chamber is obtained pursuant to Rule 72 (B) and (C), and 73 ICTY RPE; fourth, appeals

---

[49] This amendment was added for the sake of clarity, as it could have been contended that such an appeal was admissible under the first test provided for by Rule 73.

[50] Rule 72 (B) (i) explicitly provides that 'in the case of motions challenging jurisdiction . . . an appeal by either party lies as a right'.

by a State in the form of requests for review pursuant to Rule 108-*bis*; fifth, appeals against decisions rejecting a request for the production of documents by a State (Rule 54-*bis*). On the other hand, the ICTR has not adopted rules providing for appeals against preliminary motions other than those on jurisdiction, or the provisions on appeals by a State or on decisions concerning orders addressed to a State.

In the procedural system of the *ad hoc* Tribunals, initially, there has been a tendency to expand the scope of the right of appeal, which was originally limited by the provisions of the Statutes, to appeals by convicted person (implying that it could take place only after judgment). At the same time, however, there has always been the concern to avoid useless time consumption. The regulatory framework of the Tribunals has, thus, oscillated between favouring interlocutory appeals to a maximum extent and limiting them in order to reduce procedural delays.[51] Thus, on the one hand, a chance to file a motion for interlocutory appeal was granted for a larger number of decisions, but, on the other, review of the application by a bench of the Appeals Chamber was introduced to counterbalance the dilatory effects of interlocutory appeals on the proceedings. Moreover, under Rule 73 (E) of the ICTR RPE sanctions against attorneys filing frivolous motions may be taken.[52] Additionally, ICTR judges have amended their Rules, adopting Rule 108-*bis* (which is on a totally different topic from that of the corresponding Rule of ICTY RPE) providing for a Pre-hearing Judge in charge of all preliminary matters relating to appellate proceedings.[53] This certainly ensures the more effective handling of appeal proceedings, in line with the recent policy of the Tribunals

---

[51] This is confirmed by the broadening of rules on interlocutory appeals on the one hand, and by the adoption of amendments restricting resort to such appeals on the other hand, by requiring the bench to filter the motions.

[52] This rule was applied for the first time by the Appeals Chamber of the ICTR in its decision in *Akayesu* (ICTR–96–4–A), 1 June 2001. The ICTR Plenary had adopted this rule on 21 February 2000, on the basis of a suggestion made by the Group of experts appointed to review the functioning of the Tribunals. In this respect see the Report of the Expert Group to Conduct a Review of the Effective Operation and Functioning of the International Tribunal for the former Yugoslavia and the International Criminal Tribunal for Rwanda, UN doc. A/54/634, at 31 and 35, and recommendation 5. It is interesting to note that the ICTY Appeals Chamber, although the Yugoslav Tribunal has not yet adopted such a rule, has considered resorting to withholding payment of fees or costs involved in the preparation of frivolous or manifestly ill-founded motions, which were seen as an abuse of process. The Chamber, however, in the absence of an express provision in the ICTY RPE, deferred such a decision to the Registrar, who is responsible for supervising and administering the activities of assigned Defence Counsel. See the Decision on Motions for Leave to Appeal the Decision of the Appeals Chamber dated 29 May 2001, *Kupreškić and others* (IT–95–16–A), 18 June 2001, in which the Appeals Chamber requested the Registrar to consider withholding payment of fees.

[53] In this respect, one would think that the reference contained in Rule 107 to the application of the rules for trial proceedings would *mutatis mutandis* permit the appointment of a Pre–appeal Judge even in the system of the ICTY, although this is not specifically provided for in the Rules, this was, for example, the approach taken by the Appeals Chamber in *Delalić and others* (Decision 12 October 1999).

to entrust a single judge with the task of supervising the preparatory phase of both trial and appellate proceedings.

The main objective of interlocutory appeals is to save time. This was clearly set out by the Appeals Chamber in *Tadić*. The Chamber, in its well-known decision on jurisdiction,[54] clarified that a broad interpretation of rules providing for appeals on decisions relating to preliminary motions should be given. Such interpretation would serve both the interests of justice and the rights of the accused, in that it could help in preventing loss of time.

It clearly appears (also by looking at the various amendments to the Rules) that an attempt has been made to strike a balance between the rights of the parties and the interests of justice, with an eye to reducing the overall length of proceedings. The solving of problems at the appellate level by way of interlocutory decisions may reduce the length of proceedings by putting an end to controversies on procedural or substantive issues under scrutiny by a final decision by the highest judicial organ of the Tribunals. On the other hand, frivolous interlocutory appeals imply a loss of time with no benefit.[55] Hence, as far as motions for interlocutory appeal are concerned, it may generally be said that—at least in principle—they are encouraged only in so far as they aim at achieving the purpose of combining fairness and efficiency. The system of the Trial Chamber issuing a certification, however, does not seem the best way to solve this problem, and it is submitted that resort to the 'bench' of three judges (or even simply by one judge) of the Appeals Chamber would be a better solution.

(c) Against judgment

(i) General

The right of appeal against judgment is provided for by Article 25 of the ICTY Statute (Article 24 ICTR) and further implemented in Part Seven of the Rules of Procedure and Evidence.[56] Proceedings on appeal are mainly based on documents and judges clearly attempt to reduce hearings to a minimum. The aim of the appellate proceedings is to evaluate the activity of the Trial

---

[54] See Appeals Chamber Decision on Jurisdiction, *Tadić* (IT–94–1–AR72), 2 October 1995.

[55] In the ICTR system, sanctions may be resorted to both under Rule 46 and under Rule 73 for motions that are frivolous or constitute an abuse of process. Such sanctions include the non-payment of fees associated with the activity performed. It seems that these Rules are drafted simply with defence attorneys in mind. This kind of sanction, however, does not seem appropriate when referring to the Prosecution.

[56] The basic procedural rule establishes that provisions for trial proceedings may apply *mutatis mutandis* to appellate proceedings (Rule 107). Appeals are brought by way of a notice of appeal, which shall be filed with the Registry '[no] more than thirty days from the date on which the judgment or sentence was pronounced' (Rule 108). This notice, which must include the grounds for appeal, must be served upon the other parties. The Record on appeal consists of the parts of the trial record designated by the parties and certified by the Registrar. The Appeals Chamber, however, remains free to call for the entire trial record (Rule 109).

Chamber to verify whether there have been errors in two respects on facts or on law.

(ii) Scope of appellate proceedings: errors of fact and errors of law

According to the provisions of the Statutes (identical for both Tribunals) an appeal may be filed on grounds of error of law invalidating the judgment or sentence, or an error of fact leading to a miscarriage of justice. This rule implies that the Appeals Chamber should be entrusted with the twofold task of assessing the interpretation and application of the law and of reviewing, at least in part, the case on the merits. There are, thus, two main aspects of the right of appeal that should be distinguished: appellate proceedings can be seen as a process of review of the facts of the case and as a means of scrutinizing the correct interpretation and application of the law. In practice, however, it seems that the Appeals Chamber of the Tribunals has given far more weight to its function of legal supervision rather than its powers of review on factual issues.

As regards the meaning of 'error of fact', the Appeals Chamber has taken the view that appeal proceedings may not lead to substituting for the findings of the judges of first instance different findings by appeal judges. In other words, appeal proceedings should never lead to a re-trial, but should consist in an evaluation of the first instance trial on the basis of 'reasonableness'.[57] The Appeals Chamber has consistently held that a decision of a Trial Chamber on facts can be overturned only where it is proven that such decision was based on an assessment of facts that no reasonable person could endorse. This seems to clarify the scope of appellate proceedings: they cannot amount to a new trial, except where the conclusions on facts reached by the Trial Chamber are totally unreasonable. This standard, however, is very hard to apply in practice and the Appeals Chamber oscillates between a very restrictive approach and a broader one. Accordingly, it has not emerged very clearly on which basis and to what extent on appeal the facts of the case may be reviewed. For example, in *Kupreškić* the Appeals Chamber, although formally relying on the abovementioned standards set out in its previous decisions, reassessed the evaluation of the credibility of a crucial witness made by the Trial Chamber and reversed the Trial Chamber judgment.[58] According to the Appeals Chamber this was justified because

---

[57] See the Appeals Chamber Judgments, in *Tadić* (IT–94–1–A), 15 July 1999, para. 64, in *Aleksovski* (IT–95–14/1–A), 25 March 2000, para. 63, and in *Delalić and others* (IT–96–21–A), 20 February 2001, para. 491.

[58] It must be noted, however, that in this case the Appeals Chamber quashed the assessment of witness evidence made by the Trial Chamber without even seeing the relevant witness; it could at least have watched the video recording of the testimony.

the reasoning of the Trial Chamber on the credibility of this witness was insufficiently developed.[59]

In this respect, however, it seems that the approach adopted by the Appeals Chamber is too restrictive. The reasonableness test does not seem broad enough to encompass any error of fact causing a miscarriage of justice. Such error need not be unreasonable. Particularly in light of the possibility of producing additional evidence at the appellate stage, the Appeals Chamber should be entitled to overturn the findings of the Trial Chamber where this proves necessary for ensuring the proper administration of justice. As far as the rights of the accused are concerned, the Tribunal should adopt a broader interpretation allowing for a review on facts even in cases in which errors of fact, although not necessarily unreasonable, lead to a miscarriage of justice. Additionally it seems that in so doing the Appeals Chamber does not fulfil its mandate and its function. Although this may be a correct approach to prosecutorial appeals (in that it preserves the *ne bis in idem* principle in its broader interpretation), it does not seem equally convincing when confronted with the right of the accused to have his judgment or sentence reviewed by a higher tribunal. The scope of this right is certainly restricted by the approach taken by the Appeals Chamber, and one may really ask whether this was the intention of the drafters of the Statute when they established a two-step procedure. Furthermore, the power of the Appeals Chamber to review the case on factual issues must be read in close connection with the possibility of admitting new or additional evidence at the appellate stage (sub-section (iii) below). In this respect, it is submitted that the more the Appeals Chamber is in a position 'to know', the better it will be able to exercize its powers of review on factual issues.

Moving to the other ground of appeal (i.e. *error of law*); the Statute requires that it be 'an error which invalidates the decision'. The meaning of this expression, however, is not very clear. What is an error that invalidates the decision? To understand the expression correctly, it would be necessary to refer to a distinction between errors of law that can be rectified and errors that determine an absolute nullity. However, in the ICTY system there are no provisions specifying which errors produce invalidity and which do not. There is only a

---

[59] The Appeals Chamber emphasized that 'a Trial Chamber must always, in the interests of justice, proceed with extreme caution when assessing a witness' identification of the accused made under difficult circumstances. While a Trial Chamber is not obliged to refer to every piece of evidence on the trial record in its judgment, where a finding of guilt is made on the basis of identification evidence given by a witness under difficult circumstances, the Trial Chamber must rigorously implement its duty to provide a "reasoned opinion". In particular, a reasoned opinion must carefully articulate the factors relied upon in support of the identification of the accused and adequately address any significant factors impacting negatively on the reliability of the identification evidence' and added that '[where] the reasons for judgment discloses a lack of appreciation of relevant evidence and more particularly the complete disregard of such evidence, then it falls upon the reviewing tribunal to intercede'. See Appeals Chamber Judgment in *Kupre škić and others* (IT–95–16–A), 23 October 2001, para. 39.

very loose provision on procedural sanctions, which leaves it to the Chamber to determine what should be the consequence of the violation of a procedural rule (Rule 5, non-compliance with the Rules[60]). Thus, it seems that, at least in principle, no error of law automatically invalidates the decision. The evaluation of what is an error invalidating the decision will eventually depend on the determination of the Appeals Chamber. In other words, there can hardly be a filtre based on the notice of appeal. Motions for appeal will have to be heard. Only subsequently may the Appeals Chamber decline to pronounce because the error of law presented did not invalidate the impugned decision. Given this uncertainty and the broad powers of the Appeals Chamber it seems that any error of law committed by a Trial Chamber may be a legitimate ground for appeal, at least *in abstracto*, even though, naturally, only more serious errors will induce the Appeals Chamber to revise or reverse a Trial Chamber judgment.

It is interesting to note that in *Akayesu* the latter duty of legal review led the Appeals Chamber of the Tribunals to consider it appropriate to expand the scope of its powers, pronouncing also on questions of general interest beyond that specifically required by Article 25 of the Statute. These are questions which, although they do not invalidate the impugned decision, could be very important for the development of the jurisprudence of the Tribunal.[61] Additionally, in *Erdemović* the Appeals Chamber even expanded the scope of appellate review by raising issues *proprio motu*.[62] The Chamber considered in the absence of any contrary indication in the Statute or the Rules of Procedure and Evidence that it was perfectly legitimate to extend the scope of issues for consideration, where necessary to ensure a proper administration of justice.[63]

(iii) Additional evidence in appellate proceedings

The broad character of appellate proceedings is confirmed by the Rules of Procedure and Evidence that allow the admission of the entire case file of the first instance trial, which means that Appeals Chamber judges may have the whole documentation of the trial before them. Moreover, the presentation of additional evidence is possible, if the interests of justice so require (Rule 115(B) RPE). As regards the admission of such additional evidence, however, the Appeals Chamber has adopted a restrictive approach as it clearly held that 'additional evidence should not be admitted lightly at the appellate stage. [It]

---

[60] See on this issue S. Beresford, 'Non-Compliance with the Rules of Procedure and Evidence', in May *et al.* (eds.), note 46 above, 403–417.

[61] In this respect, cf. Appeals Chamber Judgment, *Akayesu* (ICTR–96–4–A), 1 June 2001.

[62] See Appeals Chamber Judgment, *Erdemović* (IT–96–22–A), 7 October 1997.

[63] This seems correct even if judicial precedents have no binding value in the procedural framework of the Tribunals. On the problem of *stare decisis*, cf. the Appeals Chamber Judgment, *Aleksovski* (IT–95–14/1–A), 24 March 2000, paras. 97–107.

is not admissible in the absence of a reasonable explanation as to why the evidence was not available at trial.'[64] In particular, previous unavailability of evidence presented in the course of appeals proceedings must not result from lack of due diligence on the part of counsel who undertook the defence of the accused before the Trial Chamber. If it results from lack of due diligence, then it is not admissible. This restrictive approach taken by the Appeals Chamber of the ICTY in *Tadić* may not prove entirely satisfactory in other cases. In *Akayesu*, for example, decided by the Appeals Chamber acting for the ICTR, the appellant contended as grounds of appeal misrepresentation in the first instance trial.[65] In such cases, it seems correct to argue that lack of due diligence is a legitimate ground for submitting additional evidence and the Chamber should admit it.[66] Thus, in reality in some cases additional evidence should be admitted even when it could have been already available at trial. The requirement of due diligence should be interpreted with some flexibility.[67] Moreover, evidence that was available at trial, but was not presented, may still be admitted in appeal proceedings—as additional evidence—whenever it is absolutely necessary to admit it to avoid a miscarriage of justice.

Finally, it is interesting to note that in *Delalić and others* and in *Kupreškić* the Appeals Chamber has considered it possible to admit evidence other than under Rule 115.[68] The reasoning is based on Rule 107 which provides that the rules for trial must apply *mutatis mutandis* in appeal proceedings. The Chamber considered that it could admit evidence under Rule 89. In *Delalić and others*, the Appeals Chamber held that '[w]hile Rule 115 of the Rules of Procedure and Evidence limits the extent to which evidence upon matters relating to the guilt or innocence of the accused may be given before the Appeals Chamber (being the issue litigated in the Trial Chamber), when the Appeals Chamber is hearing evidence which relates to matters other than the issues litigated in the Trial Chamber, the Appeals Chamber is in the same position as a Trial Chamber, so that Rule 107 applies to permit the Appeals Chamber to admit any relevant or probative evidence pursuant to Rule 89(C)'.[69] This seems a *sui generis* approach.

[64] Cf. ICTY Appeals Chamber Judgment, *Tadić* (IT–95–1–A), 15 July 1999, para. 16.

[65] In the case at issue, the Appeals Chamber dismissed the claims of the accused, by finding that he was fairly represented and assisted by counsel. Cf. Appeals Chamber Judgment, *Akayesu* (ICTR–96–4–A), 1 June 2001.

[66] Of course, other conditions may be required, such as e.g. the removal of the attorney who acted at first instance.

[67] To tell the truth, the Appeals Chamber was aware of the risk of such a restrictive approach and in its decision on the admission of additional evidence, *Tadić* (IT–94–1–A), 15 October 1998, paras. 46–50, it had already suggested that in the case of gross misrepresentation additional evidence should be admitted.

[68] Cf. Appeals Chamber Judgment, *Kupreškić* (IT–95–16–A), 23 October 2001, paras. 55 ff.

[69] Cf. in *Delalić and others* (IT–96–21–A), Order in Relation to Witnesses on Appeal, 19 May 2000; *Delalić and others* (IT–96–21–A), Order on Motion of Appellant, Esad Landzo, to Admit Evidence on Appeal, and for Taking of Judicial Notice, 31 May 2000, at 2. See also *Akayesu* (ICTR–96–4–A), Decision (Concerning Motions 2, 3, 4, 5, 6 and 8 Appellant's Brief Relative to the Following Motions Referred to by the Order Dated 30 November 1999), 24 May 2000.

It is submitted that the judges should consider amending the Rules in order to broaden the scope of evidence admissible under Rule 115, rather than to stretch the scope of the rules by means of interpretation.

(iv)   Are appeals against acquittals admissible?

Appeal against conviction is obviously the main expression of the right of appeal. Generally an accused seeks to obtain redress against a conviction or a sentence he or she considers unjust or unlawfully determined. However, there are instances in which an accused who has been found not guilty may want to appeal against acquittal. This may occur when the accused has been acquitted on grounds he or she does not find satisfactory. One can take for example the case of a person who is acquitted by the International Tribunals on the grounds that the murder he or she has committed cannot be classified as a crime within the jurisdiction of the Tribunal. The accused has an interest in challenging the other part of the reasoning that implies that he or she would indeed have committed the murder. There may be other reasons why an accused may want to appeal against an acquittal, for example in case of trial proceedings being quashed for a procedural defect.

The Statutes of the *ad hoc* Tribunals clearly state that a convicted person may file an appeal against a decision on the ground of an error on a question of law invalidating the decision or an error of fact that has occasioned a miscarriage of justice. The wording of this provision seems to imply that only convicted persons may appeal. Thus, acquitted persons would never be authorized to appeal against acquittals. This conclusion has been confirmed by the order of the Appeals Chamber in *Jelisić*. However, it should be noted that the Chamber in *Aleksovski* admitted that the acquitted person has a right to submit arguments and evidence relating to points on which the Prosecution has filed an appeal.

The interpretation set out by the Appeals Chamber is probably correct and is in keeping with the plain reading of the provisions of the Statute and the Rules. Nonetheless, it is reasonable to argue that in exceptional circumstances the interest of an acquitted person in appealing against acquittal in respect of the grounds on which such a decision was reached may also coincide with the interest of the Tribunal in clarifying the law. This seems particularly true given the dual nature of the Appeals Chamber in the procedural system of the *ad hoc* Tribunals, where it acts both as a second instance Chamber and a Supreme Court. In these cases, the Tribunal should allow such appeals, although it is true that in order to permit them it would be better to adopt an amendment to the Rules.

(v)   Conclusion

It appears that there is a tendency to over-emphasize the functions of the Appeals Chamber as a 'Supreme Court', although in some cases the Chamber has played a role on factual issues. Generally, however, the Appeals Chamber should try to exercise its supervisory duties even with respect to factual issues, even considering a broader admission of additional evidence at the appellate stage. The principle of *ne bis in idem* protects the accused, thus it cannot be breached to his or her detriment. There is no violation of the rights of the accused if the Appeals Chamber delivers a new judgment on facts *pro reo*. This approach may require new amendments to the Rules of Procedure of the Tribunals. Such amendments may be envisaged, as they would improve the implementation of due process guarantees in the *ad hoc* Tribunals' system.

(d) Against sentencing

The Statutes of the *ad hoc* Tribunals do not specifically provide for the right of appeal against sentence. However, it has been considered implicit in the Rules that an appeal may be filed even against sentence. Persons convicted by the Tribunals have often appealed against sentencing judgments. In some cases, such as in *Kambanda*[70] before the ICTR and in *Erdemović*[71] before the ICTY, appeals were filed even against sentencing judgments issued on the basis of guilty pleas. In other cases, however, for example *Tadić*, the convicted person appealed against both conviction and sentence. In these cases it is suggested that, in order to avoid unnecessary loss of time, motions should be joined in a single appeal proceedure before the Appeals Chamber. This would help in reducing the overall length of proceedings before the ICTY. In *Tadić*, for example, had the Appeals Chamber itself proceeded to revise the judgment of the Trial Chamber and subsequently the sentence the whole procedure would have been six months shorter.

The main ground for appeal against sentence has been disproportion between guilt and sentence, a principle that has now been codified in Article 81, paragraph 2, of the ICC Statute (cf. sub-section 4 below).

(e) Possible outcomes of appellate proceedings

The Statutes of the Tribunals provide that the Appeals Chamber may affirm, reverse, or revise the decision impugned (Article 25, paragraph 2 ICTY and 24, paragraph 2 ICTR). Thus, according to this rule the Appeals Chamber has the power to pronounce finally on the case under review. In practice, however, the Chamber has often decided to remit the case to the Trial Chamber for re-trial, at least on certain issues, or for the re-determination of sentence. In *Tadić*, for example, the Appeals Chamber disagreed with the interpretation of law given by the Trial Chamber, set out the correct interpretation, and

---

[70] On the Appeals Chamber proceedings in *Kambanda* see ICTR Annual Report (2000), 14 September 2001, para. 62.

[71] Cf. Appeals Chamber Judgment, *Erdemović* (IT–96–22–A), 7 October 1997.

then remitted the case to a Trial Chamber for new sentencing on the basis of the correct interpretation of the law it had given. Subsequently, however, the accused appealed against the new sentence imposed and the Appeals Chamber revised the sentence. In *Erdemović* the Appeals Chamber pronounced on the law and left it to a new Trial Chamber to ask the accused to enter a new plea and subsequently decide on the appropriate sentence. In *Aleksovski* the Appeals Chamber corrected the Trial Chamber on a point of law and increased the sentence from two and a half years' to seven years' imprisonment. In *Delalić* the Appeals Chamber remitted the case to a Trial Chamber to be nominated by the President of the Tribunal for reconsideration and adjustment of sentences imposed on convicted persons.

There are no clear rules determining which cases should be decided upon directly by the Appeals Chamber and which should be remitted to a Trial Chamber, nor to what extent they must be remitted, nor whether the proceedings should be sent back to the same Trial Chamber or to another. The Appeals Chamber has very broad powers, so it seems that, at least in principle, in order to enhance the effectiveness of proceedings, efforts should be made to resolve the matter at the appellate stage, without creating a sort of 'shuttle' between the two sections of the Tribunals. Nonetheless, the position of the ICTY Appeals Chamber, at least in theory, has been that it should not intervene in the exercise of Trial Chambers' discretion.[72] Exceptionally, as has occurred so far only in *Aleksovski*, the Appeals Chamber may directly modify the sentence originally imposed by the Trial Chamber. In that case, this position was justified by the reason that nothing had changed concerning the evaluation of facts. It was only a matter of characterization of the same facts under two different headings; thus the Appeals Chamber itself could increase the sentence. In this respect, it seems that the Appeals Chamber may act more effectively by itself modifying whatever needs to be amended. This would avoid the problem of having another appeal against the second pronouncement of the Trial Chamber. In *Jelisić* the Appeals Chamber held that the Trial Chamber had erred in its decision to acquit the accused at the close of the Prosecution case, by using a wrong criterion. However, it did not remit the case to the same Trial Chamber or a new Trial Chamber because it considered that in the interests of the expeditious administration of justice it could simply confirm the sentence imposed, notwithstanding the error committed by the Trial Chamber.[73]

---

[72] See in this respect, the Judgment of the Appeals Chamber on sentencing, *Tadić* (IT–94–1–S) 26 January 2000, para. 22.

[73] Cf. Appeals Chamber Judgment, *Jelisić* (IT–95–10–A), 5 July 2001.

4. *The right of appeal in the ICC system*

(a) General

Articles 81 to 83 of the ICC Statute deal with appeals proceedings. Article 81 sets out the grounds of appeal and who may file an appeal against a decision of acquittal or conviction, or against sentence.[74] The Prosecutor is entitled to appeal for a procedural error, an error of fact or of law. The convicted person may exercize this right on the same grounds; moreover, the drafters added that the convicted person is entitled to appeal on 'any other ground that affects the fairness or reliability of the proceedings or decision'. In other words, there has been the clear intention to offer to the individual the possibility of filing an appeal against a judgment or sentence in very broad terms. Additionally, even the Prosecutor is entitled to appeal on such a ground on behalf of the convicted person. This is an important element that contributes to, and confirms, the characterization of the Prosecutor as an *'organe de just-ice'* (cf. Chapter 2 above). Furthermore, the ICC Statute explicitly provided for the right of appeal against sentence on the ground of disproportion between the crime and the penalty.[75] In so doing it codified the Tribunals' practice.

In the ICC system the right of appeal seems more broadly conceived than in the *ad hoc* Tribunals' system. This may be explained because the draftsmen managed to overcome the tension between civil law and common law approaches to appeals proceedings, opting for a solution more close to the former. Hence, appellate proceedings include broad powers of review on factual issues. This opinion is supported both by the very broad formula that confers on the accused the right of appeal on 'any . . . ground that affects the fairness or reliability of the proceedings or decision' and by the powers of the Appeals Chamber to admit new evidence.

---

[74] Chapter 8 ICC RPE (Rules 149 to 158) has further implemented the provisions of the Statute on appellate proceedings. Like Rule 107 in the *ad hoc* Tribunal's RPE, Rule 149 establishes that the rules governing trial and pre-trial proceedings may apply *mutatis mutandis* to appellate proceedings. Rule 150 sets out the time limit for filing an appeal, which is 30 days from the date of notification of the impugned decision. The Appeals Chamber, however, is entitled to extend such time limit for good cause, upon application of the relevant party. Appeals may be filed against decisions, sentences, or reparation orders and the notice shall be filed with the Registrar. If no appeal is filed the decision becomes final (Rule 150, paragraph 4). Rule 151 provides for notification by the Registrar of the appeal notice to 'all parties who participated in the proceedings before the Trial Chamber'. Rule 152 entitles any party who has filed an appeal to discontinue the proceedings at any time. To this effect a written notice of discontinuance must be filed with the Registrar, who shall inform other parties.

[75] Article 81, para. 2 (a), ICC St. provides that 'a sentence may be appealed . . . on the ground of disproportion between the crime and the sentence'. The Appeals Chamber itself may determine the new sentence. In this case the Chamber may invite the parties to make appropriate representations.

In this respect, one should note that, although there is no specific rule on the admission of new or additional evidence in the course of appellate proceedings, there are two good reasons for believing that evidence may be introduced on appeal. First, the general rule set out in Article 83.1 provides that for the purpose of appeal proceedings 'the Appeals Chamber shall have the powers of the Trial Chamber'. This means that it is entitled to admit new evidence, if it deems it relevant. This reading is confirmed by the RPE that establish that 'the rules of evidence shall apply in proceedings before *all* Chambers'.[76] Secondly, the Appeals Chamber has the power to reverse or amend the judgment, and must not necessarily order a new trial before a different Trial Chamber. Thus it seems logical to conclude that new evidence may be admitted in appeals proceedings.

It is particularly interesting to note that the ICC Statute has explicitly recognized the principle that there cannot be the so-called *reformatio in peius*.[77] This confirms the idea that the ICC Statute contains stronger guarantees as compared with the *ad hoc* Tribunals' system, where this principle is not clearly spelt out.

Another aspect worthy of note is that separate or dissenting opinions are allowed only on points of law;[78] this draws a clear line between the role of the Appeals Chamber as a supreme court and its role as a second trier of facts.

(b) Interlocutory appeals

Unlike the provisions of the *ad hoc* Tribunals Statutes, the procedural rules of the ICC Statute have been designed specifically to protect the right of appeal other than against final decisions (Article 82, Appeal against other decisions). Article 82 distinguishes two broad categories of decisions that may be appealed: first, those against which parties are automatically entitled on the basis of the Statute to file an appeal: Article 82, paragraph 1, letter a–c; secondly, 'decision[s] that involve an issue that would significantly affect the fair and expeditious conduct of the proceedings or the outcome of the trial, and for which, in the opinion of the Pre-Trial or Trial Chamber, an immediate resolution by the Appeals Chamber may materially advance in the proceedings'. In the latter case, the RPE have required that leave to appeal should be granted by the Chamber that made the decision being impugned (Rule 155). It seems that the solution adopted by the ICTY, where appeal motions are examined by a bench of three judges of the Appeals Chamber, better ensures

---

[76] Rule 63.1 ICC RPE, (emphasis added).

[77] Article 83, para. 2 provides that 'when the decision or sentence has been appealed by the convicted person or by the Prosecutor on that person's behalf, it cannot be amended in to his or her detriment'.

[78] If there is no unanimity the judgment shall contain the views of the minority (Article 83, para. 3).

an objective evaluation of the arguments of the parties. The Chamber that made the decision may be inclined to admit motions too broadly in order not to be criticized by the appellant, or, on the other hand, may be tempted to reject motions too easily, considering that there is no need to review its own decisions. In both cases, the Chamber will inevitably appear as not being totally impartial and immune from inappropriate considerations, and this does not serve the interests of justice. On the other hand, a bench of the Appeals Chamber seems a more appropriate body to make such determinations. Additionally, such a body would have the possibility of developing a set of principles that may assist in determining which motions satisfy the requirements to obtain leave to appeal and which do not.

The RPE have further specified the procedure for interlocutory appeals,[79] providing, among other things, that in principle such proceedings must be held in writing and resolved expeditiously.

5. *The right of the accused to be protected against double jeopardy and prosecutorial appeals*

A controversial issue in drafting the procedural rules of the *ad hoc* Tribunals, but even more those of the ICC, was whether a power of appeal had to be attributed to the Prosecutor. Most authors quite correctly presented the solution adopted as a compromise between civil and common law.[80] However, more than a compromise in itself this should be seen as a concession to civil law countries in the framework of a more global package deal.

Generally speaking, it may be argued that in common law systems prosecutorial appeals would be seen as a violation of the protection against double jeopardy. On the other hand, in civil law countries the power of the Prosecutor to appeal against acquittal is a normal feature of the legal system.[81] This

---

[79] Rule 154 deals generally with appeals other than appeals against judgment, sentence, or reparation orders, which do not require the leave of the Court. In cases referred to in Rule 154 the time limit is five days, or two days for appeals under Article 82, para. 1 (c) (i.e. a decision of the Pre-trial Chamber to ensure *proprio motu* the conservation of evidence under Article 56, Role of the Pre-trial Chamber in relation to a unique investigative opportunity). Rule 156 contains the procedural rules for these interlocutory appeals, providing for an expeditious solution of the matters under consideration. In principle, appeals proceeding in these cases are in writing unless the Chamber decides to convene a hearing. Rule 157 provides for the possibility of abandonment of the proceedings. In this respect it seems that it would have been interesting to clarify whether or not to discontinue at this stage entitles the party to raise the same issue again in an appeal against the judgment.

[80] Cf. the comments by H. Brady and M. Jennings, 'Appeal and Revision', in R. Lee (ed.), *The International Criminal Court—The Making of the Rome Statute. Issues—Negotiations—Results* (The Hague: Kluwer, 1999), at 298–299.

[81] M. Delmas-Marty (ed.), *Procédures Pénales d'Europe (Allemagne, Angleterre et Pays de Galles, Belgique, France, Italie)* (Paris: PUF, 1995) and C. van den Wyngaert (ed.), *Criminal Procedure Systems in the European Community* (London: Butterworths, 1993), in particular Van den Wyngaert (Belgium), at 46, Greve (Denmark), at 70, Mylonopoulos (Greece), at 182, Corso (Italy), at 256.

difference is justified by the fact that while in common law the judgment pronounced by the trial judge is seen as final, in civil law systems the proceedings in their entirety are seen as a two-step process, comprising both trial and appellate stage. Only the judgment of an appellate court is considered final, or a judgment by a first instance judge when the time limit for filing an appeal has elapsed (i.e. the judgment is implicitly accepted by the parties). In other words, the two systems have a different understanding of the notion of the so-called *res judicata* (i.e. final judgment). However, it should be noted that even in common law systems the Prosecutor has a limited power to appeal on the ground of errors of law.

The different approaches of civil and common law are reflected in human rights provisions that protect the right of the individual not to be tried twice for the same offence. Article 14, paragraph 7, ICCPR protects the individual against double jeopardy, or better still it protects the individual against being subjected to criminal prosecution twice for the same facts. The provision reads as follows: 'no one shall be liable to be tried or punished again for an offence for which he has already been *finally* convicted or acquitted in accordance with the *law* and penal *procedure of each country*'. The reference to the law and procedure of each country indicates that the protection for anyone not to be tried again for an offence in respect of which there is already a final judgment strictly depends on the notion of final judgment in each country.

The solution adopted in international criminal procedure is certainly based more on the *civil law* approach. However, one may wonder whether such a compromise was necessary and appropriate, given the procedural system of the *ad hoc* Tribunals and the ICC.

There are arguments contending that appeals by the Prosecutor should be more limited than appeals by the convicted person, at least in so far as errors of fact are concerned.[82] On the other hand, given the function of the Appeals Chamber as an organ entrusted with the task of authoritatively interpreting the law, it is correct to allow the Prosecutor to appeal on errors of law.

The solution chosen is not entirely persuasive for several reasons. First, it emerges from the very history of the right of appeal (and revision) that such right was mainly designed as a measure of justice to protect the convicted person. This is the modern conception enshrined in human rights law and additionally strengthened by the presumption of innocence. In other words, the accused must benefit from the widest possible protection in accordance with the fundamental premise of modern criminal procedure, according to which the prosecution must prove guilt beyond reasonable doubt (see Chapter 3 above). Secondly, prosecutorial appeals do not seem to match the procedural system chosen for international criminal justice. Under the ICC system (as

---

[82] On this issue and on appellate proceedings more broadly see M. Fleming, 'Appellate Review in the International Criminal Tribunals', in 37 *TILJ* (2002) 111–155, at 117–142.

well as the *ad hoc* Tribunals' Statutes), the Prosecutor is never obliged to submit a case for the prosecution. The prosecution is the only body responsible for starting a case and it may decide at any stage of the proceedings to withdraw the indictment (or counts in the indictment), even if at the trial stage it needs approval from the Trial Chamber. These elements seem to confirm the idea that authorizing appeals on facts may essentially lead to giving a second chance to the prosecution. In any case, one may conclude that although prosecutorial appeals are not in breach of the *ne bis in idem* principle, they are not necessarily appropriate in international criminal proceedings.

The broad power of appeal conferred on the Prosecutor in international criminal procedure may be explained by the difficulties that may be encountered at international level in collecting evidence and obtaining the attendance of witnesses. It is only against such a background that one is more inclined to justify the admission of such a broad power of appeal for the Prosecutor. Nonetheless, it is suggested that some thought should be given to the possibility of restraining such a power to appeals on grounds of errors of law and only in exceptional circumstances on errors of fact.

6. An overall assessment of appellate proceedings before the ad hoc Tribunals and the ICC

The inclusion of the right of the accused to appeal against judgment or sentence is an important step in the protection of due process rights in international criminal trials.

The Appeals Chamber in the original design of the *ad hoc* Tribunals is both a second instance Chamber and a Supreme Court. This latter function of authoritative interpretation of the law, however, is the truly distinctive trait of appellate review in international criminal procedure. In this respect, it is important to note that the Security Council, when it established the ICTR, decided that the ICTY Appeals Chamber would serve as Appeals Chamber for the ICTR. This indicates the intention to ensure uniformity in the interpretation and application of international criminal law, both substantive and procedural.

An issue that poses problems with regard to the right of appeal in the framework of the *ad hoc* Tribunals is the composition of the Appeals Chamber. The principle of the rotation of judges between Trial and Appeals sections,[83] which derives from the full equality among judges in terms of both

---

[83] Rule 27 RPE reads as follow: '(A) Permanent Judges shall rotate on a regular basis between the Trial Chambers and the Appeals Chamber. Rotation shall take into account the efficient disposal of cases. (B) The Judges shall take their places in their new Chamber as soon as the President thinks it convenient, having regard to the disposal of part-heard cases. (C) The President may at any time temporarily assign a member of a Trial Chamber or of the Appeals Chamber to another Chamber': IT/32/Rev.21; 12 April 2001, as amended at the 23rd Plenary Session.

qualifications and functions,[84] makes it difficult for the Chamber to act as a Supreme Court.[85]

The right of appeal implies that the second step of the process must take place before a higher court. Generally, appellate bodies are composed of judges with more experience and higher qualifications. There is a sort of link between appeal proceedings and hierarchical organization of the judicial power.[86] Now, this link is totally absent in the framework of international criminal tribunals; all judges are on the same footing, they often rotate from trial sections to the appeals section, but also the other way round, which is seldom the case in hierarchical systems.[87]

In the international legal order, there are other examples of proceedings before appellate judges, for example, in the framework of the European Community. In this case, however, the requirements for being elected to the Court of First Instance (CFI) of the EC are different from and less demanding than those required for the European Court of Justice, which is the body that hears appeals against decision of the CFI. Thus, the right of appeal in the system of the *ad hoc* Tribunals and the ICC does not match the traditional organization of appellate bodies (national and international). Moreover, as currently organized, appellate proceedings in the Statutes of *ad hoc* Tribunals and the ICC do not ensure avoiding problems both with regard to coherence in the interpretation of the case law and to the evaluation of proceedings by the Appeals Chamber.

In particular, the rotation mechanisms by which judges move from the Trial Section to the Appellate Section does not seem proper to ensure sufficient

---

[84] ICTY/ICTR St. Articles 13–14, 12–13; Rule 17(A) RPEs: '[a]ll judges are equal in the exercize of their judicial functions'.

[85] This was also the opinion of the Expert Group: see Report of the Expert Group, UN doc. A/54/634, 22 November 1999.

[86] Cf. in this respect R. David and C. Jauffret Spinosi, *Les Grands Systèmes de Droit Contemporains* (10th edn., Paris: Dalloz, 1992), at 107 and 112. See also 'Appeal' in *Black's Law Dictionary* (6th edn., St. Paul, Minn.: West Publishing, 1990): '[r]esort to a superior (i.e. appellate) court to review the decision of an inferior (i.e. trial) court or administrative agency'.

[87] For example Judge Cassese, previously President of the Tribunal and presiding judge of the Appeals Chamber, subsequently, upon leaving the Presidency of the Tribunal, became presiding judge of a Trial Chamber. The same holds true also for other judges: Judge McDonald became President of the Tribunal, while the *Tadić* case (which she had presided over at first instance) was under appeal; and Judge Jorda who is the current President of the Tribunal while the *Blaškić* case is under appeal. There is nothing wrong from a strictly legal perspective. However, it may be inappropriate for this to occur. This idea is confirmed by the rejection of the rotation principle for the ICC Statute: Article 39, para. 3 (b), which states that 'Judges assigned to the Appeals Division shall serve in that division for their entire term of office', and para. 4 specifies that 'Judges assigned to the Appeals Division shall serve only in that division'. A more flexible approach has been adopted for judges of the Pre-trial or Trial division to be subsequently assigned to the Appeals division and for temporary assignment of judges from the Pre-trial division to the Trial division. Nonetheless, temporary assignments of judges from Pre-trial or Trial division to the Appeals division are not provided for, and thus it seems that this limits rotation to a very large extent.

independence and authority to the Appeals Chamber.[88] A Trial Chamber judge who joins the Appeals Chamber while one of the cases he or she has tried at first instance, although indirectly, may influence the decisions in the appeals proceedings. This system creates an intricate network of precedents. Additionally, the existence of separate and dissenting opinions increases risks of attempts to establish *ad hoc* compositions of the Appeals Chamber to support a certain interpretative solution. Even if this risk is only extremely remote and rather implausible, it may however, affect the image of the Tribunal and undermine the perception of the integrity of international justice.[89]

Finally, we have seen that the *ad hoc* Tribunals' Statutes and the ICC Statute provide for appeals by both parties. Thus, it is very clearly affirmed that the international Prosecutor has the power to appeal. This is an element that may be criticized on the ground that it may violate the principle of *ne bis in idem*. This argument has been objected to on the basis that the prevailing conception is based on the civil law approach, which does not consider the first instance judgment as final. Thus, an appeal by the Prosecutor does not amount to a new trial, but is simply the second step of a more complex process articulated in several stages.[90] The fact that the *ne bis in idem* principle is not directly affected does not mean that no thought should be given to the possibility of limiting prosecutorial appeals. There are sound arguments for believing that such a power may not be necessary in international criminal justice and, for example, could be submitted to an authorization by a bench of the Appeals Chamber. This bench would assess whether there are specific reasons for justifying such an appeal. If the case were not considered proven on evidentiary grounds by the Trial Chamber then it would hardly be proven before the Appeals Chamber. Appeals by the Prosecution should be admitted in only two cases: the discovery or production of new or additional evidence (subject to approval by the bench) and errors of law committed by the Trial Chamber.

III. THE RIGHT OF CONVICTED PERSONS TO REVISION

1. General

The right to revision (or review) is based on the discovery, after the closing of the proceedings, of new facts which if they had been known in time might have led to a different outcome. Generally, it is an extraordinary means of doing justice, particularly known to civil law systems, which constitutes an exception

---

[88] This point has already been made by C. Blakesley, 'Comparing the *ad hoc* Tribunal for Crimes against Humanitarian Law in the Former Yugoslavia and the Project for an International Criminal Court Prepared by the ILC', in 67 *RIDP* (1996), at 201–202.

[89] There is no need to remind the reader that '[j]ustice should not only be done, but should also be seen to be done'.

[90] First instance, Appeal, *Cassation*, and in some cases Constitutional review.

to the principle of *res judicata*.[91] Usually, national systems admit it rather broadly in favour of the convicted person, but much more restrictively *in malam partem*, that is against an acquittal.[92] This can be explained by the need to preserve the principle of *ne bis in idem* and protect individuals from prosecutorial harassment. One of the rare occasions on which a motion for review can be permitted is where an accused has interfered with the administration of justice for the purpose of offering false evidence to the court.[93] For example, revision *in malam partem* may be allowed in the event of a subsequent conviction for false testimony (induced by means of intimidation or corruption) of a decisive witness favourable to the accused, or the discovery of other forms of falsification of evidence. Given the extraordinary nature of review proceedings, the grounds on which review may be sought are generally very specific and make up an exhaustive list.

In international criminal procedure the situation is somehow different. Initially (in Nuremberg and Tokyo), this right was practically absent, despite the general provision contained in the Tokyo Charter on the power of review of the Supreme Commander. On the other hand, human rights law generally allows review proceedings. It would be very odd not to provide an innocent person with an alternative to remaining in prison, where there are new elements that may definitively lead to the conclusion that he or she is not guilty. Such a right, for example, is explicitly provided for by Article 4 of Optional Protocol 7 to the ECHR, but is implied in other provisions such as Article 14, paragraph 6 ICCPR. Human rights texts, however, do not specifically rule out review *in malam partem*.

In the framework of the *ad hoc* Tribunals, the exceptional character of review proceedings has been under-estimated, as indicated by the relevant provisions of both the Statute and the Rules, which are very broad.

The right of revision has been explicitly provided for in the ICC Statute, which thus represents a development of international criminal procedure. However, while in the *ad hoc* Tribunals' system review is admitted very broadly, in the ICC procedural system restrictions have been imposed on the power of the Prosecutor to seek revision. The provisions of the ICC Statute

[91] See Stefani, Levasseur and Bouloc, note 4 above, at 1001–1002, and Van den Wyngaert (ed.), note 81 above, at 48 (Belgium), at 161 (Germany).

[92] Scholarship in civil law countries has often criticized revision *in malam partem*: see e.g. Cordero, note 10 above, and Rassat, note 5 above, at 660, '*[en] premier lieu, c'est un régime de faveur qui ne permet la révision que dans un sens favorable à la personne condamnée*', and Ruiz Vadillo, 'Spain', in Van den Wyngaert (ed.), note 81 above, at 398.

[93] This is the case in some national systems (e.g. Italy), where review *in malam partem* operates as a sort of additional sanction against the defendant, for having interfered with the administration of justice. See Law No. 203 of 1991, which specifically deals with the case of a member of a criminal organization whose declaration was subsequently found to be false, on this issue see G. Spangher, 'Article 4 Optional Protocol 7', in S. Bartole, B. Conforti, and G. Raimondi (eds.), *Commentario alla Convenzione europea per la tutela dei diritti dell'uomo e delle libertà fondamentali* (Padua: Cedam, 2001), 960.

on revision strike a proper balance between the rights of the accused and the principle of *ne bis in idem*, by requiring that the power of the Prosecutor to request revision be exercized only in the interests of the accused.

2. *The provisions on revision in the* ad hoc *Tribunals system*

(a) General

The Statutes of the *ad hoc* Tribunals rather succinctly provide that 'where a new fact has been discovered which was not known at the time of the proceedings before the Trial Chambers or the Appeals Chamber and which could have been a decisive factor in reaching the decision, the convicted person or the Prosecutor may submit to the International Tribunal an application for *review of the judgment*' (Articles 26 ICTY St. and 25 ICTR St.). Accordingly, Rule 119 provides for the right of both the convicted person and the Prosecutor to apply for revision of a judgment (be it the Trial Chamber's or the Appeals Chamber's judgment). Rule 119 RPE specifies that '[where] a new fact has been discovered which . . . could not have been discovered through the *exercise of due diligence*, the defence or, within one year after the final judgment has been pronounced, the Prosecutor, may make a motion to that Chamber for review of the *judgment*'.[94]

The Rules have also provided for the procedure to be followed when deciding on review motions. Rule 120, entitled 'Preliminary Examination', requires that 'a majority of Judges of the Chamber that pronounced the judgment agree that the new fact, if proved, could have been a decisive factor in reaching a decision'. If there is such an agreement, 'the Chamber shall review the judgment, and pronounce a further judgment after hearing the parties'. Furthermore, Rule 122 RPE (123 ICTR) establishes that where '[the] judgment to be reviewed is under appeal at the time the motion for review is filed, the Appeals Chamber may return the case to the Trial Chamber for disposition of the motion'.

This is the regulatory framework of review proceedings in the system of the *ad hoc* Tribunals, which apparently seems rather clear. There are, however, at least *four main features* of the provisions on review proceedings in the *ad hoc* Tribunals that do not appear satisfactory and should be discussed.

First, it is unclear which decisions may be impugned through motions for review; in particular, it must be ascertained to what extent rules on review apply differently to the Defence and the Prosecution. Secondly, it must be made clear whether or not the Prosecutor is entitled to seek review *in malam partem*. Thirdly, one should explore the rather unclear relationship between appeals and review proceedings, particularly in light of the notions of additional evidence

---

[94] Rule 119 RPE (emphasis added).

(which can be submitted at the appellate stage) and new facts (which can be introduced only through a review motion). Fourthly, it is uncertain before which judges review proceedings should be taken. Finally, conclusions may be drawn on review proceedings before *ad hoc* Tribunals pointing at some areas of concern.

(b) Which decision may be impugned through a motion for review?

The provisions of the Statutes do not clarify whether a motion for review may be filed only against a final judgment, as is traditionally the case in national systems,[95] or even against non-final judgment or other decisions. A literal interpretation of the provisions of the Statutes and the Rules indicates that only a judgment may be the object of a motion for review.

Additionally, the Prosecutor and the convicted person are not placed at the same level. Rule 122 read in conjunction with Rule 119 shows that the convicted person may file a motion for review even before delivery of a final judgment. On the other hand, Rule 119 indicates that the Prosecutor may apply for review only within one year of the *final* judgment. Review proceedings may run in parallel with appeal proceedings when requested by the accused, but only after the conclusion of proceedings where requested by the Prosecutor. In both cases, however, it appears that motions for review may be filed only against judgments. Nonetheless, the Appeals Chamber rejected such a plain interpretation of the provisions on review. In *Barayagwiza* the Chamber held that a motion for review could be directed even against a decision other than a judgment, provided that the impugned decision put an end to the proceedings.[96] Therefore, the resulting system provides that the Prosecutor may file motions for review against final judgments or other final decisions, and the defence even against non-final judgments.

(c) Should the Prosecutor be entitled to seek review *in malam partem*?

It remains unclear whether or not revision may be sought to the detriment of the accused. The Statutes do not specify that the Prosecutor is entitled to request review *in malam partem*. The provisions of the Statutes could have been interpreted to the effect that the Prosecutor should seek review only in the interest of the accused. The Rules of Procedure and Evidence, however, seem to imply that a motion for review may even aim at reversing an acquittal. This refers, in particular, to Rule 119, by which the judges tried to limit the otherwise excessively broad power of the Prosecutor to apply for review by introducing a time limit of one year. Nonetheless, it is submitted that noth-

---

[95] In this respect cf. note 91 above.
[96] Cf. Appeals Chamber Decision, *Barayagwiza* (ICTR–97–19–R), 31 March 2000.

ing in the Statute requires this interpretation. The judges, in adopting the Rules, could very well have provided for the power of the Prosecutor to seek review only in the interests of the convicted. In this respect, it is submitted that the Prosecutor should be endowed with a more limited power to request review. Its current power is so broad that it turns out to be at odds with the principle of *ne bis in idem*. In other words, the Statute should not be interpreted so as to allow the Prosecutor to apply for revision in such broad terms, even within one year. *De jure condendo* the judges should consider limiting the power of the Prosecutor to seeking review only in cases of intimidation of witnesses or falsification of evidence by the defendant, or other cases, which should be specifically listed.

There are several reasons supporting this interpretation. Review proceedings instituted by the Prosecutor to obtain conviction are not very convincing with respect to individual rights, particularly the principles of *ne bis in idem* and protection against double jeopardy. Additionally, there is no international principle that requires such a broad power for the Prosecution, nor does the procedural system chosen demand it. In fact, if one considers that the Prosecutor has very broad discretion in deciding whether or not to bring a case to trial, one should logically deduce that he or she should take such a decision considering the available evidence. If the legal and factual elements of the case do not result in a conviction after a two-step criminal process (trial and appellate proceedings), then the accused should be protected by the principle against double jeopardy (even in its more restrictive civil law version).[97]

To confer upon the Prosecutor such a broad power to seek revision is a violation of international human rights principles (i.e. *ne bis in idem*), which does not seem to be justified by another rule of equal importance. True, there is a need for justice to be done; however, in the case of international prosecution one can hardly see why the Prosecutor would start a case if he or she did not have enough factual elements to obtain a conviction. The Prosecution can fail once at the trial stage, but after a failure at the appellate stage, in which the admission of additional evidence is provided for, this should not be allowed. The only circumstance that may justify a review requested by the prosecution could be when an accused (or anyone else in the interest of the accused) has threatened or bribed witnesses. These cases should, however, be specifically provided for in the Rules.

(d) The relationship between appeal and review proceedings

Generally, in national systems review proceedings may be resorted to only exceptionally, after normal proceedings have ended. However, as mentioned above, it seems that in the *ad hoc* Tribunals' system an accused may file a

---

[97] Cf. Section II.5, above.

motion for review even pending an appeal. The Appeals Chamber in *Tadić*
authoritatively confirmed this reading of the Rules; it held that new facts
could not be submitted at the appellate stage as additional evidence, but
should be submitted through a motion for review.[98] The rationale for this
holding was that additional evidence must refer to issues of fact already discussed at trial, while the expression 'new facts' relates to factual issues not
raised before the Trial Chamber. As far as this reading is concerned, it is not
very clear whether a 'new fact' under Rule 119 would include additional evidence under Rule 115. It seems that in general a broader notion should com-
prise a narrow one. Thus, on the basis of the Tribunals' case law, it seems that
whenever new facts (which include new evidence) are discovered prior to a
final judgment, these should not be introduced in appeals proceedings, but
should rather be the object of a separate review motion. On the other hand,
additional evidence may be introduced, pursuant to Rule 115, directly in
appellate proceedings, but after the end of the proceedings it may still be
introduced as a 'new fact' under Rule 119. Neither additional evidence under
Rule 115 nor new fact under Rule 119 has a very clear meaning and it seems
that the confusion that currently exists under the Rules should be clarified
through an amendment, inverting the logic of the system. The view that a distinction between appellate and review proceedings exists has been recently
confirmed in *Delić*, where the Appeals Chamber, deciding on a review
motion, held that 'the clear distinction . . . between the two procedures relate
to the nature of the additional material which may be considered in each.
Where additional material proffered consists of a new fact—that is a fact
which was not in issue or considered in the original proceedings—a review
pursuant to Rule 119 is the appropriate procedure . . . If the material proffered consists of additional evidence relating to a fact which was in issue or
considered in the original proceeding this does not constitute a "new fact"
within the meaning of Rule 119, and the review procedure is not available.'[99]
This interpretation is too narrow and does not seem to conform to the object
and purpose of review proceedings. Would it be in the interests of justice and
respectful of individual rights to refuse review proceedings on the basis that
new evidence, which may radically undermine the conclusions previously
reached, cannot be admitted because it refers to a fact that was already at
issue at trial? The most appropriate criteria for deciding on the admission
of new elements for the purpose of review proceedings are their relevance,

---

[98] On this issue, cf. the Appeals Chamber decision on additional evidence, in *Tadić*
(IT–94–1–A), 15 October 1998 and the decision on review in *Barayagwiza* (ICTR–97–19–R), 31
March 2000.

[99] Appeals Chamber Decision on Motion for Review, *Delić* (IT–96–21-R119), 25 April 2002,
para. 11.

i.e. they must, at least potentially, lead to redressing a miscarriage of justice and the fact that these elements were unknown to the party seeking review.[100]

Furthermore, in both cases, for the motion to be admissible parties are required to have exercized due diligence at the time of the proceedings resulting in the decision being impugned. This requirement of due diligence, however, was considered with some flexibility in *Barayagwiza*, but more restrictively in *Tadić*, where the Chamber strictly construed the Rules. In the former case, the Chamber considered that the requirement of due diligence was not peremptory and admitted, as new facts, elements which could have been presented in due time by the Prosecution if it had exercized due diligence. On the other hand, in *Tadić*, additional evidence in appeals proceedings was not admitted because the Chamber was not satisfied that with due diligence such evidence could not have been presented at trial.

One may wonder whether such approach is correct in light of the respect that should be paid to the rights of the accused: both flexibility and inflexibility (strict interpretation) in these cases were to the detriment of the accused. Additionally, in both cases the purpose of the proceedings seems to have been misinterpreted.

It is suggested that in respect of the elements presented to the judges the relationship between appellate and review proceedings should be reconsidered. In particular, it would seem appropriate to admit additional evidence or new facts more broadly in appeals proceedings and adopt, if necessary, a narrower standard for review proceedings. Additionally, it would seem more effective to allow for review motions only after the close of proceedings (either in first instance or on appeal, depending on which Chamber issues the final judgment).

(e) Which judges should deal with review proceedings?

The Chamber in charge of the review proceedings is the Chamber that delivered the (final) judgment.[101] Recently the Rules were amended to take into account any possible variations in the composition of Chambers. The main problem in this respect is to determine which judges should sit on a review motion. In the ICC system, as explained below, the Appeals Chamber

---

[100] There are of course new elements that, although they may have led to a slightly different result, do not, however, constitute a reasonable basis for a review motion. See, e.g., the Appeals Chamber Decision on Motion for Review, *Jelisić* (IT–95–10–R119), 2 May 2002, where the Chamber ruled out that a development in the case law of the Tribunal relating to mitigating circumstances could justify a motion for review (at 2). It is clear that in such a case there is a crucial element which is absent: the new fact, even if known at the time of the original proceedings, would not have been a decisive factor in reaching the original decision. See also the Appeals Chamber Decision on Motion for Review, *Tadić* (IT–94–1–R), 30 July 2002, paras. 33, 47, 50, and 53.

[101] See *ibidem*, paras. 22–25.

pronounces on the admissibility of the motion and it then decides whether to hear the review motion itself or remit the case to a Trial Chamber.

In the *ad hoc* Tribunals' system, Rule 121 provides for a right of appeal against '[the] judgment of a Trial Chamber on review . . . in accordance with the provisions of Part Seven'. If the Appeals Chamber delivers the judgment on review, apparently there is no right of appeal. However, given the precedents concerning the proceedings on contempt of court in which an Appeals Chamber Judgments was impugned before the same Appeals Chamber, although in a different composition, one may contend that such a right may be recognized even in the case of review proceedings.

(f) Suggestions for a different system of review proceedings before *ad hoc* Tribunals

There are some reasons for perplexity surrounding the *ad hoc* Tribunals' provisions on review. One can point to three main areas of concern: first, the non-extraordinary nature of review proceedings in the *ad hoc* Tribunals' system, particularly if one considers that seemingly the accused could seek review even pending an appeal. Secondly, the scope of the power of review of the Prosecutor is too broad. Thirdly, the decision on the admissibility of the review motion and the review itself should not be made by the same judges that issued the impugned decision, as these may be reluctant to reverse their previous findings.

Arguably, the best reading of the rules on revision would be that these proceedings should be allowed only against final judgments. Additionally, a specific catalogue of grounds for review should be established, authorizing the Prosecutor to seek review only in the case of false evidence intentionally offered by the accused.

In other words, the Prosecutor should never be entitled to resort to review proceedings simply to present evidence that was not available for submission during ordinary proceedings. This would radically undermine the principle of *ne bis in idem*, even inducing the Prosecutor to continue investigations after acquittal. The requirement that due diligence must be shown is not sufficient to avoid such risks. The Prosecutor could legitimately argue that it was impossible, even with all due diligence, for him to have known about the new fact, because of the conditions prevailing at the time of investigations (for example, ongoing armed conflict). That would be a new fact and, if decisive, might lead to a review judgment. This, however, is a solution that conflicts with the *ne bis in idem* principle without being justified by another principle of equal importance.

Under the present system, review proceedings should be held, at least in principle, before the same judges, where available. This is confirmed by the recent amendment to the Rules mentioned above, which suggests that in cases where the judges who participated in the original proceedings are no longer available, other judges should sit on review proceedings. Interpreted *a contrario*, the Rule clearly indicates that in normal cases (where the 'original' judges are available) review proceedings should be held before the same judges. In this respect, it seems that the persons of the judges should not be relevant in identifying the composition of the appropriate Chamber: true, the Chamber seized must be the Chamber that issued the impugned judgment. Nonetheless, it may be reasonable to suggest that leaving the decision on review to the same judges may not be entirely appropriate, as they may not be inclined to reconsider their previous judgment.

Lastly, along the lines of the ICC Statute, it should be considered whether to leave the decision on the admissibility of the application for revision to the Appeals Chamber, which would subsequently remit the case to the appropriate Chamber. This would ensure greater uniformity in the interpretation of the rules on review.

3. *The* Barayagwiza *case before the ICTR*

The rules on review of the *ad hoc* Tribunals' system admit these proceedings very broadly, as confirmed by the *Barayagwiza* case, in which they were tested for the first time.[102] The accused, Jean Bosco-Barayagwiza, had been held in detention in Cameroon for over a year at the behest of the Tribunal. During this period he was not charged, nor was he informed of any reason for arrest, except that it was upon the request of the ICTR. Subsequently, he was transferred to the detention unit of the Tribunal, where he remained for some weeks before being charged and informed of the allegations against him. He was then held in custody for over two months before his initial appearance took place. The accused complained of violations of his rights to both the Trial and Appeals Chambers. The Trial Chamber rejected the accused's motion. Subsequently, however, the Appeals Chamber decided that the violations of the rights of the accused had been so serious that it was justified to release the accused with the Prosecutor being barred from bringing new charges on the same facts. The Prosecutor impugned this decision, seeking review or reconsideration of the decision. The Appeals Chamber allowed the request for review on the basis that new facts were presented and an extensive interpretation of the rules on review proceedings was admissible. Eventually, on the basis of the new elements presented by the Prosecution the Appeals Chamber decided that its previous decision should be reversed because the violations of the rights of the accused were less serious than previously determined. Nonetheless, it affirmed that the rights of the accused had been

---

[102] On this case see M. Fleming, 'Appellate Review', in 37 *TILJ* (2002) 142–153, and W. Schabas, '*Barayagwiza v. Prosecutor*', in 94 *AJIL* (2000) 563–565.

violated, and thus he should be awarded reparation. Two forms of reparation were suggested: if the accused were convicted, sentence ought to be reduced taking into account the violation of his rights; if he were acquitted, he ought to receive monetary compensation.

In spite of the appropriateness of the latter solution, which constitutes an authoritative precedent on the right of compensation of individuals for violation of their rights in the *ad hoc* Tribunals' system, it seems that the Chamber erred on two grounds when admitting such request. First, review proceedings, according to the provisions of the Statutes, should be instituted only against *judgments* (convictions or acquittals). The fact that there are other decisions, not provided for by the Statute, that may put an end to the proceedings does not mean that the rules on review proceedings may be applied by analogy. To adopt an extensive interpretation of the Statute *contra reum* is not appropriate and it runs counter to the principles of strict interpretation of procedural provisions that may have penal consequences on the individual. Secondly, the opening of review proceedings depends upon the discovery of a new fact (i.e. evidence) that was not available at the time of the trial. In *Barayagwiza* the elements presented by the Prosecutor in the course of the revision proceedings were already available prior to the impugned decision, and it was the Prosecution that was responsible for their late presentation. The sensitivity of the issues involved may explain, but probably does not justify, the interpretation advanced by the Appeals Chamber.

Rules on review refer to new facts which could not have been discovered through the exercise of due diligence before the impugned decision was delivered. In the case at issue the evidence submitted as 'new' was available even prior to the decision under review and there may even have been a lack of diligence in not presenting it in due time. Hence, it was not justified to admit the motion for review on the ground that there were newly discovered elements; indeed, these elements had not been presented in due time simply because the Prosecution under-estimated the possible consequences of the proceedings.[103] The Chamber held that the requirement that the new element must not have been discovered in due time for lack of due diligence by the relevant party is a rule susceptible to derogation by the court. On the contrary, it is submitted that the Chamber should have considered it a norm not susceptible to derogation, particularly in light of the extraordinary nature of review proceedings. If the new fact could have been discovered through the exercise of due diligence, then the party requesting review committed an error. If, as often held by the Appeals Chamber, appeals proceedings are not intended to offer to the parties a way to remedy the errors committed at trial this is also true for review proceedings. In this respect, it is hard to reconcile the jurisprudence of

---

[103] Cf. Appeals Chamber Decision on Review, *Barayagwiza* (ICTR–97–19–R), 31 March 2000.

the Appeals Chamber in *Barayagwiza* with its previous decision in *Tadić*. In the latter, the Chamber held that 'additional evidence should not be admitted lightly at the appellate stage. [It] is not admissible in the absence of a reasonable explanation as to why the evidence was not available at trial. Such unavailability must not result from the lack of due diligence on the part of counsel who undertook the defence of the accused before the Trial Chamber'.[104] It is very hard to justify why the Chamber adopted a more restrictive interpretation in appellate proceedings, which are far broader than review proceedings, while it ruled rather broadly in favour of the Prosecution and in proceedings that should have an extraordinary character. Additionally, it seems unreasonable to adopt for the accused a standard narrower than that granted to the Prosecutor.

The real problem that emerged in *Barayagwiza*, however, was that there was no specific legal basis in the Statutes or the Rules for the Chambers of the Tribunal to react when confronted with egregious violations of the rights of the accused by the Prosecution or other organs acting under the authority of the Tribunal. Thus, the Appeals Chamber had to resort to the doctrine of abuse of process[105] and devised an *extra ordinem* procedural sanction (i.e. to strike out the case with prejudice for the Prosecutor to bring the charges anew). This was probably unfair to the Prosecution and to the victims of those crimes; in particular, on account of the lack of an explicit legal basis in the regulatory provisions of the *ad hoc* Tribunals.

We are thus confronted with a deplorable situation: the serious violation of the rights of an accused led to a strong reaction by the judges (i.e. release of the accused, striking out the case with prejudice for the Prosecutor). Such reaction may have been inappropriate, in that it was too drastic in the absence of an express provision. However, the subsequent remedy of the 'wrong' (the decision on the motion by the Prosecutor for review or reconsideration) from a legal viewpoint has been worse than the illness it intended to cure.

Nonetheless, the review decision led to the affirmation of a vital principle according to which violations of the rights of the accused must be compensated. The lesson to be drawn from *Barayagwiza* is the need for a system of pre-determined procedural sanctions in the *ad hoc* Tribunals' system. This issue, which is later addressed in the concluding chapter, certainly represents one of the main gaps in the protection of human rights in international criminal justice, because the absence of specific sanctions brings about a condition of uncertainty.

---

[104] Cf. Appeals Chamber decision on additional evidence in *Tadić*, note 98 above.

[105] In this respect, cf. K. Kittichaisaree, *International Criminal Law* (Oxford: OUP, 2001), at 298. On the notion of abuse of process in British cases, involving issues relating to the ECHR, cf. C. Warbrick, 'Judicial Jurisdiction and Abuse of Process', in 49 *ICLQ* (2000), 466–489.

4. Is an extra ordinem *right of reconsideration emerging in the* ad hoc *Tribunals system?*

Although a formal interpretation of the provisions of the Statute and Rules of *ad hoc* Tribunals seems to indicate that review proceedings may be instituted even against a non-final decision, a more reasonable interpretation based on the very nature of such proceedings should prevail. Therefore, review proceedings should be allowed only against final decisions. The Chambers, however, may resort to a different kind of power in order to make good wrongful decisions or rulings. It has been suggested that a party may file a motion for reconsideration. Nowhere is this provided for in the Rules. Nonetheless, there are some precedents in favour of the existence of a power inherent in Chambers or in judges to reconsider, if a party had been subjected to an unfair procedure.[106]

Initially, in *Kordić and Čerkez* and in *Delalić and others*, such a power was excluded.[107] Only with a further pronouncement by the President in *Brdjanin and Talić* was reconsideration of a decision concretely resorted to.[108] The ICTR Chambers affirmed this right, more or less in the same terms. On one occasion a motion for reconsideration was granted,[109] and the Appeals

---

[106] Judge Shahabuddeen's Separate opinion in *Barayagwiza*, 31 March 2000, concluded that in the case at issue a motion for reconsideration would not be proper because the moving party was not submitted to an unfair procedure. Respectfully, there are reasons for disagreeing with this opinion, as it seems that what the Prosecution contended was that it was taken by surprise by the decision of the Chamber. Had the Prosecutor been aware of the potential consequences of the first appeal proceedings she would have presented the elements of evidence submitted in the review proceedings earlier. The fact that the Trial Chamber exercised a power not provided for in the Statutes or the Rules impinging upon the powers of the Prosecutor could be considered as being unfair. If one believes the Prosecution contention that it was taken by surprise, one may opt for reconsidering the decision. If, on the contrary, one thinks that the Prosecutor was aware that there was the possibility that the proceedings would be terminated, then the motion for reconsideration could not have been allowed. It remains unclear why the Chamber preferred to stretch the provisions on review beyond their limits, by considering with excessive flexibility the requirement of unavailability of evidence, rather than admitting that the Prosecutor was taken by surprise by the decision of the Chamber to strike out the case. This implies that the proceedings were subjectively unfair, in the sense that the Prosecutor did not expect them to bring in a final word on the case. In other words it was not possible for the Prosecutor to predict what the outcome of the review proceedings could have been, due to the absence of a precise system of procedural sanctions in the system of the Tribunal.

[107] See Trial Chamber Decision on Prosecution's Motion for Reconsideration, *Kordić and Čerkez* (IT–95–14/2–PT), 15 February 1999, at 2. The Trial Chamber held that '[m]otions to reconsider are not provided for in the Rules and do not form part of the procedures of the International Tribunal', at 2. Along the same lines see the Appeals Chamber Order on an Emergency Motion to Reconsider Denial of Provisional Release, *Delalić and others* (IT–96–21–A), 1 June 1999, at 4.

[108] Order of the President on the Prosecution's Motion for Reconsideration, *Brdjanin and Talić* (IT–96–36–AR73.3), 11 January 2001.

[109] Appeals Chamber Decision on the motion for review, in *Imanishimwe* (ICTR–97–36–AR72), 12 July 2000.

Chamber held, *inter alia*, that '[it] may exercise its inherent power to reconsider interlocutory decisions in such cases as these, where a clear error has been exposed'.[110] The trend that emerges from the case law of the Tribunals is that Chambers are inclined to admit the possibility of resorting to this power in principle, although it has not yet been precisely clarified under which circumstances it may be applied. The main feature of this *extra ordinem* procedure is that it constitutes a unique measure for obtaining a remedy against unfair decisions.

It may be too early to affirm that a new right was born in the procedural system of the *ad hoc* Tribunals. It appears from these precedents that there is an inherent power of Chambers to reconsider their own decisions, although it remains unclear on what basis and according to what criteria. Additionally, no specific time-limits are set, nor are any other detailed guidelines for the parties given. Only subsequent practice or, perhaps more appropriately, an amendment to the Rules may clarify whether this possibility should entirely turn into a right of the parties, or whether it will simply remain a discretionary power of the Chambers.

5. The rights of convicted persons to seek revision, as envisaged in the ICC Statute

Article 84 of the ICC Statute on revision of conviction or sentence is much more complex and detailed than the corresponding provisions of the *ad hoc* Tribunals.[111] Additionally, the power of the Prosecutor to apply for revision *in malam partem* was suppressed and the Prosecution may bring an application for revision only in the interest of the convicted person. Article 84 provides that 'the convicted person or, after death, spouses, children, parents or one person alive at the time of the death of the accused, who has been given express written instructions from the accused to bring such a claim, . . . may apply to the Appeals Chamber'.

First, it has been clarified that the Appeals Chamber is the competent Chamber for ruling on the admissibility of the application for revision. Secondly, the ICC Statute has also clearly specified the grounds on which revision may be sought, in line with the extraordinary nature of revision proceedings and their main traits under existing system of criminal justice. Under the ICC Statute an application for revision may be filed where new evidence

---

[110] See *ibidem*, at 3. Additionally, the Appeals Chamber, in a subsequent decision in *Kanyabashi*, stressed its inherent power of reconsideration. Cf. Appeals Chamber Decision on a Motion for Review and/or Reconsideration, *Kanyabashi* (ICTR–96–15–AR72), 12 September 2000, at 2.

[111] In general on Article 84 of the ICC Statute see C. Staker, 'Revision of Conviction or Sentence (Article 84)', in Triffterer, *Commentary on the Rome Statute of the International Criminal Court: Observers' Notes* (Baden-Baden: Nomos, 1999), 1037–1040.

is discovered which was not available at the time of trial for reasons not imputable to the party making the application. Such evidence has to be important enough to have had an influence on the verdict if it had been known earlier, so that if it had been known it might have led to a different verdict. It is also possible to apply for revision in cases where conviction was decisively based on evidence that turned out to be false, forged, or falsified. Finally, revision may be sought when one or more of the judges who participated in conviction or confirmation of the charges has committed serious misconduct justifying removal from office under Article 46.

Having considered the motion, and having found it meritorious, the Appeals Chamber has three options: to reconvene the original Trial Chamber, to constitute a new Trial Chamber, or to retain jurisdiction over the matter. From among the three solutions, the Chamber must choose the most appropriate given the facts of each case. Where the Chamber concludes it has jurisdiction, the Chamber itself should hear the parties.

The RPE have further specified the procedural requirements for revision proceedings[112] and clarified that for the purpose of revision proceedings the Chamber has the same powers as the Trial Chamber under Part 6 and those rules must apply *mutatis mutandis* (Rule 161 paragraph 2).

Globally, it seems that provisions governing revision proceedings in the ICC system are more advanced in terms of respect of the rights of individuals than the corresponding provisions of the *ad hoc* Tribunals' systems. In the ICC system the principle of *ne bis in idem* is thoroughly guaranteed, as the Prosecutor has no power to seek revision *in malam partem* and, on the contrary, has a positive duty to apply for revision in the interests of the convicted person. Additionally, the Statute is much more specific than the *ad hoc* Tribunals' provisions on the grounds for revision.

IV. CONCLUSIONS

With regard to the rights of appeal and review a clear improvement has been made from the trials that followed the Second World War to the ICC Statute. The rights of the accused to appeal and review, absent in the Nuremberg and Tokyo Charters, are summarily provided for in the Statutes of the *ad hoc* Tribunals. However, the provisions contained in these Statutes were terse and, although they were supplemented by the RPE, still contain defects and

---

[112] Rule 159 provides that the application shall be in writing, shall set out the grounds, and be accompanied by supporting materials. It establishes that the decision must be taken by a majority of the judges (Rule 159, para. 2) and reasons for it must be notified to the applicant (para. 3). Rule 160 provides for the special arrangements that may be necessary to enable the sentenced person (who will be probably serving his sentence in a third country) to reach the seat of the Court, whenever appropriate, for the hearings.

ambiguities. For example, both parties are placed on an equal footing as regards the grounds for appeal and review.

Provisions regarding the rights of appeal and revision have been laid down in a much more detailed form in the ICC Statute. These provisions are far more balanced and in conformity with human rights standards than the provisions governing these proceedings before *ad hoc* Tribunals. They represent a further improvement towards the strengthening of human rights protection in international criminal justice.

The *ad hoc* Tribunals' provisions, from the viewpoint of the rights of the accused, certainly contain appropriate guarantees of due process. There are, however, a few problems that are still unsolved. First, the precise scope and extent of appellate and review proceedings remains rather vague, particularly as far as the notions of errors of fact and errors of law are concerned, including the power of the Chamber to pronounce on issues of general interest. In principle, the Appeals Chamber held that appellate proceedings should not be a second trial in which appellate judges substitute their findings for those of trial Chamber judges, unless such findings are totally unreasonable. In practice, however, this line is very hard to draw. Moreover, it may not respond to the interests of justice to assess errors of fact only on the basis of reasonableness. The Appeals Chamber section in the *ad hoc* Tribunals' system was also created with the purpose of assessing the case on the merits and not just the law.

Secondly, another disappointing aspect from the perspective of individual rights is that the appellate function is highly jeopardized by the rotation mechanism.

Thirdly, the scope of the power of the Prosecutor to appeal on the facts is probably too broad and should be curbed in order more effectively to protect the rights of the accused not to be tried twice for the same crime and from abuses.

Fourthly, as regards review proceedings, in the framework of the *ad hoc* Tribunals the Prosecutor is broadly entitled to seek review *in malam partem*. Notwithstanding the efforts made by the judges to limit such a risk by limiting the power of the Prosecutor to one year from the decision, it seems that these provisions are in breach of the *ne bis in idem* principle. The Statute did not provide for a power of the Prosecutor to seek review *in malam partem*. Therefore, the judges may consider amending the Rules to limit such a power. On the other hand, it is reasonable to suggest that under specific circumstances the Prosecutor should be entitled to apply for revision. This should occur in cases where an accused has intimidated or bribed witnesses or otherwise offered false evidence, and the Prosecutor becomes aware of that after the judgment.

In general, the procedural rules of the ICC system build upon the provisions of the *ad hoc* Tribunals' system. The provisions of the ICC have improved procedural rules on appellate and review proceedings in four respects. First, in the ICC system the Prosecutor has a duty to appeal and seek review in the interests of the accused. Secondly, the Statute provides that the convicted person is entitled to appeal on 'any other ground that affects the fairness or reliability of the proceedings or decision' (Article 81 paragraph 1 ICC St.). Thus, the right of a convicted person to appeal on facts is broader than the corresponding right of the Prosecutor. Where the convicted person files an appeal motion, appellate proceedings may lead to a second trial. This interpretation is certainly not contrary to the right of the accused not to be tried twice (the principle of *ne bis in idem*, or against double jeopardy), since such right is established to protect the accused and cannot be invoked to his or her detriment. Thirdly, the ICC Statute specifically provides for a ground of appeal against sentencing (i.e. disproportion between the crime and the sentence), thus codifying the practice of the *ad hoc* Tribunals and clarifying the law. Fourthly, requests for review are admitted only in the interests of the convicted person, which brings international criminal procedure more into line with a strict reading of the *ne bis in idem* principle.

Furthermore, it is suggested that the ICC Statute not only contains procedural rules for the Court but, at the same time, represents a codification of rules on international criminal procedure.[113] These rules should be considered as guidelines for the interpretation of the provisions of the *ad hoc* Tribunals' system. Hence, it is not unreasonable to argue that the ICC provisions may be relevant to the interpretation of the provisions of the *ad hoc* Tribunals' system, when these are silent on certain issues or are ambiguous. Moreover, the same should be true for express rules that are in contrast with international human rights law standards, such as the rules envisaging excessively broad powers for the Prosecutor to impugn the decisions of the Tribunals. These rules are clearly at odds with the *ne bis in idem* principle. Finally, ICC solutions should also inspire the adoption of amendments to the RPE of the Tribunals.

---

[113] The value of the ICC provisions as an authoritative statement of the international *opinio iuris* on international criminal law has been pointed out by both Trial Chambers and Appeals Chamber of the ICTY on several occasions. See e.g. the judgment of Trial Chamber in *Furundžija* (IT–95–17/1–T), 10 December 1998, para. 227, and the Appeals Chamber judgment in *Tadić* (IT–94–1–A), 15 July 1999 (para. 223). More recently, in *Milošević*, Decision, Trial Chamber (IT–99–37–PT), 8 November 2001, para. 31.

5

Penalties, Enforcement Mechanisms, and the Rights of Convicted Persons

I. THE MAJOR GOALS OF INTERNATIONAL PENALTIES AND THE LEGAL EXPECTATIONS OF CONVICTED PERSONS

1. *The* nulla poena sine lege *principle as conferring an individual right*

There is no doubt that the *nulla poena sine lege* principle aims at satisfying the need for some degree of certainty with regard to punishment.[1] Individuals must know what they can expect if they are found guilty of a particular crime.[2] Nonetheless, it is difficult to add more, unless one tries to define the *notion of law at the international level*. Naturally, it cannot be contended that this means law in the formal sense: a statute approved by a parliament. There are no statutes or parliaments in the international legal order. Therefore, it is necessary to adopt the broader notion of law propounded by the Appeals Chamber in the decision on jurisdiction delivered in *Tadić*.[3] In that pronouncement the Chamber held that the expression 'established by law' had to be interpreted in international law as meaning '*in accordance with the rule of law*'.[4] Hence, the principle *nulla poena sine lege* must be perceived as a principle of justice that, although always valid at national level, cannot be fully reproduced at international level.[5] First, there is no international legislator. Secondly, penalties have been attached to the crimes under the jurisdiction of the Court by way of judicial precedents and resort to national laws, rather than through the approval of a detailed catalogue of crimes and penalties.[6]

---

[1] The principle is contained in all major international human rights texts: cf. Article 11 UDHR, Article 15 ICCPR, Article 9 ACHR, and Article 7 ECHR.

[2] Cf. the judgment of the ECourtHR in *S.W.* v. *United Kingdom*, 22 November 1995 (Series A–335/B) **www.echr.coe.int/Eng/Judgments.htm**. The same opinion has been authoritatively expressed by G. Abi-Saab 'Droits de l'Homme et Juridictions Pénales Internationales—Convergences et Tensions', in R.-J. Dupuy (ed.), *Mélanges en l'Honneur de Nicolas Valticos—Droit et Justice* (Paris: Pedone, 1999), at 248.

[3] Cf. Appeals Chamber Decision on jurisdiction, *Tadić* (IT–94–1–AR 72), 2 October 1995.

[4] *Ibidem*, paras. 42–48 (emphasis added).

[5] Cf., in this respect, the dissenting opinion of Judge Cassese to the Appeals Chamber Sentencing Judgment, *Tadić* (IT–94–1–A), 26 January 2000.

[6] B. Stern, 'De l'utilisation du temps en droit international pénal', in *Le Droit International et le Temps, Actes du Colloque de la SFDI* (Paris: Pedone, 2001), 253–264, at 255, explains that in international law the principle *nulla poena sine lege* should be interpreted as *nulla poena sine jure*.

When the Security Council decided to establish the *ad hoc* Tribunals this problem was perceived.[7] The Secretary-General, in his report to the Security Council accompanying the ICTY Statute, affirmed that 'there is one . . . issue which would require reference to domestic practice, namely, penalties'.[8] Thus, in the *ad hoc* Tribunals' system an attempt was made formally to respect the *nulla poena* principle. Article 24 ICTY St. and Article 23 ICTR create a connection with the penalties generally applied by Yugoslav and Rwandan courts.[9] Nonetheless, on various occasions the judges have made clear that the relevance of national practice is only an indication that has no binding effect on the Tribunals.[10] The Chambers of the Tribunals have interpreted this reference to prove that the acts committed by convicted persons were considered crimes by their national States and a penalty was attached to them. In other words the Chambers have more or less clearly based their decisions on the notion that the principle is respected in so far as the crime is subject to a form of punishment under any (national) applicable law.

Therefore the principle *nulla poena sine lege* is admitted before international criminal tribunals,[11] but only to the extent that the convicted person cannot legitimately claim that neither national nor international law attached any penalty to his or her act. In other words, the *nulla poena sine lege* principle cannot really be considered as giving rise to a right of the individual: it should, instead, be interpreted as a principle of equity involving considerations of fairness and the interests of justice as a whole.[12]

A more problematic aspect concerns the concrete determination of penalties in every single case and whether a hierarchy of gravity exists among the crimes falling within the jurisdiction of the Court. In the system of the *ad hoc* Tribunals, judges determine penalties on the basis of general practice regarding prison sentences in the courts of the former Yugoslavia and Rwanda. Furthermore, the decision should take into account the gravity of the crimes and the individual circumstances of the accused (Article 24 ICTY St. and Article 23 ICTR St.). These factors have been interpreted by the Chambers of

---

[7] The projects submitted by various countries took this problem into account, see W. Schabas, 'Perverse Effects of the *Nulla Poena* Principle: National Practice and the Ad Hoc Tribunals', in 11 *EJIL* (2000) 521–539. Cf. UN doc. S/PV.3453, November 1994 concerning the ICTR.

[8] Cf. Secretary General's Report, S/25074, 3 May 1993, para. 34.

[9] This has been criticized by W. Schabas, 'Sentencing by International Tribunals: A Human Rights Approach', in 7 *DJCIL* (1997), 461–516, at 478–482.

[10] Cf., in this respect, Trial Chamber Sentencing Judgment, *Erdemović* (IT–96–22-S), 29 November 1996; and Trial Chamber Judgment, *Delalić and others* (IT–96–21–T), 16 November 1998.

[11] On the history of sentencing for international crimes by international or internationalized tribunals see W. Schabas, 'International Sentencing: From Leipzig (1923) to Arusha (1996)', in M.C. Bassiouni (ed.), *International Criminal Law* (2nd edn., Ardsley, NY: Transnational Publ., 1999), iii, 171–193, at 175–180.

[12] See, although in slightly different terms, H. Kelsen, 'Will the Nuremberg Judgement Constitute a Precedent?', in 1 *International Law Quarterly* (1947), 153, at 165.

the Tribunal and discussed thoroughly in the sentencing judgments issued so far (cf. paragraph I.3 below).

In the ICC Statute the solution adopted is that there are two types of prison sentence: a determined number of years, not exceeding thirty, and life imprisonment. The problem in respect of the principle *nulla poena sine lege* was certainly less dramatic in the ICC Statute than in the creation of the *ad hoc* Tribunals, as the permanent Court was not an *ex post facto* creation.

2. *The right of the convicted person to present evidence on sentencing issues*

At the end of the trial, when the parties have concluded their pleadings on the determination of guilt or innocence, they are also allowed to *present evidence on sentencing issues* and argue for what they believe to be the most appropriate penalty (Rule 85 (A) (vi) of both RPEs and Article 76 ICC St.). The Prosecution will try to complete its case by obtaining the sentencing of the accused to a specific term of imprisonment or even, in the most serious cases, to life imprisonment. To fulfil this task the Prosecution may call witnesses or produce documentary evidence, such as the so-called 'victim impact statements', as it did, for example, in *Tadić*.[13] On the other hand, the defence may, at this last stage, present evidence to try to assist the Chamber in tailoring the sentence to the particular defendant the sentence and to prove mitigating circumstances. The arguments made by the parties usually address questions dealing with both objective and subjective circumstances.

There are two questions which emerge at this stage. First, it is uncertain whether rules on the admission and evaluation of evidence are the same as those applied at the trial stage. Second, the Rules refer to the submission of all relevant information and do not use the term evidence. It is, thus, questionable whether this kind of information should be entirely equated to evidence within the meaning of the Rules, at least with regard to its presentation and evaluation.

In the *ad hoc* Tribunals the procedure initially provided for sentencing as a separate stage of the proceedings (cf. the two RPEs Part Six, section 4: sentencing procedure). Under that system, which was applied in a few cases before an amendment to the RPE was adopted (and entered into force), the Trial Chamber would hear evidence on sentencing issues only after it had already handed down its decision on guilt. Rule 100 of both RPEs stated that 'if the accused pleads guilty or if a Trial Chamber finds the accused guilty of a crime, the Prosecutor and the Defence may submit any *relevant information* that may assist the Trial Chamber in determining an appropriate sentence'.

---

[13] Cf. Trial Chamber Sentencing Judgment, *Tadić* (IT–94–1–S), 14 July 1997, para. 4: 'the Prosecutor offered a number of "victim impact statements" which detailed the physical and psychological injuries suffered as a result of the offences committed by Duško Tadić'.

Subsequently, the judges decided to amend the RPE and introduced a new procedure. This amendment was justified by the intention of speeding up the procedure, merging the two stages. According to this new procedure, presentation of evidence and pleading on sentencing issues occur prior to any determination of guilt or innocence. As a consequence, whilst before this amendment there were two distinct decisions: one on guilt or innocence and another, if needed, on penalties, both the establishment of guilt or innocence and the determination of the penalty or penalties to be imposed are now made in a single judgment. The system as defined by this amendment has also been adopted as a model for the ICC Statute. However, it remains unclear, in the procedure before the ICC, whether there are two distinct decisions or only one containing both the judgment and the sentence. Moreover, the accused can request specific hearings to be exclusively devoted to sentencing. It is nonetheless clear that presentation of evidence on sentencing issues will occur prior to the decision on guilt or innocence.

In the *ad hoc* Tribunals' system, the reasons for amending the Rules and merging the sentencing phase with trial proceedings are to be found in a desire for efficiency and expeditiousness. However, it does not seem that the solution found, by eliminating the two step procedure, is more effective in terms of expeditiousness of justice. Often, the defence may be induced to present a number of 'character' witnesses to testify to the personal circumstances of the accused. This does not prove to be more expeditious, since the defence may feel obliged to present an even greater number of witnesses in an attempt to influence the court prior to judgment.

It is submitted that it would have been *more consonant with respect for the rights of the accused* (in particular the presumption of innocence) to allow him or her fully to present evidence concerning sentencing issues.[14] It seems correct to argue that the *two-step procedure* better protects the rights of the accused, because it would allow the accused better to present his or her case in the sentencing phase. Once the accused knows that he or she has been considered guilty of a certain crime for some well specified reasons, he or she will be in a better position effectively to plead in mitigation. Moreover, once the accused has been convicted he or she may decide to call certain witnesses that may be counterproductive for him or her if heard prior to judgment on guilt or innocence.

The opinion that the two-step procedure is better in ensuring the protection of the rights of defendants is confirmed by the practice of the ICTY. Rule 6, paragraph (C), RPEs provides that 'an amendment shall enter into force immediately, but shall not operate to prejudice the rights of the accused in a

---

[14] This opinion seems to be shared by F. King and A.M. La Rosa, 'Penalties under the ICC Statute' in F. Lattanzi and W. Schabas (eds.), *Essays on the Rome Statute of the International Criminal Court* (L'Aquila: Il Sirente, 1999), i, 311–338, at 318.

pending case'. The procedure for sentencing was amended at the 16th Plenary Session, in July 1998, establishing that there would no longer be two separate phases. However, in *Tadić* the separation of the procedure into two stages, one for judgment and one for sentencing, was maintained even after the amendment had entered into force.[15] This was in line with the rule imposing that an amendment must not prejudice the rights of the accused in a pending case. Thus, it was implicitly admitted that the new procedure ensures a lesser degree of protection for the rights of the accused; therefore, it was not applied in cases pending at the moment of the entry into force of the amendment.

In conclusion, it is possible to argue that there is a *right to present evidence* on sentencing issues, although the formula used does not explicitly refer to evidence but simply to relevant information. This right is contained both in the Statutes of the *ad hoc* Tribunals and also in the Statute of the ICC. Ensuring the accused the right to present evidence at this stage is logical, particularly when one considers that the sentencing judgment is, at the end of the day, the decision that definitively affects the interests of the accused. Moreover, it is submitted that it would be better from the viewpoint of individual rights for relevant evidence on sentencing issues to be presented after the judgment. This reading can be supported by referring to a theological interpretation of the rights of the accused as internationally recognized in the Statutes of the International Criminal Tribunals and Court. These rights aim in the end to ensure that the accused receives a fair trial and a fair sentence.

3. The determination of penalties and the right to the individualization of sentences

(a) General

The Statutes of the *ad hoc* Tribunals establish that 'the penalty imposed by the Trial Chambers shall be limited to imprisonment'.[16] Additionally, paragraph 3 of Article 24 ICTY St. (Article 23 ICTR St.) provides that the Trial Chambers may order the return of any property and proceeds acquired by criminal conduct, including by means of duress, to their rightful owners.[17]

The provisions of the ICC Statute were drafted along the same lines. Article 77 ICC St. provides for two types of imprisonment penalty: a determined term, not exceeding thirty years, and life imprisonment. Moreover, the norms of the Statute add the possibility for the Court to impose a fine and forfeiture

---

[15] The Appeals Chamber affirmed that it would '[defer] sentencing on the Counts mentioned in sub-paragraphs (4) and (5) above [i.e. the counts on which the findings of the Trial Chamber were reversed] to a further stage of the proceedings': cf. Disposition, Judgment on Appeal, *Tadić* (IT–94–1–A), 15 July 1999, at 144.

[16] Article 24 ICTY St. and Article 23 ICTR St.

[17] On the issue of reparation (including restitution) to victims see Chapter 6 below.

on property and assets derived directly or indirectly from the crime. Furthermore, in the ICC Statute, Article 80 establishes that the provisions of the Statute on penalties do not affect the application by States of penalties prescribed by their national laws. This norm was inserted to satisfy the demands of those States whose national laws provide for the application of the death penalty (or corporal punishments). These delegations wanted to be sure that the provisions of the Statute would not be used to try to limit the range of penalties applicable under national laws. It should be noted that this rule increases the risks of the kind of unfairness that occurs in the relationships between the ICTR and national trials conducted in Rwanda. While the International Tribunal cannot impose the death penalty, the national laws of Rwanda provide for it and the courts apply it.[18] The paradox of this kind of situation is that leaders may escape death by being tried before international courts, while executors of their orders may face the death penalty if they are tried at the national level. This is a very difficult problem to address, but it may in the end jeopardize the perception of fairness of international criminal justice in its overall dimension.

The two *ad hoc* Tribunals have so far issued more than twenty judgments against more than thirty accused.[19] Six defendants have been acquitted (five

---

[18] The rejection of the death penalty in the Statute of the ICTR was one of the reasons for which Rwanda did not vote in favour of the creation of the Tribunal, for the position of Rwanda cf. the verbatim records of the session, note 4 above, at 16.

[19] ICTR (8): Kambanda, 19 October 2000 (ICTR–97–23–A): life imprisonment (notwithstanding his guilty plea); Akayesu, 1 June 2001 (IT–96–4–A): life imprisonment; Musema, 16 November 2001 (ICTR–96–13–A); Rutaganda 6 December 1999 (ICTR–96–3–T): life imprisonment; Kayshema, 1 June 2001 (ICTR–95–1–A): life imprisonment; Ruzindana, 1 June 2001 (ICTR–95–1–A e ICTR–96–10–A): 25 years; Serushago, 2 February 1999 (ICTR–98–39–S): 15 years (on the basis of his guilty plea); Ruggiu, 1 June 2000 (ICTR–97–32–S), 12 years (on the basis of his guilty plea). ICTY (11): Erdemović, 5 March 1998 (IT–96–22-S): 5 years; Tadić, 26 January 2000 (IT–94–1–A): 20 years; Blaškić, 3 March 2000 (IT–95–14–T): 45 years (appeal pending); Aleksovski, 31 March 2000 (IT–95–14/1–A): 7 years; Furundžija, 21 July 2000 (95–17/1–A): 10 years; Kunarać, Kovać , and Vuković (IT–96–23/1), 12 June 2002, sentenced to 28, 20, 12 years; Kordić and Čerkez (IT–95–14/2), 26 February 2001, 25 and 15 years; Jelisić, 5 July 2001 (IT–95–10–A): 40 years; Todorović (IT–95–9/1), 31 July 2001, 10 years (on the basis of his guilty plea); Krstić (IT–98–33) 2 August 2001, 46 years; Delalić, 20 January 2001 (IT–96–21–A): acquitted; Mucić, 9 October 2001 (IT–96–21–T): 9 years; Landzo, 9 October 2001 (IT–96–21–T): 15 years; Delić, 9 October 2001 (IT–96–21–T): 18 years; in Kupreškić and others, 23 October 2001 (IT–95–17–A), 3 accused, Zoran, Mirjan, and Vlatko Kupreškić, were acquitted on appeal and released, the 2 other defendants, Josipović and Santić, were sentenced to 12 and 18 years respectively (another co-accused in this proceeding (Papić) had already been acquitted by the Trial Chamber and the Prosecutor did not appeal); Kvocka, Kos, Radić, Zigić, and Prcac (IT–98–30/1), 2 November 2001, penalties ranging from 5 to 25 years; Sikirica, Dosen, and Kolundzija, (IT–95–8), 13 November 2001 (on the basis of their guilty plea) 15, 5, and 3 years; Krnojelac (IT–97–25), 15 March 2002, 7½ years ; Simić, 17 October 2002 (IT–95–9/2), 5 years (on the basis of this guilty plea).

7 people convicted by ICTY are currently serving their sentences: Sikirica (15 years) and Dosen (5 years) in Austria, Tadić (20 years) in Germany, Furundžija (10 years) in Finland, Josipović (12 years), Santić (18 years), and Todorović (10 years) in Spain. All persons convicted by the ICTR are currently serving their sentences in Mali, see note 40 below.

ICTY and one ICTR),[20] while the others have been convicted and sentenced to penalties ranging from three years to life imprisonment. It is interesting to note that the ICTR has issued five life imprisonment sentences out of a total of seven sentences while the ICTY has, so far, never imposed life imprisonment. This is probably due to the fact that the ICTR has tried very high officials (including the former Rwandan Prime Minister, Jean Kambanda), heavily involved in the planning of crimes of genocide, while the ICTY has so far mainly dealt with low- or middle-level accused, charged generally with war crimes or crimes against humanity. The only ICTY case in which a conviction for genocide has been entered so far is *Krstić*: the accused was sentenced to forty-six years (an appeal is currently pending).[21]

The Statutes of the Tribunal expect the Chambers to take into consideration different factors in determining the penalty to be imposed on defendants convicted of crimes within the jurisdiction of the Tribunals. Article 24, paragraph 2, ICTY St. (Article 23.2 ICTR St.) states that 'in imposing the sentences, the Trial Chambers should take into account such factors as the gravity of the offence and the individual circumstances of the convicted person'.

(b) Gravity of the offence

Rule 101 of both RPEs on penalties states that the maximum sentence the Tribunal can impose is life imprisonment. Paragraph (B) establishes that the Chamber in determining the sentence must take into account various factors including aggravating and mitigating circumstances.

It is submitted that such a vague reference to aggravating circumstances is contrary to the principle of legality of the penalties. It cannot be denied that such circumstances concretely affect the determination of the sentence. Thus they amount to a penalty that is not specifically set out. The adoption of this approach in the Rules confirms the reduced scope of the *nulla poena sine lege* principle in international criminal law, which may be explained by the relatively

---

4 sentences have already been served, and the detainees released: (1) Erdemović, in Norway (5 years), (2) Aleksovski, in Finland (7 years), (3) Kolundzija (3 years), who was released directly by order of the President of the Tribunal, having already served 2½ years in pre-trial custody at the UN Detention Unit in The Hague, and (4) Kos (6 years) who withdrew his notice of appeal and was released on 31 July 2002.

For a constant update on the proceedings before the *ad hoc* Tribunals see **www.ictr.org/ wwwroot/ENGLISH/cases/index.htm**, for the ICTR, and **www.un.org/icty/glace/profact-e.htm**, for the ICTY.

[20] These are Zejnil Delalić in the *Celebici* (IT–96–21–A), 20 February 2001, Dragan Papić, Mirjian, Zoran, and Vlatko Kupreškić in *Kupreškić and others* (IT–95–16–T and IT–95–16–A), 14 January 2000 and 23 October 2001; and *Baglishema* (ICTR–95–1–A), 3 July 2002.

[21] Trial Chamber Judgment, *Krstić* (IT–98–33–T), 2 August 2001.

primitive stage of development of this field of international law. However, the reproduction of a similar rule in the ICC Statute does not seem appropriate. Quite correctly the Rules of Procedure and Evidence have addressed this problem and have specifically laid down the aggravating circumstances.[22] Astonishingly, however, Rule 145, paragraph 2b)(vi) of the ICC Rules reintroduces the same defect, in that it leaves the door open to abuse by adding a blank reference to 'other circumstances . . . not enumerated above'. It is submitted that the drafters were conscious that such reference to other circumstances was too wide and would adversely impinge upon the rights of individuals. Hence, they added the requirement that such other circumstances not specifically mentioned might be taken into account only if 'by virtue of their nature [they] are similar to those mentioned'. This additional requirement, nonetheless, does not seem satisfactory in terms of certainty of the law. Therefore, it is suggested that the entire provision should be deleted and no aggravating circumstance, other than those specifically listed, be taken into account at the sentencing stage.

The reference contained in the Statute to the 'gravity of the offence' was not intended to enable the judges to add a *blank provision on aggravating circumstances*. On the contrary, it was aimed at inviting the judges to identify a hierarchy of gravity among the offences within the jurisdiction of the Court. There has been a great division on this issue among the judges in Chambers. It seems widely accepted that genocide should be considered the most serious crime among those attributed to the jurisdiction of the Tribunals.[23] This led the Trial Chamber of the ICTR, in the *Kambanda* case, to affirm that 'genocide was the crime of crimes'[24] and to sentence the accused to life imprisonment, irrespective of his guilty plea. In opting for such a heavy penalty the Chamber referred to the leading role of the accused during the Rwandan genocide.[25] This solution was confirmed by the Appeals Chamber, which upheld the Trial Chamber judgment. However, apart from this recognition of increased gravity of genocide, with regard to other crimes under the Statute (war crimes, grave breaches, and crimes against humanity) the situation is notably less clear. In the *Tadić* sentencing judgment, the Appeals Chamber held the view that there is no hierarchy of gravity among the crimes under the jurisdiction of the Tribunal. Judge Cassese disagreed with this interpretation, at least with reference to the single case. He specified that in principle, at this stage of development in international criminal law, no hierarchy of gravity among the crimes under the Statute can be outlined *a priori*. Nonetheless, according to his dissenting opinion a hierarchy of gravity in respect of each individual case should be recognized, whenever *ceteris paribus* (all other circumstances being equal) the very same facts imputed to an accused could be regarded as more serious depending on how

---

[22] Cf. Rules of Procedure and Evidence for the ICC, Chapter 7, Penalties, Rule 145.

[23] The crime of genocide has been defined as 'the crime of crimes': see Trial Chamber Sentencing Judgment, *Kambanda* (ICTR–97–23-S), 4 September 1998, paras. 16–25.

[24] *Ibidem*, para. 16.   [25] *Ibidem*, para. 61, point (vii).

they are characterized. In the case of crimes against humanity there is a broader context in which the crimes are committed. The fact that the accused has knowledge of the widespread or systematic context in which his acts are inscribed entails the appropriateness of a more severe punishment than if his conduct would simply have been classified as a war crime. Thus, Judge Cassese concluded that, 'whenever an offence committed by an accused is deemed to be a crime against humanity, it must be regarded of greater gravity, all else being equal, than if it is characterised as a war crime'.[26] The Trial Chamber in its second sentencing judgment of 11 November 1999, Judge Robinson dissenting, had followed a similar approach.[27]

The legal condition in this respect is certainly unclear. It seems that in *Erdemovic* the Appeals Chamber declared the plea null and void also on the basis of the conclusion that it considered the offence of crime against humanity more serious than a war crime.[28] Accordingly, the Trial Chamber that pronounced the second sentencing judgment considerably reduced the penalty, after the accused entered a guilty plea to war crimes instead of to crimes against humanity.[29]

It has been contended that in taking into account the gravity of the crime judges should refer to the so-called underlying offence, e.g. murder, extermination, plunder, etc.[30] This approach does not seem entirely persuasive since the underlying offences alone do not seem to fit the definition of 'crime', as required by the Statute. The underlying offences are *elements* of the crimes within the jurisdiction of the Tribunals: genocide, crimes against humanity, war crimes, or grave breaches. Therefore, it is clear that by referring to the gravity of the crime, the Statute did not intend to refer to the gravity of the underlying offence, but to the crime *stricto sensu*.[31]

In conclusion, given the rudimentary stage of international criminal law, it might be acceptable that a hierarchy of crimes had not yet been established. However, there are elements that seem to show that a certain hierarchy can be precisely identified. First of all, when analysing the judgments of the Tribunals it emerges that the heaviest penalties were imposed for genocide (sentences of life imprisonment by the ICTR, forty-six years of imprisonment by the ICTY). Secondly, it also emerges that the lowest penalties were

---

[26] Cf. Judge Cassese, Dissenting Opinion, 26 January 2000.

[27] Cf. Judge Robinson, Dissenting Opinion, 11 November 1999.

[28] See L.C. Green, 'Erdemovic, Tadic, Dokmanovic: Jurisdiction and Early Practice of the Yugoslav War Crimes Tribunal', in 27 *Isr. YHR* (1997), 313–364, at 324.

[29] Judge Shahabuddeen in a separate opinion in *Tadić* expressed doubts on the higher gravity of crimes against humanity *vis-à-vis* war crimes: Judge Shahabuddeen, Separate Opinion, 26 January 2000.

[30] Cf. Judge Robinson, Dissenting Opinion, 11 November 1999.

[31] More generally for a discussion of the issue see M. Frulli, 'Are Crimes Against Humanity More Serious Than War Crimes?', in 12 *EJIL* (2001), at 329, and A. Carcano, 'Sentencing and the Gravity of the Offence in International Criminal Law', in 51 *ICLQ* (2002), 583–609.

imposed for war crimes (in *Erdemović* and *Aleksovksi* the accused were sentenced respectively to five and seven years).[32] Thirdly, it is also possible to note that, after consideration of the number of people convicted of war crimes and those convicted of crimes against humanity, it becomes apparent that the penalties attached to the former are generally lower than those attached to the latter.[33]

(c) Individualization of the sentence

Moving now to the second tenet of Article 24 ICTY St. (Article 23 ICTR St.), i.e. the need to examine individual circumstances, it should be noted that the Rules of Procedure do not contain specific indications, apart from a general reference to mitigating circumstances, including co-operation with the Prosecutor.[34]

The Chambers of the Tribunal, in individualizing sentences, have usually considered the age of the accused (both at the *tempus commissi delicti* and at the moment of sentencing) and his family life. Moreover, the Chambers took into account the criminal record of the accused and his role in the context in which the crimes were committed (this element has also been taken into account as an aggravating factor). In the first sentencing judgment in *Tadić*, for example, consideration was given to the indigence of the accused and the effect of sentence on his family. Chambers also examined the character of the accused, their social background, and social behaviour prior to the commencement of the hostilities between the various ethnic groups.[35]

The meaning of individualization of the sentence, however, seems to go beyond the abovementioned elements. Individualization enshrines protection at the sentencing stage of the principle that *criminal responsibility* is an *individual form of responsibility*. In this sense it seeks to protect individuals against punishments that are not specifically addressed to *their own acts*, but are more generally aimed at punishing the crimes committed by a certain group against another. This element is closely linked to the unique features of crimes under international law, because one of the distinctive traits of international crimes is that they often occur in the midst of armed conflicts of either an international or non-international character. These conflicts usually involve opposing groups and therefore there may be the risk of punishing an individual not only for the acts he or she has committed, but also for the complex of crimes committed by one group against the other. Hence, the right to individualization contains an element of fairness. Thus, it is contended that

---

[32] Nonetheless, a Trial Chamber in *Simić and others* imposed a sentence of three years for persecution as a crime against humanity (for the accused Kolundžija): Sentencing Judgment, *Simić*, (IT–95–9–S), 13 November 2001.

[33] Cf. note 14 above.   [34] Cf. Rule 101, para. B.ii of both RPEs.

[35] See Trial Chamber Sentencing Judgment, *Tadić* (IT–94–1–S), 14 July 1997, para. 61.

Chambers should be very careful in using individualization *contra reum*. The provisions for individualization do not aim at creating a basis for aggravating the penalties to be imposed. They rather tend to represent, in the unique context of international criminal justice, a limitation to the risk of imposing the whole burden of guilt only on those few individuals who are tried and convicted. If the principle *nulla poena sine lege* has to maintain some significance at the international level, it seems that this should at least preclude the possibility of aggravating the consequences of guilt *ex post facto* on a case-by-case basis.

Individualization may also indicate that there should be efforts to try to take into account the chances of rehabilitation of the individual. However, rehabilitation cannot be construed as a right of the convicted person. It is only one of the various elements that may be given consideration at the sentencing stage. Nevertheless, it is questionable whether rehabilitation itself is outside the scope of the Tribunals' or the Court's competence. An express reference to rehabilitation is contained in Rule 125 RPE ICTY (Rule 126 RPE ICTR), dealing with the general standards for granting pardon or commutation of the sentence. This indicates that rehabilitation plays an important role, at least at the stage of execution of sentences. It seems, however, important to try to ascertain whether rehabilitation also has relevance in the determination of sentence.

4. The purpose of international penalties and the question whether there is a right of the convicted person to rehabilitation

The Chambers of the *ad hoc* Tribunals have indicated several goals for international penalties.[36] The sentencing decision of 29 November 1996 in *Erdemović* was the first sentence imposed by an international criminal tribunal since the post Second World War trials. In this decision, the Trial Chamber proceeded to review in depth the purposes of sentence. It was generally highlighted that neither the Statute, nor the Secretary-General's Report, nor the Rules contained any indication of the purposes sought through the infliction of a penalty. The Chamber examined the purposes of the penalty for crimes against humanity in the light of precedents in international law as well as national legal systems, including the former Yugoslavia. The judges assumed that the objectives envisaged by the Security Council when creating the Tribunal should be taken into account for sentencing purposes[37] and identified these elements in the concepts of *deterrence, reprobation, retribution,* and *collective reconciliation*. The Chamber recognized the importance of the concepts

---

[36] Cf. Trial Chamber Sentencing Judgment, *Erdemović* (IT–96–22–S), 29 November 1996.

[37] For a panorama on these objectives cf. T. Howland and W. Calathes, 'The UN's International Criminal Tribunal, Is It Justice or Jingoisms for Rwanda? A Call for Transformation', in 39 *VJIL* (1998) 135–167, at 150–156.

of deterrence and retribution while especially stressing reprobation as an appropriate purpose of the penalty for a crime against humanity and stigmatization of the criminal conduct underlying it. Trial Chambers in other cases[38] also followed similar reasoning.

It is certainly admissible to conclude that there is a multiplicity of purposes for international sentences and the Chambers of the Tribunal have identified most of them. However, it may be interesting to verify whether it could be argued that convicted persons have a specific right to rehabilitation and what weight, if any, should be assigned to this purpose.

Generally speaking, the Chambers of the Tribunals in imposing penalties have always tended to attach more importance to deterrence and retribution than to rehabilitation of the convicted person.[39] This, however, has usually been combined with a discussion on the need to individualize the sentence and to take into consideration the personal circumstances of the convicted person. There are two reasons that may lead to the conclusion that rehabilitation is an important goal of international punishment. First, one element indicating the willingness not to exclude in principle the possibility of rehabilitation is the refusal of the death penalty and the explicit admission of the possibility of pardon or commutation of sentence. Secondly, another element that contributes to the submission that rehabilitation plays an important role at the sentencing stage is the need for an appraisal of the personal circumstances of the accused.

In particular, the requirement of individualization of penalties imposes a duty to create a distance from the general objectives of the Tribunal. In the first *Erdemović* sentencing judgment, for example, the purposes of international penalties were identified by referring to the general objectives of the creation of the Tribunal. This approach is not completely convincing, as there is the risk of extending the scope of the punishment of individuals beyond the responsibilities they may have for the acts they have individually committed. Hence, it can certainly be admitted that it may be useful to refer to the general objectives behind the creation of the Tribunal. However, the fact that the Statute requires the individual circumstances of the convicted person to be taken into account implies that the sentence must be designed for the accused rather than for the objectives of the whole system of international criminal justice. Whilst naturally this does not automatically imply that rehabilitation should constitute one of the aims of sentencing, it does provide an interesting element for further reflection.

Leaving aside the question of precisely determining what it is meant by the term 'rehabilitation', it is interesting to note that rehabilitation as a general

---

[38] Cf. e.g. Trial Chamber Judgment, *Delalić and others* (IT–96–21–T), 16 November 1998.

[39] Retribution was certainly the main purpose of the punishment at Nuremberg and Tokyo: see Schabas, note 11 above, at 189.

goal of international penalties may prove problematic. Rehabilitation is a process linked to a determined social environment. It seems highly problematic, therefore, to invoke this kind of purpose for international penalties. Since the execution of the sentence is outside the control of the Tribunals or the Court, rehabilitation would be essentially a task for the penitentiary system. The international organ could simply recommend that consideration be given to this aspect by States agreeing to execute the sentences of the Tribunals.

Additionally, in the agreements between the United Nations and States willing to execute the sentences of the Tribunals, there is no reference to a right of the convicted person to rehabilitative treatment, or to rehabilitation more generally.

The Chambers' practice of taking into account possibilities for rehabilitation has varied and it does not seem that the Tribunals have so far considered rehabilitation as a right of the convicted person.

However, as stated by the Trial Chamber in the *Tadić* sentencing judgment of 14 July 1997, it is accepted that 'the modern philosophy of penology [is] that the punishment should fit the offender and not merely the crime'.[40] Rehabilitation affects sociological aspects and naturally does not depend only on the Tribunals. As mentioned above, an explicit reference to rehabilitation is only found in the system of the *ad hoc* Tribunals in Rule 125 RPEs (Rule 126 ICTR Rules) on general standards for granting pardon or commutation of sentences. This rule states that in determining whether pardon or commutation is appropriate, 'the President shall take into account, *inter alia*, . . . the prisoner's demonstration of rehabilitation'. Indeed, such a reference to rehabilitation clearly indicates that this must be one of the purposes of the penalty since it is one of the grounds that may justify granting pardon or commutation.[41]

Nonetheless, it is not possible to conclude, at this stage of development of the international criminal law system, that the convicted person has a right to rehabilitation.

5. *The problem of multiple sentences: concurrent versus consecutive sentences*

The Statutes and Rules of the *ad hoc* Tribunals contain few provisions on penalties. Rule 101 (C) of both RPEs, however, clearly established that 'the Trial Chamber shall indicate whether multiple sentences shall be served consecutively or concurrently'. Whilst this Rule was deleted from the ICTY RPE at the Plenary Session of December 2000 and moved into Rule 87, the content

---

[40] See Trial Chamber Sentencing Judgment, *Tadić* (IT–94–1–S), 14 July 1997, para. 61.

[41] The importance of this link between chances of early release and penalties imposed by international tribunals is pointed at by Schabas, note 9 above, at 516.

remains unchanged; thus the Rules still leave it to the judges to determine such an important issue. Furthermore, new Rule 87 (C) entrusts the Chambers with '[the] power to impose a single sentence reflecting the totality of the criminal conduct of the accused'.

This solution seems to contrast with the *nulla poena sine lege* principle, because the accused has no certainty about the outcome of sentencing. The Rules should at least provide for criteria for determining whether sentences should be served consecutively or concurrently, or when a single sentence should be imposed, including criteria for determining such a single sentence.

In this respect the solution found in the ICC Statute seems more consonant with high standards in the protection of the rights of the accused and in upholding certainty of law. Article 78, paragraph 3, ICC St. states that 'when a person has been convicted of more than one crime, the Court shall pronounce a sentence for each crime and a joint sentence specifying the total period of imprisonment'. This Article further specifies that the resulting penalty 'shall be no less than the highest individual sentence pronounced and shall not exceed 30 years imprisonment or a sentence of life imprisonment'.

In consideration of the ICC Rules it should be noted that the most recent sentences imposed by the ICTY do not seem in line with current trends concerning penalties attached to international crimes by the provisions of the Statute of the ICC. These provisions, which entered into force on 1 July 2002, should be regarded as an authoritative (and certainly the most recent) statement of the general opinion of States on this matter.[42] The Statute was approved by a positive vote of 120 States and was subsequently signed by more than 100; the process of ratification has gone rather fast, with more than sixty States having already ratified and others expected to do so in the near future.[43] At the Diplomatic Conference the only strong dissenting view on the issue of penalties was that of Trinidad and Tobago.[44] This delegation was of the opinion that the death penalty should have been allowed and for some days refused to agree to the solution found in the Statute. However, in the end, a consensus was reached on limiting international penalties to imprisonment, while explicitly providing that the provisions of the Statute would in no way limit the application by States of higher penalties as provided for by

---

[42] This has been recognized by ICTY Chambers on numerous occasions, such as e.g. Trial Chamber Judgment, *Furundžija* (IT–95–17/1–T), 10 December 1998, para. 227, and, more recently, Trial Chamber decision on preliminary motions, *Milošević* (IT–33–99–PT), 8 November 2001.

[43] Cf. <**www.un.org/icc/ratification**>, for constantly up to date information on the status of the ratification process.

[44] See position paper of the Delegation of Trinidad and Tobago, UN Diplomatic Conference for the Establishment of an International Criminal Court, 12 July 1998, arguing for the inclusion of the death penalty. On the death penalty and international law see W. Schabas, *The Abolition of the Death Penalty in International Law* (2nd edn., Cambridge: Cambridge University Press, 1997).

national legislation (Article 80 ICC St.). Moreover, it was explicitly decided to limit the term of imprisonment to thirty years (except in the case of life imprisonment). There are absolutely no elements to conclude that States believed longer terms were possible. Therefore, it is reasonable to argue that under international law a limit of thirty years has been imposed on imprisonment, unless the case justifies a sentence of life imprisonment (Article 77 ICC St. mentioned above). Thus, it is submitted that in the case of an appeal, those convicted by the Chambers of the ICTY to more than thirty years' imprisonment could seek a reduction of the sentence, asking for the application of the most recent international rules on the matter. It also seems correct to grant them an appropriate reduction of penalties in conformity with the principle of the application of the law more favourable to the *reus*.

It may be contended that it would be better to leave the choice between consecutive or concurrent sentencing to the judges. However, this approach would be problematic in terms of respect for the right of the convicted person to relative certainty about the punishment that will be imposed. To leave the choice entirely to the discretion of the Chamber does not seem appropriate. Therefore, the provisions contained in Article 78 of the ICC Statute that limit this discretion to a maximum sentence that 'shall be *no less* than the *highest* individual *sentence* pronounced and shall *not exceed 30 years*' imprisonment *or* a sentence of *life imprisonment*' is certainly more correct. Furthermore, it is important to note that so far neither the ICTY nor the ICTR has ever imposed a multiple sentence to be served consecutively. Certainly, this is a very sound and reasonable practice, which should be consistently followed in the future and should prompt an amendment to the Rules in the interest of certainty of the law.

II. THE ENFORCEMENT MECHANISMS AND THE RIGHTS OF SENTENCED PERSONS

1. Enforcement of sentences and the 'international character' of the penalty: the rights of the convicted person and the power of supervision of international authorities

(a) The enforcement of sentences in the system of the *ad hoc* Tribunals

The penalties imposed by the *ad hoc* Tribunals must be strictly enforced within the territory of UN Member States. According to Article 27 ICTY St. (Article 26 ICTR St.), 'imprisonment shall be served in a State designated by the International Tribunal from a list of States which have indicated to the Security Council their willingness to accept convicted persons'. The Secretary General clarified in his report that the Registrar will have to keep such a list.[45]

---

[45] Cf. SG Rep. note 8 above, para. 36.

210 *Rights of Convicted Persons*

Rule 103 of both RPEs reproduces the provisions of the Statute. Rule 104 RPEs also states that 'all sentences of imprisonment shall be supervised by the Tribunal or a body designated by it'.

To implement these provisions the Tribunal had to conclude agreements with some of the States that indicated their willingness to accept persons convicted by the Tribunal in their prisons. The first State to sign an agreement with the United Nations for the execution of sentences imposed by the ICTY was Italy, on 6 February 1997.[46] Thereafter, six other States have concluded such an agreement for the execution of sentences of the ICTY (Austria, Finland, France, Norway, Spain, and Sweden).[47] To date three States, Mali,[48] Benin,[49] and Swaziland,[50] have signed an agreement for the execution of sentences imposed by the ICTR. Some other States have expressed their willingness to accept convicted persons in their prisons and negotiations between them and the ICTR (on behalf of the United Nations) are continuing.

With a view to facilitating the conclusion of agreements with States for the enforcement of sentences imposed by the International Tribunals, the United Nations prepared a model agreement that was resorted to in negotiations with States. During negotiations changes were made to adapt the agreements to the different needs of national legislation.[51] All agreements are of a general nature and detail the procedure for enforcing sentences in the territory of the relevant State. The request to execute a specific sentence in a State must be made by the International Tribunal to the State concerned following the rules provided for by the agreement.

[46] The first State to sign an agreement with the ICTR was Mali. Subsequently also Benin and Swaziland signed. See <www.ictr.org>. So far (October 2002) Mali has received 5 people convicted by the ICTR, including the former Prime Minister, Jean Kambanda: see the Address by the President of the ICTR to the UN General Assembly, 26 November 2001.

[47] Cf. 1999 Sixth Annual Report of the International Criminal Tribunal for the former Yugoslavia UN doc. A/54/187 and S/1998/846, 25 August 1999.

[48] Cf. *Fourth Annual Report 1999*, ICTR, UN doc. A/54/315, 7 September 1999, **www.ictr.org**.

[49] ICTR/INFO–9–2–200, Arusha, 26 August 1999.

[50] *Fifth Annual Report 2000*, ICTR, UN doc. A/55/435, 2 October 2000, para. 82, at 14.

[51] The only agreement that corresponds entirely to a Model Agreement prepared by the UN with the Tribunal is the agreement with Norway, signed on 24 April 1998: see D. Tolbert and A. Rydberg, 'Enforcement of Sentences', in R. May *et al.* (eds.), *Essays on ICTY Procedure and Evidence. In Honour of Gabrielle Kirk McDonald* (The Hague: Kluwer, 2001), cit., 533–543. Thus, I disagree with the opinion of these authors (at 535), in that they seem to over-emphasize the role played by the Model Agreement. It does not seem that in reality such Model can be resorted to other than as a very initial basis for negotiations with States, because very often the demands of national laws on the execution of penalties require adjustments, closer to national legislation than to international demands. A latest example of this tendency is shown in the agreement between the UN and Spain, which deviates from the UN model more than previous agreements. There are two main deviations. First, the body entrusted with the task of supervising the conditions of detention of international detainees is not the ICRC (as generally provided for in the other agreements), but a parity commission appointed by the parties. Secondly, Spain will only consider the enforcement of sentences not exceeding the maximum penalty that may be imposed under Spanish law, i.e. 30 years' imprisonment.

International Tribunals, having taken into account the circumstances of each case and having heard the convicted persons, make a decision on the State for enforcement of the sentences. Subsequently, the Registrar, pursuant to the norms of the agreement with the State concerned issues a formal request and initiates the necessary proceedings. It seems that, in determining in which State the sentence will be executed, the Tribunal should follow the indication contained in the Report of the Secretary General. There it was affirmed that 'given the nature of the crimes in question and the international character of the tribunal, the enforcement of sentences should take place outside the territory of the former Yugoslavia'.[52]

Naturally, the agreements between States and the United Nations on the execution of sentences of the *ad hoc* Tribunals addressed crucial issues in the relationships between the Tribunal and States as regards the enforcement of sentences. There are two conflicting interests. The aspiration of each State uniformly in applying its laws to all persons detained in national prisons and the interest of the Tribunal in preserving the international character of the sentence.[53]

Article 27 ICTY St. (Article 26 ICTR St.) provides 'that imprisonment shall be in accordance with the applicable law of the State concerned, subject to the supervision of the Tribunal'. Moreover, Article 28 ICTY St. (Article 27 ICTR St.) further specifies that, should the convicted person be eligible for pardon or commutation of sentence, in application of the laws of the State concerned, the State must notify the International Tribunal. Furthermore, on the basis of the provisions of the Statute the final decision on this issue is for the President of the Tribunal, acting in consultation with the judges and 'on the basis of the interests of justice and general principles of law'. Accordingly, in the agreements between the United Nations and States on the enforcement of sentences it was necessary to design mechanisms that would appropriately reconcile the prerogatives of international justice with the needs of each State to apply its laws.

The Trial Chamber that issued the first *Erdemović* sentencing decision very persuasively defined the international character of penalties imposed by the Tribunals. The Trial Chamber held that a 'State may not in any way, including by legislative amendment, alter the nature of the penalty so to affect its truly international character (paragraph 71). . . . The Trial Chamber [concluded] that *two essential elements derive from the international character* of the prison sentences set by the International Tribunal: *respect for the duration* of the penalty and *respect for international* rules governing the *conditions of imprisonment*' (paragraph 72). Therefore, on the one hand, there is an absolute need to ensure that the rights of detainees are fully respected in

[52] Cf. S.G. Report, note 8 above.
[53] See S. Godart, 'L'Exécution de la Peine', in H. Ascensio, E. Decaux, and A. Pellet (eds.), *Droit International Pénal* (Paris: Pedone, 2000), 849–854, at 850.

conformity with international standards. On the other hand, the international community must have certainty about the duration of the penalties. In this respect, different solutions have been adopted by other Trial Chambers. In *Tadić*, the Trial Chamber expressly demanded that a minimum term must be served in any case, and accordingly determined it.[54] This approach, however, has not been followed by all other Chambers, which have been more flexible. It seems, however, that the requirement of a minimum term is presumably *ultra vires*. The Chambers of the Tribunal are not in any way responsible for the enforcement of the sentence. This is a duty imposed by the provisions of the Statutes and the Rules on States, on the one hand, and the President of the Tribunal, on the other. It is, therefore, correct to submit that recommendations of Chambers in this respect are not binding *per se.* For example, the minimum requirement of ten years to be served in the *Tadić* sentencing judgment is only an indication, with no direct or binding effect either on the State of execution or on the President of the Tribunal.

On 7 April 1999, the President of the ICTY, at that time Judge Gabrielle Kirk McDonald, issued the 'Practice Direction on the Procedure for the Determination of Application for Pardon, Commutation of Sentence and Early Release of Persons Convicted by the International Tribunal'.[55] These guidelines establish a procedure according to which the 'enforcing State' must notify the Registrar of the fact that a person convicted by the Tribunal has become eligible for pardon, commutation, or early release. Thereafter, the Registrar must inform the convicted person, and request reports and observations by the competent national authorities of the enforcing State on the behaviour of the convicted person and on the general conditions of imprisonment. It is also required that the Registrar should seek a detailed report from the Prosecutor on any co-operation that the convicted person may have provided to the Office of the Prosecutor. Additionally, the Registrar will have to obtain any other information that the President of the Tribunal considers relevant. All the information collected is subsequently forwarded to the President and to the convicted person. Then, the convicted person may make submissions to the President of the Tribunal, either in writing or by telephone or video-link. That information must be forwarded to the members of the Bureau, to the sentencing Chamber, and to the Office of the Prosecutor, together with any comments by the President regarding the rehabilitation of the convicted person and any other relevant information. The President decides, taking into account the views of the Bureau and of the sentencing Chamber.[56]

---

[54] The Trial Chamber set the term at 10 years from the date of transfer.

[55] Cf. UN doc. IT/146, 7 April 1999.

[56] It interesting to note that on 5 December 2001 the President of the ICTY, Judge Claude Jorda, granted release to a convicted person, Dragan Kolundžija, who had been sentenced to 3 years and had already been in pre-trial detention for 2½ years. See ICTY Press Release, 6 December 2001, and on 31 July 2002 Milojica Kos.

The constant reference made in these guidelines to the 'sentencing Chamber' does not seem to be thoroughly convincing. In all likelihood eligibility for pardon, commutation, or early release will generally occur only after a certain time from the moment of the definitive sentencing judgment. Therefore, it seems useless to refer to a sentencing Chamber that will no longer be composed of the judges who imposed the original sentence. This approach is connected with the misplaced opinion that the Sentencing Chamber has control over the enforcement of sentences, which is not the case according to the provisions of the Statutes and the Rules of the *ad hoc* Tribunals.

As mentioned above, there are two aspects of the international character of the penalty. On the one hand there is the need to respect the penalties as determined by the Chambers of the International Tribunal. On the other hand, there is the absolute necessity to ensure respect for the highest international standards in the treatment of convicted persons.

In this respect it is important to note that the Agreements concluded for the execution of sentences imposed by the international tribunals contain a set of clauses aiming at the protection of the rights of the convicted persons. First, in the preambles to the agreements the provisions of the Standard Minimum Rules for the Treatment of Prisoners and General Assembly Resolutions on the protection of all persons under any form of detention are recalled. Secondly, the need to ensure respect for these rules is reinforced in Article 3, paragraph 5. Thirdly, a monitoring system on the condition of detention and treatment of the prisoners is established, providing for inspections by the ICRC both on a regular basis and at any time. Fourthly, the enforcement of sentences can be terminated upon request of the International Tribunal at any time. Naturally, the competent organ (i.e. the President of the Tribunal) must exercise this power if it appears that the conditions of detention of persons convicted by the Chambers of the Tribunal are not in line with international minimum standards.

To sum up, it is possible to say that the Agreements between States and the UN for the execution of the sentences of the Tribunal are based on three main guidelines. First, national laws must not alter the penalty fixed by the Tribunal; secondly, the conditions of detention must respect international standards for the treatment for detainees; and finally, the Tribunal has full power (and duty) to supervise the execution of the penalty. In the exercise of this last power the Tribunal should be conditioned by the rights of convicted persons, as defined by the Statutes, the Rules, and the agreements on the execution of sentences. In particular, the convicted person should be recognized as having the right to fair treatment according to international principles concerning the conditions of detention, including a right to communicate with the Tribunal on violations of these conditions. Moreover, the convicted person has the right to argue his or her case for pardon, commutation, or early release, in cases where the application of national law would allow it. In this respect, it seems appropriate to add a specific provision providing more clearly for a right of the convicted person freely to communicate with the international Tribunals.

(b) The enforcement of sentences in the ICC system

These criteria have been upheld in the ICC Statute's provisions on enforcement of sentences, which are all grouped under Part X of the Statute. In the system of the ICC Statute, as in the *ad hoc* Tribunals, the idea that sentences are to be enforced in the territory of a State has been adopted. The Rules leave it to States to declare whether or not they are willing to accept persons convicted by the Court in their prisons and on what conditions. The Court determines the State of enforcement on a case-by-case basis. The State designated will then be notified by the Court and shall promptly inform the Court of whether it accepts or not.[57]

In making the designation the Court must take into account various factors such as the views of the sentenced person and his or her nationality. Moreover, it must also consider the application of widely accepted international treaty standards governing the treatment of prisoners and the circumstances of the crime or the person sentenced, or the effective enforcement of the sentence. Furthermore, the determination of the Court must be made on the basis of the general principle that States Parties should share the responsibility for enforcing sentences of imprisonment, in accordance with principles of equitable distribution, as provided in the Rules of Procedure and

---

[57] Article 103 reads:

'1.(a) A sentence of imprisonment shall be served in a State designated by the Court from a list of States which have indicated to the Court their willingness to accept sentenced persons. (b) At the time of declaring its willingness to accept sentenced persons, a State may attach conditions to its acceptance as agreed by the Court and in accordance with this Part. (c) A State designated in a particular case shall promptly inform the Court whether it accepts the Court's designation. 2.(a) The State of enforcement shall notify the Court of any circumstances, including the exercise of any conditions agreed under paragraph 1, which could materially affect the terms or extent of the imprisonment. The Court shall be given at least 45 days' notice of any such known or foreseeable circumstances. During this period, the State of enforcement shall take no action that might prejudice its obligations under article 110. (b) Where the Court cannot agree to the circumstances referred to in subparagraph (a), it shall notify the State of enforcement and proceed in accordance with article 104, paragraph 1. 3. In exercising its discretion to make a designation under paragraph 1, the Court shall take into account the following: (a) The principle that States Parties should share the responsibility for enforcing sentences of imprisonment, in accordance with principles of equitable distribution, as provided in the Rules of Procedure and Evidence; (b) The application of widely accepted international treaty standards governing the treatment of prisoners; (c) The views of the sentenced person; (d) The nationality of the sentenced person; (e) Such other factors regarding the circumstances of the crime or the person sentenced, or the effective enforcement of the sentence, as may be appropriate in designating the State of enforcement. 4. If no State is designated under paragraph 1, the sentence of imprisonment shall be served in a prison facility made available by the host State, in accordance with the conditions set out in the headquarters agreement referred to in article 3, paragraph 2. In such a case, the costs arising out of the enforcement of a sentence of imprisonment shall be borne by the Court.'

Evidence. The Rules of Procedure and Evidence establish that such principles should be the principle of equitable geographical distribution, the need to afford to each State on the list the opportunity to accept a sentenced person, and the number of persons already detained in each State (Rule 201).

The Statute states that the Court 'may, at any time, decide to transfer the sentenced person to a prison of another State'.[58] This is a power that in the system of the *ad hoc* Tribunals was inserted into the agreements with States.[59] The relevance of such a power is that it clearly indicates that there is a primacy of the Court in the enforcement phase. Moreover, Article 104, paragraph 2, ICC St. establishes that the 'sentenced person may, at any time, apply to the Court to be transferred from the State of enforcement'. Therefore, it is correct to consider that the rights discourse has also permeated this part of the Statute. The idea is that there is a correspondence between the powers of the Court and the rights of individuals. Furthermore, Article 105, paragraph 2, reserves to the Court the right to decide on any application for appeal or revision, and it adds that the 'State of enforcement shall not impede the making of any such application by a sentenced person'. This provision reinforces the right of the sentenced person to address the Court on various issues. Finally, Article 106, paragraph 3, completes the protection of such right, stating that 'communications between a sentenced person and the Court shall be unimpeded and confidential'. Probably, it would be appropriate explicitly to regulate in the Rules of Procedure and Evidence how this is to be ensured and through what channel confidentiality can best be protected.

As regards the enforcement of sentences, the Statute imposes that the sentence of imprisonment must be binding on States, which cannot modify it (this ensures respect for the first consequence of the international character of the sentence). This aspect is reinforced by Article 110, paragraph 1, which clarifies that the 'State of enforcement shall not release the person before expiry of the sentence pronounced by the Court'.

Moreover, Article 106, paragraph 1, ICC St., while stressing the power of supervision of the Court on the enforcement of sentences, also requires that sentences of imprisonment 'shall be consistent with widely accepted international treaty standards governing treatment of prisoners'. This provision enacts the second aspect of the international character of the sentence: the right of the sentenced person to be treated according to international standards. On the other hand, coherently with the idea of a distribution of tasks between the national and international spheres, paragraph 2 of Article 106 establishes that the 'conditions of imprisonment shall be governed by the law of the State of enforcement'.

[58] Article 104 ICC St. para. 1
[59] See Agreement with Italy Articles 3, 8, and 10 as well as Agreements with Sweden, France, and Spain: see D. Tolbert and A. Rydberg, 'Enforcement of Sentences', note 51 above, at 541 notes 39 and 40.

It is interesting to note that the provisions of Article 107 ICC St. deal with the situation of the sentenced person after completion of sentence. The norms impose a duty on States to accept and allow the sentenced person to settle down within their borders. It is unclear how this will in reality occur. However, it would seem appropriate for the Rules more specifically to indicate the criteria to be followed. Where States are unwilling to bear the costs of transferring the person from one State to another, then these will be born by the Court.

Finally, the ICC Statute establishes a review mechanism concerning the reduction of sentences. First, the provisions of Article 110 indicate that only the Court is entitled to decide any reduction of sentences, after having heard the sentenced person. It seems correct to believe that this is precisely a right of the sentenced person. Secondly, the rule establishes that the person is entitled to obtain a decision on such reduction when he or she has served two thirds of the sentence, or twenty-five years in the case of life imprisonment. The rule further states that the review must not be conducted before that time.

In deciding on the reduction the Court should take into account the co-operation of the person with the Court, both during investigation and prosecution as well as in the enforcement of judgments, including reparation to victims. Additionally, the Court should also consider 'other factors establishing a clear and significant change of circumstances sufficient to justify the reduction of sentence, as provided in the Rules of Procedure and Evidence'. The Rules of Procedure and Evidence provide that 'three judges of the Appeals Chamber appointed by that Chamber shall review the question of reduction of sentence every three years'. Such review may occur at shorter intervals if it is so decided by the Appeals Chamber in its decision pursuant to Article 110, paragraph 3, or in the case of a significant change in circumstances, by decision of the three judges (rule 224).

(c) Conclusion

In the enforcement of sentences imposed by international Tribunals and, in the future, by the ICC, there are two elements that are always combined: the need to ensure that sentences are duly executed and the constant concern about the rights of the sentenced person. The former is ensured by the prohibition of application of national laws that may lead to a reduction in the duration of the penalty and by the establishment, in the ICC system, of a minimum term of imprisonment before the activation of mechanisms for review of the penalty. In the *ad hoc* Tribunals this was attempted through a requirement of a minimum term served, which was arguably *ultra vires*.[60] However, the imposition of a minimum period of imprisonment is more effectively guaran-

---

[60] Cf. note 54 above.

teed by the provisions of the Statute and the agreements on enforcement with States, which include a power of supervision by the President of the Tribunal.

The rights of the sentenced persons are guaranteed in a multiplicity of ways. First, there is the general right to be treated according to international standards. Secondly, there are the procedural rights to apply to and communicate freely with the Tribunals and the Court. Thirdly, there is a right to review after a determined term of imprisonment for the purpose of pardon, commutation of sentence, or other forms of early release. Finally, in the ICC Statute, there is the commitment of the Statute to enforce a right of the sentenced person to relocation after completion of the sentence. This ensemble of rights affords exceptional guarantees to individuals sentenced by the international Court; all these guarantees represent a commendable example of human rights protection.

2. *The right of convicted persons to equality of treatment at the sentencing and enforcement stage*

We should now establish whether the convicted person has a right to equality of treatment at the sentencing and enforcement stage. The question is twofold: the first aspect concerns the determination of the penalty and the second its enforcement. It is submitted that general principles of non-discrimination and the right to equality before the law apply—in the context of international criminal justice—from the moment of the indictment to the enforcement of sentences, until expiration of the term of the penalty established.

As stated above, the two *ad hoc* Tribunals have issued more than twenty sentencing judgments involving more than thirty defendants. In general, it may be noted that, so far, a certain equality of treatment has been ensured in the determination of penalties. This is, however, an aspect that remains totally within the control of the Chambers of the Tribunals (and in the future of the Court).

One of the most interesting aspects is to see whether it is possible to preserve such *equality in the phase of execution* of the judgments. Persons convicted by the Tribunals are sent to different countries and naturally, in accordance with the rules on the enforcement of sentences, the conditions of enforcement will be different and depend upon the law applicable in each State. It seems acceptable that a certain degree of inequality of treatment may be determined by the application of different national laws. Nonetheless, it seems inappropriate to allow that such inequalities affect the duration of penalties, in particular when turning to the application of national provisions on pardon or commutation of sentences. It is submitted that in these cases the International Tribunals should exercise their powers of supervision to avoid disparities of treatment among persons convicted at the international level.

Rule 125 RPE ICTY (Rule 126 RPE ICTR) clearly indicates that the President, in deciding on pardon or commutation, must take into account 'the treatment of similarly situated prisoners'. This Rule is inspired by principles aimed at ensuring the equality of treatment among persons convicted by the Tribunal.

An application of these principles can be reasonably suggested in the interpretation of the agreements concluded between the Tribunals (in the name of the United Nations) and States willing to accept persons convicted by the Tribunals in their prisons. In these agreements there is a system for control over detention that leaves the supervision of the enforcement of the penalty to the International Tribunals. This power can be used for several purposes: (i) to avoid mistreatments and ensure fair standards for 'international' detainees; (ii) to prevent premature liberation of the convicted person; and finally, it is submitted, (iii) to try to ensure equality of treatment *in concreto* as regards the term of the penalty for similar offences. By way of illustration, one may take the example of two persons convicted for having together committed the same offence—both sentenced to the same penalty. Subsequently, they are sent for execution of the sentence to two different States, and after ten years one of them is eligible for early release, while the other is not. In this case it can be argued that the Tribunal should use its powers to ensure that both are treated equally.

This right to equal treatment derives from the extension of the principle of fairness to the stage of the execution of sentences; it is possible to implement it through the power and duty of supervision imposed on the Tribunal.

In the ICC Statute, the provisions of Article 106, paragraph 1, ICC St. establish that the Court is responsible for supervising the enforcement of the sentence, the conditions of which must be in accordance with international standards for the treatment of prisoners.[61] Moreover, paragraph 2 adds that such conditions of detention must 'in no case be more or less favourable than those available to prisoners convicted of similar offences in the State of enforcement'. This Rule has a dual impact. On the one hand, it aims at ensuring fair standards to persons convicted by international Tribunals. On the other hand, it reinforces the obligations of the State of enforcement to ensure at least minimum international standards to all detainees in custody in the prisons of such State. These provisions exemplify the constant impact of both substantive and procedural norms of international criminal law on municipal laws. It is part of the exemplary effect of international criminal law. The final goal is to uphold the rule of law in the international legal order.

---

[61] Article 106 reads:
'1. The enforcement of a sentence of imprisonment shall be subject to the supervision of the Court and shall be consistent with widely accepted international treaty standards governing treatment of prisoners. 2. The conditions of imprisonment shall be governed by the law of the State of enforcement and shall be consistent with widely accepted international treaty standards governing treatment of prisoners; in no case shall such conditions be more or less favourable than those available to prisoners convicted of similar offences in the State of enforcement'.

6

The Position of Persons other than the Accused

I. VICTIMS

1. General

This chapter will be devoted to a very brief discussion of the position of people other than the accused in international criminal proceedings. Of the private people involved in the proceedings two main categories ought to be discussed: victims and witnesses. This section will focus on issues relating to the situation of victims, while questions concerning the role of witnesses will be dealt with in the next section.

Victims are, in many respects, important actors in criminal proceedings. Certainly, at the origins of criminal law, victims were essential for the initiation of criminal prosecutions.[1] The most ancient mechanisms of criminal justice were based on private prosecution. Subsequently, with the transfer of criminal prosecution from the private to the public sphere the prominence of the role of victims has progressively faded.

In civil law systems, however, an effort has been made to preserve a role for victims in the criminal process in the form of a right to participate in the proceedings as *partie civile*, with the purpose of obtaining, in the context of the criminal trial, reparations and restitution.[2]

In the common law world, on the other hand, there is a strict separation between criminal prosecution, left entirely in the hands of State authorities, and civil litigation, which remains the only context in which victims can present their claims.[3]

---

[1] In Roman law prosecution was an *actio* initiated by the victim. There was no public prosecution. The roots of the adversarial inspiration can be found in that system of private prosecution. On Roman criminal law and procedure see generally B. Santalucia, *Diritto e Processo Penale nell'antica Roma* (Milan: Giuffrè, 1989).

[2] On this issue cf. G. Stefani, G. Levasseur, and B. Bouloc, *Procédure Pénale* (14th edn., Paris: Dalloz 1990), 462–463; H. Bonnard, 'La participation des victimes d'infraction au procès pénal', in *Mélanges offerts à Georges Levasseur* (Paris: Ed. Gazette du Palaix, 1992), 287–296.

[3] Cf. J. Shapland, J. Willmore, and P. Duff, *Victims in the Criminal Justice System* (Brookfield, Verm.: Gower, 1985), and J.R. Spencer, 'Criminal Procedure in England', in M. Delmas-Marty (ed.), *The Criminal Process and Human Rights* (Dordrecht: Nijhoff, 1995), at 75–76.

In international criminal law (both in Nuremberg and Tokyo as well as in the UN *ad hoc* Tribunals) victims have had only a very marginal position,[4] in that they could be heard as witnesses. They suffered as a result of the fact that the rules governing the first international criminal proceedings derived from the common law.[5] Only very recently, within the provisions of the ICC Statute, have victims been granted a more distinctive role.[6] Victims as such were not even mentioned in the Nuremberg and Tokyo Charters. In the *ad hoc* Tribunals they received some attention, albeit to a very limited extent.[7]

The increased sensitivity towards the interests of victims and their needs is something new, which has also developed in recent decades at national level. This movement for recognition and stronger protection of victims' interests has led to devoting more attention to their position in the organization of international criminal proceedings.

Of course, the problem of defining the status of victims arises. In the *ad hoc* Tribunals system the notion of victim is very narrow: a victim is only the 'person against whom a crime over which the Tribunal has jurisdiction has allegedly been committed' (Rule 2 of both RPEs). This notion seems to exclude, for example, the children (or other relatives) of a person killed. The notion adopted is too narrow; however, it might be expanded by interpretation: is not the crime committed also against people who are directly *affected by the crime*? In any event, in the system of the *ad hoc* Tribunals widening the definition of victim would not lead to a radical change in the procedural status of victims. The only effect it may have is that restitution under Rule 105 may be awarded to a broader category of subjects as well as a wider application of Rule 106 on the findings of the Chambers on compensation.

The Rules of Procedure for the ICC, on the other hand, adopted a broader definition.[8] In the ICC system, this may be counterproductive, particularly

---

[4] Cf. R. Maison, 'La Place de la Victime', in H. Ascensio, E. Decaux, and A. Pellet (eds.), *Droit International Pénal* (Paris: Pedone, 2000), 779–784, at 779.

[5] For a discussion of this issue within common law systems cf. J. Shapland, 'Victims and the Criminal Process: A Public Service Ethos for Criminal Justice?', in S. Doran and J. Jackson (eds.), *The Judicial Role in Criminal Proceedings* (Oxford: Hart Publishing, 2000), 145–157.

[6] See T. Van Boven, 'The Position of the Victim in the Statute of the International Criminal Court', in H. von Hebel, J. Lammers, and J. Schukking (eds.), *Reflections on the International Criminal Court—Essays in Honour of Adriaan Bos* (The Hague: Asser Press, 1999), 77–89. In particular, the Dutch jurist (who, among other things, has prepared, as Special Rapporteur of the Sub-Commission on Prevention of Discrimination and Protection of Minorities, a set of basic principles and guidelines on the right to reparation for victims of gross violations of human rights and international humanitarian law) writes 'the ICC Statute . . . pays special attention to the rights and interests of victims. . . . The Statute goes beyond treating the victim as an aid in criminal proceedings and . . . gives the victim standing in her or his own right' (at 77).

[7] See Van Boven, note 6 above, at 80–82 and R. Clark and D. Tolbert, 'Towards an International Criminal Court', in Y. Danieli, E. Stamatopolou, and C. Dias (eds.), *The Universal Declaration of Human Rights: Fifty Years and Beyond* (Amityville, NY: Baywood, 1998), 99–112, at 104–107.

[8] Rule 85 provides that victims are 'the natural persons who have suffered harm as a result of the commission of any crime within the jurisdiction of the Court' and may include organizations or institutions (Rule 85 (b) ICC Rules).

considering the procedural rights of victims, in that it may allow too many subjects to present their views under the relevant rules.

There is another essential question regarding the relationship between the status of victim and the position of witness. No doubt one of the central traits of a system that does not allow for direct participation of victims in the process is that the Prosecutor may, albeit involuntarily, instrumentalize victims.[9] In other words, there is the risk that victims will be allowed to participate only in so far as their claims are useful to the overall strategy of Prosecution. This naturally means that the interests of victims in respect of an individual case may not be represented if they do not coincide with those the Prosecutor intends to satisfy in the interests of justice as a whole. The Prosecutor may, for example, obtain co-operation from an accused, and thus decide not to call the victims of the crimes allegedly committed by him or her to testify. Therefore, these victims will have no opportunity at all to have their voice heard before the International Tribunal.

It is very difficult to identify *in abstracto* the interests of victims. In general, however, the objective to be achieved is to furnish the victims themselves with the appropriate instruments for trying to satisfy their needs. There are *two main methods* of trying to respond to the interests of victims. On the one hand, there is the dimension that has been called the 'service' perspective.[10] On the other hand, there is also the possibility of attributing to victims certain 'procedural' rights. This is a generally recognized framework, which is also contained in the UN Declaration of Basic Principles of Justice for Victims of Crime and Abuse of Power,[11] and it seems very useful to try to present and discuss the position of victims in international criminal proceedings.

To be clearer, it can be said that the *rights to 'service'* aim at addressing the need of victims for physical and psychological support, post-trauma assistance, and other forms of relief that largely depend on the crime suffered. Instead, the protection of victims' interests at the *procedural level* goes through the recognition of specific rights that could enable victims to contribute to prosecution, to obtain restitution or reparation, and to obtain various forms of satisfaction.

In the system of the *ad hoc* Tribunals, attention was essentially given to the 'service' dimension, while in the ICC Statute an attempt has been made to increase the procedural rights of victims and expand them to the procedural dimension.

---

[9] In this sense cf. C. Jorda and J. De Hemptinne, 'The Participation of Victims in International Criminal Proceedings', in A. Cassese, P. Gaeta, and J. Jones (eds.), *The Rome Statute of the International Criminal Court: A Commentary* (Oxford: OUP, 2002), ii, at 1372.

[10] Cf. H. Fenwick, 'Procedural 'Rights' of Victims of Crime: Public or Private Ordering of the Criminal Justice Process?', in 59 *MLR* (1997), at 317.

[11] Cf. UN doc. General Assembly Resolution 40/34, 29 November 1985.

There are also drawbacks to the involvement of victims in the criminal process. It may be argued that increasing their potential role also increases the risk of frustrating their expectations. A criminal trial, especially an international criminal trial,[12] may not be the most appropriate context for thorough satisfaction of the rights of victims. Furthermore, the grant of a well-defined procedural status for victims, coupled with the award of a direct interest in obtaining restitution and compensation, may lessen their credibility as witnesses.

2. *The rights of victims and the general ambiguity of the dual status of victim and witness*

One of the problems that has affected the consideration of victims before the *ad hoc* Tribunals is that they may often become an instrument in the hand of the Prosecutor, without any word to say about the case, nor about their personal recollection of the story. In other words, just like any other witness, victims appear before the ICTY or ICTR for their testimony alone. In the course of their testimony, victims may often be the object of attacks by defence counsel and may have no opportunity to tell their version of the facts, apart from what emerges during examination and cross-examination.[13] Of course judges can intervene and try to allow victims tell their stories in their own way, without being bound by the strategy of either party. However, under the system originally created by the Rules of Procedure of the *ad hoc* Tribunals judges had no knowledge of the facts of the case, so that their interventions could not have been really effective. With the recent modification of the procedural system judges, who are now allowed to receive witness statements (or at least a summary), are in a much better position effectively to question victims and ensure that their role is not merely at the whim of the parties.

The ability of victims to tell their stories seems to address one of the greatest concerns of victims in adversarial proceedings. Research in Britain has shown that the majority of victims who have been heard as witness in criminal trials had the feeling that their cases were not correctly presented by the Prosecution and also felt, during cross-examination, that they were the ones on trial, rather than the accused.[14]

---

[12] Apart from the more global character of international trials, which may include considerations of international politics, there is also the fact that States are reluctant to allow victims to participate to international proceedings, as there is always the idea that victims may request compensation before national tribunals.

[13] This risk certainly creates tension before the *ad hoc* Tribunals: see, e.g., ICTR Press Release ICTR/INFO–9–3–08.EN, in which the President of the ICTR responded to the allegation that a witness was treated without respect by defence counsel during a hearing and the judges in that case treated the matter inappropriately in that they did not protect the witness.

[14] See Shapland, note 5 above, at 146.

In the system of the *ad hoc* Tribunals this risk, albeit still present, has been reduced by the proactive role given to the judges. Furthermore, in the system of the *ad hoc* Tribunals problems linked to an instrumentalization of victims and witnesses could also be addressed to a certain extent by the special division, created under the Registrar's office to assist victims and witnesses. The Victims and Witnesses Unit has the general duty of providing assistance and support to victims and witnesses. In the UN *ad hoc* Tribunals' system these Units will also try to explain to victims how the proceedings are organized and what their position will be. Moreover, the Units will also warn victims and witnesses of the purpose of cross-examination and the functioning of criminal proceedings so as to try and minimize the brutality of the courtroom experience. It is clear that this kind of preventive measure does not remove the problem. However, such measures may contribute to softening the impact of trial proceedings.

The Statutes of the *ad hoc* Tribunals have imposed on the Chambers the obligation of protecting the rights of victims (Article 22 ICTY St. and Article 21 ICTR St.). However, protection of victims in the Statute has not been specifically limited to certain methods. Arguably Chambers will have to protect victims using all the powers within their competence. It may be interesting to note that according to a plain reading of Article 22 ICTY St. it could be surmised that protection of identity is a measure that can be used only for victims and not for normal witnesses. This, however, is not correct. The problem is that victims in the system of the Tribunal appear at trial only as witnesses. This is a further limitation of a system that substantially equates the status of victims to the position of witnesses.

The other provision of the Statute that may affect the rights of victims is Article 24, paragraph 3, ICTY St. (Article 23.3 ICTR St.). This rule states that 'in addition to imprisonment, the Trial Chamber may order the return of any property or proceeds acquired by criminal conduct, including by means of duress, to their rightful owners'.

Subsequently, the judges proceeded with the implementation of these norms in the Rules of Procedure and Evidence. The judges naturally recalled the right of victims to protection and decided to establish a Victim and Witnesses Unit to fulfill this task.[15] The protection afforded to victims under Rule 34 of both RPEs includes counselling, and physical and psychological support, especially in cases of rape. With regard to restitution of property, the judges adopted Rule 105 of both RPEs that establishes that 'the Trial Chamber shall, at the request of the Prosecutor, or may, *proprio motu*, hold a special hearing to determine the matter of the restitution of the property or the proceeds thereof'. While third parties can be summoned before the Trial Chamber and be given an opportunity to justify their claim to the property or

---

[15] The Unit was created under the competence of the Registrar in order to be able to treat equally defence and prosecution witnesses.

its proceeds, victims do not have any right to intervene in the proceedings to argue their case or challenge submissions made by either party. Therefore, their right to restitution is very heavily limited by the lack of appropriate procedural safeguards.[16]

In the summer of 2000 the ICTY also mandated a working group to study the issue of compensation to victims further. Following approval by the Plenary Session, on 13 September 2000, President Jorda sent the Report of the working group to the Secretary-General and the Security Council for further deliberation.[17] In particular, the Report confirms the gradual formation under international law of a right of victims to be compensated ('*indemnisation*' in French). The real problem is that mechanisms for the enforcement of this right must be implemented. The Report included recommendations on the creation of an international commission for compensation, which would deal with the claims of victims of crimes tried by the Tribunal. The conclusions of this report confirm that the Statute of the Tribunals should be amended, as little can be done for victims at the level of the international Tribunal at this stage.[18]

In conclusion, it can be affirmed that victims do not have autonomous legal standing before the Chambers of the *ad hoc* Tribunals. They are involved only in so far as they appear as witnesses. Hence, so far the service model has been the only way of trying to protect their interests.

On the other hand, the ICC Statute has substantially modified this situation. Under the strong pressure of NGOs and victim groups, a new model was adopted. It encompasses and combines both the 'service' approach and the recognition of procedural rights for victims. Therefore, under the provisions of the ICC Statute more effective participation by the witnesses in the proceedings has been allowed.[19] This can certainly be considered one of the distinctive traits of the provisions of the ICC Statute.

3. Participation of victims in the proceedings under the ICC system

The issue of participation of victims in the proceedings is a key distinction between the *civil law* and *common law* systems.[20] However, this is a difference

---

[16] On restitution of property by order of the Tribunal see S. Malmström, 'Restitution of Property and Compensation to Victims', in R. May *et al.* (eds.), *Essays on ICTY Procedure and Evidence, In Honour of Gabrielle Kirk McDonald* (The Hague: Kluwer, 2001), 373–384, at 374–379 (on the difficulties for the Tribunals in implementing such a rule, at 378–379).

[17] See Eighth ICTY Annual Report, UN doc. A/56/352, 17 September 2001, para. 49.

[18] Furthermore, this is proved by the absence of deliberations by the Tribunal specifically based on Rules 105–106 of both RPEs.

[19] In this respect see generally D. Donat Cattin, 'Protection of Victims and Witnesses and their Participation in the Proceedings (Article 68)', 'Reparations to Victims (Article 75)', both in O. Triffterer (ed.), *Commentary on the Rome Statute of the International Criminal Court. Observers' Notes, Article by Article* (Baden-Baden: Nomos, 1999), at 869–888; and 965–978.

[20] This is often mentioned as one of the advantages of civil law systems: see e.g. Spencer, note 3 above, at 88.

that does not necessarily seem to be linked to the model adopted for trial. For example, in Italy in the new criminal procedural system largely influenced by the principles of the adversarial model, which has been adopted since 1989, the option was left to victims to participate in the case as *'parte civile'*.[21] This procedural status enables victims to verify how proceedings evolve, to present motions, to call and cross-examine witnesses. In other words the Italian experience proves that it is certainly possible to combine an adversarial procedure with the possibility of conspicuous participation of victims in trials. Therefore, it seems correct to argue that the exclusion of the *partie civile* in the common law world is not due to the procedural model, but is rather linked to a different organization of judicial powers. Arguably, there are two main goals for the participation of victims in the trial alongside the Prosecutor: to seek a conviction and to obtain reparation. The final purpose of the participation of victims in criminal proceedings is justified by the idea that they can thus obtain reparation at the outcome of that trial. In systems based on total independence of the various branches of the judicial order such a dual role for criminal proceedings cannot be accepted, because the judgment in a criminal case cannot interfere with the sphere of civil litigation.

In the system of the *ad hoc* Tribunals there were no procedural rights for victims.[22] This was something new, which has been introduced into the ICC Statute as a result of lobbying by international NGOs.[23] It still remains to be seen whether this is beneficial. Certainly, what is correct is the possibility of obtaining national recognition of the findings of the Chambers of the Court. There was a similar provision in the RPEs of the *ad hoc* Tribunals. Of course, it is very difficult to say whether this provision has been of any use to victims at national level. Probably, there should be a continuing role for the Court in ensuring that compensation proceedings are conducted effectively. This could be an additional duty for the Victim and Witnesses Unit. It naturally presupposes adequate normative steps being taken by States and appropriate staffing.

Article 68 is the key provision of the ICC Statute on the rights of victims. The Court must take appropriate measures to protect the safety, physical and psychological well-being, dignity, and privacy of victims and witnesses. In so doing, the Court must have regard to all relevant factors, 'including age, gender as defined in article 7, paragraph 3, and health, and the nature of the crime, in particular, but not limited to, where the crime involves sexual or

---

[21] See Articles 75–79 of the Italian Code of Criminal Procedure.

[22] Jorda and De Hemptinne note 9 above at 1389–1390.

[23] For a number of criticisms of the role of NGOs at the ICC Conference see S. Sur, 'Vers une Cour Pénale Internationale: La Convention de Rome entre les ONG et le Conseil de Sécurité', in 104 *RGDIP* (2000), 29–45. This, however, is one of the emerging phenomena of the international arena: non-state actors will play an increasingly important role even during the negotiation of multilateral treaties.

gender violence or violence against children. The Prosecutor shall take such measures particularly during the investigation and prosecution of such crimes. These measures shall not be prejudicial to or inconsistent with the rights of the accused to a fair and impartial trial.' Paragraph 2 continues by stating that 'as an exception to the principle of public hearings provided for in Article 67' closed sessions are allowed for the purpose of protecting victims or witnesses.

In terms of recognition of the rights of victims to participate, the ICC Statute has created the appropriate framework for an effective system of procedural rights of victims. Article 68, paragraph 3, ICC St. sets out the criteria that justify the admission of applications by victims. In particular it establishes that where the personal interests of the victims are affected, the Court shall permit their views and concerns to be presented and considered at stages of the proceedings determined to be appropriate by the Court. It is also added that such presentation shall be made 'in a manner which is not prejudicial to or inconsistent with the rights of the accused to a fair and impartial trial'. Finally the rule recognizes the right of the victims to present such views and concerns through a legal representative.

The Rules of Procedure implemented the provisions of the Statute and articulated the participation of victims to the proceedings in a multifaceted way. First, the Rules restate the right to present their views and concerns (Rule 89.1 Rules of Procedure. This right, however, is submitted to a decision of the Chamber.[24] Secondly, the Rules confer on victims the right to choose a legal representative[25] (Rule 90, paragraph 1 ICC-RPE) and ensure that in order to appear such representative shall be duly qualified.[26] Thirdly, the rules also provide that 'a victim or group of victims who lack the necessary means to pay for an appointed legal representative may apply to the Registry for assistance, *inter alia*, by making available a lawyer from the Registry, and also including financial assistance'. Finally, the Chamber and the Registry are also under the obligation to ensure that 'in the selection of legal representatives, the distinct interests of the victims . . . are represented and that any conflict of interest is avoided' (Rule 90, paragraph 4). These developments are in line with the broader role victims are entitled to play in the system of the Court.

It may be feared that the participation of victims in the proceedings may delay the procedure and extend the length of trials. Nevertheless, an attempt

---

[24] It is nonetheless interesting to note that the victim retains the right to file a new application later in the proceedings: cf. Rule 89, para. 2 ICC RPE.

[25] Rule 90 ICC RPE establishes that should there be too many victims the Chamber may ask them to choose a common legal representative, and if the victims do not reach agreement the Chamber may ask the Registrar to appoint such common representative.

[26] Rule 90, para. 2, requires that 'a person shall be qualified to be a legal representative of a victim if he or she is admitted to the practice of law in a State or is a Professor of Law at a university'.

was made in the provisions of the Rules of Procedure and Evidence on the participation of victims to counterbalance this potential risk by entrusting the Trial Chamber with the task of controlling the participation of victims' representatives. Rule 91 establishes that the Chamber has the power to limit the right to participate of a legal representative of a victim to the deposition of written observations. Moreover, whenever the legal representative wants to question a witness, expert, or the accused, he or she will have to make an application to the Chamber. The Chamber may also require the legal representative to provide a written note on the questions he intends to ask and communicate it to the Prosecutor for his or her observations. Thereafter, the Chamber must issue a ruling taking into account the stage of the proceedings, the rights of the accused, the interests of witnesses, and the need for a fair, impartial, and expeditious trial. Eventually, the Chamber may also decide that it is more appropriate directly to question the witness, expert, or accused on behalf of the victim's legal representative.

4. *The right to reparation and the creation of a Trust Fund pursuant to the provisions of the ICC Statute*

(a) The right to reparation

In the *ad hoc* Tribunals' system the judges introduced rules that allow restitution, but did not really foresee possibilities for compensation (or reparation) for victims. Naturally, in drafting the RPEs the judges were bound by the Statutes and—as explained above—could not adopt provisions on restitution or compensation to victims. However, they managed to insert Rule 106 that deals with compensation to victims.[27] This rule establishes that 'the Registrar shall transmit to the competent authorities of the States concerned the judgment finding the accused guilty of a crime which has caused injury to a victim'. Subsequently, paragraph (B) restates the right of victims to bring an action in a national court or other competent body to obtain compensation. Finally, the most relevant effect of the provisions of this rule is that the judgment of the Tribunal must be considered final and binding as regards the criminal responsibility of the convicted person for the injury resulting from the offences charged. It is questionable whether this Rule is really binding on States. Certainly, the Statutes of the Tribunals did not explicitly refer to the issue of compensation. However, the power to adopt the Rules is left to the judges. Did they have the power to add a rule on compensation or did they act *ultra vires*? It is clear that, when adopting provisions on contempt of court, the judges did not exceed their powers, since punishing contempt may

---

[27] In this respect see V. Morris and M. Scharf, *An Insider's Guide to the International Criminal Tribunal for the Former Yugoslavia: A Documentary History and Analysis* (Irvington on Hudson, NY: Transnational, 1995), i, at 288–289.

be properly considered an inherent power of a court. At first sight, it may seem logical to conclude that the same reasoning cannot apply to Rule 106 and, thus, these provisions could be regarded as beyond the competence of the Tribunals. Nonetheless, this interpretation is not necessarily correct. On the contrary, it seems that one of the aspects implicit in the idea of an international court is that its findings are binding on States. If this is true, then the provisions of Rule 106 simply remind States of their obligation duly to preserve, at national level, the authority of the judgments of the Tribunals. In this light, it is inconsistent not to recognize the binding nature of the judgments of the Tribunals.

Further, the ICC Statute has been more favourable to victims' rights on the issue of compensation. Article 75 explicitly provides for a power of the Court directly to award reparation. It has been noted that the ILC Draft did not contain any provision on reparation to victims of crimes under the jurisdiction of the Court.[28] Notwithstanding many objections to attributing such powers to the Court at the end of negotiations, it was widely recognized that specific provisions on reparation could help the Court in ensuring effective reconciliation. This is also because economic compensation, albeit naturally not suitable for obliterating the crime, provides in a sense a measure of the recognition that the international community grants to victims. It may be a sign of an impoverished society, nevertheless it must be admitted that granting an amount of money to victims in compensation makes it easier to identify the restorative side of justice. It is naturally wrong to link this notion to the idea that reparation is the price of the crime committed.

Although Article 75 ICC St. is not a model of clarity, it does represent a commendable attempt to strengthen the guarantees for victims. Paragraph 1 establishes the duty of the Court to set principles relating to reparations. Moreover, it adds that 'in its decision the Court may, either upon request or by its own motion in exceptional circumstances, determine the scope and extent of any damage, loss and injury to, or in respect of, victims and will state the principles on which it is acting'. This paragraph is extremely vague and its meaning will largely depend upon the interpretation given to it by the Court. It is necessary to list briefly what the causes of uncertainty are. First, what does it mean that the Court shall establish principles relating to reparations? It is unclear whether the Court means the Chamber in its judicial capacity or the Court in general as an administrative organ adopting a sort of Practice Directions for Reparations. The Rules of Procedure are useful in this respect for clarifying the Statute.

Moving to paragraph 2 of Article 75, this Rule establishes that the Court may make an order for reparation (including restitution, compensation, and

---

[28] Cf. C. Muttukumary, 'Reparations for Victims', in F. Lattanzi and W. Schabas (eds.), *Essays on the Rome Statute of the International Criminal Court* (L'Aquila: Il Sirente, 1999), i, 302–310.

rehabilitation). This provision, however, does not explicitly grant a right to victims. The issue of such an order is entirely in the discretion of the Chamber, but it is extremely uncertain according to what rules. Perhaps the principles referred to in paragraph 1 may play a role. If this is correct why not explicitly refer to those principles? Paragraph 2 also states that the Court may decide, where appropriate, that reparations be made through the Trust Fund. This is a fund that will be created pursuant to the provision of Article 79 ICC St. and will be administered as further determined by the Assembly of States Parties. Also in this respect there is in sufficient clarity, and it would have been appropriate to provide for a more detailed procedure in the Rules of Procedure and Evidence.

The convicted person and victims, as well as other interested persons or States, may be heard on reparation and restitution. The wording of paragraph 3 is also very obscure. It states on the one hand that the Court 'may invite and shall take into account representations'. Therefore it seems that the Court enjoys wide discretion in deciding whether or not to invite representations, but once they are made it must take them into account. It would have been more correct explicitly to recognize the right of both the convicted person and the victim to be heard and present observations, and submit to the discretionary evaluation of the Chamber the admission of submissions by other subjects.

Finally, whilst paragraph 5 establishes the duty of State Parties to give effect to decisions under Article 75, paragraph 6 states that nothing in the Article 'shall be interpreted as prejudicing the rights of victims both under national or international law'.

The ICC Statute generally offers much stronger protection to the victim than that contained in the system of the *ad hoc* Tribunals. The mechanisms for this procedure actually to operate have been further specified in the Rules of Procedure and Evidence. The Rules of Procedure set out two procedures: one upon request of the interested person(s) and one by the Court of its own motion. Rule 94 deals with the former and outlines the procedure to be followed by any interested person in filing a request for compensation before the Court. Rule 95 establishes that in cases where the Court decides to proceed on its own motion, pursuant to Article 75.1, it must ask the Registrar to notify its decision to the person, or persons, against whom the Court is considering making a determination, if possible to the victims, and to any other interested person or State. It is further clarified that if, as a result of notification, a victim makes a request for reparation, such request will have to be treated as if it had been brought under Rule 94 (paragraph b). Moreover, the Rules provide for a specific duty on the Registrar to give adequate publicity of proceedings before the Court to victims, interested persons, and States. In so doing the Court may seek co-operation of States under Part 9 of the Statute and non-governmental organizations.

As regards the assessment of reparations, Rule 97 specifies that the Court may award reparation on an individualized or collective basis, taking into account the scope and extent of any damage, loss, and injury.

On the whole the rights of victims provided for by the Statute are well implemented and even strengthened by the current provisions of the Rules of Procedure and Evidence. It is clearly highlighted that the Court will have to adopt all necessary measures to make information on proceedings before the Court available to victims and victims' organizations.

(b) The Trust Fund

The ICC Statute has been innovative on the issue of reparations. Moreover, in addition to the right to obtain reparations from the convicted person, the Statute has also established the creation of a Trust Fund and the right of victims to be compensated by the Fund.[29]

Article 79 ICC St. has provided for the possibility of creation of a Trust Fund. This Fund will be established by decision of the Assembly of States Parties for the benefit of victims of crimes within the jurisdiction of the Court, and of the families of such victims. Presumably the Trust Fund will be financed both by voluntary contributions and through fines or forfeiture transferred, by order of the Court, to the Trust Fund (Article 79, paragraph 2, ICC St.). The Assembly of States Parties will determine the criteria for the management of the Trust Fund (paragraph 3).

The provisions of the Rules of Procedure and Evidence aim at implementing the norms of the Statute. Rule 98 (a) provides that, in making an order for reparations to be awarded through the Trust Fund, the Court may take into account, *inter alia*, the number of victims and the scope, forms, and modalities of reparation. It also establishes that the Court may order that an award for reparation be made through the Trust Fund to an international or national organization approved by the Court to co-operate or assist the Fund. Finally, the Court may, at any time before it has made a decision relating to reparation, order the Trust Fund to provide interim relief to victims, such as medical or psychological attention or other humanitarian assistance.

It is uncertain whether the Trust Fund will be available only for those crimes tried by the International Court and whether such approach will contribute to increase divisions, rather than contributing to national reconciliation. If the Trust Fund is available only for victims of crimes tried by the International Court, this may lead to unequal treatment of similar situations. For example, victims of the same kind of criminal transaction, committed

---

[29] On the various aspects relating to the implementation of the provisions on the Trust Fund see D. Shelton and T. Ingattodir, *Reparations to Victims of Crimes and the Trust Fund: Recommendations for the Court Rules of Procedure and Evidence* (New York: Centre on International Cooperation, New York University, 1999) (prepared for the Meeting of the ICC Preparatory Commission, 26 July–13 August 1999).

during the same conflict, may receive different treatment in terms of compensation, depending on whether the person who has committed the crime against them is tried before the ICC or before a national court.

Generally, there are three main arguments for public involvement in compensation for victims. In this respect reference can be made to the European Convention on the Compensation of Victims of Violent Crimes, in particular to the second paragraph of the Preamble. Three main reasons have traditionally been identified for awarding public compensation to victims of violent crimes. First, public involvement may be justified by the fact that States are also indirectly responsible for the crime because of having failed to prevent it. Secondly, another element that plays an important role in awarding compensation through publicly administered funds rests on reasons of social solidarity and equity. Thirdly, through compensation afforded by a Trust Fund, society shows concern and support for victims and contributes to removing the sense of injustice felt by the victims. These justifications, traditionally adopted in national law, are perfectly applicable to international criminal justice. The international community has often been considered guilty of omission in several instances. Moreover, certainly the aspiration for removing the sense of injustice is one of the objectives of reparation, and in particular when it is granted through the Trust Fund.

The European Convention has chosen an approach based on social solidarity and equity.[30] It seems that solidarity links are not easy to invoke in the context of international criminal justice. Certainly, the purpose of repairing the failure to prevent the crime is one of the ideas behind the establishment of the Trust Fund. Additionally, the idea of removing the sense of injustice felt by the victims seems very important. It is doubtful whether this is an objective that can be achieved through monetary reparation and through a trust fund. However, it is true that the idea of creating an international trust fund, which must be administered for the benefit of victims of crimes, may strongly contribute to the creation of a framework of reconciliation that also recognizes the responsibilities of the whole international community towards victims.

5. Conclusion

Thanks to the provisions of the ICC Statute, victims have acquired a more defined and active status in international criminal proceedings. In the *ad hoc* Tribunals' system, victims as such have no standing. They can be heard as witnesses for one of the parties or called by the Chambers, but cannot make autonomous representations, nor are they entitled to present their claims.

---

[30] See the Explanatory Report on the European Convention on the Compensation of Victims of Violent Crimes, at 9, General Considerations, para. 10. More generally on this issue see M. Delmas-Marty, *Pour un Droit Commun* (Paris: le Seuil, 1994), at 24–25 ('*La victime est désormais détachée du délinquant, et ce sont les fonds de solidarité . . . qui assurent son indemnisation. . . . [C']est la solidarité qui l'emporte sur la culpabilité*').

The recognition of a *greater procedural importance for victims* is particularly important, in that it leaves to victims themselves the choice of what interests they want to promote. This positive element, however, may also entail two drawbacks. First, it may increase the risks of frustration of the victim's expectations. Notwithstanding the participation of victims, the main role in the proceedings is always assigned to the Prosecutor: it is the office of the Prosecutor that conducts investigations and develops prosecutorial strategies. Therefore, the outcome may lead to results different from those sought by victims. Secondly, the participation of victims with specific economic interests in the proceedings leads to a reduction in their credibility as witnesses. It is clear that this cannot be taken as a general and *a priori* evaluation of all victims appearing as witnesses. However, it may be an element deserving some consideration at a further stage. This is a characteristic closely linked to international criminal justice. Usually, the crimes charged have been committed in the context of inter-group violence, and therefore there is a collective element that may play a role in determining the evidence given. The phenomenon of victims agreeing together on a common procedural strategy and on a given version (not to speak of the risk of having real '*syndicats de témoins*') may certainly be increased by this system, which in a certain sense forces victims to elaborate a common view. It seems that in Rwanda, in trials before national courts for crimes committed during the conflict of 1994, groups of victims agreed on a common version of the facts to satisfy purposes other than the ascertainment of the truth.

It is clear that recognition of a specific interest of victims in trial proceedings makes them parties (albeit in a particular position) to the proceedings and may therefore diminish their credibility as witnesses. On the other hand, it is extremely important for international criminal justice that victims be entitled to be involved in the proceedings. This increases the chances of achieving the objectives of reconciliation and the removal of injustice. Participation enables victims to feel that they are part of a mechanism designed to deliver justice. This may contribute to reducing a desire for vengeance and increasing the chances of a successful confidence-building process that may lead to national reconciliation and lasting peace.

II. WITNESSES

1. The specificity of the status of witnesses before international criminal courts and means of obtaining their attendance

(a) General

It is well known that one of the basic needs of criminal proceedings is to obtain the attendance of witnesses at trial. Naturally this also holds true for international trials.[31] It may, however, be more difficult for international tribunals to achieve this objective. There are at least two reasons linked to the unique features of international criminal justice that make it more difficult for international tribunals to obtain the attendance of witnesses. First, international tribunals do not control any territory, and therefore cannot directly ensure protection.[32] Secondly, the crimes charged are usually committed in the context of an ethnic or political conflict. This entails the fear of reprisals, irrespective of where the victim may reside, from other members of the group to which the accused belonged. Additionally, there are all the other classical reasons that recommend protection of witnesses in particularly sensitive criminal cases. Finally, there are classes of witnesses who are, for different reasons linked to their functions or profession, intrinsically reluctant to testify before (international) criminal courts, such as, for example, members of relief organizations, the ICRC above all,[33] members of UN missions, priests, or journalists.[33a]

In general it is possible to identify two categories of witnesses: those who are willing to testify but may fear acts of intimidation, and those who are not ready to testify unless certain specific measures are ensured. The needs of fearful witnesses are generally addressed through appropriate measures of protection, while the problem of persons unwilling to testify must be tackled in different ways. First, the Tribunal can make use of its coercive powers and issue requests for co-operation to States controlling the territory in which the reluctant witness resides, thereby imposing attendance. Secondly, the Tribunal, having identified the reasons behind the reluctance of persons to testify, can try specifically to address their worries. Often, there may be the

---

[31] See Decision on Prosecution Motion for Protective Measures, *Brdjanin* and *Talić* (IT–99–36–PT), 3 July 2000, para. 9.

[32] On the specificity of the problem of witness protection in the UN *ad hoc* Tribunals' system (particularly as compared with the Nuremberg and Tokyo Tribunals) see C. Chinkin, 'The Protection of Victims and Witnesses', in G. McDonald and O. Swaak-Goldman (eds.), *Substantive and Procedural Aspects of International Criminal Law—The Experience of International and National Courts* (The Hague: Kluwer, 2000), i, 455–478, at 455–457.

[33] The reasons for not being willing to appear may be different, but are essentially linked to the activities conducted by such organizations. The ICRC, for example, bases its activities on confidentiality. Thus its personnel cannot testify to matters known by reason of their activity (there is an analogy with professional secrets). Other relief organizations base their work on neutrality and impartiality. The involvement of their observers in criminal proceedings as witnesses may undermine their operations, in that Parties to conflicts may refuse to give access to them for fear that one day they may testify against them in Court. A Trial Chamber of the ICTY has recognized this privileged status by affirming that 'customary international law provides the ICRC with an absolute right to nondisclosure of information relating to [its] work', in *Simić and others* (IT–95–9–PT), 8 October 1999. On the issue of testimony by members of the ICRC see S. Jeannet, 'Recognition of the ICRC's Long-standing Rule of Confidentiality: An Important Decision by the ICTY', in 82 *IRRC* (2000), at 403–425. Judge Hunt, however, suggested that the determination should be made on a case-by-case basis and not as a general principle. The Tribunal should remain free to strike the balance in each case between the interests of confidentiality and the interests of justice. See Judge Hunt, Dissenting Opinion, *Simić and Others* (IT–95–9–PT), 8 October 1999.

[33a] In *Brdjanin and Talic* (IT–99–36–PT), 7 June 2002, the Trial Chamber held that once a journalist has published he has no right to refuse to answer on what he has published.

concern of being the possible object of an indictment by the Prosecutor; consequently these people are afraid of arrested upon arrival at the seat of the Court. The Tribunals have used two different methods of eliminating such reluctance: summonses to require appearance and safe-conducts to grant limited immunity from prosecution.[34]

Moreover, another method has been used: testimonies have been allowed to be given by videoconference link. Although this method has been resorted to only in exceptional circumstances, it could be more widely used, since it may be useful in reducing loss of time and risks linked to the movement of witnesses from the territories in which they reside to the seat of the Tribunal.

In Chapter 3 the impact on the rights of the accused of the various methods used by the Tribunals for obtaining the attendance of witnesses was discussed. In this section, the objective is to ascertain whether witnesses or the parties on their behalf have the right to obtain specific measures of protection.

(b) Summonses

A summons is an order issued by a court addressed to a person requiring him or her to appear. It is not necessary to summon a witness to obtain his or her attendance. The parties may call witnesses, and these usually appear spontaneously. It is clear that in such cases it is for the parties to request measures of protection. Conversely, when witnesses are summoned by the Chamber it is possible to consider that there are increased expectations of obtaining protection from the Tribunals or the Court. Whenever witnesses are reluctant to appear, the Chambers may issue summonses aimed at requiring appearance (and the assistance of States in enforcing their orders).

Summonses are explicitly provided for by Rule 54 of both RPEs and Chambers have largely resorted to them to assist the parties in obtaining the attendance of witnesses. Normally the order summoning the witness to appear contains a set of details concerning the personal data of the witness and mentions the date and hearing at which the person must appear. Sometimes Chambers have added an indication of the penalty that could be imposed in case of refusal to obey the summons. Although this power is not explicitly provided for in the Rules, the Tribunals may impose these penalties on the basis of their inherent powers.[35]

---

[34] Originally, at the 2nd Plenary Session of the ICTY 'the question of the grant of immunity from prosecution to a potential witness [was debated]. . . . However, . . . after due reflection [it was] decided that no one should be immune from prosecution for crimes such as these, no matter how useful their testimony may otherwise be' (Statement by the President made at a briefing to members of Diplomatic Missions, IT/29, 11 February 1994), reprinted in Morris and Scharf, note 27 above, ii, 649–657, at 652. Therefore, the Tribunal opted for a more limited kind of immunity from prosecution, in the form of safe-conducts, which lasts only for a very limited period of time.

[35] On the issue of inherent powers of the Tribunals see M. Buteau and G. Oosthuizen, 'When the Statute and Rules are Silent: The Inherent Powers of the Tribunal', in May *et al.* (eds.), note 16 above, 65–81.

(c) Safe-conducts

Safe-conducts are specific orders issued by the Chamber to those witnesses who fear being indicted by the Prosecutor of the Tribunal if they come to the seat of the Tribunal to testify.

Originally orders for safe-conduct were not specifically provided for in the system of the *ad hoc* Tribunals. The Trial Chamber in *Tadić* held that such an order could be made under the general terms of Rule 54 RPE. Subsequently, this Rule was amended and an explicit provision for safe-conducts was adopted. Safe-conducts usually ensure that a person travelling from one State to another to testify in open court is protected from prosecution or restrictions on personal liberty in the country of destination for acts committed prior to his or her departure. Safe-conducts are a usual feature of agreements regarding intergovernmental co-operation in criminal matters. In the context of international criminal trials it may often be necessary to provide for such a guarantee.

Orders for safe-conduct were issued to several witnesses in order to grant them immunity from prosecution or restriction of liberty while coming to give evidence before the Tribunal. In *Blaškić*, for example, the Trial Chamber had to deal with the protection of witnesses and issued a number of safe-conduct orders in favour of defence witnesses.[36] The immunity applies while the witness is giving evidence and during the witness's journey to and from the jurisdiction where evidence is given, and is restricted to acts within the jurisdiction of the Tribunal which occurred before the witness's departure from his or her home country.

(d) Videoconference link

Trial Chambers of the *ad hoc* Tribunals have granted requests to give evidence by video-link in several decisions.[37] Video-link allows the giving of evidence through a live television link with the courtroom. It enables all persons in the courtroom to see, hear, and communicate with the witness, even though the witness is not physically present. It has been stated that as a general rule a witness must be physically present at the seat of the Tribunal.[38] However,

---

[36] Trial Chamber Orders, *Blaškić* (IT–95–14–PT), 7 September 1998.

[37] Decision on the Defence Motion to Summon and Protect Defence Witnesses, and on the giving of Evidence by Video-link (25 June 1996); Decision on the Third Confidential Motion to Protect Witnesses (20 September 1996); Decision on Fourth Confidential Motion to Protect Defence Witnesses (11 October 1996); Decision on the Defence Motion Requesting Video-link for Defence Witnesses (16 October 1996); and Decision on the Defence Motion Requesting Video-link for Defence Witness Jelena Gajić (17 October 1996). Thereafter Videoconference links became a normal procedure for the *ad hoc* Tribunals: see in general ICTY Annual Report 1999, UN doc. A/54/187, 25 August 1999, e.g. paras. 36 and 151.

[38] See Trial Chamber Decision, *Tadić* (IT–94–1–T), 26 June 1996.

Trial Chambers allowed video-link testimony where it was shown that: (i) the testimony of a witness was sufficiently important to make it unfair to proceed without it; and (ii) the witness was unwilling or unable to come to the seat of the Tribunal. These criteria must be met on the face of the affidavits submitted in respect of each witness. In certain cases leave to testify by video-link was refused to witnesses because the affidavits filed by the defence did not meet the criteria.[39]

It has been held that the evidentiary value of video-link testimony, although weightier than that of evidence given by deposition, is not as weighty as evidence given in the courtroom.[40] The Chambers have held that hearing witnesses by video-link should be avoided as far as possible, as it will always be preferable for the Trial Chamber to have the benefit of the physical presence of witnesses at trial. Therefore, Chambers have expressed a general preference for safe-conducts, which allow direct participation of the witness, as opposed to video-link evidence.

In the system of the *ad hoc* Tribunals, Chambers have established a certain number of guidelines in order to ensure the orderly conduct of proceedings where testimony is given by video-link. These guidelines require, *inter alia*, that the party making the application must arrange an appropriate location and guarantee the safety and dignity of the proceedings, and that the evidence be given in the presence of a Presiding Officer appointed by the Trial Chamber.[41]

Moreover, it has consistently been held that statements made under solemn declaration through video-link by a witness must be treated as having been made in the courtroom.[42] Thus witnesses heard through videoconference may be liable for perjury in exactly the same way as if they had given evidence at the seat of the Tribunal. Sometimes videoconference may also be organized at the request of Governments for their officials.[43]

2. The protection of witnesses in court: the right of the accused to a public trial and the duty of the Chamber to afford protection to witnesses

The problem of witness protection is certainly one of the key points of the administration of criminal justice in general, but assumes even more importance in international criminal proceedings. The Statutes of the *ad hoc*

---

[39] *Ibidem.*   [40] *Ibidem.*   [41] See Rule 71 of both RPEs.

[42] Trial Chamber Decision, *Tadić*, note 37 above.

[43] In *Blaškić*, on 25 March 1999, the Trial Chamber decided *proprio motu* to call, pursuant to Rule 98, a number of witnesses, including senior officials of the UNPROFOR, the European Community Monitoring Mission, the HVO, and the Army of Bosnia and Herzegovina. Strict protective measures were granted for two of these witnesses and a videoconference was organized for one high-ranking officer at the request of his Government: *Seventh Annual Report* (1999), UN doc. A/55/273, 7 August 2000.

Tribunals solemnly proclaim the duty of the Chambers to ensure witness protection, but do not add any detail about the concrete methods and mechanisms of protection. The judges when adopting the Rules of Procedure and Evidence laid down a set of provisions aiming at the protection of witnesses. These provisions were mainly focused on the protection of witnesses in court and through procedural measures. However, with the creation of the Victims and Witnesses Unit, judges allowed the Tribunal to extend the protection of witnesses even beyond the proceedings *stricto sensu*. Naturally, State cooperation is the key for any successful implementation of measures of protection for witnesses.

The Tribunals have issued several decisions concerning protective measures.[44] Under the label of 'confidentiality measures' it is possible to include measures such as requiring that the name, address, whereabouts, and other identifying data concerning the witness not be disclosed to the public or media and be sealed to avoid their inclusion in any of the Tribunal's public records. Naturally, all hearings at which issues relating to the adoption of protective measures for witnesses are discussed must be in closed session, as well as hearings at which the witness testifies, where confidentiality is granted. Additionally, recordings and transcripts of the session(s) can be released to the public and to the media only after having been redacted and reviewed by the party calling the witness and the Victims and Witnesses Unit.

Should the witness agree to testify in open session, image- and voice-altering devices may be used to the extent necessary to prevent the witness's identity from becoming known to the public or to the media. In such cases, it is forbidden for the public and media to photograph, video record, or sketch the witness while he or she is in the precincts of the Tribunal.

Nonetheless, such protective measures did not alter the obligations of parties to communicate to each other the names of witnesses. Naturally, it was imposed on the accused, defence counsel, and people acting on their instructions or requests not to disclose any identifying data concerning the witness to the public or to the media. The only exception to this general prohibition has been to allow disclosure to the extent that may be strictly necessary to conduct adequate investigations into the witness. Obviously, such disclosure should be made whilst trying to minimize the risk of the witness's name being divulged to the public at large or the media. The complexity of this approach is confirmed by problems which occurred in several proceedings in

---

[44] Confidentiality was granted by the Trial Chamber for a total of 13 witnesses in the respective Decisions on the Prosecutor's Motions Requesting Protective Measures for Witnesses 'P', 'Q', 'R', and 'S'; the Decision on Defence Motion to Protect Witnesses (16 August 1996); the Decision on the Third Confidential Motion to Protect Defence Witnesses (20 September 1996); the Decision on the Fourth Confidential Motion to Protect Defence Witnesses (11 October 1996); and the Decision on Defence Motion Requesting Facial distortion of Broadcast Image and Protective Measures for Defence Witness 'D' (22 October 1996).

which witnesses were allegedly intimidated, with the co-operation of the accused or the defence counsel.[45]

The Chambers of the Tribunals have consistently held that fear for the lives of witnesses or their families may justify the right of the accused to a public trial and the right of the public to be informed being limited. It has usually been requested that, in order for a witness to qualify for the protection of his or her identity from disclosure to the public and media, the circumstances justifying protection (such as fear of reprisals) must be explicitly expressed in the witness's affidavit, and must be objectively reasonable.[46]

The Prosecution's submission that prior media contact by a witness rules out protection of the identity of such witness from disclosure to the public and media was rejected. The Trial Chamber held that the witnesses' fear of potentially serious consequences to them and their families must in any event be taken into account.

It has been pointed out on several occasions that protective measures should be limited to what is strictly necessary. Moreover, it is logical to affirm that, if and when protective measures are no longer necessary, they should cease to apply or less restrictive measures may be substituted in their place. This principle has been extended to a witness who proved to be unreliable.[47] This seems to imply that there is a sort of punitive effect of withdrawal of measures of protection.

Confidentiality measures consist not only in entirely withholding the identity of witnesses. Often Chambers have resorted to a less stringent form of protection that is limited to the diffusion of images in which the face and usually the voice of the witness are distorted. Protection by way of facial distortion of the visual image has been considered a sub-category of confidentiality, since in terms of legal principles the same issues are involved.[48] Naturally, these measures are accompanied by a formal prohibition on the public and media to photographing, video recording, or sketching the witness while he or she is in the Tribunal, including his or her arrival at and departure from the seat of the Court. Trial Chambers have consistently held that facial distortion of the broadcast image represents only a very minor limitation of the rights of the accused and the public right to information. It may be argued that whilst these measures offer appropriate protection to witnesses they do not limit the rights of the accused.

---

[45] See M. Bachrach, 'The Protection and Rights of Victims Under International Criminal Law', in 34 *IL* (2000), 7–20, at 18.

[46] Cf. Decision on the protection of witnesses in *Tadić* (IT–94–1–T), 25 June 1996; for the ICTR, see Trial Chamber Decision, *Bagosora* (ICTR–96–7–PT), 31 October 1997.

[47] See Decision on the Prosecutor's Motion to Withdraw Protection Measures for Witness 'L', *Tadić* (IT–94–1–T), 5 December 1996.

[48] This was the opinion of the Trial Chamber in *Tadić*, Decision on the Prosecutor's Motion Requesting Facial distortion of Broadcast Image of Witness, 31 July 1996.

In the ICC Statute, among measures of protection, Article 68, paragraph 2, refers to possible exceptions to the principle of publicity. It provides for *in camera* proceedings and allows the presentation of evidence by electronic or other special means. Obviously, these measures must not be prejudicial to or inconsistent with the right of the accused to a fair trial. In particular, such measures must be implemented in the case of a victim of sexual violence or a child who is a victim or a witness, unless otherwise ordered by the Court having regard to all the circumstances, particularly the views of the victim or witness.

Article 68, paragraph 5, states that where the disclosure of evidence or information pursuant to the Statute may lead to the security of a witness or his or her family being seriously compromised, the Prosecutor may withhold such evidence or information and may instead submit a summary of it. It is possible to withhold these elements only for the purposes of proceedings conducted prior to the commencement of the trial (i.e. they cannot be admitted as evidence). Moreover, it is specified that such measures must not be 'prejudicial to or inconsistent with the rights of the accused and a fair and impartial trial'.

Article 68, paragraph 6, ICC St. recognizes that States have the right to make applications for necessary measures to be taken in respect of the protection of their servants or agents and the protection of confidential or sensitive information.[49] In this respect it is submitted that these witnesses can always claim more protection than that which has been requested by their State or the agency to which they belong.

The expectations of witnesses to obtain protection do not really amount to a formal right to make application to the court for measures to be taken. Normally, the party calling the witness will request the necessary measures or the Chamber on its own initiative will adopt measures of protection. A very important role in this respect is given to the Victims and Witnesses Unit. This body has the duty to interact with witnesses to ascertain their needs, identify the most appropriate way of addressing them, and suggest the adoption of relevant measures to the judges.

Witnesses before international tribunals need protection even after they have testified at trial. The credibility of the tribunals depends, to a large extent, on their ability to protect witnesses after testimony. Events such as those that occurred in Rwanda, where allegedly some witnesses who had testified in the *Akayesu* trial were threatened or killed,[50] may jeopardize the endeavour of the tribunals. In particular, it has been reported that a woman was killed with all her family. It also seems that another witness was killed

---

[49] Cf. note 55 below.

[50] Cf. the Report of 1997 by the Coalition pour les droits des femmes en situation de conflit armé, 'La Protection des témoins, les femmes et le TPIR', at **www.ichrdd.ca/francais/commdoc/publications/femmes/femtri.htm**. See also Bachrach, note 45 above, at 19.

before reaching the Tribunal to testify. These events, although there is no specific evidence that they occurred, clearly show the high degree of risk which witnesses appearing before international tribunals run. The tribunals have constantly sought the co-operation of States on this issue, to protect witnesses both prior to trial and afterwards. Both the ICTY and the ICTR have regularly needed the co-operation of States in ensuring witness protection.

3. The protection of witnesses outside the courtroom: what are the legal expectations, if any, of witnesses?

The Tribunals have met with enormous difficulties in ensuring the effective protection of witnesses. This problem is naturally linked to the absence of control over the territory in which witnesses habitually reside. With the creation of the ICC this condition will, in all likelihood, remain unchanged, as the Court does not have police forces. Therefore State co-operation will be an essential element of the activity of international judicial organs in this field.

The Victims and Witnesses Units have played, and will continue to play, a fundamental role in this respect. As mentioned above these are specialist units responsible for providing support and protection to witnesses who are testifying before the Tribunals. These Units are responsible for organizing travel and accommodation for witnesses.[51] Moreover, the Victims and Witnesses Units have developed their programmes, criteria, and guidelines.[52] These include criteria for allowing witnesses to be accompanied by supporters when travelling to the seat of the Tribunals to testify. In addition, guidelines were developed for the compensation of lost earnings. This compensation will be based on standard amounts relating to minimum wages or the equivalent thereof. However, the duties of the Units are not simply limited to the handling of practical questions linked to specific witnesses in specific trials. The Units have the general responsibility of developing, under the authority of the

---

[51] In addition, during trials and other hearings, the Victims and Witnesses Unit provides a 24-hour, live-in support programme at the witnesses' place of accommodation. The live-in team consists of four witness assistants who speak Serbo-Croat but are not themselves from areas involved in the conflict in the former Yugoslavia. The live-in team provides the first point of contact for any action required at the place of accommodation. The European Union (EU), through a grant to the Rehabilitation and Research Centre for Torture Victims in Denmark, supports this witness assistance programme.

[52] The Units of the two *ad hoc* Tribunals have tried to increase co-operation. In June 1997 the Victims and Witnesses Units of both the ICTY and the ICTR met for a workshop organized in co-operation with the Co-ordination of Women's Advocacy, a non-governmental organization based in Geneva. The Units of both Tribunals met for the first time to develop procedures for harmonizing their operations. During 1997, the VWU continued to develop programmes, criteria, and guidelines for its work. An initial meeting was held between the Witness Units of the ICTY and the ICTR. This meeting laid the foundation for further collaborative work in 1998. In early 1999, a research and monitoring project was started designed to evaluate the Unit's work and assess the experience of witnesses during their attendance at the Tribunal. In addition, a project aimed at establishing common procedures and standards for the Victims and Witnesses Unit of the Tribunal and the ICTR. *Seventh Annual Report*, note 43 above.

Registrar, more global plans for action aimed at the creation of instruments which are always more effective for the protection of witnesses.

The Units have special arrangements with the police forces of the host States for rapid response to any security threat, including provisions for liaison officers to enable close co-operation in the event of action required to ensure the safety and security of witnesses. The Victims and Witnesses Unit (VWU) is also responsible for the recommendation of protective measures for witnesses who will appear before the Tribunal, and provides such people with counselling and support.

The Units have steadily expanded their contacts to increase co-operation with relevant authorities in a number of UN member States, other than the host countries (the Netherlands and Tanzania), with a view to protecting witnesses more effectively. In close co-operation with States, measures have been taken for the relocation of witnesses who cannot return to their homes after completing their testimony.

The position of witnesses before international tribunals is characterized by unique features, such as the fact of being members of one of the parties to a conflict, or the difficulties linked to the distance between their place of residence and the seat of the Tribunals. These circumstances, coupled with serious cultural problems, make the relocation of witnesses very difficult.

The Tribunals have entered into negotiations with States on relocation programmes and granting new identities in special cases. So far no general agreement on this issue, between the Tribunal and States, has been made public. Such discrete handling of these matters is certainly judicious. Obviously, the reason is linked, at least to a large extent, to the fact that at the moment it would be relatively easy for people who may be willing to harm witnesses to identify the States in which they have been relocated and how. Also, the fact that international criminal trials have so far been limited to the former Yugoslavia and Rwanda makes the chances of identification of the witnesses higher. Therefore, the approach followed by the Tribunals in not publicizing very much their activities in this field is not only understandable but also entirely justified.

4. *Justifications for witnesses refusing to answer: the protection of confidential sources of information; privilege against self-incrimination and lawyer–client privilege*

It is certainly difficult to obtain the attendance of reluctant witnesses before international tribunals, but it may also be difficult, once their attendance has been obtained, to receive complete answers.[53] Witnesses, in the system of the

---

[53] F. Hampson, 'The International Criminal Tribunal for the Former Yugoslavia and the Reluctant Witness', in 47 *ICLQ* (1998), at 50.

ad hoc Tribunals, have very limited procedural rights, but there are some provisions that may restrict their willingness fully to answer questions. These are Rule 70 on the protection of information coming from confidential sources, Rule 90(E) establishing a sort of privilege against self-incrimination, and, to a more limited extent, Rule 97 on the lawyer–client privilege. These rules may foster the unwillingness of reluctant witnesses precisely to answer all the questions.

As a general rule witnesses cannot refuse to answer a question. Rule 77 of both RPEs states that 'a witness who refuses to answer . . . may be found in contempt of the Tribunal'. The Rule adds that the Chamber may impose a penalty for contempt. However, the three above-mentioned rules may soften this general principle.

First, Rule 70 of both RPEs contains provisions protecting the source of information by allowing both the source and the information not to be to the other party. The Rule has undergone a number of amendments. Initially, it was merely designed to enable the Prosecutor to obtain information from confidential sources. Such information, however, could be used only for the purpose of generating other evidence. Subsequently, the Rule was amended to allow the Prosecutor to introduce, at least in part, such information as evidence at trial. Furthermore, the Trial Chamber added that 'notwithstanding Rule 98, [it] may not order either party to produce additional evidence received from the person or entity providing the initial information'. The Trial Chamber is thus deprived of the power to summon the person or representative of that entity as a witness or otherwise order their attendance. Additionally, it has been established that, 'if the Prosecutor calls as a witness the person providing, or a representative of the entity providing, information under this rule, the Trial Chamber may not compel the witness to answer any question the witness declines to answer on grounds of confidentiality'. This Rule, therefore, provides that a witness called to testify under Rule 70 of both RPEs may refuse to answer any question on the ground of confidentiality. Finally, this Rule was further amended to extend such a right, initially recognized only to the Prosecutor, to the defence.[54] A similar rule has been provided for in the Rules of Procedure of the ICC, in Rule 73 that provides for the protection of privileged communications and information.[55]

Secondly, the provisions compelling witnesses to answer questions are counterbalanced by the guarantee laid down in Rule 90(E) establishing that 'a witness may object to making any statement which might tend to incriminate him'. It is nonetheless further specified that 'the Chamber may

[54] J. Jones, *The Practice of the International Criminal Tribunals for the Former Yugoslavia and Rwanda* (Irvington on Hudson, NY: Transnational, 1998), (1998), at 247–249.

[55] See on this rule the comments by S. Jeannet, 'Testimony of ICRC delegates before the International Criminal Court', in 82 *IRRC* (2000), 993–1000.

. . . compel the witness to answer the question'. In such a case, however, the statement cannot be used against the witness in subsequent proceedings.

During oral arguments in the Decision on the Defence Motion to Protect Defence Witnesses (16 August 1996), the Defence requested the Trial Chamber to grant general testimonial immunity under Sub-rule 90(E) to its witnesses appearing on the basis of a safe-conduct order. The Trial Chamber denied this relief. It held that the wording of Sub-rule 90(E) did not allow blanket testimonial immunity to be granted to witnesses. However, when a witness appears before the Trial Chamber, the witness may ask for the protection of Sub-rule 90(E) by refusing to testify on the ground that the evidence may incriminate him or her.

It is submitted, however, that Rule 90(E), rather than giving a right to the witness, establishes a system of mandatory exclusion of evidence obtained by compelling witnesses to testify against themselves. In other words, the principle included in the Rules of Procedure and Evidence of the *ad hoc* Tribunals does not exactly correspond to a privilege against self-incrimination, as witnesses can always be compelled to testify. Witnesses have no right to refuse to answer, because they can always be compelled by the Chamber to answer; however, they have the limited guarantee that the declaration made will not be used against them before the Tribunal. This guarantee is insufficient, first, because it is unclear whether it would protect the witness against national prosecutions,[56] secondly, because, even if not used in evidence against him or her, the elements contained in the declaration may be used to produce or obtain evidence and the witness has no protection against this happening. Therefore, the current draft of this Rule seems inadequate thoroughly to protect the right of witnesses not to incriminate themselves.[57]

Finally, another rule that allows, but only to a very limited extent, the witness not to answer is contained in Rule 97 of both RPEs protecting communication between lawyer and client. Pursuant to this rule the content of these communications cannot be revealed in court. This rule applies also to third parties, who are prevented from revealing the content of such communications unless the client has voluntarily disclosed it to the third party. In general, it would seem appropriate to add to the *ad hoc* Tribunals' RPEs, provisions dealing specifically with the protection of professional secret.[58] However, lacking specific rules, it seems possible to extend by analogy Rule 97 to other professions (also on the basis of the broader text of Rule 73 ICC RPE).

---

[56] In this sense see A. Klip, 'The Protection of Witnesses Before International Criminal Tribunals', in 67 *RIDP* (1996), at 291.

[57] This is particularly true in light of the flexible approach to the admission of evidence, on which see Chapter 3 above.

[58] See note 33a above.

7

Concluding Remarks

I. THE ROLE OF HUMAN RIGHTS IN INTERNATIONAL CRIMINAL TRIALS: FROM NUREMBERG TO ROME

This study has shown that human rights protection before international criminal courts is, to a large extent, satisfactorily ensured. Nonetheless, human rights have not always been placed at the top of the agenda in international criminal proceedings, and indeed there still are some areas where protection needs to be strengthened.

The Nuremberg and Tokyo trials cannot really be taken as a model in this respect.[1] The regulatory instruments of those two Tribunals contained a few terse provisions on the rights of individuals involved in criminal proceedings. In particular, there were no provisions at all on the rights of suspects at the pre-trial stage, nor was there any provision on disqualification of judges or the right of appeal. Additionally, the Charters and Rules of Procedure did not confer any rights on victims and witnesses. In general, the Rules of Procedure were not detailed and the judges settled legal questions on a case-by-case basis.

Moreover, although the procedural model chosen for those trials was essentially adversarial—a model that in principle hinges, more than the inquisitorial system, on respect for the fundamental rights of the accused, some of these rights were not fully respected. For instance, there was substantial resort to documentary evidence, and affidavits offered by the Prosecution were freely admitted into evidence. Furthermore, defence attorneys mainly came from civil law countries and were not familiar with adversarial procedure, so they were not in a position to exercise their functions at their best. Finally, defence investigations were not supported and requests by the defence to the judges or to the Secretariat of the Tribunals to obtain evidence were often disregarded.

In summary, the Nuremberg and Tokyo trials cannot be said to be fair trials in modern terms. However, there are several reasons that may, at least partially, justify such unfairness. First, the Tribunals were set up very quickly

---

[1] In this respect, however, it was noted that it was precisely for having respected the right to a fair trial that the Nuremberg trials constituted a milestone in international criminal justice; in this respect see R. Badinter, 'Réflexions Générales', in A. Cassese and M. Delmas-Marty (eds.), *Juridictions internationales et crimes internationaux* (Paris: PUF, 2002), at 50, where the author wrote '*je suis convaincu que Nuremberg n'a été en quelque sorte sauvé du verdict de l'histoire que parce que Nuremberg a respecté absolument les règles fondamentales du procès équitable*'.

in a climate of controversy among the Allies on the very question of establishing such organs. Secondly, these trials were the first attempt to address, by means of criminal proceedings, *crimina juris gentium*. Thirdly, the sense of hostility towards the defendants, provoked by the atrocities committed during the war, was not easily put aside. Finally, but more importantly from a purely legal perspective, human rights protection had not yet been the object of international law-making.[2]

Only after the Second World War, with the establishment of the United Nations, were the rights of individuals solemnly proclaimed at the international level.[3] This was indeed the turning point. Moreover, on the basis of a number of human rights treaty provisions, a whole set of further resolutions and declarations were adopted.[4]

---

[2] Furthermore, protection of the right to a fair trial even at national level had not yet been thoroughly developed: D.M. Amman, 'Harmonic Convergence', in 75 *ILJ* (2000), at 820.

[3] The Universal Declaration of Human Rights (UDHR) contained fundamental provisions on the rights of persons in the administration of justice (Articles 9, 10, and 11). The Declaration, however, as is well known, was not *per se* a legally binding text. 1950 saw the adoption of the European Convention for the Protection of Human Rights and Fundamental Freedoms (ECHR). This Convention contained very important provisions for the rights of persons in the administration of criminal justice (Articles 5 and 6). Meanwhile, in the framework of the United Nations, negotiations continued with a view to drafting a treaty that—contrary to the UDHR— would directly impose legal obligations on States. Eventually, in 1966, the International Covenant on Civil and Political Rights (ICCPR) was adopted. This Covenant contained a core of fundamental rights for persons under investigation or for trial proceedings (Articles 9, 14, and 15). Subsequently, in 1969, the American Convention on Human Rights (ACHR) was signed. This text included provisions on the protection of human rights in criminal proceedings (Articles 7 and 8). Similar provisions have been included, albeit in a more synthetic form, in the African [Banjul] Charter on Human and Peoples' Rights, adopted on 27 June 1981 (Articles 5, 6, and 7) (Cf. OAU Doc. CAB/LEG/67/3 rev. 5, in 21 *ILM* 58 (1982), which entered into force on 21 October 1986). Safeguards for the right to a fair trial are also contained in the Convention on the Rights of the Child (Article 40), GA res. 44/25, annex, 44 UN GAOR Supp. (No. 49) at 167, UN Doc. A/44/49 (1989) which entered into force on 2 September 1990.

The evolution of the system of protection of human rights created under the auspices of the Council of Europe, and in particular the activity of the Court, has very deeply influenced criminal procedure rules of the Member States. See, e.g., D. Spinellis, 'Reform Movements in Criminal Procedure and the Protection of Human Rights', in 46 *RHDI* (1993), 127–148.

[4] On 20 April 2000 the UN Commission for Human Rights adopted without a vote a Resolution (2000/42) on the independence and impartiality of the judiciary, jurors, and assessors and the independence of lawyers; cf. UN doc. E/CN.4/RES/2000/42, 20 April 2000. Code of Conduct for Law Enforcement Officials, GA res. 34/169, annex, 34 UN GAOR Supp. (No. 46) at 186, UN Doc. A/34/46 (1979). Basic Principles on the Use of Force and Firearms by Law Enforcement Officials, Eighth United Nations Congress on the Prevention of Crime and the Treatment of Offenders, Havana, 27 August–7 September 1990, UN Doc. A/CONF.144/28/Rev.1 at 112 (1990). Basic Principles on the Role of Lawyers, Eighth United Nations Congress on the Prevention of Crime and the Treatment of Offenders, Havana, 27 August–7 September 1990, UN Doc. A/CONF.144/28/Rev.1 at 118 (1990). Guidelines on the Role of Prosecutors, Eighth United Nations Congress on the Prevention of Crime and the Treatment of Offenders, Havana, 27 August– 7 September 1990, UN Doc. A/CONF.144/28/Rev.1 at 189 (1990). Basic Principles on the Independence of the Judiciary, Seventh United Nations Congress on the Prevention of Crime and the Treatment of Offenders, Milan, 26 August–6 September 1985, UN Doc. A/CONF.121/22/ Rev.1 at 59 (1985). United Nations Standard Minimum Rules for Non-custodial Measures (The

In the field of the administration of criminal justice, international human rights provisions have influenced (and continue to influence), directly or indirectly, the criminal procedural rules of various countries.[5] It is nowadays largely accepted that *national* criminal procedure cannot be based on premises other than firm respect for human rights.[6] The creation of international rules governing criminal proceedings, both within the framework of the two *ad hoc* Tribunals and in the ICC Statute, must be set against this background.

In working out these procedural rules the drafters were not given a completely free hand. There were provisions of international law that imposed at least minimum criteria to be followed in national trials. Among these, *human rights law assumed a pivotal role.* All the major international standards relating to national criminal proceedings were *extended* to *international* proceedings. International criminal procedure could not be organized other than on the fundamental premise of respect for the rights of individuals, as embodied in international provisions. Accordingly, the *ad hoc* Tribunals' Statutes first, and subsequently the ICC Statute, contained provisions on the rights of defendants identical or similar to those included in the major human rights instruments.

Nonetheless, whilst respect for human rights as a fundamental feature of international trials was easily accepted, there were other problems to be faced.

Tokyo Rules), GA res. 45/110, annex, 45 UN GAOR Supp. (No. 49A) at 197, UN Doc. A/45/49 (1990). Principles on the Effective Prevention and Investigation of Extra-Legal, Arbitrary and Summary Executions, ESC res. 1989/65, annex, 1989 UN ESCOR Supp. (No. 1) at 52, UN Doc. E/1989/89 (1989). Safeguards Guaranteeing Protection of the Rights of Those Facing the Death Penalty, ESC res. 1984/50, annex, 1984 UN ESCOR Supp. (No. 1) at 33, UN Doc. E/1984/84 (1984). Declaration of Basic Principles of Justice for Victims of Crime and Abuse of Power, GA res. 40/34, annex, 40 UN GAOR Supp. (No. 53) at 214, UN Doc. A/40/53 (1985). The Basic Principles on the Role of Lawyers, the Guidelines on the Role of Prosecutors, the Basic Principles on the Independence of the Judiciary. On these standards and other activities of the UN in the field of criminal justice see R. Clark, *The United Nations Crime Prevention and Criminal Justice Program—Formulation of Standards and Efforts at Their Implementation* (Philadelphia, Penn.: Univ. of Pennsylvania Press, 1994).

[5] See e.g. the impact of the ECHR on many Eastern European countries that became members of the Council of Europe. See in this respect Council of Europe, *The Role of the Judiciary in a State Governed by the Rule of Law*, organized by the Council of Europe with the co-operation of the Minister of Justice of the Republic of Poland, Warsaw (Poland), 4 April 1995 (Strasbourg: Council of Europe Publishing, 1996); Council of Europe, *Legal Co-operation with Central and Eastern European Countries, The Training of Judges and Public Prosecutors in Europe* (Strasbourg: Council of Europe Publishing, 1996). See also, although on a different level, the adoption in the UK of the Human Rights Act 1998, on which see B. Emmerson, 'The Human Rights Act: Its Effect on Criminal Proceedings', in F. Butler (ed.), *Human Rights for the New Millennium* (The Hague: Kluwer, 2000), 85–105 and J.R. Spencer, 'English Criminal Procedure and the Human Rights Act 1998', in 33 *Isr.LR* (1999), 664–677 and the authors quoted therein, at 664.

[6] See in this respect G. Conso, 'I diritti dell'uomo e il processo penale', in *Rivista di diritto processuale* (1968) at 307; M. Delmas-Marty, *The Criminal Process and Human Rights* (Dordrecht: Nijhoff, 1995), at viii.

It was necessary to deal with issues such as the choice of authorities in charge of investigations or the role that the judges and the parties respectively should play. It was further necessary to decide whether or not it was appropriate to have jury trials, or to allow trials *in absentia*. Other important matters included the role of victims in the proceedings, the rules on admission and evaluation of evidence, etc. In other words, the need arose not only to adopt rules conforming to human rights provisions, but also to create a procedural system, and there the choice between the adversarial and the inquisitorial model became crucial.[7]

II. THE PROBLEM OF PROCEDURAL MODELS: THE NEED FOR A PRINCIPLED APPROACH TO PROCEDURE, DESIGNED TO ENHANCE RESPECT FOR HUMAN RIGHTS

Human rights provisions, even though they are the fundamental bedrock of international criminal trials, are not *per se* sufficient thoroughly to organize proceedings[8] nor do they indicate what procedural model must be followed. It was thus necessary to resort to other sources of inspiration, when it came to designing more articulated procedural mechanisms.

Moreover, human rights provisions generally set minimum standards,[9] while the Tribunals aimed at ensuring the highest standards of due process.[10] Respect for minimum standards can be ensured in different ways. There is nothing that *ipso facto* violates human rights in a system that allows for investigations to be made by a judge, such as a *juge d'instruction*. There is nothing intrinsically unfair in allowing examination of witnesses not directly by the parties but only through the judge.[11]

The choice between these or other options is a difficult one and a matter of *policy determination*, which generally requires principled decisions.[12] It was

[7] On the fundamental traits of these models see above Chapter I Section IV.

[8] In this respect, it has been noted correctly that human rights cannot determine how procedural rules should be drafted: C. Warbrick, 'International Criminal Courts and Fair Trial', in 3 *JACL* (1998), at 51.

[9] *Ibidem.*

[10] See A. Cassese, 'Opinion: The International Criminal Tribunal for the Former Yugoslavia and Human Rights', in 2 *EHRLR* (1997), at 330–331.

[11] These are all normal features of the inquisitorial system. For an in-depth analysis of these features from the perspective of international criminal procedure see A. Orie, 'Accusatorial v. Inquisitorial Approach in International Criminal Proceedings prior to the Establishment of the ICC and in the Proceedings before the ICC', in A. Cassese, P. Gaeta, and J. Jones (eds.), *The Rome Statute of the International Criminal Court: A Commentary* (Oxford: OUP, 2002), ii, 1439–1495.

[12] As the Italian philosopher Norberto Bobbio has noted, those who live according to principles do not care about the consequences of their actions, thus their actions may be noble but ineffective, while those who look only at the consequences of their actions, disregarding principles, may act effectively, but ignobly. See N. Bobbio, *Elogio della mitezza e altri scritti morali*

not possible appropriately to discuss and address these issues in the Security Council when the *ad hoc* Tribunals were created. The judges tried to deal with these problems when they adopted the Rules of Procedure and Evidence, but they had little time fully to consider these matters at that stage; in addition, they had not yet tested, through international judicial experience, the various options that were open *in abstracto*.[13] The difficulty of such a task is reflected in, and easily explains, the numerous amendments to the Rules of Procedure and Evidence of the ICTY, which the judges of the Tribunal adopted after 1994.

To a certain extent an attempt coherently to address these issues has been made in the context of the preparation of the ICC Draft Statute, although perhaps not with sufficient clarity. Naturally, at the Diplomatic Conference the main focus was on other important issues, such as the definition of crimes, the trigger mechanisms, the role of the Security Council. As regards the procedural system considered as a whole, States were always tempted to bring their own national experience into the debates without trying to extract the principles inspiring national rules and adapting them to the needs of international criminal procedure. Additionally, negotiations were very difficult for most delegations, since too many debates were going on at the same time and there was not enough time to deal with each question thoroughly. This naturally left many questions of principle unresolved and offered little guidance for subsequent interpretation.[14] These issues were further discussed within the Preparatory Commission when it drafted the Rules of Procedure and Evidence for the ICC. The spirit of compromise present in every international negotiation, however, has diminished the impact of principled decisions on issues relating to the procedural model.

Plainly, criminal procedure is a method of establishment of the truth (the so-called 'judicial truth'). Judicial truth, however, is never absolute; its correct determination depends upon full respect for the rules laid down for the establishment of guilt or innocence. As in science, where the method of reaching the truth must be pre-established and cannot be subject to change on a case-by-case basis, in criminal procedure respect for procedural rules is the only way to guarantee a fair and accurate result.

(Milan: Pratiche Editrice, 1998), at 75–78. Along the same lines see the comments by G. Abi-Saab, 'Droit de l'Homme et Juridictions Pénales Internationales—Convergences et Tensions', in R.-J. Dupuy (ed.), *Mélanges en l'Honneur de Nicolas Valticos—Droit et Justice* (Paris: Pedone, 1999), at 253, where the author warns that it must be avoided '*à tout prix ce qui procède de l'adage les fins justifient les moyens*'.

[13] Additionally, one may question whether judges would have enjoyed sufficient political legitimacy to decide on such delicate issues. Although it is true that they are elected by the General Assembly, one should keep in mind that they are elected mainly to perform judicial functions (so that Article 13 ICTY St. requires that they be eligible for the highest judicial function in their countries).

[14] In this respect, it is regrettable that the verbatim records or summary records of the *ad hoc* Tribunal Plenary Sessions and of the Diplomatic Conference are not public.

This implies that international criminal procedure should not be set out on a case-by-case basis, lest it should lead to arbitrary solutions and gross disparities of treatment among defendants. It is, thus, necessary to agree on the rules of the game and on the values behind them. This is the reason the Statutes of the *ad hoc* Tribunals required that the judges should adopt the Rules of Procedure and Evidence. These Rules are much more detailed than those of Nuremberg and Tokyo, which contained only a few very general principles, with the consequence that when specific procedural matters arose, they were decided upon by rulings made by judges on a case-by-case basis. In the ICC system, the Preparatory Commission was entrusted with the task of drafting the Rules of Procedure and Evidence of the Court. Additionally, it has been established that any future amendment to the Rules is for the Assembly of State Parties to make.

This evolution proves that States became aware of the importance of decisions concerning the Rules of Procedure and Evidence. Moreover, notwithstanding the commendable effort made by the judges of the *ad hoc* Tribunals to make the provisions of both RPEs meet the needs of international criminal justice, it seems reasonable that States decided to grant the power to amend the Rules to the Assembly of States Parties. The policy choices behind fundamental rules of criminal procedure need to be made by political organs entrusted with the responsibility of determining where the general interest lies. These organs will be in a position to strike an appropriate and fair balance between the rights of individuals and the interests of society.

The adversarial (mainly American) system was the procedural model initially chosen. This was probably due, at the outset, to prevailing historical circumstances.[15] Subsequently, however, it became a deliberate choice inspired by the notion that the adversarial system generally *better guarantees protection* of the *rights of defendants*, since it is generally more focused on the protection of individual liberties than on the interests of society. Thus, the genetic code of international criminal justice (the need to ensure the highest standards of due process) suggested the adoption of the accusatorial model, which appeared to be the fairer procedural system.

The *ad hoc* Tribunals started to operate on a fundamentally *adversarial* system. However, it soon appeared that such a model did not fully meet the demands of international criminal proceedings. It ought to be stressed that these demands, such as expeditiousness of trial and equality of arms, ultimately constituted ways of better protecting the rights of the individuals involved, in particular the defendants. Obviously, it is one thing to choose a procedural system on paper, and another to see it in operation. Modifications

---

[15] There is no doubt that the USA played a major role in the process that led to the establishment of the Nuremberg and Tokyo Tribunals, and in the adoption of the RPEs of the UN *ad hoc* Tribunals, see above Chapter 1.

to the initial system proved necessary and the judges of the *ad hoc* Tribunals, scrupulously avoiding limitations on the rights of the accused, initiated this process of amending the Rules.

The first set of amendments (Fifth Plenary Session of January 1995) aimed at strengthening the rights of the accused along the lines of a purely adversarial system. The second round of reform (July and November 1997 Plenary Sessions) was inspired by the idea of trying to crystallize the Rule of Procedure and Evidence and codify the practice of the Tribunals (including rules on Status Conferences, time limits, and more detailed procedures for guilty pleas). Finally, the third phase (from July 1998 onwards), primarily occasioned by the increasing number of apprehensions or voluntary surrenders of accused and consequent trials, was justified by the absolute necessity of reducing the length of trials and ensuring the rights of the accused to an expeditious trial.[16]

This latest set of changes began with a number of decisions by Trial Chambers aimed at accelerating the procedure, and was inspired by an overall tendency to insert into the RPE elements predominantly deriving from *inquisitorial* systems. Thus the Tribunals now operate on a procedural model which is different from the initial system. This shift was necessary on account of the situation with which the Tribunals were confronted, i.e. the increasing judicial workload and, until the decision by the Security Council to provide for *ad litem* judges, the relatively limited number of judges.

There are, however, also *reasons of principle* that required modifications of the adversarial model, such as, for example, difficulties linked to defence investigations, the risk that groups of 'organized witnesses' may interfere with trials, or misconduct by defence counsel. Moreover, some of the most relevant distinctive traits of international criminal justice, such as the need to conduct investigations in different countries, the need for State co-operation, the fact that it may often be necessary to detain defendants pending trial, make it extremely difficult for an accused to prepare his defence, as fundamentally required by the adversarial model. Hence, it became clear that in international criminal proceedings some changes to the adversarial model were necessary.

From Nuremberg to Rome there have been substantial changes in the relationship between the judges and the parties in international criminal proceedings. It appears that judges cannot simply be regarded as umpires, but

---

[16] More recent amendments have served both the right of the accused to a speedy trial, within a reasonable time, and the interest of the effective administration of justice. The introduction of the 'Pre-Trial Judge', who co-ordinates communication between the parties, thereby ensuring expeditiousness and a climate of mutual trust. The provisions on 'Pre-Trial' and 'Pre-Defence' Conferences, where the trial is organized in order to minimize losses of time. The decision that judges should be entitled to receive a whole set of documents, including witnesses' written statements and other investigative reports, that, although never turned into evidence, enable them better to conduct proceedings. Or the admission of written evidence to prove facts other than those relating to the charges in the indictment. In particular, these amendments are intended to guarantee full and timely disclosure, and the exclusion of redundant evidence, thereby ensuring shorter pre-trial detention.

must play a more active role in the conduct of proceedings. Moreover, the Prosecutor should no longer act simply as a party to the proceedings, but must operate with increased awareness of his or her impartial role towards defendants. Most of the *ad hoc* Tribunals' achievements were incorporated into the norms of the ICC Statute and, in some respect, were even improved[17] (see, for example, the role of the Pre-Trial Chamber; the duty of the Prosecutor to search for exculpatory evidence and to respect fully the rights of suspects).

Of course, it may be somewhat puzzling to look at this blending of legal traditions, and one may even be tempted to consider it dangerous.[18] Nonetheless, there is no such danger since this procedural combination is not merely the result of an abstract process, but originated from practice and has been (and is being) tested in the day-to-day functioning of the Tribunals.

The above remarks do not mean that under the system currently applied by *ad hoc* Tribunals and in the ICC procedural rules everything is satisfactory. There are still areas of concern. In particular, since *further imports from the inquisitorial system* may restrict individual rights, it would be extremely important constantly to monitor amendments in order to ensure that they do not erode or curtail the rights of defendants.

III. RESPECT FOR HUMAN RIGHTS IN INTERNATIONAL TRIALS: A FEW OUTSTANDING PROBLEMS

The experience of the *ad hoc* Tribunals has paved the way for the permanent Court. The Tribunals have begun to bridge the gaps between differing legal

---

[17] Nonetheless, the most serious problem arising in the early stages of the proceedings, both before the *ad hoc* Tribunals and the ICC, is the absence of precise determination of the status of persons in each relevant moment and the absence of a specified measure that determines the status of suspect. It is suggested that the introduction of a sort of notice of being under investigation should be provided for in the rules governing the activities of the Tribunals and the Court. This measure would enable the person to be notified timely of his or her rights and would enable him or her effectively to exercise them. Moreover, given the fundamentally adversarial nature of the proceedings, it would have the important effect of allowing the person under investigation to start defence investigations, whenever appropriate. However, in the absence of such a notice (which may be undesirable in consideration of the risk that the suspect may abscond and threaten witnesses), the uncertainty about the status of persons at this stage makes the new institutional characterization of the Prosecutor as an *organe de justice* of extreme importance. The correct exercise of his or her duties by the Prosecutor, at the early stage of international criminal proceedings, may reduce the risk of violation of the rights of individuals under investigation. Naturally, this should not be seen as a substitute for ensuring the enjoyment of individual rights to the fullest extent and should operate together with all other safeguards provided for by the Statutes and Rules of Procedure of the *ad hoc* Tribunals and the ICC.

[18] See C. Warbrick, note 8 above, arguing that 'if one model is not chosen, at least, predominantly over the other, there is a risk that compromise between the two will result in a bastardised process which is too favourable to one side or the other', at 53, and C. De Francia, 'Due Process in International Criminal Courts: Why Procedure Matters', in 87 *VLR* (2001), 1381–1439, at 1382.

systems, with a view to creating rules of international criminal procedure. In this endeavour they have continued to recognize a privileged role for the rights of defendants, notwithstanding a strong commitment to ensuring appropriate satisfaction of the interests of victims.

Generally speaking, in international criminal proceedings human rights are protected in a fairly satisfactory manner at the trial stage. Although there may be some doubts about the very broad admission of evidence (there are virtually no exclusionary rules), there are some elements that make such an approach acceptable. In particular, the fact that trials are held before professional judges, the requirement that all judgments must give detailed reasons for conviction, and the possibility of challenging Trial Chamber judgments through appeal proceedings lead to the reasonable compromise that all evidence is in principle admissible unless the judges decide otherwise.

Respect for human rights is also satisfactory with regard to appeal and review proceedings, notwithstanding the somewhat unclear nature of review proceedings. In this respect, there has been some improvement from the *ad hoc* Tribunals to the ICC Statute, since in the ICC system the power of the Prosecutor to appeal has been appropriately reduced.

Conversely, there still are some problems regarding the protection of the rights of individuals during investigations and in the pre-trial phase. These are due to the unclear status of persons at that stage and to the lack of a precise definition of the notion of suspect. In both the *ad hoc* Tribunals and the ICC systems, respect for the rights of persons during investigations very much depends on how the Prosecution exercizes its functions. Hopefully, the Pre-Trial Chamber in the ICC system will play a role in strengthening the protection of individual rights. Moreover, notwithstanding recent progress on pre-trial detention in the ICTY practice, it seems that in general it is very difficult in international criminal trials for defendants to be released pending trial. In this respect, State co-operation is crucial, since it is the only way to ensure the presence of the accused at trial and the effective protection of witnesses.

Another area in which concerns may arise is sentencing. In international criminal justice, the determination of penalties is entirely left to the discretion of the judges and there is no clear guarantee of equality of treatment among convicted persons. Penal policies usually derive from societal values: in international law shared values are generally based on a core of minimum elements, which may not be sufficiently developed to promote a common penal policy. Therefore, the judges of international criminal courts are basically without specific guidance in determining the appropriate sentence, and may rely on a broad variety of factors, which may easily lead to a disparity of treatment.

Finally, as far as the rights of victims are concerned, the provisions of the ICC Statute and Rules have broadened their rights, enabling them both to participate in the proceedings and to obtain compensation. In this respect, one should note that, notwithstanding recent important proposals made by the President of ICTY, very little has been done at the *ad hoc* Tribunals' level to protect the interests of victims.

There are, however, three broader areas of concern, which deserve some specific attention. These are (i) the length of proceedings;[19] (ii) the lack of specific procedural sanctions;[20] and (iii) the need to strengthen the protection of defendants from misconduct by defence counsel or malicious witnesses.[21]

The judges of the *ad hoc* Tribunals have effectively tried to address the issue of the length of proceedings. Amendments to the Rules of Procedure have introduced the 'Pre-Trial Judge', as well as 'Pre-Trial' and 'Pre-Defence Conferences', and broader resort to written evidence. These are all instruments for the judges better to organize the conduct of trials, to be more aware of the needs of the parties, and to control the unfolding of proceedings, particularly with regard to the discovery process. Additionally, these changes have strengthened the climate of confidence between the parties and the judges, thereby facilitating co-operation. Moreover, both by amending the Rules and by virtue of decisions of the Trial Chambers it has been admitted that judges may have access to supporting material (in particular witness statements), as well as transcripts of other proceedings. Finally, recent amendments to Rule 71 and the adoption of Rule 92-*bis* have extended the possibility of taking depositions and resorting to evidence other than oral testimony. These modifications are certainly an appropriate means for addressing the problem of the length of trials. The amendments substantially enable the judges of the Trial Chamber to have a more detailed knowledge of the facts of the case before the opening of trial, or at least prior to hearing witnesses in court. This naturally helps them to exercise more effective control

---

[19] The judges of the *ad hoc* Tribunals and the Security Council have addressed this issue, adopting several amendments to the Rules of Procedure and Evidence and providing for a pool of *ad litem* judges to enhance the ability of the ICTY and ICTR to conduct trials.

[20] In this respect it should be noted that the flexible approach adopted by the judges of the *ad hoc* Tribunals does not ensure certainty and uniformity of judgment. This, naturally, may lead to inequalities of treatment. Furthermore, resort to requests for disciplinary sanctions for misconduct do not seem very effective: for example the decisions on misconduct by prosecution attorneys by the Trial Chamber in *Furundžija* (IT–95–17/1-PT), 5 June 1998.

[21] The *Tadić* case has shown, on the one hand, the risks of legal assistance offered by defence counsel who may have interests different from those of the accused (see Appeals Chamber decision in the proceedings instituted by the Prosecutor against Milan Vujin for contempt of court, 31 January 2000). On the other hand, it has been shown that great caution should be exercized *vis-à-vis* witnesses, as evidenced by the case of witness 'L', who claimed to be an eye-witness to alleged crimes committed by the accused, but whose statements turned out to be highly untrustworthy. On this issue cf. G. McDonald, 'Trial Procedures and Practices', in G. McDonald and O. Swaak-Goldman (eds.), *Substantive and Procedural Aspects of International Criminal Law—The Experience of International and National Courts* (The Hague: Kluwer, 2000), i, 548–620, at 566–567.

over the proceedings (for example, they can more easily limit the examination of witnesses to relevant issues or more effectively shorten the lists of witnesses submitted by the parties).[22] As regards possible new amendments to the Rules, it would not seem appropriate to extend options concerning the admission of out-of-court statements (or affidavits). First, the very essence of adversarial criminal trials is testing evidence through *oral* argument between the parties. This element of adversariness must be preserved as it represents the core of the fact-finding method of criminal courts.[23] Secondly, the 'pedagogical' mission of the Tribunals requires public examination of evidence.

On a different level, in order to contribute to accelerating proceedings before the Tribunals, it would be interesting to explore the possibility of the wider use of guilty plea procedures, notwithstanding the drawbacks involved.[24] Moreover, other measures could be resorted to, such as more joint trials or trials before a single judge,[25] and some thought should be given to the possibility of creating new abbreviated procedures.[26] Furthermore, the judges should consider the idea of introducing specific procedural sanctions for actions (or omissions) causing delays in the proceedings (for example, violations of disclosure obligations).[27]

This last argument leads to the second area of concern, i.e. the lack of sanctions for procedural violations. The pre-trial phase is still too long, often due to delays in the mutual communication of documents between the parties. Only under the threat of sanctions (such as the exclusion of witnesses or exhibits in respect of which notice has not been given to the other party) will parties feel compelled to respect time limits and disclosure obligations.

---

[22] This was an interesting amendment introduced into the Rules of Procedure as a consequence of a practice already established by the Chambers. See Chapter 3 above.

[23] It is interesting to note that even inquisitorial systems are characterized by the presence of adversarial elements in the trial phase (*le principe du débat contradictoire*). See e.g. J. Pradel, 'Inquisitoire—Accusatoire: Une Redoutable Complexité', in 68 *RIDP* (1997), at 225, and G. Ubertis, *Appunti di procedura penale* (Milan: Giuffrè, 2002), at 12.

[24] Cf. Chapter 3 above, Section I.

[25] See P. Robinson, 'Ensuring Fair and Expeditious Trials at the International Tribunal for the Former Yugoslavia', in 11 *EJIL* (2000), 569–589, at 588.

[26] Such as, e.g., the possibility for the defendant to agree to immediate trial upon his or her arrival at the Tribunal on the sole basis of the material submitted for confirmation of the indictment, plus any evidence the accused may bring. One could take as a model the '*giudizio abbreviato*', provided for in the Italian Code of Criminal Procedure, whereby the trial is conducted in an expedited form before the '*giudice dell'udienza preliminare*' (a sort of reviewing judge) on the basis of the elements contained in the Prosecutor's dossier to support the confirmation of the indictment (see Articles 438–443 of the Code of Criminal Procedure).

[27] In *Furundžija* the Trial Chamber decided to re-open proceedings, while it would have been probably more appropriate to strike out the evidence of the witness (Decision of the Trial Chamber on a Defence Motion, *Furundžija* (IT–95–17/1–PT), 16 July 1998). Also in the *Blaškić* case (IT–95–14–PT), e.g., the prosecution delayed the proceedings for a very long time, even violating disclosure obligations from time to time. However, absent the adoption of rules attaching specific sanctions to these violations, breaches of their duties by prosecution attorneys do not have consequences for the prosecution, as implicitly accepted by the Trial Chamber (Decision 28 September 1998).

Moreover, the absence of procedural sanctions in the *ad hoc* Tribunals makes it necessary for the judges to find innovative and imaginative solutions designed to address violations of procedural rules on a case-by-case basis (the same holds true for the ICC). This approach may give rise to criticisms and lead in the end to a reduction of the Tribunals' credibility.[28] Furthermore, lack of procedural sanctions exposes the parties to uncertainty about the course of the proceeding. This is particularly unacceptable from the point of view of the rights of defendants, who are left without true protection against violations, for example, regarding disclosure obligations on the part of the Prosecutor. The introduction of procedural sanctions, coupled with a strong commitment by the Prosecutor to respect fundamental rights, would help accelerate proceedings, since it would considerably reduce delay in the process of discovery.

As regards the third problem area, concerning the need to protect the accused against malicious witnesses or the deviant behaviour of defence counsel, two of the abovementioned elements may prove to be useful tools in addressing the problem. A stronger commitment by the Prosecutor to the protection of fundamental rights and the deeper knowledge judges may acquire of the facts of the case (in accordance with recent amendments to the RPE) may offer an important contribution to the protection of defendants against prejudicial interference in their cases.

IV. SOME SUGGESTIONS FOR IMPROVING HUMAN RIGHTS PROTECTION IN INTERNATIONAL CRIMINAL PROCEEDINGS

It has clearly emerged that the protection of human rights is—to a large extent—satisfactorily ensured in international criminal proceedings. Nonetheless, it may be fitting to add a few suggestions for more complete protection.

First, it seems appropriate, in the system of both the *ad hoc* Tribunals and the ICC, to add *specific remedies for procedural violations*. Secondly, it is suggested that in the *ad hoc* Tribunals' system the Prosecutor should play a more active role in the protection of the rights of defendants. This could be achieved by transforming the current duty to communicate exculpatory evidence to the accused (Rule 68 RPE) into a wider obligation to search for exculpatory evidence, following the example of the ICC Statute. Thirdly, it might be useful to adopt a specific set of *provisions dealing with the consequences of violation of fundamental rights* by organs of the Court. The *right to compensation* for

---

[28] Parties to the proceedings, international media, NGOs, and above all interested States may be inclined to exercise all sort of pressures on the judges. For example, this occurred in *Barayagwiza* when Rwanda threatened to stop co-operating with the Tribunal.

unlawful arrest (and detention) or unjust conviction provided for by the ICC Statute could be expanded to cover all violations of fundamental rights. In this regard an attempt should be made to try to extend this protection to the *ad hoc* Tribunals' system.

With respect to all these suggestions it may be interesting briefly to recall the Appeals Chamber's decision in *Barayagwiza*. This case is extremely instructive in respect of the absence of remedies for violations of fundamental rights in the system of the *ad hoc* Tribunals. The Appeals Chamber of the *ad hoc* Tribunals was confronted with the impossible task of striking the right balance between two interests that had equal dignity and deserved equal consideration. On the one hand, the right of the accused not to be arbitrarily detained;[29] on the other, the effective functioning of international criminal justice.[30] In its first ruling the Appeals Chamber decided that the violations of the rights of the accused had been so serious that it was justifiable to dismiss the indictment with prejudice to the Prosecutor for bringing new charges on the same facts and release the accused. Reactions to this decision were very strong, in particular from the Government of Rwanda, which threatened to halt all forms of co-operation with the Tribunal. In the end the Appeals Chamber reviewed its previous decision and withdrew the order for release. The Appeals Chamber, however, although it recognized that violations of the rights of defendant were less extensive than previously thought (and thus release and discontinuance of the case were no longer justified), decided to grant compensation to the accused for those violations. Thus, the *Barayagwiza* saga ended and the accused remained in detention at the UN Detention Unit in Arusha pending trial.

The crucial questions at issue in this case, however, remain unanswered. In cases of this kind, in which both the expectations of the accused and the interests of the international community (and also those of victims) are in conflict, it does not seem appropriate to leave it to judges to strike the proper balance between conflicting interests. It is for pre-established *procedural remedies* to *specify* what should be the consequence of the breach of fundamental rights. In general, it seems acceptable that, in the case of a very serious breach, the consequence may be the end of the trial and release of the accused. It would be unfair to the defendant and too risky for the credibility of international justice to leave such problems for a case-by-case determination by the Chambers of the Tribunals. The *ad hoc* Tribunals (and in the future the ICC) are specialized organs with specific competence in conducting criminal trials.

---

[29] It may briefly be recalled that the accused had been held in detention in violation of several rules for a long period. Subsequently, the Appeals Chamber decided to order the dismissal of the case and the release of the accused: see the Decision of 3 November 1999 in *Barayagwiza* (ICTR–97–19–R).

[30] It is well known that the effective functioning of the ICTR depends to a large extent on the co-operation of the Government of Rwanda.

It seems that in order for them to continue to be perceived as organs of justice, there should be mechanisms designed to ensure more certainty in addressing these issues.

Finally, turning to the right to compensation, it should be noted that the Appeals Chamber in its decision in the abovementioned case held that if the accused were found not guilty at the end of his trial, he would have the right to be appropriately compensated. If, on the other hand, he were found guilty, consideration should be given to the serious violations of his or her rights when determining the penalty.[31]

There are two considerations that ought to be taken into account in this regard. First, the judges introduced, in the system of *ad hoc* Tribunals, a right to compensation that, prior to this decision, did not exist in either the Statute or the Rules of Procedure and Evidence. It is interesting to note that the Chamber limited this right to acquittal (thus it does not apply to the violation *per se*). Secondly, the Appeals Chamber judges imposed on the Trial Chamber a duty to take into account the violation of the rights of the accused should the Chamber find him guilty. The Appeals Chamber, in *Semanza*, subsequently confirmed this precedent.[32]

These cases attest to the efforts made by the judges to find balanced and imaginative solutions to complex problems. In this respect, however, it would seem useful, both to protect the judges against pressures and criticism and to ensure more certainty to individuals, explicitly to provide in the Rules of Procedure for the consequences of violations of fundamental rights. In the ICC Statute this has been done, at least to a certain extent. The right to compensation for unlawful arrest (and detention) or unjust conviction has been set out in terms (Article 85 ICC St.). The Rules of Procedure and Evidence of the Court have established a more detailed mechanism for seeking compensation.[33] Two suggestions may be made in this respect, one with regard to the ICC Statute, one with respect to the system of the *ad hoc* Tribunals. First, it would seem appropriate, in the ICC system, to extend the right to compensation to other possible violations of fundamental rights. Secondly, as mentioned above, it would seem logical to amend both RPEs of *ad hoc* Tribunals specifically to provide for compensation for human rights violations, thereby strengthening the protection of fundamental rights in international criminal procedure.

---

[31] In this respect, I submit that compensation for violation of fundamental rights should be granted to an accused irrespective of whether or not he is convicted.

[32] Cf. Decision, *Semanza* (ICTR–97–20-T), 31 May 2000.

[33] Rule 173.1 of the ICC Rules establishes that 'anyone wishing to obtain compensation on any of the grounds indicated in article 85 shall submit a request, in writing, to the Presidency who shall designate a chamber composed of three judges of the Court to consider the request'. It must also be ensured that none of the judges considering the request for compensation 'have participated in any earlier judgment of the Court regarding the person making the request'. Paras. (c) and (d) add further details concerning the proceedings and time limits.

The adoption of specific provisions on the right to compensation and procedures for its enforcement, as well as rules dealing with the specific remedies for the violation of procedural rules, would have at least two positive effects. First, it would imply an improvement in the protection of individual rights, in that disregard for procedural rules entailing a violation of the rights of defendants would be duly compensated. In addition, in the event that mechanisms for procedural sanctions were adopted, the violation of procedural duties would be more detrimental than beneficial to their authors: for example, evidence could be excluded. This would favour the impartiality of investigations and prosecutions, since the Prosecutor would not be tempted to act in violation of the rights of the defendant. Secondly, the amendments under discussion would strengthen the overall fairness of international criminal proceedings and make respect for procedural rules more stringent, thereby contributing to the enhancement of the rule of law in international criminal justice.

One of the distinctive traits of international criminal trials, at least so far, has been the flexibility of procedural rules. This feature may be explained by the relatively short life of this branch of law, and by a tradition of procedural flexibility in international courts. Today, however, with the establishment of the ICC, international criminal justice aims to become an 'ordinary' system of judicial accountability for very serious criminal offences. Therefore, increasingly flexibility in international criminal trials should be reduced: procedural rules should be drafted in more rigorous terms, and strict compliance with these rules should be ensured. Borrowing Montesquieu's words one should recall that '*les formalités de la justice sont nécessaires à la liberté*'.[34] Only by strengthening respect for procedural rules will international criminal justice be truly just and fair. It will also be perceived as such by defendants, victims, and public opinion, both in the States concerned and in the rest of the world.

---

[34] In *De l'Esprit des Lois*, Livre XXIX, Chapitre Premier.

Select Bibliography

I. GENERAL

ABI-SAAB, G., 'Fragmentation or Unification: Some Concluding Remarks', in 31 *New York University Journal of International Law and Politics* (1999), 919.

AKHAVAN, P., 'Beyond Impunity: Can International Criminal Justice Prevent Future Atrocities?', in 95 *American Journal of International Law* (2001), 7.

ARBOUR, L., and others (eds.), *The Prosecutor of a Permanent International Criminal Court* (Freiburg im Breisgau : Edition Iuscrim, 2000).

ASCENSIO, H., DECAUX, E., and PELLET, A. (eds.), *Droit International Pénal* (Paris: Pedone, 2000).

BANTEKAS, I., NASH, S., and MACKAREL, M., *International Criminal Law* (London: Cavendish, 2001).

BASSIOUNI, M. C. (ed.), *International Criminal Law*, vol. 3 'Enforcement' (2nd edn., Ardsley, NY: Transnational, 1999).

BIANCHI, A., 'Immunity versus Human Rights: The *Pinochet* Case', in 10 *European Journal of International Law* (1999), 237.

BROWN, B., 'Primacy or Complementarity: Reconciling the Jurisdiction of National Courts and International Criminal Tribunals', in 23 *Yale Journal of International Law* (1998), 383.

CASSESE, A., 'On the Current Trends towards Criminal Prosecution and Punishment of Breaches of International Humanitarian Law', in 9 *European Journal of International Law* (1998), 2.

——'Reflections on International Criminal Justice', in 61 *Modern Law Review* (1998), 1.

——*International Criminal Law* (Oxford: OUP, forthcoming 2003).

——and DELMAS-MARTY, M., *Juridictions Nationales et Crimes Internationaux* (Paris: PUF, 2002).

D'AMATO, A., 'Peace vs. Accountability in Bosnia', in 88 *American Journal of International Law* (1994), 500.

FERENCZ, B., *An International Criminal Court—A Step Toward World Peace* (New York: Oceana Publ., 1980), 2 vols.

FERRAJOLI, L., *Diritto e Ragione—Teoria del garantismo penale* (3rd edn., Rome-Bari: Laterza, 1996).

FLETCHER, G., *Basic Concepts of Criminal Law* (Oxford–New York: OUP, 1998).

GAJA, G., 'Accession by the Community to the European Convention for the Protection of Human Rights and Fundamental Freedoms', in 33 *Common Market Law Review* (1996), 973.

——'I rischi di un ruolo "complementare" del Tribunale penale internazionale' in P. Lamberti Zanardi and G. Venturini (eds.), *Crimini di Guerra e Competenza delle Giurisdizioni Nazionali* (Milan: Giuffrè, 1998), 87.

KELSEN, H., *Peace Through Law* (New York: Garland, 1973, reprint, originally published 1944).

KITTICHAISAREE, K., *International Criminal Law* (Oxford: OUP, 2001).

LATTANZI, F., *Garanzie dei diritti dell'uomo nel diritto internazionale generale* (Milan: Giuffrè, 1983).

LOMBOIS, C., *Droit pénal international* (Paris: Dalloz, 1979).

MALEKIAN, F., *The Concept of Islamic International Criminal Law: A Comparative Study* (London: Graham and Trotman, 1994).

MCCORMACK, T. L. H., and SIMPSON, G. J. (eds.), *The Law of War Crimes: National and International Approaches* (The Hague: Kluwer, 1997).

MERON, T., 'From Nuremberg to The Hague', in 149 *Military Law Review* (1995), 107.

NINO, C.S., *Radical Evil on Trial* (New Haven, Conn.: Yale University Press, 1995).

ORENTLICHER, D., 'Settling Accounts: The Duty to Prosecute Human Rights Violations of a Prior Regime', in 100 *Yale Law Journal* (1991), 2537.

OSIEL, M., *Mass Atrocity, Collective Memory, and the Law* (New Brusnwick, NJ: Transaction, 1997).

PAULUS, A., and SIMMA, B., 'The Responsibility of Individuals for Human Rights Abuses in Internal Conflicts: A Positivist View', in 93 *American Journal of International Law* (1999), 302.

PAUST, J. (ed.), *International Criminal Law: Cases and Materials* (2nd edn., Durham, NC: North Carolina Academic Press, 2000).

PRADEL, J., *Droit Pénal Comparé* (Paris: Dalloz, 1995).

RANA, G., '. . . And justice for All: Normative Descriptive Frameworks for the Implementation of Tribunals to Try Human Rights Violators', in 30 *Vanderbilt Journal of Transnational Law* (1997), 349.

RATNER, S., and ABRAMS, J. (eds.), *Accountability for Human Rights Atrocities in International Law: Beyond the Nuremberg Legacy* (2nd edn., Oxford: OUP, 2001).

ROTH–ARRIAZA, N., *Impunity and Human Rights in International Law and Practice* (New York: OUP, 1995).

SIDI (Società Italiana di Diritto Internazionale), *Cooperazione fra Stati e Giustizia Penale Internazionale* (Naples: Editoriale Scientifica, 1999).

SUNGA, L., *The Emerging System of International Criminal Law* (The Hague: Kluwer, 1997).

VAN BOVEN, T., 'Autonomy and Independence of United Nations Judicial Institutions: A Comparative Note', in K. Wellens (ed.), *International Law: Theory and Practice* (The Hague: Kluwer, 1998), 679.

WIPPMAN, D., 'Atrocities, Deterrence, and the Limits of International Justice', in 23 *Fordham Journal of International Law* (1999), 473.

WISE, E., and PODGOR, E., *International Criminal Law: Cases and Materials* (New York: Lexis Pub., 2000).

II. CRIMINAL PROCEDURE

1. General Theory

ALESSI, G., *Il Processo Penale* (Rome-Bari: Laterza, 2001).

ANGEL, M., 'Modern Criminal Procedure: A Comparative Law Symposium—Foreword', in 62 *Temple Law Review* (1989), 1087.

ASHWORTH, A., *The Criminal Process—An Evaluative Study* (Oxford: OUP, 1994).

CHIAVARIO, M., *Processo Penale e Garanzie della Persona* (2nd edn., Milan: Giuffrè, 1984).

CORDERO, F., *Ideologie del Processo Penale* (Rome: Università della Sapienza, 1997, reprint, originally published Milan: Giuffrè, 1966).

——*Procedura Penale* (6th edn., Milan: Giuffrè, 2001).

CROSS, SIR RUPERT, and TAPPER, C., *Cross and Tapper on Evidence* (9th edn., London: Butterworths, 1999).

DAMASKA, M., 'Evidentiary Barriers to Conviction and Two Models of Criminal Procedure', in 121 *University of Pennsylvania Law Review* (1973), 506.

DAMASKA, M., *The Faces of Justice and State Authority* (New Haven: Yale University Press, 1986).

DEVLIN, P., *Trial by Jury* (London: Stevens, 1966).

DORAN, S., and JACKSON, J., *The Judicial Role in Criminal Proceedings* (Oxford: Hart Publishing, 2000).

EASTON, S. *The Right to Silence* (Ashgate: Aldershot, 1991).

EMMINS, C., *A Practical Approach to Criminal Procedure* (3rd edn., London: Financial Training Publications, 1985).

FATTAH, 'The interchangeable roles of victims and victimizers: 2nd Inkei Anttila honour lecture', Dept. of Criminal Law and Jurisdictional Procedure—Helsinki— 9 September 1993, European Institute for crime prevention and control 1994.

FENWICK, H., 'Procedural 'Rights' of Victims of Crime: Public or Private Ordering of the Criminal Justice Process?', in 59 *Modern Law Review* (1997), 317.

GREVI, V., Nemo tenetur se detegere. *Interrogatorio dell'imputato e diritto al silenzio nel processo penale* (Milan: Giuffrè, 1972).

HENHAM, R., 'Truth in Plea-Bargaining: Anglo-American Approaches to the Use of Guilty Plea Discounts at the Sentencing Stage', in 29 *Anglo American Law Review* (2000), 1.

KAMISAR, Y., LA FAVE, W., and ISRAEL, J., *Basic Criminal Procedure* (7th edn., St. Paul, MN: West Publishing, 1990).

LA FAVE, W., and ISRAEL, J., *Criminal Procedure* (2nd edn., St. Paul, MN: West Publishing, 1992).

LA FAVE, W., 'Appeal', in *Encyclopaedia of Crime and Justice*, vol. 1, (New York: The Free Press, 1983), 62.

LEIGH, L., 'Liberty and efficiency in the criminal process—The Significance of Models' in 26 *International and Comparative Law Quarterly* (1977), 516.

McEWAN, J., *Evidence and the Adversarial Process: the Modern Law* (Oxford: Hart Publishing, 1998).

NEWMAN, J., 'Beyond Reasonable Doubt', in 68 *New York University Law Review* (1993), 979.

ORESTANO, R., 'Appello a) Diritto Romano', in *Enciclopedia del Diritto* vol. II (Milan: Giuffrè, 1958), 708.

PACKER, H., *The Limits of Criminal Sanction* (Stanford, CA: Stanford University Press, 1968).

PRADEL, J., 'Inquisitoire—Accusatoire: Une Redoutable Complexité', in 68 *Revue Internationale de Droit Pénal* (1997), 213.

PRADEL, J., *Procédure Pénale* (8th edn., Paris: Cujàs, 1995).

RASSAT, M.L., *Procédure Pénale* (12th edn., Paris: PUF, 1995).

SPENCER, J.R., 'French and English Criminal Procedure: a brief comparison', in B. Markensinis (ed.), *The Gradual Convergence*, (Oxford: OUP, 1994).

SPENCER, J.R., 'Orality and the Evidence of Absent Witnesses', in *Criminal Law Review* (1994), 628.

STEFANI, G., LEVASSEUR, G., and BOULOC, F., *Procédure Pénale* (14th edn., Paris: Dalloz, 1990).

WRIGHT, M., 'Victims, Mediation and Criminal Justice', in *Criminal Law Review* (1995), 187.

2. *International and Comparative Criminal Procedure*

AMMAN, D.M., 'Harmonic Convergence ? Constitutional Criminal Procedure in an International Context', in 75 *Indiana Law Journal* (2000), 809.

AYAT, M., 'Le silence prend la parole: la percée du droit de se taire en droit international pénal', in R*evue de droit international et de droit comparé* (2001), 237.

BRADLEY, C., 'The Emerging International Consensus as to Criminal Procedure Rules', in 14 *Michigan Journal of International Law* (1993), 171.

BRADLEY, C. (ed.), *Criminal Procedure. A Worldwide Study* (Durham, NC: Carolina Academic Press, 1999).

CHAMPY, G., 'Inquisitoire—Accusatoire Devant les Juridictions Pénales Internationales', in 68 *Revue Internationale de Droit Pénal* (1997), 149.

DE FRANCIA, C., 'Due Process in International Criminal Courts: Why Procedure Matters', in 87 *Virginia Law Review* (2001), 1381.

DELMAS MARTY, M. (ed.) *Procédures pénales d'Europe (Allemagne, Angleterre et Pays de Galles, Belgique, France, Italie)* (Paris: PUF, 1995).

HARRIS, K., 'Development of Rules of International Criminal Procedure Applicable to the International Adjudication Process: Arriving at a Body of Criminal Procedure Law for the ICC', in 17 *Nouvelles Etudes Pénales* (1998), 389.

HATCHARD, J., HUBER, B., and VOGLER, R. (eds.), *Comparative Criminal Procedure* (London: British Institute of International and Comparative Law, 1996).

KOKOTT, J., *The Burden of Proof in Comparative and International Human Rights Law: Civil and Common Law Approaches with Special Reference to the American and German Legal Systems* (The Hague: Kluwer, 1998).

LANGBEIN, J., *Comparative Criminal Procedure: Germany* (St. Paul, MN: West Publishing, 1977).

MAY, R. and WIERDA, M., 'Trends in International Criminal Evidence: Nuremberg, Tokyo, The Hague and Arusha', in 37 *Columbia Journal of Transnational Law* (1999), 725.

ORIE, A., 'Mechanisms of Developing Procedural Standards in International Adjudication: The Delicate Balance Between the Judiciary and the Legislative Powers in Developing the Rules of Procedure', in *Les Systèmes Comparés de Justice Pénale*, in 17 *Nouvelles Études Pénales* (1998), 383.

SAFFERLING, C., *Towards an International Criminal Procedure* (Oxford: OUP, 2001).

VAN DEN WYNGAERT, C. (ed.), *Criminal Procedure Systems in the European Community* (London: Butterworths, 1993).

III. HUMAN RIGHTS IN CRIMINAL PROCEEDINGS

ABI-SAAB, G., 'Droits de l'Homme et Juridictions Pénales Internationales—Convergences et Tensions', in René-Jean Dupuy (ed.), *Mélanges en l'Honneur de Nicolas Valticos—Droit et Justice*, (Paris: Pedone, 1999), 245.

AL AWANI, T., 'The rights of the accused in Islam', in 10 *Arab Law Quarterly* (1995), 3–16 (part I), 238–249 (part II).

ANDREWS, J.A., *Human Rights in Criminal Procedure: A Comparative Study* (The Hague: Njihoff, 1982).

BAILEY, S., 'Rights in the Administration of Justice', in Harris and Joseph (eds.), *The International Covenant on Civil and Political Rights and United Kingdom Law*, (Oxford: Clarendon Press, 1995), 185.

BASSIOUNI, M. C., 'Human Rights in the Context of Criminal Justice: Identifying International Procedural Protections and Equivalent Protections in National Constitutions', in 3 *Duke Journal of Comparative and International Law* (1993), 235.

BUERGENTHAL, T., 'Confrontation de la Jurisprudence des Tribunaux Nationaux avec la Jurisprudence des Organes de la Convention en ce qui Concerne les Droits Judiciaires (Articles 5, 6 et 13)', in Van der Meersch (ed.), *Les Droits de l'Homme: en Droit Interne et en Droit International* (Brussels: Bruylant, 1968), 263.

CANÇADO TRINDADE, A., 'The right to a fair trial under the american convention on human rights', in Byrnes, A., (Ed.), *The right to a fair trial in international and comparative perspective* (Hong Kong: Centre for comparative and public law, 1997), 4.

CONSO, G., 'Diritti Umani e Procedura Penale', in *L'Italia e l'Anno Internazionale dei Diritti dell'Uomo* (Padua: Cedam, 1969, 25.

DE SALVIA, M., 'Principes Directeurs d'une Procédure Pénale Européenne: la Contribution des Organes de la Convention Européenne des Droits de l'Homme', in *Collected Courses of the Academy of European Law*, vol. V–II, 59.

DELMAS MARTY, M., *Procès pénal et droits de l'homme* (Paris: PUF, 1992).

EDWARDS, G., 'International Human Rights Law Challenges to the New International Criminal Court: the Search and Seizure Right to Privacy', in 26 *Yale Journal of International Law* (2001), 323.

ELLERT, R., *NATO 'Fair Trial' Safeguards: Precursor to an International Bill of Procedural Rights* (The Hague: Nijhoff, 1963).

EMMERSON, B., 'The Human Rights Act: Its Effect on Criminal Proceedings', in Butler, F. (ed.), *Human Rights for the New Millennium* (The Hague: Kluwer, 2000), 85.

——and ASHWORTH, A., *Human Rights and Criminal Justice* (London: Sweet and Maxwell, 2001).

GOMIEN, D., 'The Future of Fair Trial in Europe: The Contribution of International Human Rights Legal and Political Instruments', in 9 *Netherlands Quarterly of Human Rights* (1991), 263.

GREEN, L.C., 'The Intersection of Human Rights and International Criminal Law', in 2 *Finnish Yearbook of International Law* (1991), 153.

GROTIAN, A., *Article 6 of the European Convention on Human Rights: The Right to a Fair Trial* (Strasbourg: Council of Europe Publ., 1994).

HARRIS, D., 'The Right to a Fair Trial in Criminal Proceedings as a Human Right', in 16 *International and Comparative Law Quarterly* (1967), 352.

JACOBS, F., 'The Right to a Fair Trial in European Law', in 4 *European Human Rights Law Review* (1999), 141.

JACOT-GUILLARMOD, O., 'Rights Related to Good Administration of Justice (Article 6)', in R.S.J. MacDonald, F. Matscher, and H. Petzold (eds.), *The European System for the Protection of Human Rights* (Dordrecht: Nijhoff, 1993), 381.

KLIP, A., 'The Decrease of Protection Under Human Rights Treaties in International Criminal Law', in 68 *Revue internationale de droit pénal* (1997), 291.

LILLICH, R., 'Civil Rights' in T. Meron (ed.), *Human Rights in International Law* (Oxford: Clarendon Press, 1984), 115.

——'The Paris Minimum Standards of Human Rights Norms in a State of Emergency', in 79 *American Journal of International Law* (1985), 1072.

MANN, F. A., 'Reflections on the Prosecution of Persons Abducted in breach of International Law' in Y. Dinstein (ed.), *International Law at a Time of Perplexity* (Dordrecht: Nijhoff, 1989), 407.

MARTIN, F., and TUSHNET, M., *The Rights International Companion to Criminal Law and Procedure: An International Human Rights Law Supplement* (The Hague: Kluwer, 1999).

MERON, T., *Human Rights and Humanitarian Norms as Customary Law* (Oxford: Clarendon Press, 1989).

MURDOCH, J.L., *Article 5 of the European Convention on Human Rights: The Protection of Liberty and Security of Persons* (Strasbourg: Council of Europe, 1994).

NOOR MUHAMMAD, H.N.A., 'Due Process of Law for Persons Accused of Crime' in L. Henkin (ed.), *The International Bill of Rights: The Covenant on Civil and Political Rights* (New York: Columbia University Press, 1981), 138.

PONCET, D., *La protection de l'accusé par la CEDH: étude de droit comparé* (Geneva: Georg, 1977).

PRADEL, J., 'La notion de procès équitable en droit pénal européen', in 27 *Revue générale de droit* (1996), 505.

QUIGLEY, J., 'Criminal Law and Human Rights: Implications of the United States Ratification of the International Covenant on Civil and Political Rights', in 6 *Harvard Human Rights Journal* (1993), 58.

RODLEY, N., *The Treatment of Prisoners under International Law* (2nd edn., Oxford: Clarendon Press, 1999).

SPENCER, J.R., 'English Criminal Procedure and the Human Rights Act', in 33 *Israel Law Review* (1999), 664.

SPINELLIS, D., 'Reform Movements in Criminal Procedure and the Protection of Human Rights', in 46 *Revue Hellénique de Droit International* (1993), 127.

STAVROS, S., 'The Right to a Fair Trial in Emergency Situations', in 41 *International and Comparative Law Quarterly* (1992), 343.

——*The Guarantees for Accused Persons Under Article 6 of the European Convention on Human Rights* (Dordrecht: Nijhoff, 1993).

TRAVERNIER, P., 'Le droit à un procès équitable dans la jurisprudence du Comité des droits de l'homme des Nations Unies', in 7 *Revue Trimestrielle des Droits de l'Homme* (1996), 3.

TRECHSEL, S., 'Liberty and Security of Person', in R.S.J. MacDonald, F. Matscher, and H. Petzold (eds.), *The European System for the Protection of Human Rights* (Dordrecht: Nijhoff, 1993), 277.

VAN DIJK, P., *The Right of the Accused to a Fair Trial under International Law* (Utrecht: 1 SIM special, 1983).

——'Universal Legal Principles of Fair Trial in Criminal Proceedings' in A. Rosas and J. Helgesen (eds.), *Human Rights in a Changing East-West Perspective* (London: Pinter, 1990), 89.

WEISSBRODT, D., and HALLENDORFF, M., 'Travaux Préparatoires of the Fair Trial Provisions—Articles 8 to 11—of the Universal Declaration of Human Rights', in 21 *Human Rights Quarterly* (1999), 1061.

——and WOLFRUM, R., *The Right to a Fair Trial* (Berlin: Springer, 1997).

IV. NUREMBERG AND TOKYO

BASSIOUNI, M.C., 'International Criminal Investigations and Prosecutions: From Versailles to Rwanda', in M.C. Bassiouni (ed.), *International Criminal Law* (Ardsley, NY: Transnational, 1999), iii, 31.

CASSESE, A., 'Remarks on Law, War and Human Rights: International Courts and the Legacy of Nuremberg', in 12 *Connecticut Journal of International Law* (1997), 201.

GINSBURGS, G., and KUDRIAVTSEV, V.N. (eds.), *The Nuremberg Trial and International Law* (Dordrecht: Nijhoff, 1990).

IRVING, D., *Nuremberg: The Last Battle* (London: Focal Point, 1996).

KELSEN, H., 'Will the Judgement in the Nuremberg Trial Constitute a Precedent in International Law?', in *International Law Quarterly* [1947], 143.

MARRUS, M., *The Nuremberg War Crimes Trial 1945–46: A Documentary History* (Boston, Mass.: Bedford Books, 1997).

MINEAR, R., *Victor's Justice—The Tokyo War Crimes Trial* (Princeton, NJ: Princeton University Press, 1971).

PICCIGALLO, P., *The Japanese on Trial* (Austin, Tex.: University of Texas Press, 1979).

PRITCHARD, R.J., 'The International Military Tribunal for the Far East and the Allied National War Crimes Trials in Asia', in M.C. Bassiouni (ed.), *International Criminal Law* (Ardsley, NY: Transnational, 1999), iii, 109.

RÖLING, B.V.A., and CASSESE, A., *The Tokyo Trial and Beyond—Reflections of a Peacemonger* (Cambridge: Polity Press, 1993).

——and RÜTER, C. F. (eds.), *The Tokyo Judgement* (Amsterdam: Amsterdam University Press, 1977), 2 vols.

SCHWARZENBERGER, G., 'The Judgement of Nuremberg', in 21 *Tulane Law Review* (1947), 328.

SMITH, B., *The Road to Nuremberg* (New York: Basic Books, 1981).

TAYLOR, T., *The Anatomy of the Nuremberg Trials—A Personal Memoir* (New York: Knopf, 1992).

TUSA, A., and TUSA, J., *The Nuremberg Trial* (London: BBC Books, 1995).

VARADARAJAN, L., 'From Tokyo to The Hague: A Reassessment of Radhabinodh Pal's Dissenting Opinion at the Tokyo Trials on its Golden Jubilee', in 38 *Indian Journal of International Law* (1998), 233.

VON KNIEREM, A., *The Nuremberg Trials* (Chicago, Ill.: Regnery, 1959).

WALLACH, E., 'The Procedural and Evidentiary Rules of the Post-World War II War Crimes Trials: Did They Provide An Outline For International Legal Procedure?', in 37 *Columbia Journal of Transnational Law* (1999), 851.

WOETZEL, R., *The Nuremberg Trials in International Law* (London: Stevens and Sons, 1962).

V. ICTY AND ICTR

ACKERMAN, J.E., and O'SULLIVAN, E., *Practice and Procedure of the International Criminal Tribunal for the Former Yugoslavia* (The Hague: Kluwer, 2000).

AFFOLDER, N., 'Tadic, the Anonymous Witness and the Sources of International Procedural Law', in 19 *Michigan Journal of International Law* (1998), 445.

ALVAREZ, J., 'Rush to Closure: Lessons of the Tadic Judgement', in 96 *Michigan Law Review* (1998), 2031.

——'Crimes of States/Crimes of Hate: Lessons from Rwanda', in 24 *Yale Journal of International Law* (1999), 365.

ARBOUR, L., 'The Development of a Coherent System of Rules of International Criminal Procedure and Evidence Before the Ad Hoc International Tribunals for the Former Yugoslavia and Rwanda', in *Les Systèmes Comparés de Justice Pénale*, 17 *Nouvelles Études Pénales* (1998), 371.

ASCENSIO, H., 'The Rules of Procedure and Evidence of the ICTY', in 9 *Leiden Journal of International Law* (1996), 467.

——and MAISON, R., 'L'Activité des Tribunaux Pénaux Internationaux pour l'Ex-Yougoslavie (1995–1997) et pour le Rwanda (1994–1997)', in 43 *Annuaire Français de Droit International* (1997), 368.

——and ——'L'Activité des Tribunaux Pénaux Internationaux', in 44 *Annuaire Français de Droit International* (1998), 370.

——and ——'L'Activité des Tribunaux Pénaux Internationaux', in 45 *Annuaire Français de Droit International* (1999), 472.

——and ——'L'Activité des Tribunaux Pénaux Internationaux', in 46 *Annuaire Français de Droit International* (2000), 285.

——and PELLET, A., 'L'activité du Tribunal pénal international pour l'ex-Yougoslavie (1993–1995)', in 41 *Annuaire Français de Droit International* (1995), 101.

BASSIOUNI, M. C., and MANIKAS, P., *The Law of the International Criminal Tribunals for the Former Yugoslavia* (Irvington on Hudson, NY: Transnational, 1996).

BENVENUTI, P., 'The ICTY Prosecutor and the Review of the NATO Bombing Campaign against the Federal Republic of Yugoslavia', in 12 *European Journal of International Law* (2001), 503.

BERESFORD, S., 'Unshackling the Paper Tiger—the Sentencing Practices of the ad hoc International Criminal Tribunals for the Former Yugoslavia and Rwanda', in 1 *International Criminal Law Review* (2001), 33.

BLAKESLEY, C., 'Comparing the Ad Hoc Tribunal for Crimes Against Humanitarian Law in the Former Yugoslavia and the Project for an International Criminal Court, Prepared by the International Law Commission', in 67 *Revue Internationale de Droit Pénal* (1996), 139.

——'Atrocity and Its Prosecution: The Ad Hoc Tribunals for former Yugoslavia and Rwanda', in T.L.H. McCormack and G.J. Simpson (eds.), *The Law of War Crimes: National and International Approaches* (The Hague: Kluwer 1997), 189.

CARTER, K., 'Proof Beyond a Reasonable Doubt?: Collecting Evidence for the International Criminal Tribunal for the Former Yugoslavia', in 31 *Canadian Yearbook of International Law* (1993), 235.

CASSESE, A., 'Opinion: The International Criminal Tribunal for the Former Yugoslavia and Human Rights', in 2 *European Human Rights Law Review* (1997), 329.

CHINKIN, C., 'Due Process and Witness Anonymity', in 91 *American Journal of International Law* (1997), 75.

CONDORELLI, L., 'Le Tribunal Pénal International pour l'ex-Yougoslavie et sa jurisprudence', in 1 *Cursos Bancaja* (1997), 241.

CRETA, V., 'The Search for Justice in the Former Yugoslavia and Beyond: Analyzing the Rights of the Accused under the Statute and the Rules of Procedure and Evidence of the International Criminal Tribunal for the Former Yugoslavia', in 20 *Houston Journal of International Law* (1998), 381.

CRYER, R., 'One Appeal, Two Philosophies, Four Opinions and a Remittal: The Erdemovic Case at the ICTY Appeals Chamber', in 2 *Journal of Armed Conflict Law* (1997), 193.

DAVID, E., 'Le Tribunal International Pénal pour l'ex-Yougoslavie', in 25 *Revue Belge de Droit International* (1992), 565.

——and KLEIN, P., and LA ROSA, A.M. (eds.), *Tribunal pénal international pour le Rwanda: recueil des ordonnances, décisions et arrêts 1995–1997* (Brussels: Bruylant, 2000).

DE WAART, P., 'From "Kidnapped" Witness to Released Accused "for Humanitarian Reasons": The Case of the Late General Djordje Djukic', in 9 *Leiden Journal of International Law* (1996), 453.

FALVEY, J., 'UN Justice or Military Justice: Which is the Oxymoron? An Analysis of the Rules of Procedure and Evidence of the International Tribunal for the Former Yugoslavia', in 19 *Fordham International Law Journal* (1995), 475.

FLEMING, M., 'Appellate Review in the International Criminal Tribunals', in 37 *Texas International Law Journal* (2002), 111.

FORSYTHE, F., 'Politics and the International Criminal Tribunal for the Former Yugoslavia', in 5 *Criminal Law Forum* (1994), 401.

GAETA, P., 'Is NATO Authorized or Obliged to Arrest Persons Indicted by the International Criminal Tribunal for the Former Yugoslavia?', in 9 *European Journal of International Law* (1998), 174.

GALLANT, K., 'Securing the Presence of Defendants Before the International Tribunal for the Former Yugoslavia', in 5 *Criminal Law Forum* (1994), 557.

GREEN, L.C., 'Erdemovic—Tadic—Dokmanovic: Jurisdiction and Early Practice of the Yugoslav War Crimes Tribunal', in 27 *Israel Yearbook of Human Rights* (1997), 313.

HAFNER, G., 'Limits to the Procedural Powers of the International Tribunal for the Former Yugoslavia', in K. Wellens (ed.), *International Law: Theory and Practice* (The Hague: Kluwer, 1998), 651.

HAMPSON, F., 'The International Criminal Tribunal for the Former Yugoslavia and the Reluctant Witness', in 47 *International and Comparative Law Quarterly* (1998), 50.

HOWLAND, T., and CALATHES, W., 'The UN's International Criminal Tribunal, Is it Justice or Jingoism for Rwanda: A Call for Transformation', in 39 *Virginia Journal of International Law* (1998), 135.

JONES, J., *The Practice of the International Criminal Tribunals for the Former Yugoslavia and Rwanda* (2nd edn., Andsley, NY: Transnational, 2000).

KLIP, A., 'Witnesses before the International Criminal Tribunal for the Former Yugoslavia', in 67 *Revue internationale de droit pénal* (1996), 267.

——and SLUITER, G. (eds.), *Annotated Leading Cases of International Criminal Tribunals* (Antwerp: Intersentia, 1999), i.

LA ROSA, A.M., 'Défi de taille pour les tribunaux pénaux internationaux: conciliation des exigences du droit international humanitaire et d'une procédure équitable', in 80 *International Review of the Red Cross* (1997), 677.

——'Réflexions sur l'apport du Tribunal pénal international pour l'ex-Yougoslavie au droit à un procès équitable', in 101 *Revue Générale de Droit International Public* (1997), 960.

LAKATOS, A., 'Evaluating the Rules of Procedure and Evidence for the International Tribunal in the Former Yugoslavia: Balancing Witnesses' Needs Against Defendants' Rights', in 46 *Hastings Law Journal* (1995), 909.

LAMB, S., 'The Powers of Arrest of the International Criminal Tribunal for the Former Yugoslavia', in 70 *British Yearbook of International Law* (2000), 165.

LATTANZI, F., and SCISO, E. (eds.), *Dai Tribunali Penali Internazionali Ad Hoc a una Corte Permanente, Atti del convegno* (Naples: Editoriale Scientifica, 1996).

LEIGH, M., 'The Yugoslav Tribunal: Use of Unnamed Witnesses Against Accused', in 90 *American Journal of International Law* (1996), 235.

——'Witness Anonymity Is Inconsistent with Due Process', in 90 *American Journal International Law* (1997), 80.

LINTON, S., 'Reviewing the Case of Draćzen Erdemoviž: Unchartered Waters at the International Criminal Tribunal for the Former Yugoslavia', in 12 *Leiden Journal of International Law* (1999), 251.

MARRO, D., and MAISON, R., 'Quelle répression internationale des crimes commis dans l'ex-Yougoslavie? Le bilan d'une année d'activité judiciaire du Tribunal pénal international de La Haye', in *Gazette du Palais* (17–21 mai 1996), 2.

MARTIN, P.M., 'La compétence de la compétence', in *Recueil Dalloz*, 19 cahier, (1996), 157.

MAY, R., and others (eds.), *Essays on ICTY Procedure and Evidence: in Honour of Gabrielle Kirk McDonald* (The Hague: Kluwer, 2000).

MCDONALD, G., and SWAAK-GOLDMAN, O. (eds.), *Substantive and Procedural Aspects of International Criminal Law—The Experience of International and National Courts* (The Hague: Kluwer, 2000), 3 vols.

MERON, T., 'War Crimes in Yugoslavia and the Development of International Law', in 88 *American Journal of International Law* (1994), 78.

MOMENI, M., 'Balancing the Procedural Rights of the Accused against a Mandate to Protect Victims and Witnesses: An Examination of the Anonymity Rules of the International Criminal Tribunal for the Former Yugoslavia', in 41 *Howard Law Journal* (1997), 155.

MORRIS, V., and SCHARF, M. (eds.), *An Insider's Guide to the International Criminal Tribunal for the Former Yugoslavia: A Documentary History and Analysis* (Irvington-on-Hudson, NY: Transnational, 1995), 2 vols.

——and ——(eds.), *The International Criminal Tribunal for Rwanda* (Irvington-on-Hudson, NY: Transnational, 1998), 2 vols.

MUBIALA, M., 'Le Tribunal International pour le Rwanda: Vraie ou Fausse Copie du Tribunal Pénal International pour l'ex-Yougoslavie', in 99 *Revue Générale de Droit International Public* (1995), 929.

MUNDIS, D., 'Improving the Operation and Functioning of the International Criminal Tribunals', in 94 *American Journal of International Law* (2000), 759.

——'From "Common Law" Towards "Civil Law": The Evolution of the ICTY Rules of Procedure and Evidence', in 14 *Leiden Journal of International Law* (2001), 367.

NIANG, M., 'Le Tribunal Pénal International pour le Rwanda: Et si la Contumace Était Possible!', in 103 *Revue Générale de Droit International Public* (1999), 379.

NICE, G., 'Trials of Imperfection', in 14 *Leiden Journal of International Law* (2001) 383.

NOUVEL, Y., 'La Preuve devant le Tribunal Pénal International pour l'ex-Yougoslavie', in 101 *Revue Générale de Droit International Public* (1997), 905.

NSEREKO, D.N., 'Rules of Procedure and Evidence of the International Tribunal for the Former Yugoslavia', in 5 *Criminal Law Forum* (1994), 507.

PATEL-KING, F., 'Public Disclosure in Rule 61 Proceedings Before the International Criminal Tribunal for the Former Yugoslavia', in 29 *New York University Journal of International Law and Politics* (1997), 523.

——and LA ROSA, A.M., 'The Jurisprudence of the Yugoslavia Tribunal: 1994–1996', in 8 *European Journal of International Law* (1997), 123.

PELLET, A., 'Le Tribunal Criminel International pour l'ex-Yougoslavie, Poudre aux Yeux ou Avancée Décisive', in 98 *Revue Générale de Droit International Public* (1994), 7.

PRUITT, R., 'Guilt by Majority at the ICTY: Does This Meet the Standard of Proof Beyond Reasonable Doubt?', in 10 *Leiden Journal of International Law* (1997), 557.

ROBINSON, P., 'Ensuring Fair and Expeditious Trials at the International Criminal Tribunal for the Former Yugoslavia', in 11 *European Journal of International Law* (2000), 569.

RONZITTI, N., 'Is the Non Liquet of the Final Report by the Committee Established to Review the NATO Bombing Campaign against the Federal Republic of Yugoslavia Acceptable?', in 82 *International Review of the Red Cross* (2000), 1017.

SCHABAS, W., 'Sentencing by International Tribunals: A Human Rights Approach', in 7 *Duke Journal of Comparative and International Law* (1997), 461.

——'Perverse Effects of the *Nulla Poena* Principle National Practice and the *Ad Hoc* Tribunals', in 11 *European Journal of International Law* (2000) 521.

SCHARF, M., 'A Critique of the Yugoslavia War Crimes Tribunal', in 13 *Nouvelles études pénales* (1997), 259.

——*Balkan Justice: The Story Behind the First International War Crimes Trial Since Nuremberg* (Durham, NC: Carolina Academic Press, 1997).

——'The Prosecutor v. Dokmanović: Irregular Rendition and the ICTY', in 11 *Leiden Journal of International Law* (1998), 369.

——'Trial and Error: An Assessment of the First Judgement of the Yugoslavia War Crimes Tribunal', in 30 *New York University Journal of International Law and Politics* (1998), 167.

SCHUTTE, J., 'Legal and Practical Implications, from the Perspective of the Host Country, Relating to the Establishment of the International Tribunal for the Former Yugoslavia', in 5 *Criminal Law Forum* (1994), 423.

SHESTACK, J., 'A Review and Critique of the Statute of the International Tribunal', in Y. Dinstein and M. Tabory (eds.), *War Crimes and International Law* (The Hague: Kluwer, 1996), 197.

SJOCRONA, J., 'The International Criminal Tribunal for the Former Yugoslavia: Some Introductory Remarks From a Defence Point of View', in 8 *Leiden Journal of International Law* (1995), 463.

SLOAN, J., 'The International Criminal Tribunal for the Former Yugoslavia and Fair Trial Rights: A Closer Look', in 9 *Leiden Journal of International Law* (1996), 479.

SLUITER, G., 'Obtaining Evidence for the International Criminal Tribunal for the Former Yugoslavia: An Overview and Assessment of Domestic Implementing Legislation', in 29 *Netherlands International Law Review* (1998), 87.

SWAAK GOLDMAN, O., 'The ICTY and the Right to a Fair Trial: A Critique of the Critics', in 10 *Leiden Journal of International Law* (1997), 215.

TOLBERT, D., 'The International Tribunal for the Former Yugoslavia and the Enforcement of Sentences', in 11 *Leiden Journal of International Law* (1998), 655.

TOMUSCHAT, C., 'International Criminal Prosecution: The Precedent of Nuremberg Confirmed', in 5 *Criminal Law Forum* (1994), 237.

VASSALLI, G., 'Il Tribunale internazionale per i crimini commessi nei territori dell'ex-Jugoslavia', in *Legislazione Penale* (1994), 335.

WALD, P., 'To Establish Incredible Events by Credible Evidence: The Use of Affidavit Testimony in Yugoslavia War Crimes Tribunal Proceedings', in 42 *Harvard International Law Journal* (2001), 535.

WEDGWOOD, R., 'International Criminal Tribunals and State Sources of Proof: The Case of Tihomir Blaškić', in 11 *Leiden Journal of International Law* (1998), 635.

WLADIMIROFF, M., 'The Assignment of Defence Counsel Before the International Criminal Tribunal for the Rwanda', in 12 *Leiden Journal of International Law* (1999), 957.

YEE, S., 'The *Erdemović* Sentencing Judgement: A Questionable Milestone for the International Criminal Tribunal for the Former Yugoslavia', in 26 *Georgia Journal of International and Comparative Law* (1997), 263.

V. ICC

AMBOS, K., 'The Role of the Prosecutor of an International Criminal Court from a Comparative Perspective', in 58–59 *Review of the International Commission of Jurists* (1997), 45.

——'Les Fondements Juridiques de la Cour Pénale Internationale', in 10 *Revue Trimestrielle des Droits de l'Homme* (1999), 739.

AMNESTY INTERNATIONAL, 'Establishing a Just, Fair and Effective International Criminal Court', October 1994, AI index IOR 40/05/94.

——'The International Criminal Court: Making the Right Choices, Part I—Defining the Crimes and Permissible Defences and Initiating a Prosecution', January 1997, AI index: IOR 40/01/97.

——'The International Criminal Court: Making the Right Choices—Part II, Organizing the Court and Ensuring a Fair Trial', July 1997, AI index IOR 40/01/97.

ARSANJANI, M.H., 'The Rome Statute of the International Criminal Court', in 93 *American Journal of International Law* (1999), 22.

BEHRENS, H.J., 'Investigation, Trial and Appeal in the International Criminal Court Statute (Parts V, VI, VIII)', in 6 *European Journal of Crime, Criminal Law and Criminal Justice* (1998), 113.

BERESFORD, S., and LAHIOUEL, H.,'The Right to be Defended in Person or Through Legal Assistance and the International Criminal Court', in 13 *Leiden Journal of International Law* (2000), 949.

BITTI, G., 'Les Tribulations de la Justice Pénale Internationale au 20ème Siècle: La Création d'une Cour Criminelle Internationale Permanente—Affrontement ou Conciliation des Dogmes en Procédure Pénale?', in *Les Systèmes Comparés de Justice Pénale*, in 17 *Nouvelles Etudes Pénales* (1998), 395.

BOAS, G., 'Comparing the ICTY and the ICC: Some Procedural and Substantive Issues', in 47 *Netherlands International Law Review* (2000), 267.

BOS, A., '1948–1998: The Universal Declaration of Human Rights and the Statute of the International Criminal Court', in 22 *Fordham International Law Journal* (1998), 229.

BOURDON, W., 'Rôle de la Société Civile et des ONG', in *La Cour Pénale Internationale* (Paris: La Documentation Française, 1999), 89.

BROWN, D., 'The International Criminal Court and Trial in *Absentia*', in 24 *Brooklyn Journal of International Law* (1998), 763.

CASSESE, A., 'The Statute of the International Criminal Court: Some Preliminary Reflections', in 10 *European Journal of International Law* (1999), 144.

——GAETA, P., and JONES, J. (eds.), *The Rome Statute of the International Criminal Court: A Commentary* (Oxford: OUP 2002), 3 vols.

CLARK, R.S., 'The Proposed International Criminal Court: Its Establishment and Its Relationship with the United Nations', in 8 *Criminal Law Forum* (1997), 411.

CONDORELLI, L., 'La Cour Pénale Internationale: Un Pas de Géant (pourvu qu'il soit accompli . . .)', in 103 *Revue Générale de Droit International Public* (1999), 7.

CRAWFORD, J., 'The ILC's Draft Statute for an International Criminal Court', in 88 *American Journal of International Law* (1994), 140.

——'The ILC Adopts a Statute for an International Criminal Court', in 89 *American Journal of International Law* (1995), 404.

FORSYTHE, D., 'International Criminal Court: A Political View', in 15 *Netherlands Quarterly of Human Rights* (1997), 5.

GALLANT, K., 'The Role and Powers of Defense Counsel in the Rome Statute of the International Criminal Court', in 34 *International Lawyer* (2000), 21.

GOWLLAND-DEBBAS, V., 'The Relationship Between the Security Council and the Projected International Criminal Court', in 3 *Journal of Armed Conflict Law* (1998), 97.

——'The Role of the Security Council in the New International Criminal Court from a Systemic Perspective', in L. Boisson de Chazournes, and V. Gowlland-Debbas (eds.), *The International Legal System in Quest of Equity and Universality, Liber Amicorum G. Abi-Saab* (The Hague: Nijhoff, 2001), 629.

HALL, C., 'The First Two Sessions of the UN Preparatory Committee on the Establishment of an International Criminal Court', in 91 *American Journal of International Law* (1997), 177.

HALL, C., 'The Third and Fourth Sessions of the UN Preparatory Committee on the Establishment of an International Criminal Court', in 92 *American Journal of International Law* (1998), 124.

—— 'The Fifth Session of the UN Preparatory Committee on the Establishment of an International Criminal Court', in 92 *American Journal of International Law* (1998), 331.

—— 'The Sixth Session of the UN Preparatory Committee on the Establishment of an International Criminal Court', in 92 *American Journal of International Law* (1998), 548.

KATZ COGAN, J., 'International Criminal Courts and Fair Trials: Difficulties and Prospects', in 27 *Yale Journal of International Law* (2002), 111.

KIRSCH, P., and HOLMES, J., 'The Rome Conference on an International Criminal Court: The Negotiating Process', in 93 *American Journal of International Law* (1999), 2.

KRESS, C., 'Investigation, Trial and Appeal in the International Criminal Court Statute (Parts V, VI, VIII)', in 6 *European Journal of Crime, Criminal Law and Criminal Justice* (1998), 126.

LATTANZI, F. (ed.), *The International Criminal Court: Comments on the Draft Statute* (Naples: Editoriale Scientifica, 1998).

—— and SCHABAS, W. (eds.), *Essays on the Rome Statute of the International Criminal Court* (L'Aquila: Il Sirente, 1999), i.

LEE, R. (ed.), *The International Criminal Court, The Making of the Rome Statute—Issues, Negotiations, Results* (The Hague: Kluwer, 1999).

—— and others (eds.), *The International Criminal Court: Elements of Crimes and Rules of Procedure and Evidence* (Ardsley, NY: Transnational, 2001).

MacSWEENEY, D., 'International Standards of Fairness, Criminal Procedure and the International Criminal Court', in 68 *Revue Internationale de Droit Pénal* (1997), 233.

NSEREKO, D.N., 'The International Criminal Court: Jurisdictional and Related Issues', in 10 *Criminal Law Forum* (1999), 87.

PAUST, J., 'The Reach of ICC Jurisdiction Over Non-Signatory Nationals', in 33 *Vanderbilt Journal of Transnational Law* (2000), 1.

POLITI, M., and NESI, G. (eds.), *The Rome Statute of the International Criminal Court. A challenge to impunity* (Aldershot: Ashgate, 2001).

RASMUSSEN, M.A., 'Rules of Evidence for the International Criminal Court', in 64 *Nordic Journal of International Law* (1995), 275.

RUDOLF, B., 'Considérations Constitutionnelles à propos de l'Établissement d'une Justice Pénale Internationale', in 10 *Revue Française de Droit Constitutionnel* (1999), 451.

SAROOSHI, D., 'The Statute of the International Criminal Court', in 48 *International and Comparative Law Quarterly* (1999), 387.

SADAT, L., *The International Criminal Court and the Transformation of International Law: Justice for the New Millennium* (Ardsley, NY: Transnational, 2002).

SCHABAS, W., *An Introduction to the International Criminal Court* (Cambridge: Cambridge University Press, 2001).

SCHEFFER, D., 'Staying the Course with the International Criminal Court', in 35 *Cornell International Law Journal* (2002), 47.

SHAW, M., 'The International Criminal Court: Some Procedural and Evidential Issues', in 3 *Journal of Armed Conflict Law* (1998), 65.

SHELTON, D. (ed.), *International Crimes, Peace, and Human Rights: The Role of the International Criminal Court* (Ardsley, NY: Transnational, 2000).

STAPLETON, S., 'Ensuring a Fair Trial in the International Criminal Court', in 31 *New York University Journal of International Law and Politics* (1999), 535.

SYMPOSIUM, 'The International Criminal Court: Consensus and Debate on International Adjudication of Genocide, Crimes Against Humanity, War Crimes and Aggression', in 32 *Cornell International Law Journal* (1999), 431.

TOCHILOVSKY, V., 'Rules of Procedure for the International Criminal Court: Problems to Address in Light of the Experience of the *ad hoc* Tribunals', in 46 *Netherlands International Law Review* (1999), 343.

TRIFFTERER, O. (ed.), *Commentary on the Rome Statute of the International Criminal Court. Observers' Notes, Article by Article* (Baden-Baden: Nomos, 1999).

VAN BOVEN, T., 'The Position of the Victim in the Statute of the International Criminal Court', in H. Von Hebel, J. Schukking, and J. Lammers (eds.), *Reflections on the International Criminal Court* (The Hague: T.M.C. Asser, 1999), 77.

WARBRICK, C., 'International Criminal Courts and Fair Trial', in 3 *Journal of Armed Conflict Law* (1998), 45.

WEDGWOOD, R., 'The International Criminal Court: An American View', in 11 *European Journal of International Law* (1999), 93.

ZAPPALÀ, S., 'Il Procuratore della Corte Penale Internazionale: Luci e Ombre', in 82 *Rivista di diritto internazionale* (1999), 39.

Index

Lightning Source UK Ltd.
Milton Keynes UK
08 December 2009

147228UK00002B/20/P